# PADDLING
# PACIFIC
# NORTHWEST
# WHITEWATER

## THE BEST WHITEWATER
## IN WASHINGTON AND OREGON

NICK HINDS, RYAN SCOTT, JACOB CRUSER,
AND SCOTT WAIDELICH

**FALCON**GUIDES®

GUILFORD, CONNECTICUT
HELENA, MONTANA

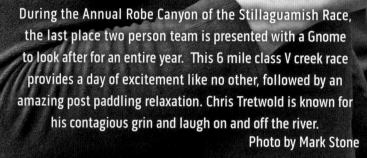

During the Annual Robe Canyon of the Stillaguamish Race, the last place two person team is presented with a Gnome to look after for an entire year. This 6 mile class V creek race provides a day of excitement like no other, followed by an amazing post paddling relaxation. Chris Tretwold is known for his contagious grin and laugh on and off the river.

Photo by Mark Stone

# HERE'S TO HOPPY

EMPLOYEE OWNED

NEW BELGIUM
CITRADELIC
TANGERINE IPA

NEW BELGIUM
SLOW RIDE
SESSION IPA

NEW BELGIUM
RANGER
INDIA PALE ALE

NEW BELGIUM
RAMPANT
IMPERIAL IPA

FIND A RANGER IPA, JOIN THE GRAND CRU AND
DOWNLOAD BEERMODE AT NEWBELGIUM.COM

## FALCONGUIDES®

An imprint of Rowman & Littlefield
Falcon and FalconGuides are registered
trademarks and Make Adventure Your Story is
a trademark of Rowman & Littlefield.

Distributed by NATIONAL BOOK NETWORK

Copyright © 2016 Rowman & Littlefield
Maps © Rowman & Littlefield

**Library of Congress Cataloging-in-
Publication Data available**

ISBN 978-1-4930-2306-6 (paperback)
ISBN 978-1-4930-2307-3 (e-book)

The paper used in this publication meets
the minimum requirements of American
National Standard for Information Sciences—
Permanence of Paper for Printed Library
Materials, ANSI/NISO Z39.48-1992.

Keel Brightman

A team from the PNW about to explore a new first descent

# STAY ALERT!

Welcome to the Pacific Northwest! Before we get started—and you get on the river—there are a few things we want to make clear.

**This is simply a guidebook—**a collection of knowledge from expert sources around the PNW about the best places to paddle whitewater in Washington and Oregon. Only you can decide what you should and shouldn't paddle, and you should exercise your own best judgment in doing so. If you feel you have the skills to test yourself on any of the whitewater mentioned in this book, however, just keep in mind that this is only a guide. It can get you to the river and give you somewhat of an idea of what to expect, but that's about it. We are not responsible for your actions. You are. Please, paddle with caution, and don't get in over your head.

**Whitewater kayaking is an inherently dangerous sport.** However, that risk can be managed responsibly. (By you!) Seek out professional instruction before ever attempting whitewater kayaking. Many local shops from Hood River to Portland to Seattle and throughout Oregon and Washington offer whitewater instruction. There are many skills and logistics that go into paddling whitewater, and the purpose of this book isn't to provide instruction on any of it. It's your responsibility to educate yourself and to be the safest paddler you can be.

**Classification** has always been subjective, but here is a general guideline of river classifications:

Class I — Easy
Moving whitewater with small ripples, no obstructions in the rapid.

Class II — Moderate
Easy rapids in swift-moving water, wide and clear passages with little maneuvering required.

Class III — Intermediate
Swifter, more challenging whitewater with obstructions in the flow and more complex moves to avoid the hazards.

Class IV — Advanced to Expert
Longer, more difficult rapids requiring sharp decision making while dealing with very turbulent whitewater. Swims and self-rescue become very difficult, usually requiring assistance to avoid long swims.

Class V — Expert
Long, complex, steep, highly congested violent whitewater! Significant danger to life and limb.

Class VI — Extreme in every sense
Ridiculous whitewater with marginal or no chance of survival.

**Keep in mind this scale is just a guideline.** Expert whitewater can be anything from a 10-foot waterfall such as Husum Falls, to a steep trickle of a rapid like those found on Lava Creek, or even a big-volume beast like Benham Falls on the Deschutes. Point being, be prepared for whitewater! Stay alert, be attentive to your surrounding and ALWAYS scout before you paddle into anything you are uncertain of.

**Always wear your PFD** (Personal Flotation Device) and carry a whistle. The more you move up in the whitewater Classification the more safety gear you may need—throw ropes, pin kits, first aid kit, dry storage bags, extra clothes, etc. Always check the forecast and know what weather condition you are dealing with. The water here in the PNW is always COLD. Always. Drysuits, warm socks, head heaters, and insulating fleece clothing can make all the difference between a very fun run and a downright miserable one. Please dress for the conditions.

**Water crafts are a personal choice.** Hardshell kayaks are a favorite because they are so maneuverable and easy to transport. Self-bailing rafts, catarafts, inflatable kayaks, prone river boards and standup paddle boards are all popular forms of watercraft these days, too. There are recommendations per page for rafts in this book. For more Standup Paddling information seek out local knowledge.

**Water levels can be unpredictable to the untrained eye.** The PNW is full of aquifers and underground springs that charge many of the rivers here. On the other hand, we have some rivers that are mostly affected by rainfall and rise quickly. The water flow recommendations in this book are based off years of combined experience and research particular to each run. Classification usually rises with water flow, by a substantial factor in some cases. Flooding rivers are extremely dangerous and never predictable; avoid them at all costs.

**With high water comes change.** Always be on the lookout for new logs and trees in the river. Keep in mind that rocks roll and rapids change. If you're skeptical of a rapid, get out and scout! I have seen four different versions of Lower Zig Zag on the Green Truss and seen many other rapids change with new lines opening up, old lines closing and vise versa.

**Whatever you do, stay alert!** As always, you are responsible for your actions on and off the water.

**Scout well and have fun!**

# CONTRIBUTORS

## CONTRIBUTING AUTHORS

**Aaron Lieberman** A southern Oregon man born and bred, Aaron loves to be on the water year-round, whether it be leading inflatable kayak trips down Idaho's Classics, high-water raft runs on the Rogue, or winter kayaking in Chile. It may be that the only thing he respects as much as whitewater are the words of the English language.

**Adam Griffin** A gold medalist in the Loghaven Log Olympics and crowned Mr. Soccer in his home state of Tennessee, Adam Griffin, is a Southeast transplant who is known for his easy-going style and silky-smooth lines. He now spends his free time exploring the wild splendor of the Olympic Peninsula.

**Ben Hawthorne** California whitewater raised this river explorer who has paddled much of the V+ from the high Sierras to the Grand Canyon of the Stikine. Currently he is studying to be a Naturopathic Physician.

**Brett Barton** A Washington-raised local who has construction chops, decidedly an explorer of the far-reaching paddling options off the beaten path. Over his long paddling career, Brett has shifted from freestyle to creeking, and now documents this with quality photography.

**Brian Pernick** Originally from Michigan, Brian has started a rafting company called Adventure Cascades based in Darrington, Wash. Along with his wife Katie and his dog Chief, Brian can be found up on the Sauk River or nearby drainages.

**Brian Vogt** Brian is known for working at the University of Washington and paddling inflatable kayaks around the Northwest on many rivers and creeks. If there is an overnighter that serves up a logistical problem he has the solution.

**Chris Korbulic** Chris travels the world with his boat, seeking adventure and putting together some of the world's most challenging river puzzles. He exudes humility, and it is not uncommon to see him paddling his hometown runs with friends from Grants Pass, Oregon, between his worldly travels.

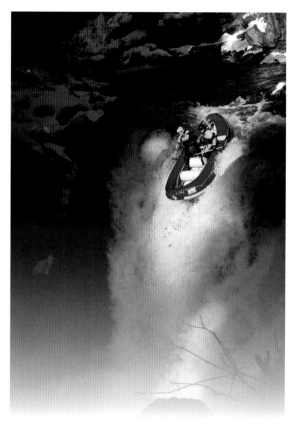

**Chris Totten** Totten has taught many a kayaker to boat during his time as an instructor, and keeps his finger on the pulse of the Seattle scene. Trained in the E.R., he and Steven Cameron actually reduced the shoulder of a certain compiler of this book on the Ohany.

**Chris Tretwold** Construction master and boofing scientist, Chris hails from Bellingham and is one of the most seasoned Class V kayakers in the Northwest. Having ventured around Canada, Oregon, Idaho and beyond, Chris is known for his upbeat nature and optimistic outlook.

**Christian Knight** A mainstay of Seattle paddling, this Kirkland City PR/Outreach guy once paddled alongside Tao Berman in the 'Twitch' series. He also worked at *Paddler* magazine and has a wife and three children that keep him in line.

**Dan Patrinellis** Once a Navy submariner, Dan resides in Port Orchard, Washington, but doesn't mind a ferry ride for Class V action. This man is known for high-quality video edits and being a heavy contributor to the American Whitewater cause. Dan's father taught him to shred on the South Fork of the American River in California in the early 90s.

**Darren Albright** "Little D" grew up under the wing of some of the best boaters around, and it shows in his race results (usually first) around the Northwest. A fireman and a family man, Darren can be found both floating with his son Cody on the Wenatchee or tackling Icicle Creek at flood stage.

**Darren Dangerdeeds** Emile loves all things water: He is an expert surfer, playboater, exploratory squirt-boater and creekboater. Fun to be around and never afraid of an adventure, there may not be a better all-around watersport athlete in the Willamette Valley.

**Ellie Wheat** Now studying to be a nurse, Ellie grew up paddling whitewater in Colorado with a father who wrote the guidebook there. Since transplanting five years ago to the Northwest, she has tackled some of the toughest haystacks and hydraulics.

**Erik Weiseth** Erik was only 6 months old when his father first took him out on the Rogue River. Over the years, Erik's love for rivers and adventures grew as he tackled some of the more ambitious rivers and runs in the West. Now as the general manager of inflatable kayaking outfitter Orange Torpedo Trips, Erik has continued to pass along his passion for rivers to guides and guests alike.

**Hans Hoomans** Hans is a part-time raft guide and full-time father who thrives in the outdoors. Hans pushed the envelope for a few years in exploratory rafting, inspiring many paddlers to look beyond the 'guidebook runs.'

**Hunter Connolly** As of this book's publication, Hunter is a young gun with many Class V runs under his belt. This skillful southern Oregon boater has the fire for paddling that will not likely go out anytime soon.

**Jacob Cruser** While just as happy to travel downriver via tube, raft, inflatable or hardshell kayak, Jacob treasures exploratory boating over all other forms, documenting his adventures at mthoodh2o.blogspot.com.

**Jason Rackley** Full of enthusiasm and a zest for exploration, Jason is the moderator and founder of oregonkayaking.net, Oregon's most used online resource for paddling. Without the efforts of Jason and his team, paddling in Oregon would not be the same.

**JD Gaffney** A longtime mainstay of the kayaking scene, JD is solid on and off the water. Family man and an epically smooth kayaker, this silverback keeps charging the gnar.

**Jed Hawkes** Kayak and raft guide extraordinaire, Jed was born in Massachusetts then moved out west for college and now works at SEA-LECT Designs. His attention to detail and tireless river logging helped this project immensely.

**Jeff Bennett** A lawyer by trade, but also an author of the region's last paddling guidebook (*A Guide to the Whitewater Rivers of Washington*), which showcases Jeff's exuberance for whitewater (read the intro for proof). Without his footprints to follow, the Washington, portion of the book would have been much less complete.

**Johnathan Ellinger** A former raft guide on the east side of Washington, Johnathan and his wife now live in the greater Seattle area, one a mental health counselor and one a Ph.D.-totting professor who both are avid whitewater boaters.

**Johnny Ott** Johnny is a Portland, Oregon-based whitewater enthusiast with an impressive personal list of runs under his belt.

**Jon Crain** Known as Jon "Wayne" Crain in many circles, this family man can sure set you on the right path to the put-in. His energy, input, patience, and expertise was greatly welcomed on this project.

**Jon Dufay** This Navy veteran now teaches in the greater Seattle area. With a joking smile and a quick laugh, Jon worked his way from the Bellingham scene down to the big metropolis.

**Jon Shelby** A High school teacher and dedicated family man, Jon has brought his Kentucky good nature to the banks of many Washington rivers.

**Kris Wilson** Using Gary Korb's paddling guidebook and a tattered gazetteer, Kris keeps on searching the Olympic Peninsula. These days Kris creeks, canoes, and fishes in his drift boat all over Washington. His wealth of backyard knowledge was a great contribution.

**Lane Jacobs** Lane has run some of the toughest rivers on the planet and to no surprise he calls the PNW home. His infectious drive and attitude for adventure are unmatched.

**Lucas Rietmann** A founding member of the CCC out of Corvallis, Lucas is always up for a challenge. He has the skill and desire to run tough whitewater, but enjoys fishing and Class II just the same.

**Luke Spencer** Luke has been at the forefront of paddling in Portland, Oregon, for decades. He grew up paddling inflatables, then took to hardshells, logging more runs on Classic, obscure creeks, and large waterfalls around the greater Portland area than nearly anyone. Luke's whitewater abilities go far beyond the kayak as he started Clackamas River Outfitters and offers instruction on many whitewater crafts.

**Matt King** A man of extreme competence with a zest for life that is as contagious as his smile, Matt is know as the "labrador of the river." Though Matt travels extensively, he has spent the last half-decade calling La Grande, Oregon, home, where he has explored and shared the bounty of the Wallowa Mountains.

**Mike Hagadorn** A transplant from Summit County, Colorado, Mike and his wife call Duvall, Washington, home now. With an amazing eye for photography and only a few years of touring the Pacific Northwest, he has turned some of the most amazing scenes into something you will find in this book.

**Mike Harms** Mike is our Index-Skykomish local, always in the drainage and always willing to share sage water-level advice. Mike, and his wife and son enjoy a charmed life in the beautiful valley. His generosity and spirit are known throughout the paddling community.

**Mike Nash** Mike is a Kiwi, an engineer by training, a carpenter, a real estate agent, a rodeo rider, a sailor, and a Class V+ charger. The man can build about anything and exudes New Zealand's legendary pioneer spirit. He is always about adventure!

**Nate Herbeck** Not only does Nate ride ambulances and save lives, he is a professional videographer and photographer. Living so close to some of paddling's best training grounds, Nate and his wife enjoy the quiet town of BZ Corner, Washington, but also take advantage of their backyard whitewater.

**Nate Pfiefer** Nate has helped fill the information void that occurred when oregonkayaking.net desisted content production. If you are interested in a river in the Willamette Valley, chances are wheelsandwater.blogspot.com has the information you are looking for.

**Nick Hinds** Learning to paddle whitewater canoes and guiding rafts in the mountains of North Carolina, Nick didn't start kayaking until he went to school in Colorado. Work in the paddlesports industry took him farther west to Seattle, where he lives and paddles as much as possible with his wife.

**Paul Meier** Not many people have more fun on the river than Paul. While he has plenty of Class V runs under his belt, he has just as much fun catching eddies on a Class III run or SUPing down the rivers near Portland, Oregon.

**Pete Giordano** The owner of Blue Sky Rafting out of Estacada, Oregon, Pete spent much of the '90s and early 2000s exploring the undocumented rivers around Portland. There are a number of runs in the area that are only paddled because of the efforts of Pete and his paddling partners. Now exploring the joys of fatherhood, Pete still finds time to get out on a few new runs each winter.

**Ron Reynier** Ron is a down-to-earth and unassuming judge who still tackles hard whitewater. He was one of the original explorers of the Northwest's whitewater.

**Ryan Scott** Ryan is the unofficial whitewater steward of the Columbia River Gorge. Having been a part of nearly every exploratory mission taking place within its boundaries over the past decade, Ryan knows this area like no one else. Add to that a marginally believable amount of descents down the Little White and Salmon River Canyon, and you know why if there is a question to be asked about the Gorge, he is the man to answer it.

**Sam Grafton** Seeing Sam come up over the years to super-charger status has been quite the ride. This EMT often works at night and mostly paddles during the day, having now charged some of the largest volume rivers in the Northwest, New Zealand, and Norway.

**Scott Baker** Scott has been exploring the Pacific Northwest and beyond for years. Technically a resident of Bend, Oregon, this traveling/paddling nomad at heart is always ready for any whitewater adventure.

**Scott Gerber** Since '72, "Old Man River" has been running the rio with style, starting in western Colorado and now based with his wife in Portland, Oregon.

**Scott Matthews** You will probably never meet anyone who has paddled more of Washington's rivers and creeks than Scott. With rare descents into the headwaters of nearly every drainage in the state, many of Scott's exploratory runs in the late '80s and early '90s have yet to be repeated. On any given weekend he is still quietly charging into the hills to his favorite whitewater runs.

**Scott Waidelich** Born and raised in the PNW, Scott Waidelich grew up paddling whitewater with his father in the early 90s. Known by the old guard as "Fish," he started out rafting, cat-boating, and eventually moved into hardshell kayaking. Scott's influence on the runs and beta in this book reflect decades spent on these rivers in different craft. Living in Seattle, Robe and Ernie's are his backyard favorites, and he will usually drop everything in favor of a good multi-day self support trip with friends.

**Sean Lee** Colorado-trained charger transplanted to the Northwest, Sean contributes his photos and adventures. This guy is out getting sick every chance he gets.

**Thomas O'Keefe** One of the reasons our Northwest rivers have great access is the past and continued work of American Whitewater's Pacific Northwest Stewardship Director. With a Ph.D. from the University of Wisconsin in aquatic ecology, Tom has a key understanding of what is at stake. His passion for preserving our waters, gaining access, and taking down dead-beat dams continues to yield results.

**Tony Skrivanek** Tony is a Portland, Oregon, resident who spends much of his time anticipating the next Class V mission. He is a big waterfall paddler and whitewater enthusiast with experience growing up on the rocky runs of Minnesota's steep creeks before making the move to the Pacific Northwest.

**Will Volpert** Will Volpert was running rivers before he knew it, literally. As the son of an outfitter and guide, Volpert took his first trip down the river at 6 months old and hasn't let up. He now owns and operates his own river company, Indigo Creek Outfitters, based out of Ashland, Oregon In addition, he has also expanded his company into the fabrication business. The guy is inexhaustible and one heck of human being.

## CONTRIBUTING PHOTOGRAPHERS

Due to the vast quantity of contributing photographers, we unfortunately do not have room here to give each a bio. Many of the authors also contributed photos. It is clear that their imagery is what brings this book to life. Each photo has a credit, so I will let their work speak for them. We are amazed that so many professional and amateur photographers donated professional level material—and thankful!

| | | |
|---|---|---|
| Adam Elliott | EJ Etherington | Leif Embertson |
| Abe Herrera | Emile Elliot | Logan Ferrel |
| Ben Sigler | Eric Mickelson | Mark Stone |
| Bill Cavali | Jason Shappart | Matt Kurle |
| Bill Tuthill | Jermy Bisson | Matt Vogt |
| Bryce Jenkinson | Joe Keck | Michael Dyrland |
| Bryon Dorr | Joe Vogt | Michael Freeman |
| Cade Waud | Jordan Kourupes | Nate Pfiefer |
| Charlie Munsey | Katey Kelley | Paul Thompson |
| Chris Korbulic | Katie Campbell | Priscilla Macy |
| Darcy Gaechter | Keel Brightman | Tait Troutman |
| David Brigg | Kevin Cripps | Taylor Hazen |
| David Pool | Kira Marley | |
| David Spiegel | Kory Kellum | |

Dan Patrinellis

# WASHINGTON

Robe Canyon of the South Fork Stillaaguamish, Dave Costello

# FOREWORD

### Jeff Bennett

Take a second and thumb through the pages of this guidebook. Take a look at some of the photos. Do you feel that. Do you feel ... that?!

That feeling—the excitement and anticipation that surrounds whitewater pursuits—is what bonds river runners. Whether poised above a rapid, or reading about it from afar, we can hear the rapid's roar, feel its energy, and succumb to its draw. And like so many paddlers, we want to share ... that!

In the mid-1980s, I was a snot-nosed kid, eager to run rivers well above my fledgling skill level. I was surrounded by better paddlers, inundated by curiosity, and eagerly aspiring to more challenging runs. Gear was quickly evolving: self-bailing rafts were supplanting "bucket boats"; generic kayaks were evolving into playboats and creekboats; and layers of wool and neoprene were giving away to polypro and drysuits. All the while, a few new license plates were beginning to appear at our local put-ins. Where we used to know every paddler by the color of his boat or make of his car, we were seeing new rigs appear, with license plates from Idaho, California ... West Virginia. Something was happening here. People were driving to Washington to check out our rivers! They didn't have Internet or GPS. Google didn't yet exist. These paddlers were hearing about this place, and coming here en masse.

Alas, while the general population was immersed in newly glamorized common runs, many of us went searching for something new, something obscure, something ... upstream. Every first descent—and there were many—begged the question: What would we find if we put in seven miles higher? And that's what we did. We put in upstream, again, and again, and again.

By 1990, I had paddled countless rivers, throughout Washington and along its borders. I'd worn out a couple of old Washington guidebooks, two pickups, a half-dozen kayaks, and every topo map I'd ever purchased. In their place were new toys, reams of river notes, phone numbers, and plethora of great friends. And, in the midst of that turbulent joy, a guidebook emerged.

In my many years on the river, I'd gained much from the paddling community, and it was time to give something back. Something big. Something like, *A Guide to the Whitewater Rivers of Washington.*

The book was a shared celebration of time, place and people. Emerging from the last vestiges of topo maps, cassette tapes and 35-millimeter film, *A Guide to the Whitewater Rivers of Washington* embodied the water-stained notes of the region's best paddlers and campfire tales of first descents gone awry. It was the glue that bound together countless outings, and the springboard that launched many a paddler's career. For nearly 25 years, it was the single guidebook you placed on your dashboard, so as to let the world know you were part of something. So, yeah, it was a hell of a guidebook, but more importantly, it was an embodiment of a collective feeling ... that feeling!

In the decades since its first publication, Washington's paddling scene has evolved further than I could have ever imagined. Many of the world's best paddlers now call this area home. Washington's rapids and paddlers adorn Web pages, calendars and videos. But, most importantly, Washington's rivers occupy our psyche.

*Paddling Pacific Northwest Whitewater* provides an exciting and new perspective into that collective psyche. The photos are captivating and the descriptions are current. Recently discovered runs lure veterans toward obscured canyons, while renowned runs are polished with new perspectives and insights. It's a great book. It's a hell of a guidebook. It's the book you'll want to put on your dashboard, so as to let the world know that you are part of something.

Yet, it is in the heart of *PPNWW* that we find something modern yet timeless. For *PPNWW* does an unparalleled job of conveying that feeling. Yes ... that feeling!

Jeff Bennett on Champagne
Rapid, Canyon Creek Lewis

NF Nooksack
(Horseshoe Bend)
Class IV+

Little
Beaver
Class IV+

Clearwater Creek
Class V

Lost River
Class V

Chewuch R
Class III-IV

MF Nooksack
(Canyon Run)
Class V

Skagit River
(S Bends)
Class III+

Thunder
Creek
Class V

**Northwest**

Cascade
River
Class V

Bridge Creek
(Stehekin)
Class V

Pilchuck Creek
Class IV

Deer Creek
Class V

Sauk River
Class
III (IV)

SF Stillaguamish
(Robe Canyon)
Class V

North Fork Sauk River
Class IV+

Canyon Creek
Class IV+

Upper Sultan
Class IV+

North Fork Skykomish
Class IV+

Little
Wenatchee River
Class IV(V)

Entiat River
(Canyon)
Class IV+

Sol Duc River
Class III-IV

Upper Sitkum River
Class V

Elwha River
(Lower)
Class III-IV

Dungeness River
Class III-IV

SF Calawah River
Class IV

Elwha River
(Grand Canyon)
Class IV-V

Big Quilcene
(Upper)
Class IV-V

Lower Sultan
Class IV+

Skykomish River
Class III (IV)

Rapid River
Class IV+

Nason
Creek
Class IV-V

Wenatchee River
(Tumwater)
Class IV-V

Matheny Creek
(Lower)
Class IV+

Quinault River
Class IV+(V+)

Dosewallips River
(Elkhorn Canyon)
Class V-V+

Beckler River
Class III

Wenatchee Rive
(Play Run)
Class III (IV)

NF Snoqualmie
(Ernies Canyon)
Class V+

Miller River
Class IV+

Top Tye
Class V

Matheny Creek
(Upper/Middle)
Class IV+

Jefferson Creek
Class IV-V

Icicle Creek
(Upper)
Class IV(V)

MF Snoqualmie River
(Middle Middle)
Class IV

Foss River
Class IV+

MF Satsop River
(Fools Canyon)
Class IV-V

SF Skokomish River
Class IV-V

Green River
(Gorge)
Class IV+

Ingals/Peshastin Creek
Class IV

**Olympic Peninsula**

SF Snoqualmie River
(Fall in the Wall)
Class IV/V

Cle Elum River
(China Gorge)
Class IV-V

Carbon River
Class V

Cooper River
Class IV-V

Mashel River
Class IV/V

Ohanepecosh River
Class IV-V

NF Tilton
River
Class IV

Clear Fork Cowlitz
Class IV-V+

Tieton River
Class II-III

Tilton River
(Lower)
Class III-IV

Grays River
(SF/Main)
Class IV+(V)

**Southwest**

Cispus River
(SuperSlides)
Class IV-V(V+)

Hoffstadt Creek
Class IV-V(V+)

Upper Upper Cispus River
Class IV-V

McCoy Creek
Class IV-V

NF Lewis River
Class II-V+

Kalama River
(Park & Huck)
Class III-IV

White Salmon River
(Green Truss)
Class IV-V

Summit Creek
Class V+

Canyon Creek
(Lewis)
Class IV+(V)

Wind River
(Upper)
Class IV(V)

White Salmon River
(Middle)
Class III-IV(IV+)

EF Lewis (Waterfalls)
Class IV

Little White
Salmon
Class V

Washougal
River
Class III-IV

Wind River
(Lower)
Class IV-V

Rock Creek
Class III-IV(V)

Trout Creek
Class IV-V

Sullivan Creek
Class IV-V

Trail

Castlegar

Columbia

SELKIRK
MOUNTAINS

Spokane River
Class II-III+

Post Falls

Spokane

Eastern

Snake

Pullman

Lewiston

Kennewick

HEAVEN

Walla Walla

HILLS

● River Trip Location

N

| 0 | 7.5 | 15 | 30 |
Miles

| 0 | 15 | 30 | 60 |
Kilometers

# INTRODUCTION

## BY NICK HINDS

I have a vast library of guidebooks accumulated over the last two and a half decades of kayaking that has kept me dreaming of travel and of new rivers to experience. Each of the four main compilers of this guidebook shared in that same simple dream bound together in all those information-packed pages: Provide the details of how to get to that next new experience, what you may encounter, the wise water levels, and some excellent photographs. The four of us all someday hope to gain new experiences from the collective knowledge now bound in the pages of this inspirational tutorial on Class III-V+ kayaking in the Pacific Northwest.

There are many lifetimes of paddling options in the Pacific Northwest, even just in the states of Oregon and Washington alone. After growing up paddling in the Southeast, I kayaked through my college years in Boulder, Colorado, adding another five years in Steamboat Springs honing my skills on Class V before finding the Northwest at age 28. What I learned in the eight years since is that the variety of runs and the consistency of water found up here is unparalleled. There is a good argument that many of the best runs in the world are right in our region. Not to mention that our rivers run almost all year except August and September, given a typical annual snowpack.

Basing out of Seattle can yield amazing paddling experiences—if you can find the time and avoid the rush-hour traffic. This spring (and every spring) I tried to paddle every Classic local run, plus get in at least one trip down to the Hood River area. We have Robe Canyon of the Stillaguamish, Tumwater Canyon of the Wenatchee, the Green River Gorge, the Fall in the Wall section of the Snoqualmie, the Top Tye River, and plenty more just within an hour or two of the city center. Ninety minutes more and you're at the Little White Salmon takeout in Hood River, Oregon, or up in B.C. exploring the Coast Mountain Range.

Whitewater paddling has been the driving force in my adult life, paying me back with joy for every bit of effort I have put into the sport. Over the years I have guided rafts, instructed whitewater canoeing and kayaking, worked in advertising sales for a variety of magazines, written articles, worked retail sales, and now am trying to pay a bit back: taking a stab at compiling a guidebook just like ones that led me on so many adventures. Those experiences include paddling rivers in Ecuador, Costa Rica, Mexico, Canada, and much of the U.S.

*Continued on page 12*

Classic would never have been possible without the help of Jeff Bennett and the amazing explorations in the '80s and beyond. Anyone who knows me can attest that my sense of direction isn't the best. Getting to the put-in can be difficult. Thank goodness for smartphones. Fortunately, within this book you will find contributions from many of the pioneers of this area's world-class whitewater, as well as the keepers of each drainage. Without the endless enthusiasm and selfless collaboration from the Pacific Northwest paddling community this book would not be in your hands. Photographic contributions from some of the region's most talented photographers bring to life that same tireless passion that brings us together, draws us to exploration and challenge, keeps us going year-round, and will always sustain us as Pacific Northwest paddlers.

Too often we get locked into comfort, staying local and enjoying our favorite runs. I implore you to go out and drive that extra three hours to see the gems at the end of your day-trip. Surround yourself with positive paddlers that inspire you and motivate you to get out on the water. And above all, be safe out there. Stick to a progression and get proper instruction before tackling any difficult whitewater.

I've witnessed more than my share of folks stepping up too soon and suffering horrendous swims. Seeking thrills is the inherent nature of the sport. It's nothing short of amazing when things go right. Paddle whitewater long enough, however, and you will likely encounter friends who drown doing what they love. (I've known five, one a close partner for many Colorado seasons.) The risk is real even on Class II-III whitewater. So minimize it with proper Swiftwater rescue training, hold informal rescue clinics with your friends, practice with your throw bag, scout and set safety on problematic rapids, and always be prepared with the right gear for the weather and for the river.

A good friend from New Zealand learned to kayak on rivers without a roll, relishing the beat-down feedback that hard rivers can dish out. Learning to paddle at a camp, on easy water and taking a slow progression, I have a much more cautious, slow and steady approach. Whichever mindset you apply, there is one universal truth about when to step up your paddling: No progress in whitewater is made without taking your licks. Treat each as a rite of passage, not an deterrent. Learn from each swim. Stay positive. Many paddlers will go out of their way to help on the river, but hiking off, getting hurt, or worse can happen if you are charging in above your abilities. Please use this guidebook as a reference. Only you know your abilities. So please boat cautiously and realize that rapids change and wood moves. Stay safe and enjoy the unending beauty of this region from the best perspective possible: on the water!

Thanks go out first to Ryan Scott and Jacob Cruser, who did a fine job of mostly writing and proofing the entire Oregon half of this book. Ryan diligently balanced a large writing workload while compiling the work of many other authors and photographers. Jacob used his intimate knowledge of the Oregon hills to make the runs come to life. These two basically helped this book become a two-state affair.

Scott Waidelich and I have explored many of the rivers in the Wash., half of this book, originally dreaming of updating the Bennett book eight years ago. I appreciate his motivation and safety skills when I have been out of my kayak. Jon Crain is the man with regards to finding any putin and has helped a lot with great advice.

This book was edited heavily by my good friend and cohort David Shively of *Canoe & Kayak* magazine. He is a word-smith that has helped my writing come out smoothly when it was originally rough for more years than I care to admit. A quick shout out also is needed to my man Dave Costello with Falcon publishing, thanks for pushing me into this book and keeping me on track. It has been a long road.

My wife Alyson Hinds has been supportive and helpful the entire way, helping me get organized and edited. Thank you for being my rock, feeding me through it all, and exploring the world with me. Without you I would've never tackled this project. This book is dedicated to you.

Mike Hagadorn

Chris Tretwold and Chris Totten walk into Robe

David Spiegel

Ben Luck charging the top of Granite Falls Rapid

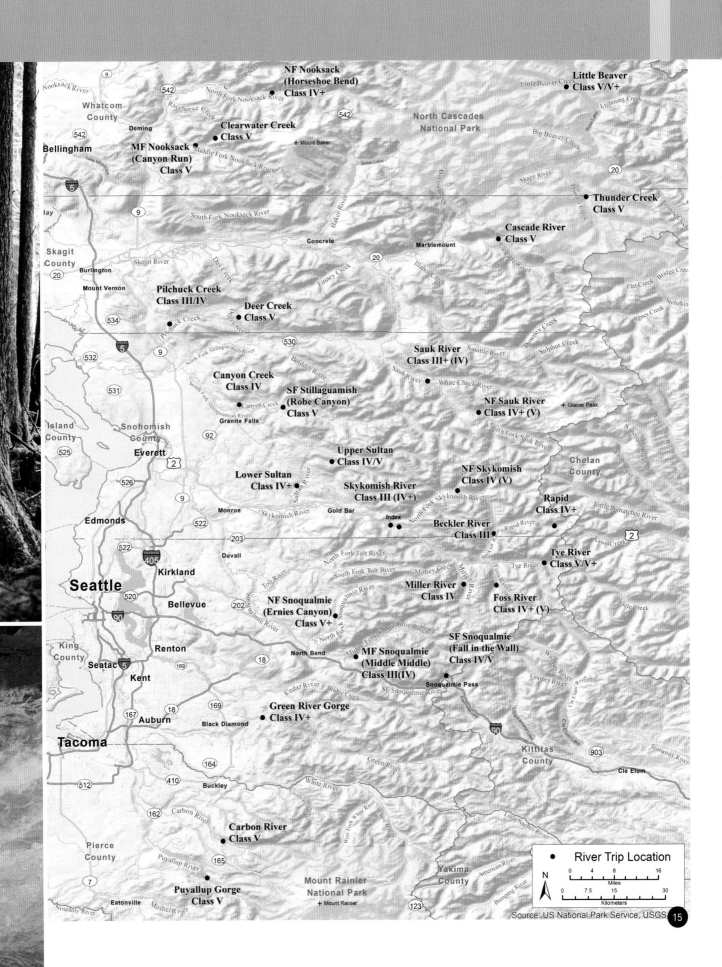

NF Nooksack
(Horseshoe Bend)
Class IV+

Little Beaver
Class V/V+

Whatcom
County

North Cascades
National Park

Deming

Clearwater Creek
Class V

Bellingham

MF Nooksack
(Canyon Run)
Class V

+ Mount Baker

Baker Lake

Thunder Creek
Class V

Concrete

Marblemount

Cascade River
Class V

Skagit
County

Burlington

Mount Vernon

Pilchuck Creek
Class III/IV

Deer Creek
Class V

Sauk River
Class III+ (IV)

Canyon Creek
Class IV

SF Stillaguamish
(Robe Canyon)
Class V

NF Sauk River
Class IV+ (V)

+ Glacier Peak

Granite Falls

Island
County

Snohomish
County

Everett

Chelan
County

Upper Sultan
Class IV/V

Lower Sultan
Class IV+

Skykomish River
Class III (IV+)

NF Skykomish
Class IV (V)

Rapid
Class IV+

Edmonds

Monroe

Gold Bar

Index

Beckler River
Class III

Tye River
Class V/V+

Kirkland

Duvall

Seattle

Bellevue

Miller River
Class IV

Foss River
Class IV+ (V)

NF Snoqualmie
(Ernies Canyon)
Class V+

King
County

Renton

MF Snoqualmie
(Middle Middle)
Class III(IV)

SF Snoqualmie
(Fall in the Wall)
Class IV/V

Seatac

Kent

North Bend

Snoqualmie Pass

Auburn

Black Diamond

Green River Gorge
Class IV+

Tacoma

Kittitas
County

Cle Elum

Buckley

Pierce
County

Carbon River
Class V

Puyallup Gorge
Class V

Eatonville

Mount Rainier
National Park

+ Mount Rainier

Yakima
County

River Trip Location

N

0   4   8        16
Miles
0    7.5   15        30
Kilometers

# HORSESHOE BEND

## OF THE NORTH FORK NOOKSACK

The Bend is more than just the staple for Bellingham and Glacier boaters, with ample flows through July, people come from all over to test their skills or perfect their eddy turns and boofs late into the boating season. While the highway is never far away, nor the hiking trail, paddlers are treated to a pristine river valley with plenty of wildlife and views of nearby Church Mountain.

From the put-in, the Bend starts gradually and offers up some good catch on-the-fly waves and challenging eddy hopping and attainments. After about a mile the river makes a left-hand turn and tears through sticky offset holes and boulders as it romps through Entrance drop. Shortly downstream the river sways back to the right and filters through Bender rapid, a boulder garden with a 3-foot ledge near the bottom. Stay on your toes here since wood sometimes accumulates on the left side of the river. Bender rapid signifies the beginning of the Class IV, if you're not comfortable with the difficulty, the trail is close by on river-right. More continuous boulder gardens lie below Bender with a couple sneaky holes that can get munchy at higher flows.

Bench Drop is the next rapid of concern that boaters encounter. Scout on river-right and choose your line wisely as the main ledge has separated more than a few good boaters from their respective craft. Two more powerful rapids lie in wait downstream before the lead-in to S.A.T.

S.A.T. is the jewel of the Bend: it's a 100-yard-long challenging, steep, boulder garden. Scout well because the moves are often more challenging and powerful than they look from the top. You can get a look at this rapid with a short walk up the Horseshoe Bend trail from the takeout, or on the water, from an eddy above it on river-right. A couple more fun Class III rapids lie below S.A.T. before the takeout at the bridge.

Option: Continue downstream from Douglas Fir Campground to Glacier for some more Class III action in the Canyon.

*—Chris Tretwold*

## THE RUNDOWN

Worth spending all day doing laps or mixing it up with some nearby mountain biking or hiking. Continue downstream 1.8 miles through the Canyon to the town of Glacier for some great Class III.

**Difficulty:** Class IV (IV+)

**Gauge:** USGS #12205000—North Fork Nooksack below Cascade Creek near Glacier, WA; NWRFC #NFNW1—NF NOOKSACK NEAR GLACIER

**Flow Min-max:** 500-1800 cfs (Higher flows possible and frequently paddled up to 2500 cfs, but run becomes continuous Class IV+-V below Bender Rapid.)

**Gradient:** 84 fpm average, 127 fpm in last .75 mile

**Takeout:** Two miles east of the town of Glacier across from Douglas Fir Campground. River is accessed from the parking lot on the south side of the highway on river-right.

**Put-in:** 2.4 miles east of Douglas Fir Campground, look for three pullouts and park in the last one. There is a nice put-in trail to the river here.

**Length:** 2.24 miles

**Hitchability:** Pretty good on weekends, plan on biking/ running shuttle mid-week

**Season:** Year-round

**Camping:** Douglas Fir Campground at the takeout has hand-pump water and vault toilets open May 16 to September 28. Various good dispersed campsites on river-left above the put-in.

**4WD Needed?** No

**Best Close Food/Beers:** Grahams for burgers and atmosphere, Chair 9 for pizza, and Milanos for delicious Italian food. All located within 1 mile of Glacier.

**Quality (out of 5):** 5, only negative is the length of the run.

**Raft Recommendations:** Advanced rafters in small rafts only over 1,000 cfs.

## SHUTTLE DIRECTIONS

From I-5 take state Hwy. 542 east toward the town of Glacier (approx. 32 miles). Continue through Glacier for 2 miles until you cross the river at the Douglas Fir Campground, park on river-right upstream of the bridge. Continue for another 2.4 miles until three consecutive pullouts appear on the south side of the road, pull into the last and largest pullout and find the put-in trail.

**Put-in: 48.904568, -121.875328**
**Takeout: 48.901911, -121.911893**

Eric Michelson 📷

Unknown paddler navigating down a rapid 👁

Nick Hinds 📷

Ellie Wheat navigates a boulder garden 👁

# THE CANYON

## OF THE NORTH FORK NOOKSACK

### THE RUNDOWN

Glacier meltwater when other runs are going dry.

**Difficulty:** Class II–III

**Gauge:** USGS #12205000—North Fork Nooksack below Cascade Creek near Glacier, WA

**Flow Min-max:** 600-2,000 cfs

**Gradient:** Average of 53 fpm

**Takeout:** Warnick Bridge

**Put-in:** Douglas Fir Campground

**Length:** 4.5 miles

**Hitchability:** No

**Season:** Late spring to early fall

**Camping:** Yes, check at ranger station

**4WD Needed?** No

**Best Close Food/Beers:** Chair 9

**Quality (out of 5):** 4

**Raft Recommendations:** Narrow canyon, unique to Class III in the area.

After many other runs around the state have become too low to boat, the North Fork Nooksack continues to be fed by the glaciers of the North Cascades, providing dependable flows well into August. For intermediate boaters looking for a good run in the summer, the North Fork Canyon is short but features high-quality whitewater. The Class III segment of this run is short and you can easily lap it. This river is also a good destination for multi-sport trips. Stack the rack and enjoy a weekend of paddling, mountain biking, and hiking along the Mount Baker Highway while camping with family or friends—this is an ideal destination for the kids—at one of the great Forest Service Campgrounds.

From the put-in at Douglas Fir Campground the river soon enters the canyon and a stacked series of Class III drops begins. At lower summer flows, the rapids are easy to boat-scout. More advanced

Warnick Bridge by Tom O'Keefe

paddlers enjoy the wild ride that winter storms bring. The river corridor is incredibly scenic, but the good whitewater ends all too soon as the canyon opens up and a wider alluvial section begins near the mouth of Glacier Creek. You can take out here on the downstream side of Glacier Creek and shoulder your boat for the short hike into the community of Glacier. Alternatively, you can enjoy the Class II float down to the Warnick Bridge or a public access near Milepost 21. This section features some good fossil hunting, spectacular views up the valley of Mount Baker, and good salmon viewing in August. This later attribute has resulted in voluntary guidelines to avoid boating this reach when flows are below 900 cfs from August 15 to October 15 as the salmon are spawning and most impacted by disturbance.

—Tom O'Keefe

### SHUTTLE DIRECTIONS

Access continues to be a challenge on the North Fork Nooksack. While the put-in is located on Forest Service land **(48.901911, -121.911893)**, no formal takeout exists (a situation American Whitewater is working to change).

# CANYON RUN

## OF THE MIDDLE FORK NOOKSACK

The Middle Fork (MF) canyon is the Class V staple for Whatcom County boaters. With a combination of its headwaters originating from dramatic Deming Glacier and a large mid-elevation basin, the waters of the MF giveth! The canyon section can often be run most of the winter off rain events, while spring runoff lasts until late July.

The first glimpse of the canyon sets the story: Water dripping from the lush vegetation off overhanging cliffs, snarling, foaming, whitewater churns from wall to wall. It is the kind of place where only hearty kayakers get to read the canyon's true deep secrets.

As you snap your sprayskirt on, slide into the milky water below the dam and begin the descent; the rapids tend to be pushy and fast. Hopefully you scouted the first drop from the bridge, Icebox Paradise, as the seemingly innocuous small holes stack up on river-right with a tight, snaking line just to their left. Below Icebox, eddy-out a few hundred feet down on the right and stare over your shoulder to boat-scout Leap of Faith. Here the river constricts down to a 10-foot-wide slot flanked by vertical walls. While we have never seen wood accumulate here, it would be devastating to enter the canyon and find this slot unrunnable, hence the name. (That said, it can be scouted with some difficulty on river-left before dropping into the canyon.) There is not really a usual line here. Just keep in mind the hole in the constriction has kept many boaters in its grip for

## THE RUNDOWN

The most scenic run near Bellingham.

**Difficulty:** Class V

**Gauge:** USGS #12208000— Middle Fork Nooksack near Deming, WA; NWRFC #MFNW1—MF NOOKSACK NEAR DEMING

**Flow Min-max:** 350-700 cfs

**Gradient:** 118 fpm average (208 fpm first .5 mile)

**Takeout:** River-left at the bridge over the Middle Fork Nooksack on Mosquito Lake Rd.

**Put-in:** Short hike down to diversion dam off FS Rd. 38

**Length:** 2.74 miles

**Hitchability:** Difficult, bike shuttle ok

**Season:** Nearly all year, or during small rain events in the fall and winter. Best from June to July.

**Camping:** At takeout or various spots on FS Rd. 38

**4WD Needed?** No

**Best Close Food/Beers:** North Fork Beer Shrine just a couple miles farther east on State Hwy. 542. Bellingham if after 9 p.m.

**Quality (out of 5):** 5

**Raft Recommendations:** Possibly at higher flows in small two-persons rafts (experts only)

Leif Embertson

Chris Tretwold

short rides, and tail-stands abound for those who do not make it far enough left. At flows above 750 cfs, this hole gets stickier and tends to span the whole slot!

Below the Leap of Faith rapid, the canyon peels back and house-sized boulders start filling the river as it proceeds through a few nice pool-drop rapids. The next notable horizon line can be scouted on river-right before entering the drop, or from a river-right eddy midway down the rapid. This rapid is named Hawaii 5-O for an 8-foot-tall curling wave-boof that has since disappeared. With that move gone, run options are a a sneaky line down the left and over a small ledge, or down the right and into the sticky hole. Beware of the center line; there is potential for a nasty pin. The rapid finishes with a small ledge drop that is best run down the middle.

Around the corner, catch the next big eddy on the left behind the house-size boulder and scout Bullshit. Your best bet is to run the center slot off the right side of the boof, landing just inches from the rooster tail. This should send you to the right and (possibly) clear of the mank. Catch an eddy quickly as S-turn lurks downstream.

Being a landslide-type rapid, the main flow in S-turn pushes left against the tall cliff wall. The rapid begins with lines to either side of a large midstream boulder, then returns together and tumbles through some powerful reactionaries, and a large hole at the bottom. Below S-turn lies a fun flume that leads into Super Boof, a great 5-foot boof down the middle and over a meaty hole.

Rapids begin easing up from this point on and there are fun, boulder-slalom moves everywhere—though it's best to keep your wits about you as a powerful slot known as Cheesegrater awaits downstream. Find the boulder slide and avoid being grated!

The final float out continues to provide magnificent canyon views and a few fun Class III rapids all the way to the takeout bridge on Mosquito Lake Rd.

—*Chris Tretwold*

## SHUTTLE DIRECTIONS

From I-5 take the Sunset St./State Hwy. 542 exit and head east approximately 17.7 miles to Mosquito Lake Rd. Take Mosquito Lake Rd. 5.8 miles to the bridge that crosses the MF Nooksack, cross the bridge and take the first right to a nice pullout next to the river. This is the takeout. To get to the put-in, go back over the bridge and drive about a half-mile to FS Rd. 38, go right on FS 38 and continue approx. 2.6 miles to a gated gravel road on your right, there should be an interpretive sign full of gunshot holes here. Walk down the gated gravel road 10 minutes and put in below the diversion dam on river-left.

**Put-in: 48.771278, -122.073743**
**Takeout: 48.784687, -122.113263**

Leif Embertson

Todd Gillman

21

# CLEARWATER CREEK

## OF THE MIDDLE FORK NOOKSACK

Clearwater (C-Dub) may be the finest whitewater in Whatcom County. With 35 boulder and bedrock rapids in 1.25 miles, and a gradient of 320 fpm, this little creek boasts a multitude of tricky moves to beguile even the best kayaker. The same high gradient that attracts whitewater paddlers, however, has also attracted hydropower developers. American Whitewater is working to secure permanent protection for this creek as a Wild and Scenic River.

Straight out of the gate the first quarter-mile is replete with small boofs and fun curling reactionaries to make ready any weary kayakers. Then the crux begins with the Canyon comprised of the Slippery Slit, Tony's Tumble, Slide for Life, and finally Hairy Ferry. This canyon can be scouted from directly below the parking pullout at the put-in and provides a good chance to assess if your skills are up to the Clearwater challenge.

Below the canyon, the creek opens up again but the rapids persist in abundance. From Island Drop (which requires a precision boof to miss a piton) through Orange Slice, Boofs-per-minute, Horseshoe Hole, and Bark-no-bite. The creek funnels kayakers down a nearly continuous, boisterous ride of back-to-back ledges, ping-ponging reactionaries, and sticky holes.

Now you are only two-thirds finished with the run, but Ski-jump (an unavoidable hole), and Owens Rapid will test your bracing abilities prior to using the force at Jedi Hole. A few 'tweener rapids leads into the Donut Shop, which is a large, low-angle lead-in hole followed by a twisting, churning luge between bedrock on the left and boulders to the right. This constriction indicates the last few rapids before Rocky Road, the rapid seen from the takeout bridge. If the flows are right, and you had a good run this may be the day to engage the toughest rapid of the creek, or take out above it, which you hopefully scouted ahead of time on river-left. Then go get another lap!

—*Chris Tretwold*

## THE RUNDOWN

If flows are on the low side it may be possible to kayak the Bellingham "right-hand-turn," which includes Clearwater through the upper and lower Middle Fork's runs! Best Class V in the county!

**Difficulty:** Class V

**Gauge:** USGS #12208000— Middle Fork Nooksack near Deming, WA. Stick gauge at put-in. NWRFC #MFNW1—MF NOOKSACK NEAR DEMING

**Flow Min-max:** 800-1,200 cfs (snowmelt), 1,400-2,000 cfs (rain-fed). Stick gauge: 0.6-1.3´

**Gradient:** 320 fpm.

**Takeout:** Bridge over Clearwater Creek on FS Rd. 38

**Put-in:** Short hike (.25-mile) upstream of takeout

**Length:** 1.25 miles

**Hitchability:** You are better off jogging the shuttle

**Season:** Early spring runoff, fall and winter rain events, or rain on snow events

**Camping:** At takeout

**4WD Needed?** No

**Best Close Food/Beers:** North Fork Beer Shrine, a few miles farther east on state Hwy. 542

**Quality (out of 5):** 5

**Raft Recommendations:** Not recommended, scout entire creek first.

## SHUTTLE DIRECTIONS

From I-5 take the Sunset St./State Hwy. 542 exit and head east approx. 17.7 miles to Mosquito Lake Rd. Take Mosquito Lake Rd. 5.3 miles to a left turn onto Forest Service Rd. 38. On FS 38 travel 4.5 miles to the bridge over Clearwater Creek, this is the takeout **(48.7745667, -122.04518)**. To find the put-in, drive back down FS 38 a quarter-mile to the first un-named gravel road on your right. Go up this road about 1.2 miles to a small pullout/decommissioned road, park here, and hike up the decommissioned road 10 minutes (a quarter-mile) to a USGS gauge and put in here **(48.7892418, -122.02251)**. This is where the custom stick gauge is located on river-left where you get in the water.

Eric Michelson

Jamie Klein

Tait Trautman
Eric Parker and Fred Norquist enjoy the Canyon

Mike Hagadorn
Orange Slice, Hilary Neevel

# LITTLE BEAVER CREEK

If you are looking to quench your thirst for adventure in just a couple days, look no further. Prior to our June mission during the drought of 2015, Little Beaver Creek had only been run once, but we found it to be an instant Classic. The Thunder Creek gauge was reading 1,600 cfs which was a perfect medium flow for Little Beaver. Complemented by epic scenery from around Ross Lake, this is one of the finest backcountry runs within North Cascades National Park. We arrived to the Little Beaver Creek Campground mid-afternoon after 90-minute motorboat ride, shouldered our kayaks and proceeded up the Little Beaver Trail for close to an hour until we reached a point to scramble down to the put-in. Like any remote Class V creek, Little Beaver requires thorough scouting, so plan on at least three hours for the run itself. We completed the run before dark and camped at the takeout. The hike to the lake, the motorboat ride, the hike up the creek, and the paddle can all be done in a day. Camping at the takeout is an attractive option or the ambitious crew could try to rally back across the lake and hike back out to the cars.

## THE RUNDOWN

Über-high adventure factor when not much else is running. Epic scenery from around Ross Lake. Hike, motorboat, hike, paddle, camp, motorboat, etc. Explore the other creeks and waterfalls of Ross Lake on your way in or out. Great for a family trip.

**Difficulty:** Class V-V+

**Gauge:** USGS #12175500—THUNDER CREEK NEAR NEWHALEM, WA; NWRFC #THNW1—THUNDER CREEK NEAR NEWHALEM

**Flow Min-max:** 1,200-1,800 cfs on Thunder Creek (still experimental, only been run a few times)

**Gradient:** 250 fpm.

**Takeout:** Ross Lake

**Put-in:** ~1 mile upstream from Ross Lake

**Length:** 1 mile

**Hitchability:** Trail from takeout to put-in well above water level.

**Season:** Mid to late summer

**Camping:** Yes

**4WD Needed?** No

**Best Close Food/Beers:** Marblemount

**Quality (out of 5):** 4

**Raft Recommendations:** No

Sean Lee
Ari Walker

Sean Lee

Jordy Searle

After scrambling down to the creek from the trail, things pick up quickly and you will find yourself running quality V- rapids. You will be mostly walled in so scout the horizon lines and know your next eddy as the run is pretty stacked. The creek offers 1 full mile of high-quality rapids with the crux (V+) coming toward the end of the run.  Totally gorged in, this rapid includes a small entrance ledge quickly followed by an almost vertical 12-footer. The twisting currents and angle of the drop make it extremely difficult to boof. The falls land next to a deep undercut wall on the left compounded by a cave on the right. The crux rapid was successfully run by both Ari Walker and Will Grubb from our group. The rest of our group portaged with some basic rope work, a short rappel and a sweet seal launch. After the crux there are a couple more V- rapids before you find yourself in the calm of the lake with a giant smile on your face. Be sure to put this one on your annual calendar!

—Sean Lee

## SHUTTLE DIRECTIONS

Park your car and hike down the Ross Lake Resort Trail with gear from the Ross Lake Resort trailhead. Paddle across the lake and rent a motorboat from the resort. Take the motorboat 8 miles up the lake to Little Beaver Creek Campground.  Hike up Little Beaver Creek Trail 2 miles until you can scramble down to the river. (Boating to Little Beaver from the Canadian side of the border is another option.)

Boat Rental: $90 per day from Ross Lake Resort. Call ahead for reservations (206) 386-4437.

Camping: Backcountry Permits are required and are only issued in-person on the day of or up to one day before your trip on a first-come, first-served basis. Visit the ranger station in Marblemount for reservations.

Put-in: 48.916194, -121.102778
Takeout: 48.915773, -121.074368
Ross Lake Resort Trailhead: 48.727578, -121.062435

# THUNDER CREEK

Thunder Creek delivers the goods to trail-weary boaters with fast-moving bedrock ledges and boulder gardens set in steep gorge walls—welcome to the North Cascades! Downstream from the put-in, the river rushes around a slight right bend and over Trial Falls, so be on your toes and scout/portage on river-left. Most boaters will portage at all but the lowest flows. Below the falls is a nice 5- to 6-foot ledge called Chopsticks. Below here are a few more Class IV rapids. The action is fast-paced so catch eddies and watch for wood. The next rapid of significance is Dim Sum, two back-to-back 8- to 10-foot ledges run down the middle. Below Dim Sum is the confluence with Neve Creek, marking the end of the first gorge, but not the end of the whitewater.

The start of the second gorge begins with Mandarin Palace. It is not uncommon that paddlers will find themselves boating into Mandarin without realizing it and having no option to scout. So when in doubt, scout! Mandarin is the first of two multi-tiered boulder rapids, and is usually run from left to right around the house-size boulder and off the right side of the final folding ledge—not a place you want to read-and-run.

Shortly downstream is the other multi-tier rapid. This one can get quite meaty with higher flows. Below here, boaters will find themselves hemmed in by gorge walls above the final rapid of the run, Triple Threat. I have been able to claw my way up the canyon walls from an eddy on river-right just above the right slot to scout, and if you have the means, do so, as wood tends to accumulate in this rapid. We have run either slot at the entrance of the rapid moving to the left and through the boulder garden. Where the rapid makes a sharp right turn, be ready to square up to the Lurker.

The river quickly runs out of steam as you float beneath the footbridge. Before long the river will meander into a quarter-mile-long logjam as it gives way to the lake. We tend to take right channels as long as possible then usually make a few portages before finding a way through the jam. Take out at a beach in the campground.

—*Chris Tretwold*

Leif Embertson

Hilary Neevel boofs Mandarin Palace ledge

## SHUTTLE DIRECTIONS

From I-5 in Burlington take state Hwy. 20 approx. 75 miles east to Colonial Creek Campground. From the campground, hike just over 4 miles up the Thunder Creek Trail. Mile 4 is approx. the third footbridge on the trail starting from the trailhead. Head down to the river just beyond this bridge. If you hike until a clearing/scree slope you have gone about .3 miles to far; backtrack the .3 miles and descend down to the river. Upstream are a few marginally kayak-able falls and large slides but the difficulty of portaging them rarely seems worth the extra effort. The first mile of the hike is relatively flat and the remainder is of a pretty consistent, mellow grade, which makes this a pretty reasonable hike in.

**Put-in:** 48.646051, -121.055254
**Takeout:** 48.685239, -121.092939

## THE RUNDOWN

Recently discovered gem of the PNW. River flows come from one of the largest glaciers in the state. Thus, Thunder Creek was at one time considered for hydropower development, but has been protected as wilderness since 2012.

**Difficulty:** Class IV-V (V above 1,100 cfs)

**Gauge:** USGS #12175500—Thunder Creek Near Newhalem; NWRFC #THNW1— THUNDER CREEK near NEWHALEM

**Flow Min-max:** 600-1,100 cfs (up to 1,400 for expert boaters who know the run and wood situation)

**Gradient:** 89 fpm average, up to 150 fpm in the last 1.25 miles of the canyon.

**Takeout:** Colonial Creek Campground

**Put-in:** A 4-mile hike through old growth from the Thunder Creek Trailhead in Colonial Creek Campground

**Length:** 4 miles

**Hitchability:** Trail from takeout to put-in well above water level

**Season:** Summer and fall. Often one of the latest-running rivers in the state.

**Camping:** Camp at Colonial Creek Campground or drive back west on state Hwy. 20 to find dispersed camping up Bacon Creek.

**4WD Needed?** No

**Best Close Food/Beers:** Marblemount. Barbecue next to the Chevron station.

**Quality (out of 5):** 5. Wilderness boating at its finest!

**Raft Recommendations:** Probably not impossible, but there are some tough must-make eddies. Raft at your own risk!

Dan Patrinellis

Dan Rubado gets air time

In our family garage growing up, there was a picture of my dad cat-boating Monster on the Cascade River in the early '90s. I remember him telling me it was the hardest river he had ever done. Ten years later I, too, would catch my first glimpse of the crystal-clear blue waters that tumble from the snowfields and glaciers above. "This is a river, not a creek," I first remember thinking. Generally running from June into late August on good snow years, and during the rainy season, the Cascade has a wide runnable range, and flows when many other runs have dried up. Considered a classic by most paddlers, this run offers a fantastic big-water experience at the higher end of the flow range, and more bouldery options at the lower range.

Putting in, you have a brief warm-up before Starts with a Bang. This long and continuous Class V rapid can be scouted above on river-right, and is also normally run the right as well, avoiding the large holes in the center. At the bottom, the river bends to the right and you can either eddy-out right or left, and scout the bottom section. Only a brief respite separates the next rapid, Bridge Drop, which is great boulder slalom and keeps you on your toes for a while before winding down into continuous Class IV boogie. Premium is a named rapid soon up: Run right off the boof if you can find it. Monster comes next and is the biggest rapid on Rundown: Scout above on the left and walk down to catch a great view. Monster has several lines depending on water level, and is a bit junky at the lower flow range. I like to start right, in the eddy above, and work center left or center right at the bottom. Below Monster on river-left is a great waterfall with the deepest and softest moss you have ever seen or felt—a great spot to relax for a few. Down below, the river tapers off into fun Class III-IV with some fun surf-waves, slowing down until the takeout at the bridge.

*—Scott Waidelich*

## THE RUNDOWN

Flows in late summer when other rivers have dried up.

**Difficulty:** Class IV/V

**Gauge:** USGS Cascade at Marblemount

**Flow Min-max:** 1,000-3,500 cfs

**Gradient:** 80 fpm

**Takeout:** Bridge at intersection of Cascade Rd. and Cascade-Rockport Rd.

**Put-in:** Marble Creek Campground

**Length:** 8 miles

**Hitchability:** Possible in summer on weekends

**Season:** Spring-summer, rain events

**Camping:** There is camping at the put-in and takeout areas.

**4WD Needed?** No

**Best Close Food/Beers:** BYOB

**Quality (out of 5):** 5

**Raft Recommendations:** Great Class V raft/cataraft run!

## SHUTTLE DIRECTIONS

There are two possible takeouts. The bridge at the intersection of Cascade Rd. and Cascade-Rockport Rd. Or shorten the run and flatwater by parking 2 miles upstream on the left at a large pullout where a trail runs down to the river along a steep hillside. The put-in is up Cascade River Rd. 7.5 miles. Turn right into Marble Creek Campground and follow down until you see a big grassy area with picnic tables and a huge spruce tree. Put in here.

**Put-in:** 48.532942, -121.282962
**Takeout (roadside pullout):** 48.518228, -121.363656
**Takeout (bridge):** 48.526638, -121.415468

Leif Embertson
Randall Reinders dropping into Monster

Mike Hagadorn
Cascade Lounging: Jed Hawkes, Nick Hinds, Katie and Mike Hagadorn

# S BENDS

## OF THE SKAGIT RIVER

Once considered for hydropower development, this section of the Skagit River is a great place for advanced beginners to go and learn from an experienced paddler. Due in part to regulation of flows by hydropower dams that provide a large percentage of Seattle's electricity, the Skagit is one of the rare rivers that flows throughout the year making it a great place for a midsummer float.

The run starts at the put-in with easy Class II rapids. It's a good practice section with strong eddylines and occasional wave trains that continue on downstream past gravel bars which make for good lunch spots in summer. The excitement of the run comes with the S Bends, a series of three distinct rapids separated by short stretches of flatwater in between. The big wave trains can be either exciting or terrorizing for first-time paddlers. They normally rate Class III. They become bigger and faster with higher water levels (6,000+ cfs), but it would be hard to call them anything more difficult than III+. Stay alert for a hole that could cause trouble near the middle of the rapid. Otherwise everything flushes straight through. The S Bends can be scouted from the road near mile 114.

The river calms down considerably after leaving the S Bends and continues along at any easy pace to the takeout. Downstream of this section the river passes through the communities of Marblemount and Rockport where hundreds of bald eagles over winter, attracting paddlers looking for a mellow winter float and eagle watching.

*—Thomas O'Keefe*

### THE RUNDOWN

Consistent dam release flows along a beautiful river.

**Difficulty:** Class II-III (III+ at higher flows)

**Gauge:** Skagit River at Newhalem

**Flow Min-max:** 1,500-15,000 cfs

**Gradient:** 15 fpm

**Takeout:** Copper Creek

**Put-in:** Marble Creek Campground

**Length:** 8.9 miles

**Hitchability:** Lots of traffic on state Hwy. 20, can be difficult to get drivers to stop.

**Season:** Throughout the year. Dam release modulates the annual hydrograph, but weekly hydrographs are closely tied

to power demand. Seattle City Light works to operate their dams in a manner that is protective of the rich fishery resources of the Skagit River.

**Camping:** The put-in is at the Goodell Creek Campground. Stay overnight and do the run again the next day.

**4WD Needed?** No. You can do this one in a Prius.

**Best Close Food/Beers:** Birdsview Brewing Company and some other good options in Marblemount.

**Quality (out of 5):** 4

**Raft Recommendations:** Great raft trip for the whole family.

### SHUTTLE DIRECTIONS

State Hwy. 20 parallels the run.

Put-in: Goodell Creek Campground at Mile 119.4 on State Hwy. 20 **(48.6737671, -121.27104)**. The boat launch and information sign is at the downstream end of the campground. Be sure to leave room for rafters to access the launch by parking cars outside the campground on the dirt road.

Takeout: At Mile 111.7 on state Hwy. 20 look for the dirt road (NPS Rd. 213) leading south to the river (just before you reach the Ross Lake National Recreation Area sign). Follow the dirt road and take the left fork to a takeout about 200 yards from the highway **(48.5927849, -121.37886)**. Parking options are limited. Leave room for others including commercial rafting groups that use the takeout. If you have a large group, extra vehicles should be parked at the put-in.

# THE SAUK RIVER

The Wild and Scenic Sauk exemplifies everything that is great about paddling in the North Cascades.

The Sauk itself is divided into three sections, and with other options in the drainage including the North Fork Sauk (Class IV+), Upper and Lower Suiattle (Class III+, II-III) and Whitechuck (Class IV) there is something for everyone to enjoy.

The Upper Sauk begins at Bedal Campground on the North Fork just above its confluence with the South Fork. This section contains numerous II-II+ rapids with one Class III near the start, just above the confluence, and one at the end called Rocky Road. The wood on this section can be a real pain, and the season is shorter than the Middle Sauk. The boaters who manage to see this remote stretch will be treated to some of the best mountain views the Sauk has to offer. (Some make it into an overnight trip.)

The Class III+ Middle Sauk begins below the confluence with the Whitechuck River. The Whitechuck flows down from Glacier Peak, and its high-elevation drainage sustains good flows on the Sauk late in the season. The Whitechuck has also carried volcanic lahar debris originating on Glacier Peak, which has deposited many of the big boulders that make this such a fun section of whitewater.

## More complete vision of the drainage below

The consistent flows sustained by high elevation snowfields and a glacially clad volcano, plus great whitewater, wildlife, mountain views, old-growth trees, and the remote, forested valley make any trip out to Darrington well worth the added distance compared to the more well known Seattle-area staples.

Factors including frequent high flows capable of rearranging the river, widely spaced waves of use, and head butting between outfitters have lead to there not being much consensus in regards to modern rapid names. There are names for all of the rapids, but only the ones that have lasted over the years are included here.

Below the Whitechuck Raft Launch, the action starts immediately. The first mile consists of four Class II-III rapids collectively called the Warm Ups. these smaller rapids provide a great opportunity to tune up your paddle crew before getting into the bigger stuff.

## THE RUNDOWN

Darrington is an outdoor mecca for multiple outdoor adventures.

**Difficulty:** Class III+ (IV)

**Gauge:** USGS #12187500—Sauk River at Darrington

**Flow Min-max:** 1,000-8,000+ cfs

**Gradient:** 42 fpm

**Takeout:** Backman County Park

**Put-in:** Whitechuck Boat Launch

**Length:** 7.5 miles

**Hitchability:** OK

**Season:** Year-round

**Camping:** Yes. Clear Creek Campground is 3 miles south of Darrington on the way to the put-in. It has vault toilets but no potable water.

**4WD Needed?** No. You can do this one in a Prius.

**Best Close Food/Beers:** River Time Brewing

**Quality (out of 5):** 4

**Raft Recommendations:** Yes

## SHUTTLE DIRECTIONS

To reach Backman from SR530 head south on the Mt. Loop Hwy for 1.5 miles. Look for signs indicating a left turn to Backman Co. Park. This is Clear Creek Rd, and Backman will be on the left in 0.5 miles.

To get to the put in at Whitechuck from Backman, continue south on Clear Creek Rd to where it rejoins the Mt. Loop. Turn left and continue south for 6 miles. Just after a bridge over the Sauk, turn left on N Sauk River Rd. (NF 22) and cross a bridge over the Whitechuck. The Putin is just beyond the bridge on the left.

# THE SAUK RIVER

Barbecue Bend, a Class II wave train at the apex of a big bend to the left is the last of the Warm Ups, and signifies the start of the steepest set of rapids. The next mile or so is stacked with eight great III-III+ rapids, and while recovery pools exist at medium and low flows, high water turns this section into a nonstop rollercoaster ride with many great catch-on-the-fly surfs.

After the Warm Ups are two closely spaced Class IIIs followed by a short pool and a 3rd long III. The 4th rapid in the set, called Jaws, used to have a bad reputation and stood out as the crux of the run. It has mellowed a bit in recent floods, and is no longer much harder than any of the other big rapids in the run. After a long lead in, a set of beautiful waves leaves. As the rapid steepens, Midstream boulders and holes force paddlers to commit to an improbable looking slot between the right shore and the Demon Seed, a large boulder at the very bottom of the rapid. Don't try to get right too hard though, as the water tends to put you right through the slot.

While it has been widely accepted that "Jaws" is the correct spelling, there has been a recent debate as to whether "Jah's" may have been the intended name.

Another significant rapid comes not long after Jaws. Whirlpools starts after a wide bend to the left and is the steepest rapid on the run. The flow is focused into a narrow channel with offset waves and holes. The only run is down the middle, so square up for the big stuff and hang on.

Below Whirlpool the gradient eases. Don't let your guard down though. Many more good rapids remain, and if you survived this far, the rest of the run is full of opportunities to challenge your skills, and become more confident in Class III and beyond.

—*Brian Pernick*

Thomas O'Keefe

...uests enjoy the scenic beauty of the Sauk with Adventure Cascades

# NORTH FORK OF THE SAUK

The North Fork of the Sauk and Sloan Creek come together after draining the east and west slopes of Johnson Mountain, respectively, to create a Class IV-V boulder garden run. The North Fork is a fast and concentrated run with rapids from directly below the put-in right to the takeout. Its short length makes it possible to get multiple laps in a day and still have time to do something else in the area.

Before I go into any details about the run, I'm going to yell at you to SCOUT THE TAKEOUT! The takeout is directly above the North Fork Falls which is an unrunnable 30- to 40-foot waterfall with an enticing lead-in rapid. The rapid that leads into the falls looks similar to all the rapids on the run. If you were boat-scouting, it would be easy to drop into the lead-in canyon, which is full of potholes and eddies that feed upstream into sieves. So, SCOUT THE TAKEOUT!

The run is a boat-scouting boulder-garden boof-fest. A veteran Class V paddler will enjoy eddy-hopping their way down the run, and a Class IV boater stepping it up will be able to scout the larger rapids on the run. All the rapids are very manageable when taken one at a time and the run is a reasonable place to get a taste for Class V at the lower end of flows. As I'm sure you've already determined from this guidebook, the biggest unknown on this run is going to be wood. So watch out for Lincoln Logs and Swizzle-Sticks, wood in the river is no game.

Just below the put-in is Where's Scott, an S-turning ledge that you can scout from the left. This is one of the only big horizon lines on the run and is worth a scout because the boof is a sweet lefty when you stick it. You can also scout this drop before putting on from a trail on river-right at the put-in by cutting through the campsite. After this, boat-scout and eddy-hop as necessary.

The larger rapids are about midway through the run and lines can change from year to year so be sure to scout for wood or new boulders in rapids. There is also an island rapid that historically has been run to the right, but has had wood in it half the time, so proceed with caution on your first lap.

Once you have this run dialed, you can lap it to your heart's content; the short shuttle makes it possible to do several in a day with car or bike shuttle. I recommend running the Sauk or Suiattle while you are in the area to round out a good trip in the North Cascades. If you have any questions about the region or logistics, drop into Adventure Cascades Rafting in Darrington and talk to Brian, he can point you in the right direction.

—*Jed Hawkes*

## THE RUNDOWN

Late Spring or summer run that takes out just upstream of North Fork Falls. Hike down the short trail for a really nice view of the falls and lead-in rapids. The area also has exploratory Class V on Sloan Creek. Runs later in the summer season and is usually best to get after peak flows have passed.

**Difficulty:** Class IV+ (1,000-1,400), IV-V (1,400-2,000), V at high water

**Gauge:** USGS #12186000—Sauk River above Whitechuck River near Darrington, WA NWRFC #WCHW1—Sauk Above Whitechuck

**Flow Min-max:** 1,000-2,900 cfs (rainy season); 1,000-2,000 cfs (snowmelt)

**Gradient:** 187 fpm

**Takeout:** SCOUT THE TAKEOUT! UNRUNNABLE FALLS BELOW.

From Darrington, take the Mountain Loop Highway south away from Darrington for 16 miles until you can take a left onto NF-49. Drive up some switchbacks and past the trailhead for North Fork Falls and look for a small, undeveloped trail/bushwhack on the right that will take you down to the river. 48.098925, -121.368802

**Put-in:** From the takeout drive 1.3 miles until the road comes right next to the river with a big beautiful beach and eddy. Put in either above or below the rapid at the top of the eddy. 48.094279, -121.345606

**Length:** 1.3 miles

**Hitchability:** No, bike shuttle OK

**Season:** Year-round. Flows off of rain, and is a late spring and summer treat depending on snowpack.

**Camping:** Prime free spot next to the river at the put-in, which can be popular so make sure to grab it early. Also Bedal Campground is just downstream of the takeout, run by the Forest Service (vault toilet but no water, open May 16 to September 7). Sloan Creek Campground is above the put-in, a dispersed camping site commonly used by horsepackers.

**4WD Needed?** No

**Best Close Food/Beers:** Darrington—Burger Barn. Name says it all.

**Quality (out of 5):** 3.5

**Raft Recommendations:** Yes for an experienced R-2 raft crew that has sharp read-and-run skills in steep whitewater.

Katie Campbell

Jed Hawkes about to boof out of the shadows

SNAP DRAGON DESIGN

www.snapdragondesign.com

photo © Patrick Levesque

oto © Barnabas Young

# ROBE CANYON

## OF THE SOUTH FORK STILLAGUAMISH RIVER

This canyon run makes living in Seattle amazing for any Class V kayaker who craves escaping the city. Just an hour from downtown, a moss-covered deep-walled riverbed challenges experienced and first-time paddlers alike, who will benefit from local knowledge as wood does move and some of the longer boulder gardens have distinct routes. There are a plethora of Class III and IV drops plus many of the 13 larger drops require careful navigation. Robe has a dark feel since the canyon gets little sun on a short winter day. The logging upstream has increased, and with it, so has the potential for flash floods and quick-rising levels with heavy rain. Robe Canyon ends near Granite Falls, with one of the sportiest seldom run Class V+ drops in the area. I have always taken out at the bridge above this drop on river-left. Many folks enjoy the canyon run between 5 and 6 feet on the gauge, some chargers enjoy it higher. The best first-time flow is between 5.1-5.4 feet.

Robe begins with mellow warmup water that ends in a little over a mile. As canyon walls steepen you know that you have arrived at T-1 Rapid. Flows above 11 feet can shift boulders; all the rapids have changed over the years, and T-1 is particularly prone to shifting. The old railroad bed on river-right allows for easy scouting while river-left provides a view or a bank to portage on. This is where the gorge picks up and the next two miles are seriously steep and continuous. T-2 just downstream gives you another taste of the river's push and feel. The river-right path provides good scouting for the first three big rapids.

Last Sunshine can be your best friend or worst enemy, consistently flipping boaters on the left wall, which is where you enter the rapid. There is ample recovery time for the next series of drops. The river bends and winds through many splashy Class IV drops as you approach the next Class V just a third-mile downstream. This section is the most continuous of the run and at high flows Last Sunshine through Hotel California can be almost one rapid.

Following up Hotel is Hole in the Wall, Dead Deer, Faceplant (scoutable on the left), Catcher's Mitt (scoutable right bank), Z-Turn before you come up on a huge landslide on river-right. A giant boulder signals the portage route on the right bank. The points of egress from the canyon seem to be river-right until you portage Landslide Rapid (if you choose to run, scout it well as there are two sieves in this V+ rapid). Below it a river-left hike-out would be possible. The portage is at river level (beware the landslide is active).

Scott Waidelich

J.P. sending the line into Last Sunshine

The lower half of the run is more spread out with a little taller and bigger rapids like Garbage, Twenty Footer, Off Broadway, Conversation and Mrs. Robinson all providing Class V excitement. Keep an eye out for the Fluid-Fish Lounge on river-right once the canyon opens back up. I can't say enough about how bountiful the boofs are on this run, once you get to the lounge don't let your guard down because below lurks Miracle Fabric (renamed Sobriety Check).

—*Nick Hinds*

## THE RUNDOWN

Gnomes in the canyon lurk ready to cause mischief. It has a big-water feel. Annual race in the spring.

**Difficulty:** Class V (V+ or one suggested portage)

**Gauge:** USGS #12161000—SF Stillaguamish River near Granite Falls WA; NWRFC #GFLW1—SF Stillaguamish near Granite Falls

**Flow Min-max:** 5-6 feet

**Gradient:** 56 fpm, max of 180 fpm

**Takeout:** Upstream of Granite Falls on river-left just under the bridge.

**Put-in:** Across the street from the Paca Pride farm and down the road from the Old Robe Trailhead.

**Length:** 7.8 miles

**Hitchability:** Yes

**Season:** Spring, fall, winter

**Camping:** Paca Pride rents spaces for tents, Gold Basin Campground has drinking water and flush toilets, open May 16 to September 28.

**4WD Needed?** No. You can do this one in a Prius.

**Best Close Food/Beers:** Omega Pizza in Granite Falls

**Quality (out of 5):** 5 stars

**Raft Recommendations:** Yes above 5.4 and below 5.8

## SHUTTLE DIRECTIONS

Take Mountain Loop Highway out of Granite Falls east to the bridge just a half-mile from the town—beware of prowlers looking to break into your car. This is the takeout. You can hike down from here and take a look at Granite Falls Rapid, a proper Class 5+ rapid run in the low 5-foot range. When you reach the bridge take out directly underneath on river-left. You can drive 5.8 miles east to river access that crosses private land downhill (just east) of the Old Robe Trailhead. If you use this access, go with a local who knows the current arrangement with the landowners including where to park. Public access is available by continuing up the road to Verlot Campground which is Forest Service land.

**Takeout: 48.1027985, -121.95263**
**Put-in: 48.1076962, -121.84960**

Scott Waidelich
Ellie Wheat dropping into Catcher's Mitt Rapid

Brett Barton

Tretwold exits stage right through the curtain at Off Broadway

# CANYON CREEK

## OF THE SOUTH FORK STILLAGUAMISH

This is a great run and those that live near it are lucky. It is short, about 1 mile and has about six to seven rapids. None are overly difficult and the majority of the run can be boat-scouted and figured out pretty quickly. There is a good mix of boulder gardens and ledges, making it an ideal spot to hone creekboating fundamentals. The first rapid, considered by many as the most difficult, is immediate. The obvious horizon line can be scouted from the bridge or either side of the river shortly after the put-in.

### THE RUNDOWN

Short run, less than 10 minutes to route it (the shuttle is just as long), the tidiest package is four boaters, one rig, and each one takes a turn out to run shuttle. A great resource to learn how to creekboat and step it up, and also a place to go if Robe is just a bit too full.

**Difficulty:** Class IV+ (V at higher flows)

**Gauge:** Use the South Fork Stillaguamish (Robe Canyon run) as a proxy. USGS #12161000 — SF STILLAGUAMISH RIVER NEAR GRANITE FALLS, WA; NWRFC GFLW1 — NWRFC #GFLW1—SF Stillaguamish near Granite Falls

**Flow Min-max:** Look for flows between 5.5-6.5 cfs

**Gradient:** 100 fpm. At put-in: approx. 400 feet in elevation

**Takeout:** Fishing access on river-right, just downstream of the confluence of Canyon Creek with the South Fork Stillaguamish

**Put-in:** Fishing access off of Canyon Creek Road (if you go over a bridge with a big rapid underneath, you have gone too far)

**Length:** 1.3 mile

**Hitchability:** Not the easiest, and potentially shady.

**Season:** Fall, winter and spring rains

**Camping:** Up the Mountain Loop Highway for great Forest Service camping, both pay sites and primitive about a 20-minute drive away (see Robe Canyon entry for details).

**4WD Needed?** No

**Best Close Food/Beers:** Granite Falls—Barbecue Bucket, mediocre Mexican food at Playa Bonita

**Quality (out of 5):** 4

**Raft Recommendations:** On the higher side of flows.

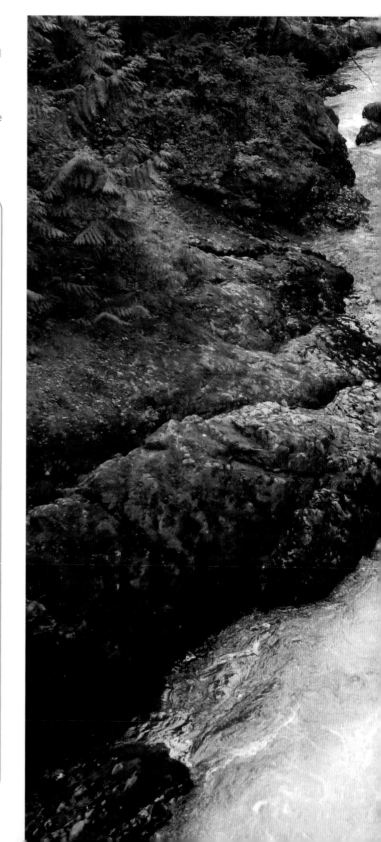

From there, the river enters a tight and scenic canyon. There are about six more rapids downstream which deserve mention. They can all be scouted and have obvious lead-ins with short pools and eddies in between. Immediately after a double-drop, you come to Landslide Rapid. It is one of the last rapids (and also the longest) and is marked by a small landslide mess of boulders on the right with obvious constrictions and a horizon line with a bunch of slots. Hop out and scout the entrance from the right as this area is pretty shifty. Run a few more rapids and right after the confluence with SF Stilly, look for the takeout on the right. Good times, eh!

*—Jon Dufay*

## SHUTTLE DIRECTIONS

The run is just a few minutes outside of Granite Falls and the shuttle is super quick. If you are driving all over the place in the middle of nowhere, you are probably lost. To get to the takeout, just before reaching Granite Falls on state Hwy. 92 (heading east), take the Quarry Road exit at the traffic circle, stay on Quarry Rd. through another traffic circle and around town. At the third traffic circle, take the second exit to Jordan Rd. (heading north, not south at the first Jordan Rd. exit). In a short distance, you should go over the SF Stilly. Once you get over the bridge, look for a fishing access immediately on your right and back toward the river. To reach the put-in, head back on Jordan Rd. to the traffic circle and go all around it, take the second Quarry Rd. option (the fourth exit at the traffic circle, the opposite way you came in), follow Quarry until it runs into the Mountain Loop Highway. Take a left (north) on the Mountain Loop Highway and go past Granite Falls proper and over the bridge (the takeout for Robe Canyon). In less than 1 mile after that bridge, take a left on Canyon Dr. The put-in is a small fishing access on the right less than 1 mile down Canyon Dr., just as the road takes a sharp left turn. There is another small fishing access a few hundred yards down the road on the left, which can be used directly above the bridge that goes over the first rapid. If you hit the bridge, you have gone too far.

**Put-in: 48.1151237, -121.96392**
**Takeout: 48.0960388, -121.97335**

Scott Waidelich

Ally Kaufman, Tammy Ritchey, Brad Xanthopoulos and Ellie Wheat

# DEER CREEK

This run is not a creek, it's a river! At low flows it's six miles of Class IV+ read-and-run whitewater with three to four Class V rapids probably too low to run. With medium flows, it's V- with harder rapids marginally runnable. With high flows, Class V with harder rapids V+. Don't swim!!

—*Mike Nash*

## SHUTTLE DIRECTIONS

River-right put-in: Drive up Lake Cavanaugh Rd., turn right onto Deer Creek Rd., turn right onto Northshore Dr., then take the first gated Forest Service road on the right. If the gate is open, drive up 2.7 miles (miles are painted on trees). Do not take the left turn a mile or so in. Drop boats at clearcut on right. There was a road here but it has been blocked with tree stumps and tank traps. Take vehicle back to gate, which could be locked at any time. Hike down clearcut track then down through trees on the left to river. **48.33630595247177,-121.96426392300054**

River-left put-in: Take Northbrooks Creek Rd., go left at fork. If gate is closed, river-right is the best option even if the river-right gate is closed. If gate is open, carry on, not taking any side roads until you reach the next gate. If open, continue past staging area and take the first hard-left turn. Proceed down to river until road ends. Drop boats and return vehicle to closest gate. Hike boats through overgrown road, then bush-bash to river. Do not drop down to the creek on the right. **48.34517177929733, -121.96475029340945**

(If gates on river-right and river-left are both closed, river-right is best option with hike of around 2.7 miles, versus ~5 miles on river-left.)

Takeout: At the bridge with the gauge. **48.27044873330835, -121.9337081926642**

Mike Nash

## THE RUNDOWN

In my opinion, the most underrated run in Washington. This gem, just one hour from Seattle, runs when everything else is too high. Catch it when levels are dropping to avoid rapidly rising water. There is no paddle in and maybe a half-mile paddle out with lots of fun, challenging whitewater in a wilderness environment.

**Difficulty:** Class V (V+ above medium flows)

**Gauge:** NWRFC #SNFW1— NF Stillaguamish at OSO; USGS #12166300 — NF STILLAGUAMISH RIVER NEAR OSO, WA
*see photo at left below for gauge at bridge at put-in (L, M H)

**Flow Min-max:** 217.25 ft.-220 ft. If Robe Canyon is 6.3-7 feet and dropping, this run may be in. The online NF Stillaguamish gauge is the only other reliable indicator. Look at how the graph is trending and catch it on the drop. Park behind the store next to bridge the and check the level painted on the footing: high, low or medium. The takeout gauge is setup to reflect the level on the river if it is dropping quickly as it often does . So if it is at a stable flow, a low reading on the gauge will actually be a medium. With the river dropping, low is a good low, not boney and high is high! And should be considered a 5+ run overall. Swim and you will most likey loose your boat. If it's too high or low at the takeout, carry on another hour and run the Cascade.

**Gradient:** 114 fpm, 719 feet of elevation drop from put-in at 917 feet

**Takeout:** Bridge at Oso over state Hwy. 530, elevation 198 feet

**Put-in:** Fishing access off of Canyon Creek Road (if you go over a bridge with a big rapid underneath, you have gone too far).

**Length:** 6.6 miles

**Hitchability:** No

**Season:** Fall, winter, and early spring

**Camping:** No

**4WD Needed?** No

**Best Close Food/Beers:** Oso General Store at the takeout

**Quality (out of 5):** 4

**Raft Recommendations:** Would be a great expert raft run at medium-medium high level with only one short, 20-foot portage. River-right put-in would be easiest with a quarter-mile hike down to river if gate was open.

Sean Lee

Rob McKibbin above the Goods

David Spiegel

Xavier Engle on a high-water descent

# PILCHUCK CREEK

Pilchuck Creek is a low-elevation creek that can rise and fall very quickly during the large rain events of Pacific Northwest winters. If optimal flows coincide with the weekend, you can expect a crowd on this local Class III/IV favorite. Any boater who runs Pilchuck Creek should be extremely cautious for wood. There is an abandoned logging road on river-right for much of the run, making egress from the river best on river-right the entire trip.

From the put-in on Lake Cavanaugh Rd., you'll run about 1.5 miles of Class III whitewater before the first Class IV rapid. The creek will turn sharply to the left with water piling up around a pyramid-shaped center rock. Run left of the rock and through the remaining 100 yards or so of read-and-run ledges. Be alert for wood in this section. Last chance eddies above the pyramid rock exist on the right. Another mile of read-and-run whitewater brings you to the next Class IV section. At high water this section can push Class V. There are many lines to run through the boulders and ledges that lead into the last ledge, which holds a nice boof on the left side. After another two miles of read-and-run whitewater there is an island (stay left), after which the river will turn sharply to the right into a corridor with many big boulders along river-right. This is the entrance of the last Class IV rapid on the upper section known locally as Pil Pusher. Catch an eddy on river-right to scout using the abandoned logging road. Here a section of large waves and holes lead to a ledge drop tucked against a house-size boulder on river-right. Run it on the right. One more rapid below here and the whitewater tapers off for the remainder of the "upper" section.

Soon you'll arrive at a campsite on river-right and a bridge over the creek. This access point can be used as a takeout for the upper or a put-in for the middle. Keep in mind that there is a gate that may be locked to access this location by vehicle. If the gate is locked it's a 1.3-mile hike to or from the river. Peaceful floating below the bridge ends with a Class III rapid into a headwall. The power lines overhead signal Pilchuck Creek Falls. There are two rapids between the headwall and the falls. Run these rapids down the right and power through the eddyline on the right to scout, run or portage Pilchuck Falls. Avoid the left side of the river above the falls, especially at high flows as strong currents move toward the

## THE RUNDOWN

Continuous whitewater through a low-elevation, second-growth forest corridor.

**Difficulty:** Class III-IV, Class V at high water

**Gauge:** Washington DOE — 05D070 Pilchuck Cr. at Bridge 626

**Flow Min-max:** 800-3,000 cfs

**Gradient:** 88 fpm for the upper section, 61 fpm for the middle section, and 76 fpm for the upper and middle sections combined. Put-in elevation, 920 feet.

**Takeout:** Old Highway 9 bridge

**Put-in:** Large gravel pull-off on Lake Cavanaugh Rd. where the creek and road meet.

**Length:** 10 miles

**Hitchability:** Not good, bring a road bike

**Season:** November to April (during prolonged rain events)

**Camping:** There is a campsite on Pilchuck Creek, but road to it is gated.

**4WD Needed?** No

**Best Close Food/Beers:** Skagit River Brewery or Conway Tavern

**Quality (out of 5):** 4

**Raft Recommendations:** Experts in self-bailers

unfriendly left side of the falls. The conventional line at the falls is to boof-scrape the deepest tongue of water on the right side. Below the falls there is more scenic, Class III+ whitewater. About 1.5 miles below the falls is a ledge-drop rapid with severe bank erosion on river-right. Keep alert for wood in this drop. After 2.5 more miles of scenic whitewater you'll arrive at a canyon section. High water and wood will spice up this half-mile, mostly Class III+ canyon section. More scenic floating to the old Hwy. 9 bridge takeout. Don't forget to check the USGS gauge on river-right as you float by!

*—Jon Crain*

Jon Crain

Adam Griffin below the falls

## SHUTTLE DIRECTIONS

Paddlers meet at the old Highway 9 bridge north of Arlington to check the visual gauge and coordinate shuttle. If you're going to run both sections then this is the takeout, but if you're just doing the upper, start heading upstream. From the old Highway 9 bridge, get back on state Hwy. 9 and drive 0.3 miles north and turn right onto Finn Settlement Rd. In 4.5 miles, you will reach a Y on a sharp curve. The gated road to the Pilchuck Creek campsite access is here to the right. To reach the put-in for the upper section, go left at the Y (around the sharp curve) to Lake Cavanaugh Rd. Go right on Lake Cavanaugh Rd. and continue 4 miles to a gravel pull-off where the road and creek meet.

Takeout: 48.265456, -122.165672
Put-in: 48.343163, -122.088469

# SKYKOMISH DRAINAGE

Source: US National Park Service, Sources: Esri, USGS, NGA, NASA, CGIAR, N Robinson, NCEAS, NLS, OS, NMA, Geodatastyrelsen, Rijkswaterstaat, GSA, Geoland, FEMA, Intermap and the GIS user community

## MAIN SKY

The waters of the Skykomish start far up the drainage in the snowfields and lakes of the Wild Sky Wilderness and Alpine Lakes Wilderness. Running free to the ocean, the Skykomish has boatable flows most years late into summer.

At normal flows this run is Class III, with the standout exception of Boulder Drop (IV+), allowing beginners and novices to work on basic moves from eddy hopping and ferries to small boofs. When flows bump above 5,000 the run provides advanced paddlers with some more challenging options and is often paddled as a cool down after doing several other local runs.

There are three options for putting in. The North Fork in Index is the most popular, extending the run by a country mile. The second option is known as Cable Drop on the South Fork. This access extends the run by a half-mile, and carries more water than the North Fork, making it a good alternative when levels are low. The final option is to put in at the confluence under the Hwy 2 bridge, for a quick lap or for when levels are low.

Boulder Drop is located one mile downstream from the confluence of the SF and NF at the U.S. Hwy. 2 bridge. The generic name is appropriate given the large house-sized rocks that break up the drop. It has three distinct parts each with its own options for entry, thus the rapid has many different lines depending on water levels.

At the top is a large house-sized rock that splits the river. The right side provides a couple optional lines weaving through the entry holes. The middle channel contains a picket fence of rocks creating several slots to choose from, with names from left to right: Airplane Turn, Chris's Crack, Ned's, the Needle, Paul's, and Mercy Chute. Ned's offers a clean water boof but can be retentive at flows above 4,000 cfs. Mercy Chute (far right) opens up at high water (above 7,000 cfs). Boulder Drop's final section consists of splitting the difference between the house-sized boulders that guard the exit. There are many different ways to run this rapid, at a variety of water levels. Sometimes paddlers will hike up the drop multiple times running a different line each time through, providing a challenge for the creative advanced paddler.

*Continued on page 48*

# THE SKYKOMISH RIVER

## THE RUNDOWN

Year-round boating on a scenic stretch.

**Difficulty:** Class III (IV+)

**Gauge:** USGS #12134500—SKYKOMISH RIVER NEAR GOLD BAR, WA; NWRFCGLBW1—SKYKOMISH NEAR GOLD BAR

**Flow Min-max:** 500- 20,000 cfs

**Gradient:** 20 fpm

**Takeout:** Split Rock

**Put-in:** North Fork, South Fork, or Confluence

**Length:** 2.3 miles from the confluence to Split Rock, 3.8 miles from Index on the NF, and 3 miles from Cable Drop on the SF

**Hitchability:** Probable

**Season:** All year long!

**Camping:** Yes

**4WD Needed?** No

**Best Close Food/Beers:** Index or Gold Bar

**Quality (out of 5):** 5

**Raft Recommendations:** Yes, for sure!

Below Boulder Drop, the river continues its playful romp down through rapids named the Weir, Lunch Hole, and Aquagasm. Split Rock usually forms a decent surfable wave between 5-6,000 cfs. It's fast and bouncy, with a good eddy. Just downstream is the takeout near the road access one mile below Boulder Drop. It is private property, so please pick up trash and don't park on the river-side of the road. Below the railroad trestle bridge is the alternate takeout. The walk is longer but it does provide one more Class III rapid.

**A note on flows.** This river gets attention at all flows. It has been run above 45,000 cfs (FLOOD) on a number of occasions. Runs above 10,000 cfs are commonplace now, but swims at those levels can be long. Exercise good judgement. Wood is rarely an issue but always be on guard.

—*Michael Harms*

David Spiegel

Jonathan Blum at the Entrance of Boulder Drop

### SHUTTLE DIRECTIONS

Split Rock has been the unofficial takeout for years now but it's on private property so please use courtesy. It's an obscure pullout on the right side of the road if you're driving eastbound, just before MM 33. Boulder Drop can be scouted on the trip up at MM34. The confluence is one more mile upriver. To reach the South Fork put-in, turn right onto Mount Index Rd. just before crossing the U.S. Hwy. 2 confluence bridge. Follow it back roughly a half-mile to a large pullout on the left under powerlines. Do not leave valuables in car. A Forest Service parking permit is now required. Alternatively, the North Fork put-in is located in the town of Index at the Outdoor Adventure Center River House. Please check in and sign a waiver if this is your first visit.

**Index put-in: 47.819816, -121.554011**
**SF at Cable Drop put-in: 47.809167, -121.572049**

**Split Rock takeout: 47.827104, -121.619603**
**Big Eddy takeout: 47.836194, -121.657373**

# NORTH FORK OF THE SKYKOMISH

## DRUMBEATER TO TROUT CREEK

Putting on below Drumbeater (V) is standard operating procedure. Drumbeater is a small, sticky ledge with wood in the exit. The canyon proper is short, pool-drop in nature and boat-scoutable except at higher flows. The first series of rapids are offset holes and small ledges leading to Let's Make a Deal, a picket-fence of large river rock clogged with wood across the center channels. It is visible from the eddy above and easily portaged on river-right. Some years, the far right slot is open. Exiting the canyon, stay in the right channel, where you'll pass Troublesome Creek, and arrive at a large horizon line near the road. This is Rooster Tail (V), about a mile downstream from the put-in. There are two channels, the left being narrower with a pinch and a rock forming a rooster tail. Paddlers have flipped in the pinch, hitting heads on said rock; the right side has a large bedrock ledge forming a sticky hole easily skipped over in a creekboat. Playboaters have had trouble here. The runout has a couple more holes to dodge. The right line is considered the best option. Scout and portage along the road.

Downstream, the river drops through continuous Class III and easy IV, going under Galena bridge, passing Silver Creek confluence, before arriving at El Nino, a fun IV, where there are some holes to dodge or bash through. By this point, the river has widened and contains a few braided channels. All go, but watch for wood hazards. A mile downstream is Minefield (IV), where a couple holes can be boofed or skirted around, and provide some excitement at high flows! Look for a beach on the left bank just before the river breaks off into braided channels: This is the takeout if you parked upstream of the washout. Pre-scout this spot! If you parked below the washout at Trout Creek or Index then take the right channel, as the left channel leads into the woods and onto the old road debris (washout). Downstream, Trout Creek will be obvious entering on the left. The river continues for a splashy (Class III) five miles down to Index.

—*Michael Harms*

## THE RUNDOWN

A great splashy, scenic Class IV option when the Sky is above 10K.

**Difficulty:** Class IV (V)

**Gauge:** USGS #12134500— Skykomish at Gold Bar; NWRFC #SNGW1—NF Skykomish at Galena

**Flow Min-max:** Visual 2,000- 8,000 cfs on NF. That translates to roughly 8,000- 20,000 cfs on the Main Sky at the Gold Bar gauge.

**Gradient:** 72 fpm average (130 fpm max)

**Takeout:** Beach at the end of the road above Trout Creek (or continue down to Index)

**Put-in:** Below Drumbeater

**Length:** ~5 miles

**Hitchability:** No

**Season:** Spring snowmelt, fall rains, winter if Index-Galena Rd. is open

**Camping:** Good; Troublesome Creek Campground is paid camping with water, vault toilets, and several scenic spots along river, open May 16 to September 16.

**4WD Needed?** No.

**Best Close Food/Beers:** Index— pack your own beers!

**Quality (out of 5):** 4

**Raft Recommendations:** Put in below Rooster Tail.

## SHUTTLE DIRECTIONS

As of 2015 the Galena-Index Road remains impassable at Trout Creek. Until the road has been repaired (2018), access is over Jack's Pass, using Forest Service Rd. 65 reached just east of the town of Skykomish. After crossing the North Fork, veer left at the junction with FR 63. The put-in will be approx. 3 miles from this junction in a very small pullout on the south side of the road. It's an obscure spot; look for a trail leading down a short ways to the river. There's also a large Douglas fir tree downstream of the pullout. The takeout is easily reached by driving downstream to the road's end. There is a beach that should be scouted as the takeout. Laps can be rallied if time allows. One can continue downstream but the shuttle from Index to the put-in will take an hour.

**Put-in: 47.895164, -121.393313**

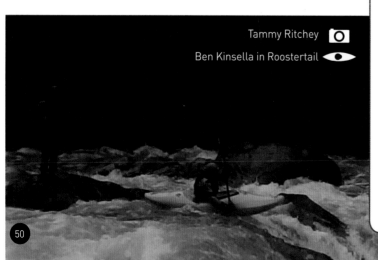

Tammy Ritchey 📷

Ben Kinsella in Roostertail 👁

The Upper North Fork of the Skykomish features three 30-some-foot waterfalls, one of the state's best rapids and a bedrock gorge. The warmup is short and punchy, beginning with a series of six or seven one-move ledge drops. The next drop is 25-foot Swordfight Falls, which many paddlers have run on the left—either by plunging down the left slot's throat or by accelerating left along the wall and landing flat in the pool. The landing here matters immensely because just downstream is Pillage, a tight 10-foot plunge into a room of doom. Several paddlers have run this at a variety of flows, but it is an intimidating rapid. Just below Pillage is a short, steep rapid, followed immediately by Gangplank Falls, a 25-foot waterfall with an obvious line down the center. This leads into a short canyon section and culminates in the rapid Plunder. Plunder begins with an 8-foot boof, followed by a micropool—just enough time to catch an eddy—before plunging down a series of ledges.

The creek's gradient disappears for a half-mile before the last major drop: Cannonball Falls, a 35-foot waterfall that most paddlers run far right. The portage is on the left and requires ropes and as much courage as running the waterfall itself.

The last few hundred yards of the Upper North Fork is bedrock Class III+ or Class IV.

*—Christian Knight*

## THE RUNDOWN

A great splashy, scenic Class IV option when the Sky is above 10K.

**Difficulty:** Class V+

**Gauge:** 4,000 to 8,000 cfs on USGS #12134500—Skykomish at Gold Bar

**Flow Min-max:** 250-500 cfs visual, 4,000 to 8,000 cfs on gauge

**Gradient:** 303 fpm

**Takeout:** The washout of the Index-Galena Road doubled the length of time necessary to access the Upper North Fork. Now, the only access is via Jack's Pass. To reach it, turn north on Beckler River Road, also called NFD 65 Rd., a mile east of the town of Skykomish. Continue on this road for 15 miles. It turns to gravel and becomes NFD 63. Turn right to stay on NFD 63 for another two miles. This is the takeout.

**Put-in:** Hike 1.5 miles up the decommissioned road to its end, then through the forest down to the river.

**Length:** ~1.5 miles

**Hitchability:** No

**Season:** Summer (high-elevation snow prevents winter runs)

**Camping:** None

**4WD Needed?** No.

**Best Close Food/Beers:** BYOB

**Quality (out of 5):** 4

**Raft Recommendations:** No

Brett Barton

Ari Walker

Nice Yalan savors Aquagasm rapid

# EAGLE FALLS

Eagle Falls on the South Fork of the Skykomish is a somewhat unknown rapid. At low flows it's a ledgy Class V drop. At high water, it becomes one of the largest runnable rapids in the Lower 48, consisting of three large waves, the first of which is run on a seam on the right side. The second wave, Oceanic, is run center this feature is notorious for flipping paddlers. The slack water between Oceanic and the final wave is extremely boiley, making rolls difficult. The final feature is run either center or on the right. Running center is usually a guaranteed mystery move. The right line consists of battling your way onto a diagonal and riding it back left. If you choose to step up to the plate and run Eagle Falls, do so with extreme caution: This rapid has dished out some major beatings.

—*Sam Grafton*

## THE RUNDOWN
Comparable to V-Drive on the Stikine

**Difficulty:** Class V-V+ (VI)

**Gauge:** Skykomish

**Flow Min-max:** 1,000-18,000 cfs

**Gradient:** 72 fpm average (130 fpm max)

**Takeout:** U.S. Hwy. 2 Mile Marker 39

**Put-in:** U.S. Hwy 2 Mile Marker 39

**Length:** Park and Huck

**Hitchability:** No

**Season:** Fall through spring

**Camping:** No

**4WD Needed?** No

**Best Close Food/Beers:** Sky Deli

**Quality (out of 5):** 5

**Raft Recommendations:** Not recommended although it has been run by rafting legend Dan McCain

## SHUTTLE DIRECTIONS
Roadside U.S. Hwy. 2
**Location: 47.795571, -121.514157**

Brian Burger

Sam Grafton on rowdy flows

# SUNSET FALLS

## OF THE SOUTH FORK SKYKOMISH

The first time someone ran western Washington's 275-foot Sunset Falls, 2,000 people—including journalists and Hollywood moviemakers—slipped through the fir and the spruce to claim a spot on the polished granite bedrock. That was 1926 and the guy everyone had gathered to watch was Al Faussett, a 46-year-old logger who discovered the exit door from the hard life when MGM announced a $5,000 prize to the person who provided the "best footage of a stunt going over a falls." Faussett charged 10 cents for admission—most didn't pay—and he wore an oxygen tank, running the furious slide in a 32-foot spruce dugout he called the *Skykomish Queen*.

The next time someone ran the slide was on a lunch break. Four people gathered that October day in 2008 to watch—and to perform what seemed like an inevitable rescue.

Christian Knight

Rob McKibbin saucing out the Kayak First Descent

The person they had come to watch was Rob McKibbin, a 43-year-old, 300-days-a-year kayaker, who arrived at the falls exactly 10 minutes past noon.

"We have to hurry," he said. "I have to be back at work at 1."

Returning to work—house construction—seemed presumptuous for a guy who was minutes from running a cataract that has killed dozens. But McKibbin avoided the lethal cave near the top, cut right, disappeared for eight seconds at the 20-foot rooster tail and emerged downstream of the boil. Since then, McKibbin has run Sunset Falls two other times as well as a handful of other expert paddlers have since styled the drop:

**Put-in: 47.8038737,-121.5531259**

*—Christian Knight*

# TOP TYE

Shortly after its discovery in 1996, kayakers frequently paddled all 2.2 miles of the Top Tye. Nowadays, most paddlers cut the run in half, by putting in at Box Drop, the second tier of Log Choke Falls. It's probably a wise decision. But it's a decision that costs them the opportunity to experience the U.S. Hwy. 2 corridor's most Classic waterfalls. The upper section of the Top Tye has seven runnable waterfalls—depending on your definition of "waterfall" and "runnable." None of them are tall—the tallest is shorter than 20 feet. And none of them are easy.

The run begins along U.S. 2, roughly a mile east of Deception Falls State Park. Within a few hundred yards, the river cascades over a short boulder garden, which ends with an 8-foot slide. Downstream a few hundred yards, the river drops over a 6-foot folding ledge with an underwater piton rock before the granite-lined river bends hard to the left. The Old Cascade Highway on river-right offers paddlers their last easy exit at this point before looming granite walls replace the boulder-lined banks. The next drop, immediately downstream, is the best and most challenging drop on the top section. The Spout begins with a ledge that transitions directly into a ramping 15-foot waterfall that lands at the base of the granite wall on the right. Paddlers have run this a variety of ways, including backwards and upside-down. But the most common way to run the Spout is to slide off the river-left shelf and land flat in the pool. That's because directly downstream is Skin-So-Soft, another funky 12-foot drop, which must be run far right. Both the Spout and Skin-So-Soft require more water than the lower section of the Top Tye. Once through Skin-So-Soft, paddlers navigate through a steep, fast boulder garden, through a few steep, braided channels and more bedrock rapids before encountering the top section's last three commonly run drops: Monkey Cage, Crack in the Earth, and the U-Ledge.

Monkey Cage is the easiest of the top section's major drops. Most paddlers run it down the center. Although, at higher flows a few paddlers have run it far left and far right. At Crack in the Earth, the river takes a symmetrical right turn through granite bedrocks. It's a 7-foot drop into a second 4-foot ledge. That ledge has induced dozens of swims—some of them quite dramatic. The last concern for paddlers is the U-Ledge, an intimidating 6- to 7-foot U-shaped ledge that has caused few swims. Speed and a delayed boof stroke are all a paddler needs to get past the U-Ledge's boil line.

From here, paddlers enjoy the creek's impressive conifers as they meander through Class III+ to Class IV boulder gardens to the lip of Log Choke Falls and the beginning of the more popular lower section.

*Continued on page 59*

## THE RUNDOWN

Rarely run waterfalls—Log Choke and Alpine—mark the ends of the Top Tye's upper and lower sections, respectively.

**Difficulty:** Class V-V+ (VI)

**Gauge:** South Fork Skykomish at Skykomish; Skykomish at Gold Bar; or sapling, downstream of the takeout bridge

**Flow Min-max:** 550-750 cfs, 6 feet on the South Fork Skykomish gauge; 5,000-7,500 cfs on the Skykomish at Gold Bar gauge during snowmelt, or at the sapling to four inches above the sapling downstream of the takeout.

**Gradient:** 380 fpm

**Takeout:** U.S. Hwy 2 bridge, 200 yards east of Hwy. 2 junction with Old Cascade Highway

**Put-in:** U.S. Hwy. 2, one mile east of Deception Falls State Park for the whole run

Or, put in just below Log Choke Falls off Old Cascade Highway for the house run. From Hwy. 2, head east on Old Cascade Highway about 0.6 miles and park in a pullout on the right. Hike down to Log Choke Falls and put in below the falls, but make sure to run Box Drop, the second tier of the drop.

**Length:** 2.2 miles

**Hitchability:** Good

**Season:** Summer snowmelt, winter after heavy rains

**Camping:** Head west on U.S. Hwy. 2 to Money Creek campground or the Beckler River Campground, both have vault toilets and water, open May to September

**4WD Needed?** No

**Best Close Food/Beers:** Skykomish Deli on U.S. 2 in Skykomish has good sandwiches and beer for takeout.

**Quality (out of 5):** 4.5

**Raft Recommendations:** No

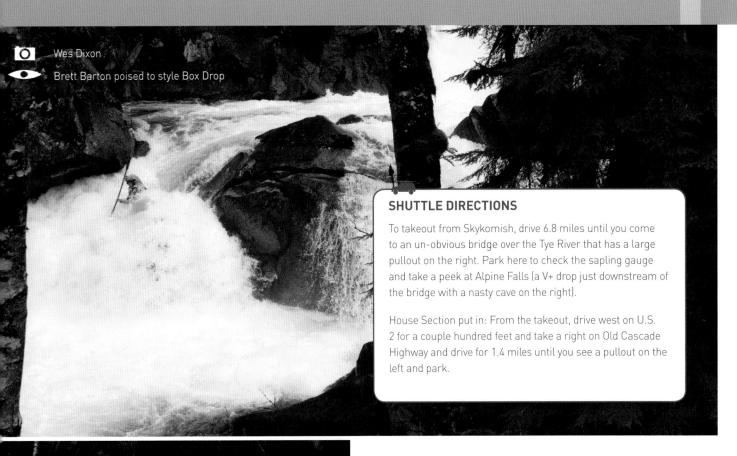

Wes Dixon

Brett Barton poised to style Box Drop

The lower run begins at the base of Log Choke Falls and the lip of
12-foot Box Drop. Paddlers can scout and photographers can shoot
the waterfall from atop the granite boulder on river-right. The next
rapid is Initiation, a long Class IV+ boulder garden with wood and a
10-foot ledge at the end. Most paddlers prefer to run the ledge with
right-to-left momentum and left angle. From here paddlers enjoy
long stretches of high-quality Class IV boulder gardens before the
creekbed narrows, twists and plunges over one of the Top Tye's
most notorious rapids: Paranoia. Paddlers scout and portage this
rapid on the left.

The next major rapid is Stairway to Heaven, a granite bedrock-
formed series of short ledges and slides. Paddlers run this Classic
rapid left of center, right of center and far right. All three are fun
lines. The left-of-center line is perhaps the most challenging. The
far-right line might be the easiest. But that doesn't mean it is any
less fun than the left-of-center line.

The last two major rapids are Godzilla and Witch's Brew,
respectively. The crux of both of these rapids involves slightly
undercut walls at the bottom of the rapid. Paddlers rarely, if ever,
have problems with the wall at the bottom of Godzilla. Some
paddlers spend time in the left wall at the bottom of Witch's Brew—
an inconvenience, for sure, but not much more than that.

—*Christian Knight*

Mike Hagadorn

Brad Xanthopoulos above Paranoia

Nick Hinds

Joe Howard stomping Box Drop

Scott Waidelich

Rob McKibbin below in the rapid below Paranoia

# LOWER TYE

The Lower Tye offers a worthy consolation prize for Top Tye seekers if the Top Tye is too high—or if a few in the crew aren't feeling up for it. The first mile contains three high-quality Class IV-IV+ rapids with impressive house-sized granite boulders forming them. The lower mile features three punchy, Class III rapids and several high-quality Class II boulder gardens.

## THE RUNDOWN

**Difficulty:** Class III-IV+

**Gauge:** Skykomish at Gold Bar; South Fork Skykomish at Skykomish

**Flow Min-max:** 6-7 ft on the South Fork gauge.

**Gradient:** 85 fpm

**Takeout:** For the two-mile run, which includes several quality Class III rapids and some high-quality Class II, takeout at the U.S. Hwy. 2 bridge 2.3 miles east of Skykomish. For the more compact version, takeout at on Foss River Road. To reach it, drive two miles east from Skykomish. Turn right onto Foss River Rd. and drive 1.2 miles to a small pullout on the left. A large boulder in the river marks the spot.

**Put-in:** Continue .9 miles past the takeout onto the unnamed, gravel road, which is on the left of the fork. Foss River Road is on the right fork. Park in a small pullout, which overlooks the section's first Class IV rapid.

**Length:** Two miles, but can be shortened to one mile

**Hitchability:** Poor

**Season:** Snowmelt or after heavy rains

**Camping:** No

**4WD Needed?** No

**Best Close Food/Beers:** BYOB

**Quality (out of 5):** 3 and woody

**Raft Recommendations:** yes

Mike Harms

Christian Knight

# FOSS RIVER

The first mile of the Foss is a fun, challenging stretch of Class IV creeking. A warmup through continuous boulder gardens leads to the only named rapid: Ken and Barbie (IV+), which is about a half-mile downriver from the put-in. Easy to scout from the bank on river-right, large boulders create an S-turn with a brief pause before a picket fence offers optional slots to choose, middle and right being preferred. There are some holes to bash through and wood can be lodged in the slots, so scout carefully. The action continues through nondescript boulder gardens with several ledges offering up some good boofs. At lower flows the riverbed can be a bit manky, so keep your nose up! At higher flows this section becomes continuous Class V. The first mile takeout is at the high railroad bridge. Below is another mile of Class III. Like many creeks in this region, wood is a constant-changing, ever-present hazard.

—*Mike Harms*

## THE RUNDOWN

Link up the Foss with Top Tye, Rapid River, and Sky for an awesome day!

**Difficulty:** Class IV+, V at high water

**Gauge:** USGS #12134500—SKYKOMISH RIVER NEAR GOLD BAR, WA

**Flow Min-max:** 7,500-10,000+ cfs on spring snowmelt. More is needed for rain runoff. For visual reference, check the downstream side of the first bridge for a large, flat table rock. Water 6 inches below its top is medium.

**Gradient:** 160 fpm (first mile), 80 fpm after that

**Takeout:** Railroad trestle pullout or continue down to bridge at Foss River Grove.

**Put-in:** Pullout one mile up from pullout at high railroad trestle

**Length:** 2 miles

**Hitchability:** No

**Season:** Fall rains, spring runoff

**Camping:** Beckler River Campground is managed by the Forest Service and has vault toilet and hand-pump water. Open May 1 to September 7. Also lots of free camping on Forest Service land.

**4WD Needed?** No, unless ice or snow-covered road in winter

**Best Close Food/Beers:** Skykomish Deli on U.S. Hwy. 2 in Skykomish

**Quality (out of 5):** 3

**Raft Recommendations:** Yes

## SHUTTLE DIRECTIONS

Turn right two miles east of Skykomish onto Foss River Road-NF 68. Drive until you cross a one-lane bridge. This is a good spot to check flows, and it's also an optional takeout. Drive to a junction with FR 6820. There is a small pullout near a high railroad bridge. This serves as the takeout if you're just interested in the best stretch of Class IV. Drive one mile upstream to another road junction with FR 6830 and park in the small pullout on right. A steep trail leads to the river.

**Put-in: 47.672812, -121.293950**
**Takeout: 47.687496, -121.297747**

# MILLER RIVER

The Miller is a great boulder garden run that is too often forgotten, but we wanted to shed some light on this great run again. It starts pretty quickly building from Class III to IV rapids and you can boat-scout most everything. At the confluence of the East and West Fork Miller, the rapids increase in size and constriction creating more powerful drops than above the confluence. The run is dotted with medium-sized boulders giving it a great slalom feel. The whitewater keeps you smiling for almost 2 miles then lets up into Class II braided channels until the takeout. Most pair this run with others in the drainage like the Foss, Lower Tye, or Sky to make it a full day.

—Scott Waidelich

## SHUTTLE DIRECTIONS

Take Miller River Rd. (FR 6410). Drive past the West Fork bridge (Mile 3.5) to a put-in where the river approaches the road anywhere near Mile 4.3 at 1,290-feet of elevation, you'll see a large slide area that allows you to see the river. The Bennett book says to put in at the West Fork bridge, which you can, but it does skip some good whitewater.

**Put-in:** 47.689196, -121.390822
**Takeout:** 47.716893, -121.393782

## THE RUNDOWN

One of the first creeks paddled in the Skykomish drainage.

**Difficulty:** Class IV

**Gauge:** USGS #12134500 SKYKOMISH RIVER NEAR GOLD BAR, WA

**Flow Min-max:** 5-10,000 cfs Skykomish at Gold bar (400-900 cfs visual)

**Gradient:** 115 fpm

**Takeout:**
option 1: 47.689196, -121.390822
option 2: 47.716893, -121.393782

**Put-in:** 47.661808, -121.380921

**Length:** Option 1, 4.25 miles; Option 2, 2.2 miles

**Hitchability:** No

**Season:** Peak snowmelt May, June, also high-water rain events

**Camping:** Miller River campground is run by the Forest Service and has hand-pump water and vault toilets, open May 18 to September 28

**4WD Needed?** Not usually

**Best Close Food/Beers:** Skykomish Deli on U.S. Hwy. 2 in Skykomish has beer, sandwiches and other grub.

**Quality (out of 5):** 3.5

**Raft Recommendations:** Small rafts OK

Dan Patrinellis

Jah Bisson exploring a Fork of the Miller

The Rapid is a very continuous Class IV run from top to bottom, it's a great run to hone your reading and running skills and only has a few spots that are steep enough that you can't see the bottom of the rapid.

The run is a little tricky to nail down flows, I've done it at 10,000 cfs (Skykomish at Gold Bar) and it felt low; I've done it at the same flows and it was nearly flood stage and felt like a Class V run, so use discretion when you get to the takeout. If the rapid at the takeout is pretty much eddy-less, has no rocks showing, and has several stomping holes, it's high.

There are two traditionally used access points: The third bridge that crosses the river as you drive upstream, or below the Class V+ triple drop at the undeveloped campsite three miles up from the takeout. If you put in below the triple drop, you get to run the longest and steepest rapid on the run—though this rapid has historically had a lot of wood and demands a good scout. Shortly after this series, the gradient flattens for about a mile and a half before you arrive at the bridge where the rapids start again. Putting in at the third bridge allows you to run the meat and potatoes of the run and is about a mile and a half long. It's best to start from the higher put-in on your first run, then do laps on the lower stretch from the third bridge.

The triple drop at the put-in is worth a look, but I've never seen it when there wasn't wood in it. Put in below the runout of this rapid and shortly downstream the gradient will increase and the river will bend to the left; scout this rapid on river-right. This rapid can also be scouted from the road before putting on and only requires some light bushwhacking.

## THE RUNDOWN

Can be combined with the Beckler River if you have Class II-III paddlers in your group.

**Difficulty:** Class IV

**Gauge:** USGS #12134500—SKYKOMISH RIVER NEAR GOLD BAR, WA NWRFC #GLBW1 SKYKOMISH—NEAR GOLD BAR

**Flow Min-max:** 10,000 +/- cfs

**Gradient:** 111 fpm

**Takeout:** At confluence with Rapid and Beckler River

**Put-in:** Below V+ Triple Drop

**Length:** 3.3 miles

**Hitchability:** No

**Season:** Rainy and peak snowmelt

**Camping:** Beckler River Campground is managed by the Forest Service and has vault toilet and hand-pump water. Open May 1 to September 7. Also lots of free camping on Forest Service land.

**4WD Needed?** Not usually

**Best Close Food/Beers:** Skykomish Liquor and Deli has beer and good breakfast sandwiches on U.S. Hwy. 2 in Skykomish.

**Quality (out of 5):** 3

**Raft Recommendations:** Yes with an experienced crew and knowledge of the wood situation.

## SHUTTLE DIRECTIONS

Takeout: From Skykomish drive 0.8 miles east on U.S. Hwy 2 and take a left on Beckler River Road. Drive 7 miles until the pavement ends at a large dirt intersection, where the road crosses the Rapid near the confluence of the Rapid and Beckler.

Put-in: From the takeout, drive east on NF-6530 and follow the river as is criss-crosses the Rapid. You can either put-in at the third bridge you cross (1.2 miles from the takeout) or drive to the end of the road (3 miles from the takeout), where there is a primitive campsite on the right—park here or a pull out if the site is full.

**Put-in: 47.661808, -121.380921**

**Takeout option 1: 47.689196, -121.390822**
**Takeout option 2: 47.716893, -121.393782**

Once you've reached the bridge, the gradient picks up—and doesn't let up—until you reach the takeout. There aren't any defined rapids, but there are two steeper drops that you can identify by the river bending sharply to the left. The rest of the run is a checkerboard of holes, pour-overs, and waves. Once you know the run and feel confident about the lack of wood you can really crank up the flow for a rocketship ride to the takeout. Much of the run can be scouted on the drive to the put-in so take your time on the way up.

—*Jed Hawkes*

Nick Hinds

Jon Shelby floats into the fog

# UPPER SULTAN

The Upper Sultan River is a Class IV wilderness adventure run in close proximity to Seattle. Less than 40 miles as the crow flies from the Space Needle, the Upper Sultan remains dewatered for much of the year. After three decades of involvement, American Whitewater reached a settlement agreement with the Snohomish PUD, resource agencies, and Tulalip Tribe to restore access to this amazing whitewater resource. With the relicensing, the PUD is required to offer ecological pulse flows that are designed to benefit fish and river health, and to provide an average of four whitewater opportunities each year. Typically scheduled in the spring and fall, the Culmback Dam releases a metered dose of rejuvenating water into the upper Sultan.

Access to the remote canyon requires hiking your boat just over a mile from the Culmback Dam parking lot. Follow the gated road to the Sultan Canyon Trail. This recently constructed trail descends swiftly through old-growth cedar, fir, and hemlock forests to its terminus at the river's edge. On the water there's time to take a few casual strokes and enjoy the spectacular scenery the Sultan has to offer. With each passing bend in the river, the remoteness increases as you become more immersed in the Sultan Canyon's wilderness.

A logjam will likely be your first obstacle in the canyon. Landslides and the absence of natural floods allow the Sultan to collect an impressive amount of timber. Much of the wood has amassed in large piles in the upper portion of the run, several of which must be portaged. Also, it is not uncommon to find smaller, hard-to-spot wood lurking in any number of the canyon's boulders slaloms.

Over five miles into the run are the first of two diversion dams. The City of Everett has made it clear that kayakers are not to attempt the first dam. Please honor their requests and portage on river-right along the maintained trail. Soon after the diversion the action picks up with a quality Class IV section of stacked drops. This section of the canyon contains the largest drop on this stretch: Landslide, which is shallow, sharp, and chunky. A quick look is enough to send many boaters scrambling over the loose scree on river-right. After a few more beautiful bends the second diversion dam marks the end of the Upper Sultan.

## THE RUNDOWN

Due to the hard work of American Whitewater and the cooperation of the great people at Snohomish County Public Utility District, we now have secured recreational releases on this section in the spring and fall.

**Difficulty:** Class IV+ (V)

**Gauge:** USGS #12137800—SULTAN RIVER BELOW DIVERSION DAM NEAR SULTAN, WA

**Flow Min-max:** 400-1,500 cfs

**Gradient:** 81 fpm

**Takeout:** Trout Farm Road

**Put-in:** NF-6120

**Length:** 11 miles

**Hitchability:** No

**Season:** Scheduled recreational releases in the fall and spring as well as after extremely heavy rain that raises the lake level over the spillway.

**Camping:** No

**4WD Needed?** No

**Best Close Food/Beers:** Lots of options in Sultan and Monroe, Sultan Bakery is a staple but can be crowded and doesn't serve beer.

**Quality (out of 5):** 4

**Raft Recommendations:** Yes

Most trips continue beyond the second diversion dam through the short but exciting Power House run. The action starts quickly and before long you are lining up to Last Nasty, a solid Class IV+ rapid with a tricky lead-in and a chunky ledge-hole. To make things worse the whole left bank is lined with sieves and undercuts. The scout and portage for Last Nasty is on river-right.

With Last Nasty in the rearview you can now relax and enjoy the last boulder slaloms of the Sultan River. It is not long before the canyon opens up and the fishing access takeout appears on river-left.

The Upper Sultan releases are a direct reflection of American Whitewater's stewardship efforts. It is important that each of us takes part in these events that aid in preserving the opportunity to travel through such a magnificent river canyon.

—Mike Hagadorn

📷 Mike Hagadorn

👁 Ben Hawthorne hitting the landslide rapid

## SHUTTLE DIRECTIONS

Takeout: From Monroe drive on U.S. Hwy. 2 for nine miles until you come into Sultan. Take a left on Third Street. and then immediately onto Main Street. Main St. bends to the right in 200 feet and turns to First St. Follow First St. for just under a mile until a stop sign at Trout Farm Road. Turn left on Trout Farm Road and follow for 1.3 miles until you see fishing access parking on the left. Park here but be considerate about other users as it's a very small lot. **(47.887999, -121.833921)**

Put-in: From the takeout drive back out to US-2 and turn left and drive for 2 miles until you can turn left at a light for Sultan Basin Road. Follow Sultan Basin Rd. for 13.3 miles until a left onto NF-6120 (there will be a large sign for culmback dam access) and continue for 1.6 miles until you see a gate on the left and a parking area on the right. Park here to start your hike to the trailhead and down to the river. **(47.971537, -121.701330)**

📷 Mike Hagadorn

👁 Jed Hawkes and Adam Griffin route a beauty

# LOWER SULTAN

The Lower Sultan is a great Class III-IV boulder garden run with one large and consequential IV+ in the first half of the run. Due to the fact that Snohomish PUD captures water behind Culmback Dam and releases it at a relatively steady rate, this section of river has reasonable flows for the majority of the year and has quality rapids throughout.

At the put-in, park at the top of the hill that leads down to the diversion dam. There is a check-in kiosk where you will need to register, though there is no fee. Registration is important to quantify recreational usage in the river and on the public lands so please be sure to register, this helps American Whitewater advocate for usage on this section. Please park here and carry your boats down the road to the river. PUD does not want vehicles down by the dam, so, in the name of maintaining access, please park up top. From the parking area carry down the road and follow it until the bridge crosses the river. Here, duck off the road to the right and a small path will lead you to a weir that at most flows is dry and provides a nice place to gear up and launch.

Once you leave the put-in there are two distinct rapids. The first you enter right, in some shallow shoals, staying right of an island. The second rapid is a series of boulders with several fun options. The third rapid should be taken seriously because it is the lead-in rapid to Last Nasty and it is a slightly blind rapid. You have two options from here to scout Last Nasty: from above this rapid, or run it then scout (there aren't many great eddies below here and you need to scout on river-right). Several large boulders split the current, so eddy out on the right above this to scout. THIS IS ONE OF THE SKETCHIEST RAPIDS AROUND. It may only be rated IV+ but it has some of the worst sieves on any run. The river-left side of the rapid has several large sieves that can be tough to see on the scout. Last Nasty is three moves, where a controlled boater can slow down and eddy-hop, though it's easy to get pushed around and have to run the whole rapid in one go. Scout carefully and be aware.

Below Last Nasty, the character and quality of the run changes to the takeout: basically fun Class III with a couple of light Class IV read-and- run rapids. A motivated paddler can really get their money's worth as they S-turn and eddy-hop their way down. Every rapid has a quality boof to be slayed and fun eddy to catch. At low flows this run still channelizes well and provides a good option if the area is in a dry spell. I've gotten reports about high-water runs through Last Nasty (3,000 cfs) and all told tales of terror as the rest of the run was really great. Best flows are from 1,200-1,700 cfs.

—Jed Hawkes

## THE RUNDOWN

A nice addition to a lap on the Skykomish. Gate to put-in closes at 6 p.m. daily.

**Difficulty:** Class IV+

**Gauge:** USGS #12138160—Sultan river below powerplant near Sultan, WA; NWRFC #SLTW1—Sultan-Near Sultan

**Flow Min-max:** 500-3,000 cfs

**Gradient:** 50 fpm

**Takeout:** Fishing Access on Trout Farm Rd.

**Put-in:** Lake Chaplain Road PUD check-in kiosk

**Length:** 2 miles

**Hitchability:** Bike Shuttle, but long (8 miles)

**Season:** Winter, spring, early summer in big snowpack years

**Camping:** No

**4WD Needed?** No

**Best Close Food/Beers:** Old School BBQ, hard to miss pair of old school buses parked in the parking lot of the Reptile Zoo. Good ribs and a distraction for the kids.

**Quality (out of 5):** 3.5. Great run, long shuttle.

**Raft Recommendations:** Yes, but with either a talented guide or a solid experienced crew.

## SHUTTLE DIRECTIONS

Takeout: From Monroe drive 7.5 miles until you come to the town of Sultan, take a left on Third St., followed immediately by a left on Main. Follow Main as it bends right and turns into First. St. for 2 miles. At the stop sign take a left onto Trout Farm Road and follow for 1.3 miles. On the left you will find a fishing access that is a small dirt pullout. **(47.887996, -121.833630)**

Put-in: Drive back out to U.S. Hwy. 2, take a right and follow for just over half a mile before taking a right at the light for Owen Rd. Follow Owen for another half-mile and take a right onto Reiner Rd., staying on it 3 miles until a very sharp right onto Lake Chaplain Rd. Follow it for a final 1.3 miles until you see a kiosk on the right to park here and walk down to the river. **(47.912920, -121.816538)**

# ERNIE'S CANYON

## OF THE NORTH FORK SNOQUALMIE

Sean Lee

Xavier Engle on Cool Rapid

Ernie's Canyon is a Pacific Northwest ultra-classic. It's also considered one of the most challenging and dangerous runs in the region. The technical and powerful rapids test and reward expert kayakers who travel from far away to run this unique section. Located only 40 minutes from downtown Seattle, the North Fork Snoqualmie flows regularly from the abundant rains in the fall and winter and snowmelt in the spring and early summer. Despite convenient access and regular flows, the difficulty and unforgiving nature of Ernie's means it is paddled much less frequently than some of the other nearby Class V runs. For a small group of locals, it is the clear favorite of the whitewater offerings in the area.

First explored in the mid-'80s, and regularly run for periods on-and-off since the '90s, Ernie's has generated a reputation of challenging and humbling the region's top kayakers. Floods in the early 2000s have dramatically rearranged most of the rapids on the run, rendering early photos unrecognizable. While individual rapids have changed, the nature of the river has not: The 2-mile whitewater section consists of high-quality, creeky, boulder-garden drops nestled within a dark canyon. Even at low flows the rapids feel pushy and powerful, and numerous undercuts and sticky holes will severely penalize paddlers who are pushed off line. As long as you can catch tight eddies in fast-moving whitewater, all of the rapids can be scouted, and capable crews regularly descend the river without a guide. Since most of the lines can be described quite simply, a first-time run with someone who knows the routes will make the trip much smoother.

Ernie's Canyon can be divided into two sections: above and below Jacuzzi Falls. From the put-in there are a couple miles of Class II-III warmup. After a single IV drop, the rapids swiftly become Vs, arriving at Ferry Land, a maze of boulders that paddlers usually run on the left and finish right. The next ledge is run on the right, which lands directly above Raft Cache, a tight-slot boof on river-right. The whitewater remains powerful and complex, with numerous unforgiving holes and ledges with short recovery pools in between. After a dozen or so Class V rapids, the section culminates with the Big Three: Cool Rapid (Big Nasty), Split Falls (Vertical Vortex), and Toilet Bowl. This last rapid is especially dangerous: The paddler must negotiate across a boiley room on river-left and then over a 6-foot drop. After rolling up after the all-too-probable flip, you must charge hard right to avoid a terminal sieve lurking 30 feet downstream of the drop. Sound sketchy? If you lack basic skills (read: roll quickly and reliably), this river is not for you. Toilet Bowl can be portaged by rappelling off of a tree on river-right, or boofed on the right at sufficiently high flows.

*Continued on page 70*

# ERNIE'S CANYON (CONTINUED)

## OF THE NORTH FORK SNOQUALMIE

Below Toilet Bowl is a stretch of Class II-III whitewater. After nearly a mile, you may see some logs on the river-left bank. Best to eddy out on the left sooner than later. The river turns to the left, quickly changes to Class IV, and then plunges over Jacuzzi. There is a last-chance eddy on river-right at the lip of the falls, but best not to mess with this. Although most choose to portage, an increasing number of paddlers have recently successfully run Jacuzzi, usually at lower flows. In the likely scenario that you boof into the left cave at the base of the falls, stay in your boat and paddle out aggressively. Ensure safety is set up from river-right so that a swimmer can be roped out of the cave. Below Jacuzzi are a few more rapids, culminating in Crash Test Dummy. Enjoy the spectacular views of Mount Si as you float to the takeout.

*—Ben Hawthorne*

### THE RUNDOWN

Nearly year-round flows and incredible whitewater in close proximity to Seattle.

**Difficulty:** V+

**Gauge:** USGS #12142000—NF SNOQUALMIE RIVER NEAR SNOQUALMIE FALLS, WA

**Flow Min-max:** 300-900 cfs

**Gradient:** 107 fpm

**Takeout:** Three Forks Park

**Put-in:** Hike 1 mile east from Spur 10 Gate to North Fork Bridge. Need Hancock Access Pass ($8/day). Or drive 4-5 miles upriver from Spur 10 Gate to legal access point at bridge. Note: One Class V rapid directly downstream of bridge, then Class II (see Upper North Fork description).

**Length:** 6.5 miles

**Hitchability:** Poor

**Season:** September/October to June/July

**Camping:** No

**4WD Needed?** No

**Best Close Food/Beers:** North Bend Bar & Grill, or check out the Sureshot for cheap tacos and a local vibe. **Quality (out of 5):** 5

**Raft Recommendations:** No, but has been run in rafts.

Kira Marley

Scott and Hans survive a high speed run through Crash Test Dummy

### SHUTTLE DIRECTIONS

From Seattle Take I-90 East for 24.5 miles to Exit 27. At the end of the ramp turn left onto Winery Rd. toward Snoqualmie Falls/Snoqualmie. Stay right onto SE North Bend Way for .7 miles. Turn left at Meadowbrook Way SE and follow for 1.4 miles until it crosses the Snoqualmie river and becomes SE Reinig Way. Turn left in a quarter-mile to stay on SE Reinig Way, continue for 1.8 miles. On your right is the small parking lot. On the southern end of the lot there is a trail that goes down to the river.

Takeout: 47.522000, -121.769594
Put-in: 47.579477, -121.715404

# MIDDLE MIDDLE

## OF THE MIDDLE FORK SNOQUALMIE

The Middle Middle is a Class III training ground for boaters in the Seattle area, with one longer Class IV drop called House Rocks. Boat-scouting is required as the land along river-left and -right is privately owned at this one tougher rapid. Find fellow boaters almost every Friday afternoon during the winter, spring and fall at the takeout. This run provides great, meandering boulder garden training, and at many levels, small, enjoyable playspots. Most people choose to shorten the run and focus on the lower half, which contains the majority of the action.

If you put in higher at the bridge, Class II rapids bend around corners until you reach the first major rapid below the lower put-in called A-frame (note the A-frame house looming at the top of the hill overlooking this rapid). If you don't like what you see, walk off on river-left, with access to the lower road. As the river continues, rapids increase in difficulty with many Class IIIs as well as a very continuous section leading into a right-hand eddy above House Rocks. Be careful, this rapid has two tiers, generally run left to right on the first half. Not much room for recovery exists before the second half, which is generally run center-left, fading right at the bottom. This rapid and run in general has retentive holes, so Class II-III boaters should beware and find a capable partner for a safe personal first descent. Boat on down until you hit the takeout near the Tanner Rd. intersection with SE North Bend Way.

—*Nick Hinds*

### THE RUNDOWN

Closest Class III near Seattle with dependable flows and decent play (at ~2,000 cfs). Big-water Class IV at high flows, gets rowdy above 5,000.

**Difficulty:** Class III (IV)

**Gauge:** USGS #12141300—MIDDLE FORK SNOQUALMIE RIVER NEAR TANNER, WA NWRFC #TANW1—MF SNOQUALMIE NEAR TANNER

**Flow Min-max:** 1,000 cfs (Class III), 1,500-4,000 cfs (Class III-IV), 4,500+ (Class IV-V)

**Gradient:** 43 fpm

**Takeout:** Tanner Road

**Put-in:** Two options, at the bridge upstream, or at an established pullout at a bend on river-left.

**Length:** 7 miles in total, or just lower 4 miles for more action-packed shorter version

**Hitchability:** No

**Season:** Winter, spring and fall

**Camping:** Yes, lower put-in is great

**4WD Needed?** No

**Best Close Food/Beers:** Snoqualmie Brewery or North Bend Bar & Grill

**Quality (out of 5):** 4 stars

**Raft Recommendations:** Yes, below 3,500 cfs

### SHUTTLE DIRECTIONS

Put-in: Two exist. Head east from the takeout .2 miles and turn left on SE 140th St. Turn left onto SE Middle Fork Rd. for 3.5 miles through a residential zone and past Valley Camp, continuing into the Mine Creek Day Use Recreation Area. The river comes right up against the road at this site that serves as your lower put-in option. If you seek a little more Class II-III, then continue another 1.5 miles upstream to the Granite Creek access at the bridge.

Takeout: To reach the take out, get off I-90 at exit 32 go north for 0.6 miles. At the T junction turn right onto North Bend Way and go 0.7 miles. At this point, past the spot where the river runs near the road, turn left onto SE Tanner Road. Take this road 0.5 down to a power-line right-of-way that crosses the river and provides access. The City of North Bend has been working to formalize this access point as new development in the neighborhood proceeds and King County considers a larger access and day-use area downstream.
**47.4781723, -121.73911**

While the Middle-Middle is the most popular run on the Middle Fork Snoqualmie, beginners looking for one of the most scenic runs in the region will enjoy the Upper Middle which has several good class II+ rapids and impressive views of Mt. Garfield, Pratt Valley, and Russian Butte. Designated as a Wild and Scenic River and less than an hour from downtown Seattle, this section of the river also has a few good places to camp if you want to enjoy an overnight trip with simple logistics. The run begins just downstream of the Taylor River confluence. Many take out at Russian Butte View, a day-use site on DNR land but you can also continue downstream through easy class II down to the Granite Creek access and the start of the Middle-Middle.

Another popular run, and one of the best for instruction is the Lower Middle which starts from the Middle-Middle take-out and continues down to Blue Hole or the Three Forks Natural Area.

—Thomas O'Keefe

## SHUTTLE DIRECTIONS

From Exist 34 off I-90 head north on 468th Ave half a mile to the Middle Fork Road. Five miles up the road is the Granite Creek Access (aka Concrete Bridge) which serves as a take-out. An intermediate access 8 miles up the road at Russian Butte View serves as an alternate take-out that let's you shorten the run while still enjoying the best whitewater and scenery. The put-in is 11.3 miles up the road at Bridgeview, a roadside pull-out just downstream of the Middle Fork Trailhead. Alternate access points are available further upstream for those seeking a longer river trip.

Put-in: 47.5471, -121.5420
Takeout: 47.4950, -121.6410

## THE RUNDOWN

Incredibly scenic run just off Interstate 90.

**Difficulty:** Class II

**Gauge:** Middle Fork Snoqualmie Near Tanner provides flow information for this reach.

**Flow Min-max:** Optimal flows are 1000-3000 cfs. It can be lower but you will hit rocks. As flows increase features begin to wash out.

**Takeout:** Granite Creek Access

**Put-in:** Bridgeview Access

**Length:** 8.3 miles

**Hitchability:** Possible on weekends in spring. During cold winter days you will be waiting a while.

**Season:** Winter rainy season through the end of spring snowmelt.

**Camping:** Camping is available at the Middle Fork Campground or a few dispersed sites along the river.

**4WD Needed?** No

**Best Close Food/Beers:** North Bend Bar and Grill or Scott's Dairy Freeze for shakes.

**Quality (out of 5):** 4

**Raft Recommendations:** A great raft float that shows of the beauty of this river valley.

# FALL IN THE WALL

## OF THE SOUTH FORK SNOQUALMIE

### THE RUNDOWN

Roadside Class IV-V slides, a walkable shuttle, perfect for after-work laps.

**Difficulty:** Class IV+, V- or V depending on level

**Gauge:** SF Snoqualmie/Visual— shortly after passing under I-90 there is a stone wall on the right. Look for a "cup" rock at the base of the overlook of Fall in the Wall Falls. Seeing the cup rock indicates a medium flow; if it's underwater, the flow is high (see photos for visual).

**Flow Min-max:** 250-700 cfs (snowmelt), 500-1,200 cfs (rain)

**Gradient:** 370 fpm

**Takeout:** River left above 70 foot Franklin Falls—scout if you plan to run Root Ball, or the big slide after it, as most take out above Root Ball.

**Put-in:** Under the I-90 overpass, below Fall in the Wall Falls

**Length:** .4 miles

**Hitchability:** Earn your strokes!

**Season:** Spring

**Camping:** Not great, but this is the Summit Ski Area. Some small pull-outs on NF-58 downstream of takeout.

**4WD Needed?** Yes, but only in early spring before road is plowed.

**Best Close Food/Beers:** No great options at the Summit (Family Pancake House), we usually rally to North Bend to eat.

**Quality (out of 5):** 4-5

**Raft Recommendations:** No

This is the kayaker's skatepark creek. It hides directly beneath the east- and westbound lanes of I-90 at the Summit at Snoqualmie (on Snoqualmie Pass) and is a staple after-work run for Seattle-area paddlers. With over 10 drops between 5-9 feet and tons of small ledges in less than a half-mile, this creek will surely make you smile. This is not a difficult run at medium to low flows, but the drops are stacked and require scouting your first time down. If the water is low, put in under the overpass and run the first falls: Fall in the Wall! Otherwise, head 80-100 yards down and beat your way to the creek to seal-launch in. Quickly you'll reach the Fearsome Foursome, a series of four stacked slides (run the bottom two ledges on the center/right). More ledges and small drops remain until you exit the short canyon and reach the Green Room. This sloping ledge is run down the middle and tends to hold boats down before releasing you like a breaching whale! Take out just downstream on the left—we park above a pullout in the road. Once you know the lines, you'll be doing laps and crushing the sweet spots. Careful, Franklin Falls is just downstream; make sure to scout the takeout.

—Scott Waidelich

### SHUTTLE DIRECTIONS

Shuttle: From Seattle, take I-90 east 51 miles to Snoqualmie Pass and take exit 52 for West Summit. At the end of the ramp, turn left and pass under the highway, staying left to parallel the highway and passing under I-90 one more time. You should soon see a small pullout on the right with a stone wall; park here to check the water level. Continue a few hundred feet downstream to a pullout on the left; park here and hike down to river level above the Fearsome Foursome. **(47.427709, -121.425842)**

Takeout: The road is a straight shot down to the takeout. The river comes very close to the road and has a small pullout. Hike back to your car from here and earn your strokes. **(47.425669, -121.430710)**

Chris Totten

Paddler: Scott Waidelich drops the Fearsome Foursome

# DENNY CREEK

The Franklin section of the SF is easily added on to FITW or can be done by itself. Your first time down, it's best to scout the drops from the hiking trail, making sure it's clear of wood, as that will determine your takeout. After putting in at the base of Franklin Falls, the river heads into a pin-ey boulder garden that bends to the left and then back to the right. A few smaller drops follow in the gorge proper, before arriving at the main event,: two back-to-back waterfalls. The first drop, Superboof, bends around a huge boulder, slides over an entrance ledge, and then ramps off a 15-foot falls. Drive left to avoid the sticky hole on the right. There's time to regroup in the pool, before 20-foot Ankle Breaker, which is a great free-falling drop that should be run far right to avoid a bad shelf.

After the two big falls, there are some smaller ledges leading to Z-Turn, which is an exciting 8-foot slide to a hard, banking right turn. This turn lands in the pool above Beater, which is the last drop of the Franklin section. Beater starts with a couple boulder moves before a 5-foot boof landing in a narrow canyon. Eddy-out left in the pool and climb up, out, and above a 25-foot falls that lands on rock.

If you're looking for more, or the water levels are too high for FITW and Franklin, don't despair: The Denny section awaits. Climb down from the trail, where it's next to the road, and put in above the Plunger (10 feet), which can live up to its name at higher flows. Fun little boulder gardens continue as you pass the Denny Creek

## SHUTTLE DIRECTIONS

Drive east of North Bend on I-90 for 16.5 miles and take exit 47 toward Denny Creek/Asahel Curtis. Go left (north) over I-90 and then make a right onto FR 9035. You'll quickly reach a bridge over the South Fork. You can take out here for the full Denny stretch, or just around the corner in Asahel Curtis Picnic Area. To reach the put-in for the Denny section, or just the Franklin section, head back toward I-90 and turn upstream on FR58 for 2.75 miles to Denny Creek Campground, where you check the stick gauge at the trailhead for Franklin Falls. The put-in for the Denny stretch is just up the road another quarter-mile where you'll see the gorge close to the road, and parking for a car or two. To get to the Franklin stretch put-in, keep going upstream for not quite a mile to a hard right turn. Find somewhere to park and then walk down the trail for a few minutes to Franklin Falls.

**Denny Stretch**
Put-in: 47.418564, -121.438774
Takeout: 47.394234, -121.473541

**Franklin Stretch**
Put-in: 47.422951, -121.43383
Takeout: 47.418564, -121.438774

## THE RUNDOWN

Two runs that are alternatives or additions to the classic Fall in the Wall stretch.

**Difficulty:** Franklin V, Denny IV – V

**Gauge:** USGS SF Snoq. at Garcia (downstream quite a ways).

**Flow Min-max:** Franklin section 350-750 cfs, Denny section 700-1,500 cfs

**Gradient:** Franklin 300 fpm (put-in 2,600 ft.), Denny 200 fpm

**Takeout:** Asahel Curtis Picnic Area

**Put-in:** Below Franklin Falls

**Length:** 4 miles

**Hitchability:** You can walk the shuttle for the 1-mile Franklin stretch, or bike the FR for Denny stretch; may be able to thumb on the weekends with more hiking use.

**Season:** March-June (snowmelt); Oct.-Nov. (fall rains) before road is snowed in.

**Camping:** Denny Creek Campground is near the put-in; may be able to find "free camping" below the takeout on the south side of I-90.

**4WD Needed?** Yes, but only in early spring before road is plowed.

**Best Close Food/Beers:** Good food and beers at North Bend Bar and Grill

**Quality (out of 5):** 3

**Raft Recommendations:** Has not been rafted, and is not recommended.

confluence, which can add a bit of volume. Below the confluence the Bridge series offers some great moves in a mini-gorge. Scout the drop below the bridge to make sure the landing is clear. As you finish this great series, you'll pass a stick gauge on the left (should be 3.1–4.2 feet), as the river becomes gravel bars down to the next bridge.

As you pass the second bridge, a few interesting moves are required before the seocnd canyon. Keep your eyes peeled for a third bridge, which signals a nasty undercut drop, with a dicey line center-right. Scout/portage on the right. Next up is the Final Four: starting with Septic Tank, a great zig-zagging drop with a sticky hole at the bottom; and then Taco Bobs, which can have a great center boof at higher flows. After Taco Bobs, grab a quick eddy, and look for a scouting/portaging eddy near the lip of Denny Falls (10 feet), which has a tight line to avoid landing on a rock. Denny Falls runs out over a fun two-step ledge that marks the end of the bigger drops and a short float to Asahel Curtis Picnic Area.

*—JD Gaffney*

Nick Hinds

Brian Pernick on Island Drop

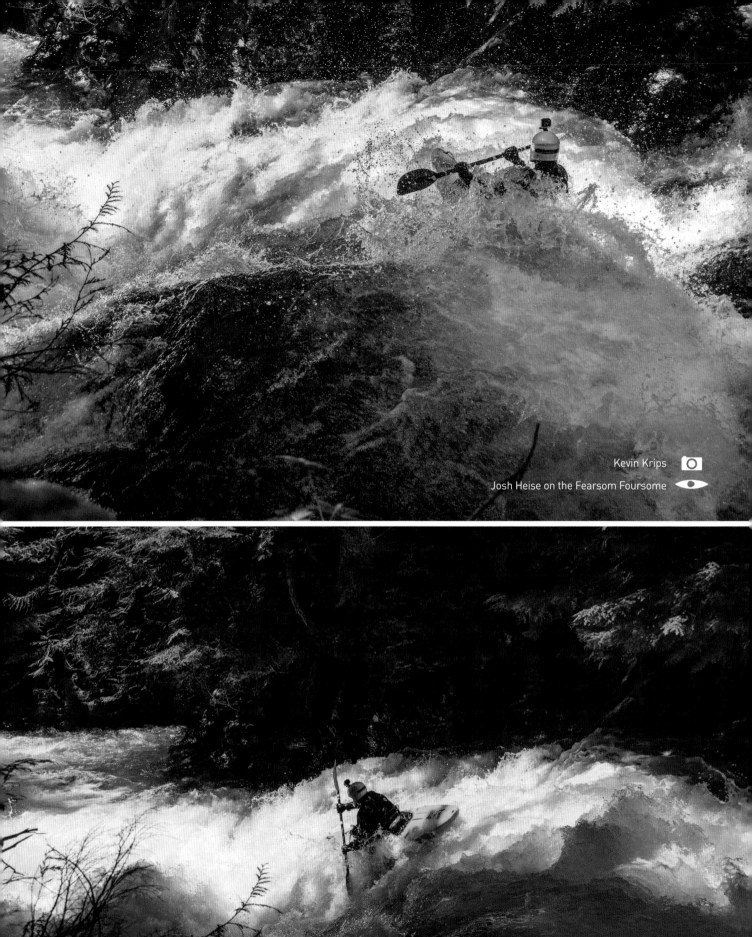

Kevin Krips

Josh Heise on the Fearsom Foursome

Kevin Krips

Josh Heise dropping in

# UPPER GORGE

## OF THE GREEN RIVER

The Green River Gorge is considered by many to be one of the most classic runs in the state. This pristine sandstone gorge has towering cliff walls set in a lush canyon just an hour from Seattle. Hidden in the foothills of the Cascades, the gorge offers paddlers a Class III-IV paradise that can be run at a wide range of levels. The Green Gorge has arguably more fun moves and drops pound-for-pound than most rivers in its class—and easily the best scenery for paddlers of all levels. At moderate flows between 1,200-3,500 cfs the green is a fun Class III-IV river; from 5,500-7,000 cfs it takes on a bigger water Class IV+ to V- feel with big, clean wave trains and boiling eddies. At any level the real crux of the run is a stacked set of rapids called Mercury and the Nozzle. The gorged-in nature of the run makes it a semi-committing for intermediate paddlers, though still beautiful and exciting enough for most seasoned kayakers. Despite the fact that it's dam controlled and primarily only runnable in the rainy winter months, if you could only choose one river to kayak for the rest of your life, the Green River Gorge might just be it.

Putting in at Kanaskat-Palmer State Park, the river starts right off with Ledge Drop 1, a short Class III warm-up as you flow down through the park with fun surf waves and continuous Class II+. A huge red danger sign at the end of the park on river-right marks the entrance to the gorge and the last good spot to exit the river. Around the corner is Ledge Drop 2 followed by more continuous Class III read-and-run as you twist through the winding canyon for a couple miles until you reach a headwall where the river pools up

## THE RUNDOWN

First Saturday in May is the Green River Cleanup. Bonus: hot springs.

**Difficulty:** Class III-IV, (V at high flows)

**Gauge:** USGS #12105900—Green River below Howard A Hanson Dam, WA
NWRFC: Green—Below Howard Hanson Dam

**Flow Min-max:** 1,100-4,000 cfs (III-IV), 4,100-7,000 cfs (IV-V)

**Gradient:** 30 fpm

**Takeout:** Flaming Geyser State Park, or Franklin Bridge, Paradise Trail (kayak only)

**Put-in:** Kanaskat-Palmer State Park

**Length:** 12 miles

**Hitchability:** Hitching a ride is moderately difficult being a rural area. However, this run is very popular when running so shuttle is often easy on weekends.

**Season:** Rainy season. Best October to February before the reservoir begins filling.

**Camping:** At put-in, the Kanaskat-Palmer State Park has many nice campsites, yurts and bathrooms with showers, small spots in the canyon.

**4WD Needed?** No

**Best Close Food/Beers:** Black Diamond Bakery

**Quality (out of 5):** 5

**Raft Recommendations:** Best between 1,500 and 4,000 cfs

Mike Hagadorn

and splits—take either channel and prepare for Pipe Line, a Class III+ rapid just downstream. Pipe Line comes up quickly with a busy lead-in as the river bends left and back to the right. Take the current to the left and square up to the lateral as you punch through the bottom wave-hole. The river then winds through big sandstone cliffs and more high quality Class III boogie as you boof your way down a couple miles looking for the power lines. Once you cross under the power lines, note a beach on river-left with a good size eddy before the river splits downstream. This signifies the entrance to the Class IV+ section with Mercury and the Nozzle and offers a good place to regroup. Run the the main current to the right of the island as the river will bend to the left and spill over middle holes leading into Mercury, a steep boulder wave train spanning the river. Mercury is run left, middle and right, but at moderate flows there are eddies on river-right and -left below it (and right above the Nozzle) to break up the two drops.

The Nozzle is formed as the river bends back to the right and constricts with two car-size boulders blocking the middle channel. This drop is typically run down the center chute, looking for a green tongue through the center boulders. At higher water the holes behind the boulders can get sticky, but the tongue in the middle seems to flush at most levels with a sneak to the right and left opening up at higher flows. Don't celebrate too soon; the river doesn't let up, turning the corner into hole-dodging moves flowing into three bigger offset boulders called Let's Make a Deal. Pick

a channel early (the conservative "safe" route is to go left of the boulders). Below Let's Make a Deal, the river mellows and pools as the gorge walls pinch down as you drift through the lush fern-covered canyon often lead by mergansers and great blue herons. Two more miles are littered with fun Class III-III+ rapids all the way to another island (run on the left) beneath a waterfall pouring down from the hundred-foot-tall gorge walls on river-left.

After the pool through this narrowest spot in the gorge, the Franklin bridge takeout trail is on river-right, above Paradise Ledge, a popular park-and-play spot. While the trail goes straight up to the parking lot, a mile and a half of fun Class II-III boogie lies downriver with an old coal-fire hot springs hidden in a side creek on river-left just above the lower takeout—the last takeout on river-right before the lower gorge.

Another 6 miles of paddling to Flaming Geyser State Park, the lower gorge of the Green is a grade easier than the upper gorge, but still has some of the best scenery on the river with towering sandstone cliffs and meandering Class II-III rapids with good surfing and fun whitewater. This is a great intermediate run for kayakers looking for the feel of the gorge, but who don't want to paddle Class IV. Rafters are committed to running down the 6 miles to Flaming Geyser as the hike out from Franklin bridge is very steep and only accessible by kayak.

—*Chris Totten*

## SHUTTLE DIRECTIONS

Kanaskat-Palmer to Franklin Bridge (the upper gorge)

Franklin Bridge to Flaming Geyser (the lower gorge)

To reach the takeout, take state Hwy. 18 east from I-5 or state Hwy. 167. Follow signs to Flaming Geyser State Park 8 miles up SE Green Valley Road. To reach the put-in, drive back out toward SE Green Valley Road. Go right, up the hill and out to state Hwy 169. Turn right, cross the Green River, then take a left at Crane Corner on S 400th St. This will T-bone with Veazie Cumberland Rd. SE. Go left and follow signs to Kanaskat-Palmer State Park. A Discovery Pass is needed at both parks.

**Put-in: 47.321851, -121.907235**
**Takeout: 47.274945, -122.031356**

Scott Waidelich

Green River Gorge Paradise

# PUYALLUP GORGE

## OF THE PUYALLUP RIVER

Originating from the west slope of Mount Rainier, the Puyallup River flows through a narrow and dramatic canyon that evokes comparisons to the incomparable Carbon Gorge. The Puyallup Gorge may even have a better overall quality of whitewater than the Carbon. Unfortunately, instead of its rightful status as a Seattle classic, the Puyallup is almost completely unappreciated due to two main issues. The first is that Hancock Forest Management has completely restricted a large swath of the upper watershed—driving in using the road that provides easy access to the gorge requires a $375 annual pass. If caught on the property hiking, or even sitting in the car of someone with a pass, you risk a trespassing citation and a $500 fine. The second obstacle to kayaking the Puyallup Gorge is catching a stable flow in the narrow optimum range, which is complicated by the river-right diversion dam that removes 400 cfs above the canyon (meaning the gauge at Electron should read 800-900 cfs for ideal flows in the canyon).

In 2006, a group ran the Puyallup by putting in on the South Fork Puyallup after hiking in on West Side Road. This involves a long hike and paddle in as well as a potential portage around an upper canyon. On my one run in January 2011 we accessed the run by paddling the Mowich River, which joins the Puyallup River about 5 or 6 miles upstream of the gorge—a reasonable day-trip with an early start. We hiked into the Mowich from a turnout on state Hwy. 165 a short distance east of the Mount Rainier National Park boundary and got to the river near the confluence of Meadow Creek. The most tedious part of the trip is the first few miles of the Mowich, which is braided and shallow with many log portages. Hiking into the lower portion of the Mowich from WA 165 would be extremely difficult due to the towering cliffs on river-right. The second half of the Mowich is more channelized and had few portages. The section of the Puyallup before the gorge is unmemorable Class II-III. Downstream of the Mowich, you will pass the diversion dam, final destination of the "World's Crookedest Railway."

## THE RUNDOWN

Slightly easier version of its sister drainage the Carbon River.

**Difficulty:** Class V

**Gauge:** USGS #12092000—PUYALLUP RIVER NEAR ELECTRON, WA NWRFC #ELEW1—PUYALLUP NEAR ELECTRON

**Flow Min-max:** 400-500 cfs is ideal (800-900 cfs on the gauge at Electron, located just upstream of the powerhouse diversion which removes up to 400 cfs from the river.)

**Gradient:** 120 fpm

**Length:** 9 miles

**Hitchability:** Bike shuttle

**Season:** Rain or snowmelt

**Camping:** Not reliable, mostly private logging land surrounds the Puyallup

**4WD Needed?** No

**Best Close Food/Beers:** Town of Graham has lots of food options.

**Raft Recommendations:** No

With the gauge reading 850, the whitewater in the gorge is high quality. I would have been comfortable returning with a significantly higher flow except for one notable rapid. After about five rapids, there is gravel bar on river-left at the top of an entry rapid. Directly below the river makes a right bend, and around the corner there is a river-wide hole at a narrow spot in the canyon. The scout from the gravel bar does not afford a full view of the hole. I boofed through this drop on the right and got stuck in the eddy on river-right, and it took many attempts to paddle out. This hole should be run center going straight across the boil (see this hazard on video at tinyurl. com/puyallupgorge, with a clean line at 2:50). The similarity of this feature to Rick's Slide on the Carbon is eerie, although Rick's is steeper, more challenging, and more powerful.

—Ben Hawthorne

## SHUTTLE DIRECTIONS

Put-in: north on Orville Rd. Take a right on 162 E, right on 165 (S). Put-in is down the second to last road on the right before you get to a "Mount Rainier" sign. Hike down the right fork then follow the switchbacks until the road is gone. Follow the lightly used trail down to an old road. Stay on the road until it hits a floatable section of the river.

Takeout: (directions cited from Americanwhiter.org) Head south on Orville road from Highway 162. After 6.7 miles there is a turnout on the left, with large boulders blocking a road that goes through the forest to the river. It is a little more than a half-mile north of Electron Rd. At Electron Rd. there is another road leading to a bridge directly upstream of the takeout. If you crossed this bridge and headed upriver, it would lead you to an easy put-in above the gorge. Absolutely no trespassing here. **(46.993225, -122.177297)**

Draining the Carbon Glacier on the Northwest side of Mount Rainier, the Carbon River flows through one of the most spectacular canyons in Washington. In places only a boat-length wide, all who pass through will be awed and humbled by this special place. The experience does not come without danger, however. The upper section of this river contains the proverbial river nightmare: Rick's Slide. This fearsome, unportageable rapid has an eddy on river-right that is difficult-to-impossible to escape depending on the water level. In order to avoid running Rick's, the Carbon River canyon is typically accessed by a rappel on river-right a short distance downstream of Rick's Slide. At the cost of three or four rapids and half-mile of amazing scenery, paddlers can experience much of the canyon, including the most dramatic Classic Canyon section without the hazard entailed by Rick's Slide.

Despite the risk, to those who are up for the challenge I can't help but recommend running the canyon from beginning to end. The experience, including the anticipation, commitment, and danger, makes this one of the most special rivers in the area. Please approach this with the utmost respect. Exploring a canyon this tight without recent beta that it is clear of wood entails extra risk and should be approached cautiously.

From the upper put-in, a few miles of meandering Class II precede the canyon. The rapids turn to Class IV as the Fairfax Bridge comes into sight. As the canyon narrows, the holes begin to pack a punch. Welcome Rapid consists of a lead-in and then a pinch that tends to throw paddlers into the right wall. After a few more rapids, you reach a blind horizon line. This is Lobsterclaw, which is typically run on river-right with a delayed boof. A couple small ledges later you will be in the pool above Rick's Slide. Unless the rock is slippery from rain, it should be possible to get out on the right to scout, but

it is impossible to set good safety or to portage. Rick's Slide is a steep drop where much of the current is shunted to the right into an eddy rather than downstream. The line is to enter center-left and charge through the hole on the left and NOT get pushed right. At flows below 300 cfs it may be necessary to enter more center and then drive left. There is a river-left eddy across the current from the recirculating eddy on river-right. It is conceivable that a rope could be thrown from a boat to effect a rescue, but it would not be easy.

Below Rick's Slide is another ledge, which is right above the normal rappel-in point on river-right. Downstream is a sizable boof over a recirculating hole and right around the corner is the 14-foot waterfall. Although this drop is a fairly straight-forward move, it has a sizable cave behind it and is often portaged. After a number of rapids, you will arrive at Classic Canyon, a great, fairly straightforward Class IV rapid that culminates in the narrowest section of the Carbon. After that constriction the canyon begins to open up but there is still fun whitewater. The Class V Landslide deserves a scout. After another rapid, Utter Undercutter, you pass private property on the right and the river turns to Class II with a few miles to the takeout.

Flow note: Although I have heard of runs up to 800 cfs, I would recommend flows of 250-400 for the upper canyon. At 400, a strong paddler was able to paddle out of Rick's, although it was not easy. A swimmer flushed out of Rick's at 550 cfs after being recirculated for over a minute. The rapid becomes more difficult with higher water as the hole on river-left gets bigger, increasing the chance that you will be pushed right into the eddy. At 250, the river is runnable but definitely bony in places. Rick's is still challenging at that flow. The lower section is regularly run up to 800 cfs though 600 is optimal.

*—Ben Hawthorne*

Mike Hagadorn

Joe Keck revels in the Carbon

# LOWER CARBON

(See Carbon River entry by Ben Hawthorne on page 74)

## SHUTTLE DIRECTIONS

Put-in: Best to have a boater with you who knows where the rappel is located.

Takeout: head east out of Orting on state Hwy. 162 and turn right on 177th St. East. Drive just over 2 miles to the end of the road. To reach the put-in: Return to state Hwy 162 E for 6.5 miles until the intersection of WA 162 and WA 165, stay right on 165 south toward Wilkeson and the Carbon River Ranger Station. In 7.2 miles you cross the Carbon River and Fairfax Bridge, then in .5 miles the road forks; take the left fork and drive 1.8 miles to Burnett-Fairfax Rd. and head down to the river.

## THE RUNDOWN

Spectacular narrow granite gorge only 6 feet wide in spots.

**Difficulty:** Class V

**Gauge:** USGS #12094000—CARBON RIVER NEAR FAIRFAX, WA

**Flow Min-max:** 300-700 cfs

**Gradient:** 80 fpm

**Takeout:** 177 St. east, off state Hwy 162. Drive just over 2 miles to end of the road.

**Put-in:** Rappel in above Ricks, best to have an experienced boater/ climber

**Length:** 9 miles

**Hitchability:** Not good

**Season:** Rainy season, July to August

**Camping:** No

**4WD Needed?** No

**Best Close Food/Beers:** Restaurants in Wilkeson

**Quality (out of 5):** 4

**Raft Recommendations:** No

# MASHEL RIVER

If you've made it to the put-in, the adventurous boater will enjoy 10 miles of river that includes bedrock gorges, quality boulder gardens and a few rewarding Class IV+/V rapids that will require scouting and line selection. However, getting to the put-in requires some route planning, a 4WD vehicle with significant clearance, a little luck and at least an hour and a half to drive to the put-in.

After removing all the brush and devil's club from your boat, slide into the Mashel and enjoy a couple miles of Class III with likely at least one wood portage until you reach the first major drop worth a quick scout. It's a straightforward triple drop with a final ledge-hole requiring a strong boof. Read-and-run Class III-IV continues to a distinct end of the first gorge.

After a couple miles of flatwater, the second gorge begins with the crux: a Class V rapid with a right-hand entrance off a broken ledge followed by a right-hand turn committing you to the next set of rapids with vertical bedrock walls. Be sure and scout this corner and runout for wood. Below, there's a few more miles of Class III-IV before one final Class III gorge as you see the railroad trestle overhead. The takeout is less than a mile downstream. Hopefully you arranged a shuttle driver. If not, get changed and start your shuttle, you'll have plenty of time to warmup in the car.

—Adam Griffin

## THE RUNDOWN

Spectacular narrow granite gorge only 6 feet wide in spots.

**Difficulty:** Class IV-IV+

**Gauge:** USGS #12087000— Mashel River Near La Grande, WA

**Flow Min-max:** 800-1,300 cfs

**Gradient:** 90 fpm

**Takeout:** Center St. Bridge in Eatonville

**Put-in:** Confluence of Busy Wild Creek and Mashel River

**Length:** 10 miles

**Hitchability:** Conventional shuttle required

**Season:** Fall and winter (best after storms with high snow levels because of the elevation)

**Camping:** Plenty of camping around the put-in but when it's running you won't be looking to camp

**4WD Needed?** Yes

**Best Close Food/Beers:** Available in Eatonville and Ashford

**Quality (out of 5):** 4

**Raft Recommendations:** It's been done but an early start can't be emphasized enough.

## SHUTTLE DIRECTIONS

From the takeout bridge in Eatonville, get comfortable and put the best navigator on your team in the passenger seat. Continue south on Center Rd., which becomes Alder Cutoff Rd. until state Hwy. 7, then turn left toward Elbe. At Elbe, turn left again on state Hwy. 706 toward Ashford. About two miles before Ashford, turn left onto SF-1142 (aka Stoner Rd.). Shortly after a few switchbacks and crossing the small Busy Wild Creek, turn left (downhill) to a parking area primarily used by the off-road driving community. If there's no snow here, that's good news for you.

From here, you continue on the 4WD to the north for 3-4 miles until a distinct pullout on the left that's been graded into the hillside. At this point, you're on the ridge between Busy Wild and the Mashel and the general idea is to walk downhill toward the confluence. There are trails and one road that we turned left onto but none with a clearly defined route. It's recommended to go with someone who's been before or do a lot of homework. In both cases, get a very early start!

Put-in: 46.843524, -122.12603
Takeout: 46.86359, -122.25246

# HONORABLE MENTIONS

## OF THE SEATTLE AREA

**Limp Wrist Falls** on the South Fork Snoqualmie River is the best park-and-huck option near Seattle, and you likely drive past it all the time without even knowing it! Nestled along the westbound lanes of Interstate 90, this clean 30-foot falls is only 30 minutes from downtown Seattle, and runs throughout the fall and spring. Limp Wrist is usually running when the MM Snoqualmie gauge is between 4,000-7,000 cfs. The SF Snoqualmie also has a gauge, but we never dialed it in for the falls. Note that there is a diversion, so the SF gauge will read higher than what you will find at Limp Wrist. The normal line is on the center-left. Be sure to set safety at the bottom as there are more falls around the corner a ways after the pool.

Directions: From Seattle head east on I-90 to Exit 38. Get back on the freeway headed back west for a half-mile or so. Pull over along the right shoulder, the falls is beside the highway, marked by the blasting of the wall and rock piles.

**The East Fork Miller** is full day of Class V+ paddling in only two short miles. Bring your A game, and a good pair of footwear, as there is a fair bit of portaging. With an easy 1-mile hike in, the trail follows the run for a ways as you begin to see the gradient and continuous nature. It's only a mile hike to the put-in bridge over the river where you see the massive granite put-in slide! The EF Miller has a bit of everything: huge slides, manky, continuous boulder gardens, ledges, small waterfalls and several portages. There aren't a lot of eddies; it just keeps coming at you. If you're looking to mix it up and run some next-level slides and chunky drops, the extra effort is worth it. It's easy to scout everything and move around, plus you can put in lower to shorten the run and pick off your favorite drops. The put-in slide is great, then your reach Drag Strip halfway in, a few small waterfalls, then the biggest of them all: a 70-foot granite slide called Smoothie. For levels, you want the USGS Skykomish River at Gold Bar gauge between 6,500-8,500 cfs.

To reach the takeout, head east from Index on U.S. Hwy 2. Turn right onto NE Old Cascade Hwy. toward Money Creek Campground then turn right again on Miller River Rd., and almost to the end of the road, look for a pullout before Lake Dorothy Trailhead (white road markers just down from the pullout mark the takeout). To reach the put-in, continue up Dorothy Lake Trailhead 1 mile and put in near the bridge.

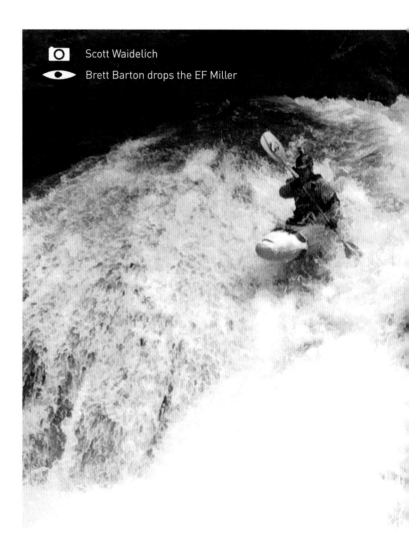

Scott Waidelich

Brett Barton drops the EF Miller

the West Fork bridge. You can scout along the way, and pick and choose what you want to run. By no means a classic, The WF Miller does have some stout, runnable falls and extremely steep boulder gardens. The upper falls is known as Borderline, and the lower is Immigration Falls. It runs when the Skykomish (at Gold Bar) is between 8,000 -11,000cfs.

The takeout of this run is also the put-in for the Miller River. Turn right off U.S. Hwy 2 onto NE Old Cascade Hwy. toward Money Creek Campground then turn right again on Miller River Rd. (FR 6410), following it a few miles until the West Fork bridge. Hike up the old path on river-left.

**Money Creek** feels like paddling a flooded drainage ditch. Often running when the Sky is between 11,000-15,000 cfs; this Class IV-V roadside torrent is one long, continuous boulder slalom that has a few sticky ledges up top, and a harder section in the middle that contains tight moves. Wood is a constant danger on this run; scout the run on the way up and hold on!

To reach the takeout take the U.S. Hwy. 2 exit toward Money Creek Campground, follow NE Old Cascade Hwy. a mile, go right to Miller River Rd. NE, quickly turn right on NE Money Creek Rd (NF-6420) follow it .6 miles to the takeout bridge on Money Creek. The put-in is 2+ miles up the road; scout along the way for wood.

Scott Waidelich

Alex Podolak on the EF Miller

# HONORABLE MENTIONS

## OF THE SEATTLE AREA

**Beckler River** features 7 miles of Class III with the occasional piece of wood, heading south down to its confluence with the South Fork of the Skykomish River. (Exit U.S. Hwy 2 onto Beckler Rd., which parallels the river for simple shuttle logistics.)

**Seattle Gorge** on the South Fork Snoqualmie is a short stretch of sweet whitewater in a pretty canyon after a couple miles of pleasant Class II. There are six or seven distinct rapids with small eddies in between; be sure to scout them all your first time down. The character is bedrock slides with boulders. At 350 cfs (low side of good), most of the rapids are Class IV except for the final drop, which is Class V. At 650 cfs, the rapids have more of a Class V feel with more difficult scouting. Downstream of the takeout are more rapids and slides, though a diversion removes most of the water. With a high enough flow, these runs should be linked together. It may even be worth continuing downstream through 30-foot Limp Wrist Falls which is subject to a second diversion (just be sure to take out above the massive Twin Falls). Both put-in and takeout are accessed off of I-90. The takeout is off Exit 38: eastbound, drive up Homestead Rd. 2 miles, where parking is located shortly past the I-90 bridge; if westbound, turn right after the ramp to find parking immediately (47.431295, -121.632391). Put in at the Tinkham Road bridge accessed from Exit 42 (47.415326, -121.587049).

**The North Fork Tolt** is the nearest Class V river to Seattle and it ranks high in terms of scenery and whitewater quality. Unfortunately, due to access restrictions, it is rarely paddled. Unlike the Puyallup River, which has no entry permitted whatsoever, the Tolt can be accessed with a pass purchased through Hancock. The run has some nice III-IV+ whitewater broken up by two distinct and beautiful canyons. The first is over a mile long and contains some challenging rapids, and for the most part is not inescapable. The second canyon is much more committing, but it is also shorter and has less whitewater, though its spectacular geology is reward enough—overall, worth the effort. Due to the nature of the whitewater and the difficulty of access however, this river should be treated as an exploratory run and only attempted by those prepared for such undertakings. An ideal flow was 350 cfs; anything over 500 would be quite pushy. Take out at the fishing access along Tolt River Rd. Put-in at a bridge just above the confluence with Yellow Creek.

**Sloan Creek** runs best in the spring or after rains when the Sauk River near Whitechuck is reading between 1,700-3,000 cfs, or when the NF Sauk is running—best to just run both NF Sauk and Sloan together to make a full day of creeking. This fun but short run is a mile of continuous boulder gardens. The takeout is at Sloan Creek Campground, just before the confluence. The put-in is a mile up from the NF Sauk bridge to a campsite near the river.

## 1

Brett Barton

Phil Kast in Sloan Creek

# OLYMPIC PENINSULA

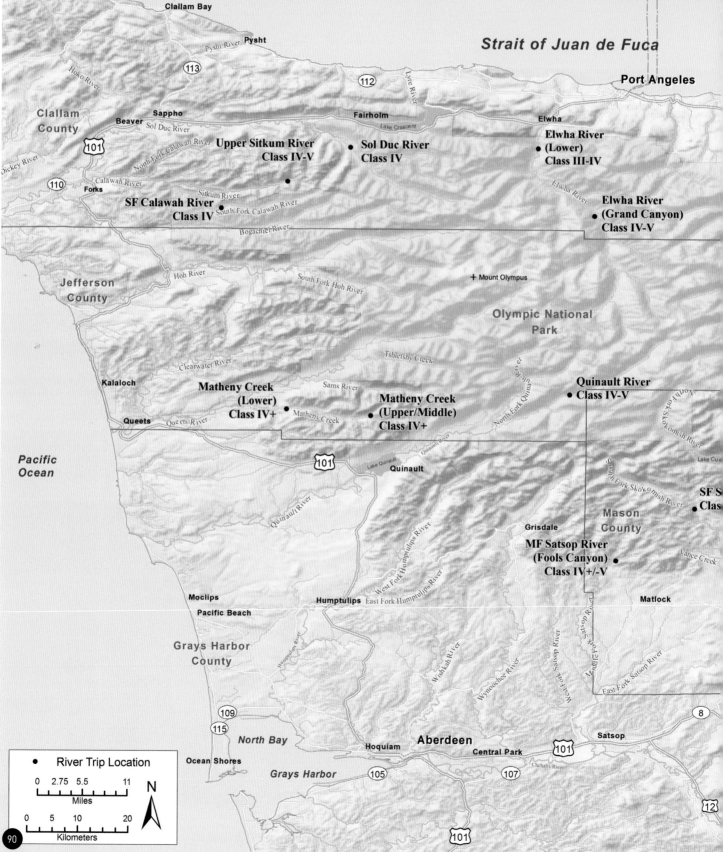

Clallam Bay

Pysht River  Pysht

**Strait of Juan de Fuca**

113

112

Lyre River

**Port Angeles**

Hoko River

Fairholm

Lake Crescent

Elwha

**Clallam County**

Sappho

Beaver

Sol Duc River

101

North Fork Calawah River

**Upper Sitkum River Class IV-V**

**Sol Duc River Class IV**

**Elwha River (Lower) Class III-IV**

Dickey River

110

Calawah River

Forks

Sitkum River

**SF Calawah River Class IV**

South Fork Calawah River

Elwha River

**Elwha River (Grand Canyon) Class IV-V**

Bogachiel River

**Jefferson County**

Hoh River

South Fork Hoh River

+ Mount Olympus

**Olympic National Park**

Clearwater River

Tshletshy Creek

North Fork Quinault

North Fork Skokomish River

Kalaloch

**Matheny Creek (Lower) Class IV+**

Sams River

Matheny Creek

**Matheny Creek (Upper/Middle) Class IV+**

**Quinault River Class IV-V**

Queets

Queets River

**Pacific Ocean**

Quinault River

Lake Quinault

Quinault

101

Quinault River

South Fork Skokomish River

Lake Cus

**SF S Clas**

**Mason County**

Grisdale

**MF Satsop River (Fools Canyon) Class IV+/-V**

Vance Creek

West Fork Humptulips River

Moclips

Humptulips

East Fork Humptulips River

Matlock

Pacific Beach

Humptulips River

Wishkah River

Wynoochee River

West Fork Satsop River

Middle Fork Satsop River

East Fork Satsop River

**Grays Harbor County**

109

115

**North Bay**

Hoquiam

**Aberdeen**

Central Park

Satsop

8

Ocean Shores

105

107

101

12

**Grays Harbor**

Chehalis River

● River Trip Location

0   2.75  5.5      11
Miles

0    5    10      20
Kilometers

N

90

Island
County

Coupeville

20

Port Townsend

Sequim

20

River

104

ungeness River
Class IV

Quilcene

Big Quilcene
(Upper)
Class IV-V

Big Quilcene River

River
nyon)
IV-V

Dosewallips River

305

Brinnon

Silverdale

Seabeck

30

3

a River

101

Kitsap
County

son Creek
ss IV-V

Bremerton

Hood Canal

3

16

Hoodsport

302

kokomish

106

Pierce
County

3

Shelton

Olympia

Tumwater

510

Thurston
County

5

121

507

Tait Trautman

Dan Patrinellis

Source: US National Park Service, USGS TNM

# GRAND CANYON

## OF THE ELWHA RIVER

The Grand Canyon of the Elwha is one of the most classic sections of whitewater surrounded by stunning scenery within canyon walls. An 8.5-mile hike with self-support gear has been the most prevalent way of tackling this run, hiking in one day and boating out the next. This two canyon, Class IV and V multiday run has must-run rapids that reward a prepared and capable group.

After about a mile of some quality warmup rapids, you arrive at the Grand Canyon—from the rock formations, to the moss, to the wood up high, it truly delivers some of the most unique and stunning scenery imaginable. And once through the entrance rapids, Eskimo Pie is a Class V rapid with staggered holes feeding into a left wall, the first of several must-run rapids. Soon after you will be forced to get out on river-right and scout as the river cuts through a spectacular gorge. This is the rapid above Nightmare. You can see the top of Nightmare deeper in the canyon as you have to commit to the gorge to get a look; enter with caution.

Some great Class III-IV brings you to the confluence with the Lillian River. After passing the confluence, paddlers arrive to Pebbles & Bam Bam, and then Dagger. At low flows groups may want to portage Dagger. Downstream is the longest rapid in the Grand Canyon, Landslide, consisting of amazing boulder garden after boulder garden.

Next up is Geyser Valley, a popular camping spot for those who want to break up the trip. Downstream of Geyser Valley is Rica Canyon and the Goblin Gates. The river bends 90 degrees to the right as it enters the second and final canyon of the trip. This impressive rapid has a few lines, normally run along the right wall, though other creative routes can be found with a nice recovery pool at the bottom. Below are the Secret Chutes, recently littered with wood, but still runnable. The rest of Rica Canyon is quality Class IV boulder gardens and chutes with some powerful holes thrown in the mix.

## THE RUNDOWN

One of the gems of the OP and a challenging mission.

**Difficulty:** Class V

**Gauge:** ELWHA RIVER ABOVE LAKE MILLS NR PORT ANGELES, WA

**Flow Min-max:** 600-1,200 cfs

**Gradient:** 570 fpm

**Takeout:** Two options (see shuttle directions)

**Put-in:** Hike 8.5 miles upriver from Whiskey Bend Trailhead

**Length:** 11 miles

**Hitchability:** Hike for your strokes

**Season:** Spring-summer

**Camping:** Paca Pride rents spaces for tents, Gold Basin Campground

**4WD Needed?** Yes

**Best Close Food/Beers:** Town of Elwha

**Quality (out of 5):** 5

**Raft Recommendations:** OK. This has been done by Class V rafters—very tight in spots.

Scouting and portaging options present themselves. There are several must-run rapids and many places to get creative with your scouting technique. Approach this run with respect. The whitewater is committing and the canyon is beautiful, making the entire trip is grand in every sense—a true OP Classic!

—Nick Hinds and Scott Waidelich

"This run is so special it goes beyond words. The whitewater ... the canyons ... the wildlife ... the riverside camping ... it's the Elwha! It has canyons so beautiful yet dangerous that it gives you a sacred almost forbidden feeling. A group could find the river blocked by logs or rock and be forced to leave the river ... IF possible."

— Gary Korb, A Paddler's Guide to the Olympic Peninsula

## 2

### Map labels

Port Angeles

112

101

Lake Sutherland

Indian Creek

Little River

Olympic Hot Springs Rd

Mount Storm King
4537 ft

Mount Baldy
4642 ft

Barnes Creek

Hughes Creek

Elwha Campground

Elwha Ranger Station

Altair Campground

Griff Peak
5118 ft

South Branch Little River

Mount Angeles
6342 ft

Clallam
County

Grand Canyon
Elwha Take-out

Boulder Creek
Campground

Boulder Creek

Whiskey Bend Rd

Rica Canyon

Olympic Hot Springs

Schoeffel Creek

Goblin Gates

Elwha River Trail

Elwha River

Lillian River

Cat Creek

Mount Fitzhenry
6040 ft

Long Creek

Grand Canyon
Elwha Put-in

Mount Carrie
6972 ft

Windfall Pe
5964 ft

Elkhorn Ranger Station

Mount Scott
5902 ft

0  1.5  3  6
Miles
0  2.5  5  10
Kilometers

N

Source: US National Park Service, USGS TNM

## SHUTTLE DIRECTIONS

At Mile 239.5 on U.S. Hwy 101, take Olympic Hot Springs Rd. south through the National Park entrance. Continue 4 miles up this road and take the left-hand turn up to Whiskey Bend. You will reach the historic Glines Canyon Dam rapid at mile 1.2. Continuing up the road to mile 4, a trail leads down to the exit from Rica Canyon and the historic start of the Mills Reservoir. This has been a popular takeout option for those who want to end their run with Rica Canyon, although it requires a steep climb up a .4-mile trail. The Whiskey Bend Rd. ends at Mile 4.4, which is the trailhead (47.968104, -123.582586). The trail starts out fairly level for the first couple miles. At mile 4.7 you cross the Lillian River. At about 8.5 miles, just downstream of Prescott Creek, you come to a sandy bar by the river: This is the put-in (47.905963, -123.492546). For those who want to taste the whitewater on a day-trip, you can walk into Rica Canyon. It is 1.2-mile hike up to the junction of the Rica Canyon Trail, which heads .5 miles down to the river.

With Glines Canyon Dam now removed, the reservoir paddle is now replaced with a paddle through the recovering riparian zone. It is possible to hike out to Whiskey Bend from shortly above the dam site via the NE Terrace Trail. Current debris is still moving downstream of the dam site, Rebar has been spotted in bad areasBe very careful if you decide to boat all the way down. Just below the short Class IV Glines Canyon lies Altaire, a campground on river-left. This is an oft-used put-in for the Class III water below and has convenient riverside road access.

# SOL DUC

The most commonly run section of whitewater on the Sol Duc River begins at Salmon Cascade. This Class V rapid sees a taker every now and then, but most paddlers put in at the base of Salmon Cascade and enjoy the continuous Class III+ and IV whitewater down to the FR 2918 Bridge.

Below Salmon Cascade, paddlers will encounter many Class III+ rapids and some really beautiful playspots. The biggest rapid on this section comes up after the South Fork Sol Duc enters on river-left. This rapid is difficult to scout from your boat and can collect wood on river-right. A large hole develops right of center that most will want to avoid (scout or portage on river-left). The river then tapers off to Class II to the FR 2918 Bridge, below which there is more Class III whitewater to one of the access points on Hwy. 101.

When water levels are higher you can put in at Salmon Cascade and paddle down to a gravel parking area on W. Snider Creek Rd., where Snider Creek joins the Sol Duc. This parking area is just above the Riverside takeout and right after the first Hwy. 101 bridge over the Sol Duc. Paddling down to this spot from Salmon Cascade makes a 10-mile Class III/IV trip, with everything below FR 2918 bridge being Class III.

*—Jon Crain*

## THE RUNDOWN

Incredible scenery paired with miles of high quality intermediate whitewater make this one of the most popular rivers on the OP.

**Difficulty:** Class III-IV

**Gauge:** No official USGS or DOE gauge currently active but AW has developed a virtual gauge.

**Flow Min-max:** 800-3,000+ cfs

**Gradient:** 92 fpm

**Takeout:** FR 2918 Bridge is the most common

**Put-in:** Salmon Cascade, put-in Elevation is 1,365 feet

**Length:** 3.1 miles

**Hitchability:** Fair; bring a bike

**Season:** November through June. Most dependable during winter rain events when things are moderately high. During good snow years it can run from snowmelt in May and June.

**Camping:** There is free camping up FS Rd. 2918 on river-left near Goodman Creek or within the Olympic NP at Sol Duc Campground (open year-round) on river-right

**4WD Needed?** No

**Best Close Food/Beers:** Port Angeles if headed east on U.S. Hwy 101; the Hungry Bear Cafe if headed west on U.S. 101 (11 miles west of Sol Duc Rd.)

**Quality (out of 5):** 4.5

**Raft Recommendations:** OK.

## SHUTTLE DIRECTIONS

To reach Salmon Cascade, take U.S. 101 to MM 219.2 and go south on Sol Duc Hot Springs Rd. into Olympic National Park. The takeout can be reached at Mile 4.2, where you park on a small gravel pullout in front of a gate. On the other side of the gate is FR 2918. It's a short walk down to the FR 2918 takeout bridge over the Sol Duc. **48.04746612172695,-123.97187114838743**

The put-in is at Mile 7.3 on Sol Duc Hot Springs Rd., at the viewing area for Salmon Cascade. Note that Sol Duc Hot Springs Rd. can be closed for snow or during inclement weather if the rangers think there is a danger from falling branches and trees—check with Olympic N.P. for the latest conditions. The Forest Service Road (FR 2918) on river-left is usually left open, but it moves away from the river at the South Fork confluence. You can still put in at the South Fork confluence and float down to an access point on Hwy 101. **48.0225001748713, -123.92437459246139**

The South Fork Sol Duc (SFSD) is a tight, fast-moving creek with few eddies, blind corners, and potential for wood with disorganized Class III and IV rapids that lead into Ross's Rapid (Class V) followed by bedrock Class IV rapids down to the takeout. The run has quality, tight gorges and commitment you would expect from the more difficult Olympic Peninsula runs.

The small drainage of the SFSD means that it has the potential for collecting wood in some years and being spotless in others. So when you drop in, it's best to do so under the assumption that you need to be aware of wood hazards. The first third of the run is mostly disorganized boulder gardens and small ledges, which at medium flows will be a bit on the scrappy side. Downstream the rapids will become more organized and formed by bedrock, and a series of twisting Class IV slides followed by a sharp left turn mark the lead-in to Ross's Rapid: a very straight-forward Class V that is tricky to scout but is unreasonable to portage. When we last ran it (March 2013), a vertical log in the right side of exit meant some extra maneuvering that was easy enough.

Scout Ross' son river-left from a raised peninsula that requires a marginal scramble but gives you the best view of the rapid. The rapid is a tight triple drop with sliding ledges that are not strong holes—the middle ledge is the tallest and a bit blind from the scout. The last pinch looks like a tall ledge but is really a nice slide.

Below Ross's, the bedrock Class IV rapids continue down until you approach Tom Creek which tumbles into the riverbed from river-left. The takeout is a short ways below here.

During the early fall and late spring you can drive up to the Salmon Cascades section of the Sol Duc, which is a nice one-two punch to round out a good day on the water.

*—Jed Hawkes*

## SHUTTLE DIRECTIONS

Takeout: From Port Angeles: Drive on U.S. Hwy. 101 for 30 miles, turn left onto FS Rd. 2918 and follow it for 3.6 miles. Bear left at the fork and continue to a bridge over the South Fork Sol Duc. **48.038482, -123.954434**

Put-in: From the takeout, drive back, take a sharp left at the fork and follow for just under a mile until your first left onto NF-2946. Drive 4.5 miles until the next intersection. Take a left onto an unnamed road and follow for it for .7 miles. At the next major fork, take a left and follow for 6 miles, to the next intersection, and another left onto NF-2920 for 1.5 miles until it crosses the South Fork Sol Duc river. **48.021011, -123.937676**

## THE RUNDOWN

After running the South Fork, get in a fast lap on the Sol Duc Salmon Cascades section at medium-high flows for a great day of boating.

**Difficulty:** Class IV+ (V)

**Gauge:** Hoh, USGS #12041200—HOH RIVER AT US HIGHWAY 101 NEAR FORKS, WA; Calawah, USGS #12043000—CALAWAH RIVER NEAR FORKS, WA

**Flow Min-max:** Correlation between the Hoh (4,000-8,000 cfs) and Calawah (3,000-6,000 cfs)

**Gradient:** 130 fpm.

**Takeout:** TK

**Put-in:** Salmon Cascade, put-in elevation is 1636.4 feet

**Length:** 1.6 miles

**Hitchability:** Fair; bring a bike

**Season:** Winter, rainy

**Camping:** Lots of Forest Service opportunities in the area

**4WD Needed?** No

**Best Close Food/Beers:** Port Angeles if headed east on U.S. Hwy. 101; the Hungry Bear Cafe if headed west on U.S. 101 (11 miles west of Sol Duc Rd.)

**Quality (out of 5):** 3

**Raft Recommendations:** No

# UPPER UPPER

## OF THE SITKUM RIVER

Starting at the top with the Upper Upper, you may wonder upon reaching the river how such a small flow will boat. Yes, there will be scraping in the flats. Fear not, because when you reach the first set of ledges the channelized nature of this slip-sliding run instantly reassures. Several slides in the top of this section are all runnable, though there can be big holes at some flows.

The crux series is a triple in a small gorge; scout on the left. You will then have a couple more individual ledges and a waterfall, which has several lines at higher water with less options at lower flows. I like the middle at all flows, taking care to stay out of the left of the base, where some funky rock may be undercut. After a couple cool down-drops you arrive at the put-in for the Upper. With a magic overlapping water flow, you may continue for a higher water descent of the Upper too—a rare treat. Often a good way to complete both is with an Upper Upper run Day One and the Upper on Day Two as flows drop.

For the Upper, put in at the confluence with a seal launch. The first drop sets the tone for the run: It's a 4-foot ledge into a hole. There's rumor of rebar in it, though I have not seen it. This is the only drop in the first canyon. The next gorge contains Severe Reality: a steep and chunky drop. You can portage the entire canyon on the right. Next is Claustrophobia, a double set of holes that can be sticky. Your next obstacle is a long, almost good, steep boulder garden: The Boulder Factory. It is manky, mean, and just tempting enough for someone to give it a try. Most, if not all, will make the carry on river-left. There is a cool split drop next, which I like to boof left. You will then have some cool down, so watch for the Peninsula's last remaining wild steelhead if you are here in February to April.

The North Fork enters from the right, which is good because a short hike upriver on the North Fork reveals a totally runnable and clean falls. They are probably in the mid-20-foot class—boof or plug, the choice is yours. There's even a cool surf hole right at the lip at some flows, providing an opportunity for some real showboating. You are now on the Middle Sitkum float, with just a couple of drops in this 6-mile stretch. They are Class IV and very clean and enjoyable as well as being easy to read and run from the cockpit. Don't pass the takeout on the the right.

—*Kris Wilson*

## THE RUNDOWN

Slides on the Upper Upper—something we don't get a ton of out here. Followed by classic OP gorges.

**Difficulty:** Class IV-V (Upper Upper); Class V (Upper); Class IV (Middle); Class II-III (Lower)

**Gauge:** USGS #12043000 CALAWAH RIVER NEAR FORKS

**Flow Min-max:** 3,000-4,000 cfs (Upper Upper); 2,000-3,500 cfs (Upper)

**Gradient:** 150 fpm (avg.)

**Takeout:** Several (see shuttle directions)

**Put-in:** Several (see shuttle directions)

**Length:** 2.5 miles (Upper Upper); 3.5 miles (Upper); 3 miles (Middle); 3 miles (Lower)

**Hitchability:** Not a chance

**Season:** Fall through early spring, exclusively rain-fed

**Camping:** Pick a spur. Located on logging company land, check policies.

**4WD Needed?** No, but it is a rugged logging road so be smart about your choice.

**Best Close Food/Beers:** Forks

**Quality (out of 5):** 4-4.5

**Raft Recommendations:** Possible for those on the fringe of modern creek-style rafting.

## SHUTTLE DIRECTIONS

About a mile north of Forks on U.S. Hwy 101, FR-26 heads up the Sitkum River. Follow it up to Mile 8, and just before the Hyas Bridge turn right down a spur road to the confluence with SF Calawa: This is the takeout for the Lower **(47.960514, -124.256579)**. Continue up FR-26 a few miles to a right turn onto 2913. The bridge crossing the river is the takeout for the Middle/Lower put-in **(47.950656, -124.196679)**. Continue up FR-26. Just under a half-mile past the bridge over the NF there is a trail to the right that follows the NF down to the confluence: This is the Upper takeout/Middle put-in **(47.947209, -124.147201)**. Continue up FR-26 to Mile 17.6. Just before the Brandeberry Creek bridge you can see the Sitkum: This is the Upper Upper takeout/Upper put-in **(47.952738, -124.079411)**. Continue up FR-26, about 2.5 miles where the road has failed and Class II river is seen from the road: This is the Upper Upper put-in **(47.963637, -124.044852)**

Jon Crain

Adam Griffin enjoying the scenery

Jon Crain

Jed Hawkes

# SOUTH FORK OF THE CALAWAH

# 2

The South Fork Calawah is a great way to experience quality Class III and IV rapids in the Olympic National Park that has a 3.5-mile hike to the put-in. If you are looking for a little bit of adventure on the OP and you're not ready to step up to the harder Class V runs, this is a good place to test your mettle on a hike-in day-trip.

The majority of the rapids are in the first half of this 8.9-mile run and are mostly bedrock in character. All Rapids are easily boat-scoutable or scout-from-shore depending on your comfort level. The rapids begin shortly after putting on the water with a double ledge called West Virginia. The rapids then continue for several miles through old-growth forest and mossy draperies. About halfway through the run, the rapids flatten and turn into Class II rapids sprinkled with the occasional Class III boulder gardens down to the takeout near Hyas Creek.

From the Rugged Ridge Trailhead hike to the put-in for 2.8 miles with an elevation gain of 407 feet over a moderately maintained trail that had several downed trees along its length. That mileage on paper doesn't sound so bad, but this hike has lots of up and down with several steep pitches—it took us more than an hour the last time we ran it. You cross 10-15 micro-drainages before attaining an obvious high point that descends down to the river. It's tough enough that it was worth having a backpack system for the carry. The hike divides the SF Calwah from the Sitkum drainage and you soon enter the Olympic National Park after leaving the trailhead (see alltrails.com for more detailed info on the hike).

*—Jed Hawkes*

## THE RUNDOWN

The entire run is in the Olympic National Park and is surrounded by old-growth forest. Would be an ideal pack-rafting trip.

**Difficulty:** Class III-IV

**Gauge:** USGS #12043000—CALAWAH RIVER NEAR FORKS, WA

**Flow Min-max:** 2,000-4,000 cfs

**Takeout:** Hyas Creek

**Put-in:** Rugged Ridge Trail

**Length:** 8.9 miles

**Hitchability:** No

**Season:** Rainy season

**Camping:** Lots of Forest Service land on way to put-in; find a pullout and stake your claim.

**4WD Needed?** No

**Best Close Food/Beers:** Forks—In Place restaurant is middle of the road diner fare with no *Twilight* series memorabilia on the walls.

**Quality (out of 5):** 2.5

**Raft Recommendations:** Not recommended

## SHUTTLE DIRECTIONS

From Forks drive north on U.S. Hwy. 101 for 1.7 miles. Turn right onto Sitkum-Sol Duc Rd. and follow for 4.4 miles (the road will change names several times, but stay in the flow until you cross Hyas Creek). Shortly after Hyas, a pullout on the right goes down to the river. Park here to take out. **47.960261, -124.256239**

To get to the put-in from the Hyas Creek pullout, drive east on NF-29 for 3.1 miles until a slight right puts you onto NF-2913 (you'll cross the Sitkum river shortly after the turn). Follow it for 2.6 miles until the road ends in a grassy turnaround. The trailhead is slightly back down the road on the left from where you park your car. **47.936599, -124.160244**

# SUPPORTING PADDLERS SINCE 1971

www.pyranha.com

# MATHENY CREEK

Again, taken from the top-down, hopefully you have around 10,000 cfs for your first trip down the Upper. You may still wonder why you are banging a quarter-mile down the North Fork. Watch out for wood—at the time of press you could get through without portage. Once on the main stem, a bedrock gorge quickly greets you to some high quality Class III. The first real rapid is a 5-foot ledge that is boat-scoutable, just mind the hole. Following this are several ledges and gardens to negotiate, most scoutable with ease. A narrow constriction ledge after a fast Class III rapid is worth a look as it's always full of wood and sometimes not runnable, portage right if necessary. The creek again resumes a pleasant pace of ledges and gardens. The next notable feature is Shark Fin Falls: difficult to scout and mean at ultra high flows (in my opinion the limiting factor for the Upper section). The line is about 8 feet off the right wall, find the flake and use it.

## THE RUNDOWN

Fun rain-fed river with a lot of variety.

**Difficulty:** Upper & Middle Class IV+, Lower Class III-IV

**Gauge:** USGS # 12040500 QUEETS RIVER NEAR CLEARWATER

**Flow Min-max:** 7-15,000 cfs (Upper/Middle); 5-25,000 cfs (Lower)

**Gradient:** 60-80 fpm

**Takeout:** Upper/Middle at FS 21 bridge, Lower at Q-1000 Bridge (next one down)

**Put-in:** Upper, bridge over North Fork Matheny Creek; Middle, FR 2160-080 bridge; Lower, FS 21 bridge

**Length:** Upper and Middle 9 miles, Lower 4.3 miles

**Hitchability:** No

**Season:** Rainy

**Camping:** Put-in for the Lower is nice

**4WD Needed?** No but roads are rough

**Best Close Food/Beers:** Amanda Park, Internet Cafe

**Quality (out of 5):** 4.5

**Raft Recommendations:** Lower would be fine at high water

Brian Vogt

Nick Boretti and Michael Franz Hornern in Ledges in Upper

Brian Vogt

Lower Matheny Bowling Ball, Michael Franz Horner

After another short rapid series, you pass under the bridge that marks the put-in for the Middle. The drop after the bridge can pack a serious punch; get a good boof over the hole. From here down, the creek goes through many miles of Class III. The action cools the farther down you paddle, but remains interesting. Soon you will be at the put-in for the Lower: FS 21 bridge. If the Upper was good, you are in for some fun river running. If you came to run the Lower, at high water you're in for some big-water fun in a small riverbed. Most of the rapids are read-and-run and at low flows are a Class III+ affair demanding solid Class IV skills to lead. Again this goes out the window at higher flows when the point value doubles and anything can happen. A couple standout drops include Call 911 and Bowling Ball. There are multiple routes down each, while it is most common to run them on the left of center at most flows. Read or scout your line knowing that the drops are fun, clean, and have a good cadence to them—not what I would call continuous barring high flows, but no frog-water either. There are two distinct canyon sections on the Lower. Once you emerge from the second canyon it is a short float down to the Q-1000 Bridge.

—*Kris Wilson*

## SHUTTLE DIRECTIONS

Take West Boundary Rd. (aka Forest Service Rd. 21/NF-2405) off U.S. Hwy 101 approximately 10 miles north of Amanda Park, Wash. Eight miles up this paved road you will come to a bridge over Matheny Creek with a great place to park on the right, far side of the bridge. This is the put-in for the Lower and takeout of the Upper-Middle combo **(47.571426, -124.038800)**. To reach the takeout for the Lower, go past this bridge and make the next left (under a half-mile). Make another left onto the Q-1000 Road. Continue 2.5+ miles and you will arrive at a bridge over the creek which is your takeout **(47.5668, -124.076861)**. To reach the put-in to the Upper, return to the bridge on West Boundary Rd. and continue upstream on FR 2160 (NF-2433), along river-right. Go 7.4 miles, stay right at the Y and head down to the bridge over the North Fork of Matheny Creek. This is your put-in **(47.560820, -123.886867)**. There is also access downstream that could be used to put in and run the Middle section alone **(47.554507, -123.932100)**. It is 4.7 miles up FR 2160, taking the only other major right turn (FR 2160-080/NF-030) off the drive up to the Upper put-in. There is a steep trail on the river-right, near side of the bridge. It is a pain in the ass, rope will help.

# QUINAULT GORGE

## OF THE QUINAULT RIVER

Once you arrive at Pony Bridge, the mesmerizing emerald green water enchants you to put on automatically. Getting to this point, however, requires a 3-mile hike at a steady uphill grade through old-growth stands of Douglas fir, big-leaf maples and western red and Alaskan cedars. After crossing the bridge over Graves Creek at the trailhead, the trail contours away from the river and behind a small ridge that allows you to ignore the sounds of whitewater and appreciate the unparalleled forest. After swapping back to a shoulder that's already tired of carrying, the trail takes a 90-degree left-hand turn followed by a second dogleg to the right: This is your opportunity to evaluate the crux, Dolly Falls.

Like other gorges in the Olympics, the entrance has boulders choking the flow and allows few egress options. Dolly Falls is a three-tiered, Class V+ drop that most will want to portage. If water is too high or wood is in bad places it could render it impassable and a total nightmare. With the right wood conditions, it can be sketchily portaged at river level (river-right), requiring some careful footwork and the toss-and-jump method. The second and third tier of Dolly can be easily portaged on river-right after negotiating the crux. There is an alternate access via rappel below this first short canyon. Furthermore, this makes the run boatable at higher flows for a more padded experience.

Below Dolly is a short canyon with a couple of smaller drops in it. After emerging from the canyon, the river resumes a Class IV nature, arriving to a split falls of about 10 feet or less. This marks the rappel access; you will see the small drainage coming in on the left. Traditionally these falls were run left, but the channel has moved to the right currently—beware of wood. You then enter a

### THE RUNDOWN

The Quinault Rain Forest is a temperate rain forest known as the "Valley of Rain Forest Giants" because of its numerous record-size trees. The largest specimens of western red cedar, Sitka spruce, western hemlock, Alaskan cedar and mountain hemlock are all found in the Quinault Valley, which receives on average over 12 feet of rain per year!

**Difficulty:** Class IV+ (V+)

**Gauge:** USGS #12039500— Quinault River at Quinault Lake

**Flow Min-max:** 750–1,800 cfs (gauge); 200–500 cfs (estimated in reach)

**Gradient:** 108 fpm

**Takeout:** Graves Creek Campground

**Put-in:** Pony Bridge

**Length:** 3 miles

**Hitchability:** N/A

**Season:** Summer

**Camping:** There is a campground at the takeout, but it can be crowded in the summer

**4WD Needed?** No but roads are rough

**Best Close Food/Beers:** Basic provisions/breakfast at the Quinault Lodge store. Also Amanda Park Internet Cafe, or Salmon House in Quinault Village

**Quality (out of 5):** 4

**Raft Recommendations:** Doable but the portage or rappel access would be burly

### SHUTTLE DIRECTIONS

Take the Quinault Village or South Shore Rd. through the village of Quinault. Keep on this road as it will eventually turn to gravel. There will be one intersection: Stay right and continue upriver on river-left. You will eventually come to Graves Creek Campground, your takeout **(47.574419, -123.578525)**. To reach the trailhead, pull out of the campground and head left a third of a mile up the hill. Start walking.

The put-in has options. If Dolly is known to be clear then putting in at Pony Bridge about 2.5 miles up the trail is the best option **(47.596714, -123.540806)**. If not, or if the water is too high to make the portage, you have to rappel in for a fluffy day. Describing the spot is near impossible and not necessarily legal as you are bushwhacking off-trail, an activity not looked upon kindly by the Park. That said, when you reach the rotting picnic table, which may soon be gone, you exit the trail and head left toward the canyon. The picnic table is at the "summit" on the trail about 2.1 miles in. You then work your way to the canyon edge at a blowout creek (there are two, and one is taller than a climbing rope will allow with no beach). Rule of thumb: If you can see the landing area, you are at the right one. It may be helpful to scout without your boat first. Good luck.

second narrow hallway without rapids. Don't forget to check out the innumerable bull trout and steelhead holding in some of the river's calmer sections or the dark basalt canyon with unimaginable high-water lines.

The river increases pace here with Class IV+ read-and-run water. The next rapid is a sliding drop with a cave on the left; scout on the right and run more or less down the middle. The bottom is narrow and the cleft of rock on the left is a factor should you get mucked with by the hole that feeds here. Luckily, safety can be set on the right and access is easy (as is the portage if you are not feeling it). After this is more read-and-run until you get to the Wolf Trap: signified by a narrow passage run on the right followed by another narrower passage with a corner in it, also run on the right. This second drop (Wolf Trap proper) can be run, or snuck on the left at higher flows. Once again you will encounter more read-and-run for the duration of the canyon. There are some narrow slots and wood is a constant threat so use prudence. The canyon exit is a twisting drop run on the right. The pace then slows with a quarter-mile of Class II-III before passing the Graves Creek confluence and the takeout campground just downstream.

—*Adam Griffin and Kris Wilson*

Thomas O'Keefe

Stephen Canale

105

# FOOL'S CANYON

## OF THE MIDDLE FORK SATSOP

Fool's Canyon is a unique bedrock gorge with tight S-turning walls funneling quality Class IV rapids in a Class V environment that has a high possibility for wood.

Fool's is a great run with lots of rapids in a short length, the entirety of which can be scouted from the rim despite being impossible to escape from the river. The river enters the canyon shortly after leaving the put-in at the confluence of the Middle Fork Satsop and Baker Creek. The run features a few immediate Class III rapids before the walls rise around you, creating mostly bedrock ledges and flumes with one manky landslide rapid.

—*Jed Hawkes*

### THE RUNDOWN

Driving from Olympia you will see the cooling towers of the incomplete nuclear power plant that was constructed by the Washington Public Power Supply System (WPPSS) in the 1970s. Swayed public opinion after the 1979 Three Mile Island accident plus a swollen budget halted the WPPSS plans for this plant as well as the reactors on the Hanford Reservation. While the towers now loom off the highway on the southern edge of the Olympic Peninsula's foothills, the location has been converted to a business park. Fool's can be converted into a combo run with Baker Creek, though Fools is a higher quality run and Baker is manky and woody.

**Difficulty:** Class IV-V

**Gauge:** USGS #12035000—Satsop River near Satsop, WA

**Flow Min-max:** 2,500-7,000 cfs

**Gradient:** 115 fpm

**Takeout:** Decommissioned logging road that goes from the river up to NF-2199

**Put-in:** Confluence of Baker Creek and the Middle Fork of the Satsop

**Length:** 1.5 miles

**Hitchability:** No (bike shuttle recommended)

**Season:** Winter (rain-fed)

**Camping:** Lots of Forest Service land surround the Satsop drainage, just find a pull-out that looks like a good camp spot for the night.

**4WD Needed?** No

**Best Close Food/Beers:** Lots of roadside dive bars in the area. The Rusty Tractor in Elma has diner fare.

**Quality (out of 5):** 3.5

**Raft Recommendations:** Possible with a very narrow and short raft at medium-high and high water

### SHUTTLE DIRECTIONS

From Shelton, take City Center/Matlock exit off of U.S. Hwy. 101 and follow Shelton Matlock Rd. west for 15 miles. Turn right onto W. Beeville Rd., and follow for 2.7 miles. Bear left onto W. Beeville Loop Rd., for 2.3 miles, then take a slight right onto W. Kelly Hall Rd. Follow it for 1.3 miles to a closed logging road on the left (there will be a tank trap and a place to pull out). Walk down to the river and scout your takeout.
**47.296340, -123.460722**

Put-in: Drive north on W. Kelly Hall Rd. for .2 miles and take a left onto W. Kelly Hall Rd./NF-2199/NF-2341 and follow for 1.4 miles until you cross a bridge over Baker Creek. From here you can put on or continue up Baker Creek and notch two runs in one day.
**47.312104, -123.452992**

Welcome to the Washington flood zone! As one of the first rivers to flood each year, this run is often paddled in winter or early spring during dependable flow windows. It's quick to rise and respond to rain due to the extensive logging in this region. You have to start early as this 11-mile run always seems to take longer than anticipated and darkness comes quick this time of year. The run starts easy for the first 2 miles then takes a hard right turn where the walls begin to tower above. Welcome to the first of two gorges, true O.P.-style! You'll run some great Class IV, and most things can be boat-scouted or scouted on river-left.

Then you arrive at Big Momma Jomba, a standout rapid with a fun bottom hole. After some easy paddling, the second gorge is 3.5 miles in length, and where you commit to the run. The actions starts quickly with slot moves and more steep, boulder-filled rapids until you soon see a huge steel bridge over the river: This is High Steel Falls (scout right). I've run right on all my trips, crashing into the big hole at the bottom. Next is Bobbing for Butler (scout right), which is a landslide rapid that always seems to be changing. From here amazing gorge scenery takes over and you can finally look up and experience the paradise you're passing through. The last rapid is Mr. Toad's Wild Ride, which usually feels a bit manky, but boats well over 900 cfs. There's still 3.5 miles to the takeout, so paddle fast ... it's likely getting late.

—Scott Waidelich

## THE RUNDOWN

This is the first river to flood in Washington once the steady rains arrive.

**Difficulty:** Class IV-V

**Gauge:** USGS #12060500 SOUTH FORK SKOKOMISH RIVER NEAR UNION

**Flow Min-max:** 650-1,300 cfs

**Gradient:** 36 fpm avg., 90 max

**Takeout:** Skokomish Valley Rd. A large pullout along the river just before Vance Creek bridge.

**Put-in:** 8.5 miles up FR 23 to Spur Rd. 220

**Length:** 11 miles

**Hitchability:** No

**Season:** Early spring/winter

**Camping:** Brown Creek Campground just upstream from the put-in

**4WD Needed?** No

**Best Close Food/Beers:** BYO, not much around here

**Quality (out of 5):** 4.5

**Raft Recommendations:** Though it has been rafted and cat-boated, not recommended

Brian Vogt

Mike Hoover taking it all in

## SHUTTLE DIRECTIONS

At U.S. Hwy. 101, turn west onto Skokomish Valley Rd. Go 4.5 miles and look for a large pullout along the river just before Vance Creek bridge. This is the takeout (**47.315549, -123.251301**). To reach the put-in, continue another 1.2 miles to a right turnoff on Govey Rd. (FR 23). Stay on FR 23 toward Brown Creek Campground around 8.5 miles to Spur Rd 220 down to the river (where the big Forest Service sign is). Likely gated, walk 15 minutes down the hill to the river (**47.402186, -123.311980**).

# JEFFERSON CREEK

If you like nonstop whitewater and incredible scenery, Jefferson Creek is for you. Many joke there is only one rapid on Jefferson, but it's really two miles of constant ledges, boofs, blind corners, steep horizon lines, a couple slides and a portage. And when the water gets high you really notice the 300 fpm. It gets FAST!

There is no warmup. As water pours out of Elk Lake, the action picks up immediately. About a quarter-mile downstream, the river widens, gets shallow for a 100 feet and is followed by a horizon line. This rapid is worth a scout on the right bank. If the level seems too high at this point, hike out here. There is a nasty, blind piton rock at the bottom left that can be avoided by staying center. The biggest rapid on the run is a few hundred yards downstream.

Island Drop sneaks up after a left-hand bend. It should be scouted by getting out at the top of the Island. This can be challenging if levels are high. The common line is the right channel. The ledge downstream is also run right.

The rapids below the island are a blur. Attempting to describe them is pointless, especially if you've made it this far as you'll be scouting a bit. The combination of wood potential and Jefferson's blind nature make the first run take an hour or two. After you get the all-clear, it only takes about 30 minutes to cruise, including the portage, which is a little less than halfway. When you notice a couple trees spanning the river and an abrupt left-hand corner, get ready to eddy river-left. The horizon line is obvious, but comes up fast and can catch you off guard. Although it is commonly portaged, it does get run.

The last notable drop is after several tall, steep cliffs. The river gorges up into a mini-canyon and drops 6-8 feet down a steep chute. Stay to the right and avoid the recirculating room-of-doom on the left. There is usually a fixed rope to help if you end up over there.

The hardest part about Jefferson Creek is catching it at a good flow. The low side tends to be hard on boats and the high side can get scary if you don't know the wood situation or where you're going. Elk Lake helps hold the flow for a while, but normally it only runs for a day or two after heavy rains. It's best to catch it on the way down. For a first-time run, aim for 1,200-1,400 cfs on the NF Skokomish gauge. Above 1,600, things start to speed way up. And below 1,200 it gets very boney. The numbers are not an exact science either. And be sure to disregard the marks painted on the rocks at the put-in and takeout.

—*Darren Albright*

## THE RUNDOWN

Basically one long rapid!

**Difficulty:** Class V

**Gauge:** USGS #12056500— North Fork Skokomish River below Staircase Rapids near Hoodsport (USGS). Look for 3-5" precipitation in 24-hour period—NF Skok near. Staircase or Jefferson Creek RAWS

**Flow Min-max:** 1,000-2,000 cfs

**Gradient:** 300 fpm

**Takeout:** NF-2480 bridge at Jefferson Creek

**Put-in:** Elk Lake

**Length:** 2 miles

**Hitchability:** Bad

**Season:** Late October to April during moderate to heavy rains. Short snowmelt season.

**Camping:** Available at both put-in and takeout. Plus Hamma Hamma Campground.

**4WD Needed?** No

**Best Close Food/Beers:** Hoodsport

**Quality (out of 5):** 4 (3 when low—hard on boats)

**Raft Recommendations:** Yes, swims will be long.

## SHUTTLE DIRECTIONS

From U.S. Hwy. 101 go west on FS Rd. 25 (Hamma Hamma Recreation Area). FR 25 is approx. 14 miles north of Hoodsport. Go 6.5 miles on FS 25 to the junction of FS Rd. 2480. Turn left on FR 2480, go over the Hamma Hamma River and follow it downstream, staying left at the Y. Continue until the next bridge; take out here **(47.582717, -123.106418)**.

Put-in: Continue on FR 2480 for about a mile to FS Rd. 2401 and turn right. Go 2.5 miles to a small road on the right (FR 2401-012). Drive 200 yards down steep spur road or park on the side of road and walk down **(47.573902, -123.131954)**.

Joe Keck

Chris Totten getting past the horseshoe

# ELKHORN CANYON

## OF THE DOSEWALLIPS RIVER

The Elkhorn Canyon section of the Dosewallips River is an Olympic Peninsula classic for a reason: quality Class V rapids with a fast, chunky feel. The water is cold, fast and beautiful. There is not much of a warmup, but thanks to that hike in, your hips and shoulders will already be tired. Stay on your toes! This river collects wood and is a step up from nearby runs like the Big Quilcene or Matheny Creek. A steep-sided gorge with tight, technical boulder gardens broken up by numerous 4- to 6-foot non-uniform ledges reinforce a very remote and isolated feel.

Putting in just downstream of Dosewallips Falls, the first of the larger rapids comes at you quickly. As you bebop down through some smaller broken ledges and bedrock-pinch hydraulics, you gain a feel for the canyon and what to expect downstream. After the first couple ledges, the canyon walls will briefly open back up with a large pile of ancient deadwood directly in front of you. A debris field on the right gives you an impression of just how high the water gets here, while the left looks like the river falls into Middle Earth. Some house-sized boulders on river-right/center are perfect for scouting and portaging. Scout here and gain a feel for the style and difficulty of the run below this rapid.

Run this rapid by starting down the left side, dodge the trees in the middle and then exit through the slot on river left or center (depending on flow). Beware: The large boulders midstream and on river-right are extremely undercut and the last hole in this rapid is hungry. This rapid gives you a feel for the complexity and nature of the run.

Below this rapid you are truly in Elkhorn Canyon. The rapids do not let up and there is minimal margin for error, so if you're walking this rapid, begin thinking of an exit strategy. At multiple points, this entire river will push through slots barely 6 feet wide. As you pass Tumbling Creek on river-right, the river constricts and banks hard left. There is a very distinct, fan-shaped rock in the riverbed. Paddle just left of this rock and then fall left into the inside corner of the rapid to avoid the nasty pocket on river right.

## THE RUNDOWN

**Difficulty:** Class V-V+ at normal flows

**Gauge:** Visual at Nightmare rapid: River should look filled in but not big or pushy. You should see clear channels through the boulders in Nightmare, but not hydraulics of concern.

**Flow Min-max:** 600-1,000 cfs

**Gradient:** 115 fpm

**Takeout:** Elkhorn Campground or as close as you can get due to landslide just downstream

**Put-in:** Below Lower Dosewallips Falls

**Length:** 3 miles

**Hitchability:** Not an option.

**Season:** November to July. Snowmelt in the spring and after rainstorms on the east side of the Olympics.

**Camping:** Dosewallips Campground is nearby

**4WD Needed?** No

**Best Close Food/Beers:** Town of Brinnon

**Quality (out of 5):** 4.5

**Raft Recommendations:** Possible for the truly daring and those who just don't care about their sanity

Midway in the trip you will have an 8(ish)-foot entrance ledge into a narrow chunky boulder garden. Boof right of center on the entrance, then keep left and pick a side of the gunsight, boofing for glory.

Catch your eddies and scout habitually, Elkhorn canyon is one of the premier reasons to visit the east side of the Olympics. Pack a lunch, a couple extra Snickers bars, maybe even a headlamp, and give this little slice of whitewater heaven the respect it deserves.

—Daniel Patrinellis

## SHUTTLE DIRECTIONS

From U.S. Hwy. 101, turn west onto Dosewallips Rd/FS Rd. 2610. Dosewallips Rd. used to provide access right to the put-in, but a 2002 flood washed it out below The Maze Rapid, and the ranger station at the trailhead has been abandoned ever since. Drive up Dosewallips Rd. as far as you can and then begin hiking. The trail is an old overgrown road and the incline is forgiving, but a pack system is preferred to shouldering for this hike. Access is tricky. After you pass the campground around the 2.5-Mile Mark, note an area of old burn on your left. Begin looking for a way to scramble down the slope to put in below Dosewallips Falls. There is no trail to river level and you will be scrambling through old-growth and devil's club, so wear your old drysuit. If you made it to Dosewallips Falls, turn around and start looking for access downstream.

**Put-in Lower Falls: 47.730428, -123.148938**
**Takeout (Elkhorn Campground): 47.728643, -123.095091**

# BIG QUILCENE

The name "Big Quilcene" invokes thoughts of large volume and big whitewater, but this run normally only sees what locals call boat-able levels between 200 and 500 cfs.

At normal flows, the put-in will have you guessing whether or not there will be enough water in the riverbed. As a good friend once stated about a similar creek in the Cascades, "If the put-in looks boat-able, walk away." The same rule of thumb applies here.

The riverbed and the fold in the land that you paddle down will look and feel like a scene from a Tolkien book: massive mossy boulders, enormous old-growth trees (some of which will be in the river) and water so colorful that you will feel drab in your neon drysuit.

The Big Q fits the Olympic Peninsula cookie-cutter description: steep and full of wood, but awesome! This shallow creek is a solid Class V run based on consequence of the swim or loss of gear and run intensity. This creek is steep and the recovery pools are very small. The riverbed is so narrow in some places that you can touch both sides and need to duck under a tree. Some years there are more wood portages than rapids, but the spirit of adventure and complete lack of consistency are what make this little creek so enticing as well as rewarding. Bring your best river shoes and a PowerBar as both will be needed for a pleasant jaunt down the Big Q. The run starts off with a lot of wood and a very shallow riverbed.

Casserly's Falls was named in honor of Justin Casserly who notched the first descent in the late '90s. Casserly's is a two-tiered, 17(ish)-foot drop with a Big Brother-style cave on river-right. Enter the drop either center or on river-right, moving with left angle and delay that boof stroke ...

The nature of the run changes dramatically after Casserly's. The gradient picks up and the gorge stays narrow. From here out the Big Quilcene takes on a more characteristic OP feel, with bedrock ledge drops and basalt boulders with undercuts to spice things up. Several of the larger rapids occur where the river has hit a dense layer of rock and taken a 90-degree turn. These cutbacks also tend to be undercut and full of wood.

## THE RUNDOWN

It's always an adventure!

**Difficulty:** Class V-V+ (Upper), IV+ (Lower)

**Gauge:** Visual at the put-in. Stick gauge at the fish hatchery.

**Flow Min-max:** 200-600 cfs

**Gradient:** 115 fpm

**Takeout:** U.S. Hwy. 101 bridge over Big Quilcene

**Put-in:** Lower, Rainbow Campground at Mile 299.7 on U.S. 101; Upper, off Rd. 2700

**Length:** 2 miles (Upper), 3.2 miles (Lower)

**Hitchability:** Don't count on it

**Season:** Runs on snowmelt briefly and after rains in the northeast Olympics

**Camping:** Stealth camping or camp near Dosewallips

**4WD Needed?** No

**Best Close Food/Beers:** Quilcene or Brinnon

**Quality (out of 5):** 4

**Raft Recommendations:** No

Describing individual rapids below Casaly's Falls is all but useless. This river bed changes on a yearly basis and wood keeps things interesting. Instead, in preparing for the big quilcene be ready for wood obstacles and sieve piles. Very small scout Eddie's, super committed, steep walled canyons. And moss on everything.

Beaware of the weir above the lower takeout. Take out above it on river-right.

—Daniel Patrinellis

## SHUTTLE DIRECTIONS

The lower takeout is 2 miles south of the town of Quilcene where the U.S. Hwy. 101 bridge goes over the Big Quilcene River **(47.811110, -122.910545)**. To reach the Lower put-in, head south on U.S. 101 for 3 miles to Rainbow Campground **(47.773279, -122.917270)**. To reach the Upper put-in, head north on U.S. 101 to a left on Penny Creek Rd. In 1.4 miles, take a left onto Big Quilcene River Rd/FR-27. In 1.8 miles take a left onto Road 2700. Continue 2.4 miles to where the road comes close to the river **(47.780484, -122.954656)**.

Dan Patrinellis

Joe Howard dropping in

# UPPER DUNGENESS

The scenery at the put-in bridge is incredible with towering, old-growth cedars and firs on the steep ridgelines framing a river whose color is best described as glacial and enchanting. Seal-launch into the river from a rock covered in moss thick enough to swallow your hand as you push off and enjoy the first half-mile of warmup Class II-III boogie. This is the character of the Upper with many fun small boofs and slots. Proceed carefully and always assume wood in blind corners. The Dungeness doesn't flush as often or as thoroughly as other OP rivers because of the rain shadow. Expect to make at least three portages due to wood—the quality of the rapids and especially the scenery still make this a very worthwhile run. The best rapid, Mouse Trap, is at the very end of the Upper and within eyesight of the bridge and Dungeness Forks Campground.

Take out at the campground if you're only doing the Upper, otherwise, it's recommended to continue and do both sections. After the Forks campground, the Dungeness and Gray Wolf converge, combining similar flows of distinct colors to create a visible mixing zone as you approach the first Class III boulder gardens on the Lower section. The scenery continues as you eddy-hop Class III rapids for 2-3 miles before the gradient lessens to Class II and braided channels for another couple of miles to the takeout. Pre-scout the takeout, as you can't see your car from river: It's just after the concrete diversion that feeds the hatchery.

A bare minimum for both sections is 800 cfs with 1,000 cfs being a good low. Both sections have been boated up to 2,000 cfs, which is a very enjoyable flow for the Lower and a manageable pushy for the Upper (if you know the run).

—Adam Griffin

## THE RUNDOWN

The Dungeness is located on the northeastern corner of the Olympics, a rain shadow created by the high peaks and ridges of the range. The rain shadow receives on average 13 inches of rain per year which is an order of magnitude less than locations as close 40 miles away! The Dungeness is also known as one of the steepest watersheds in the country, dropping 7,300 feet from Mount Mystery and Mount Deception over 32 miles to the Strait of Juan de Fuca.

**Difficulty:** Class III-IV

**Gauge:** USGS #12048000—Dungeness River near Sequim, WA

**Flow Min-max:** 800-2,000 cfs

**Gradient:** 125 fpm (Upper); 59 fpm (Lower)

**Takeout:** Fish Hatchery (Lower), Dungeness Forks Campground (Upper)

**Put-in:** Confluence of Gold Creek and Dungeness, access by FS Rd. 230 via 2870

**Length:** 3 miles (Upper), 5.5 miles (Lower)

**Hitchability:** Shuttle required. Very long bike shuttle.

**Season:** Winter, brief snowmelt window in spring

**Camping:** Dungeness Forks Campground

**4WD Needed?** No

**Best Close Food/Beers:** Longhouse Deli in Blyn (U.S. Hwy. 101)

**Quality (out of 5):** 3.5

**Raft Recommendations:** Not recommended because of small riverbed

## SHUTTLE DIRECTIONS

Take U.S. Hwy 101 to the northwest corner of the Peninsula and turn onto Palo Alto Rd. In approximately 8 miles, turn right onto NF-2880 and descend downhill to the Dungeness Forks Campground: the takeout for the Upper and put-in for the Lower. To get to the Upper put-in, continue past the campground and uphill to the first left onto 230. Then take 230 (NF 2860) left, downhill and to the trailhead parking and end of the road. Walk another half-mile down this roadbed to the bridge over the Dungeness (47.9421196, -123.09516)

To get to the Lower put-in, turn onto Taylor Cutoff Rd. just west of Sequim. At the first turn in the road, turn left onto Hatchery Rd. and park in the gravel lot on the left a quarter-mile past the Hatchery (48.02448566, -123.13693). From here, head back to Dungeness Fork Campground using NF-2870 (instead of going back up Taylor Cutoff Rd. to U.S. 101 and Palo Alto Rd.).

2

# HONORABLE MENTIONS

## OF THE OLYMPIC PENINSULA

**The East Fork of the Humptulips** is known as the Narrows, with old-growth in a beautiful secluded gorge. Beware of logjams that might need portaging. There is also a fish ladder on river-right that usually goes well. Run typically between 800 and 15,000 cfs, this 5-mile stretch, at 24 fpm, is perfect for intermediates.

**The WF Humptulips Gorge** is short and sweet (at 3.5 miles) with a handful of Class IV+ rapids in a beautiful gorge. The first section can be scouted from the put-in bridge. The final rapid can be seen from the canyon rim on the left with some work. Once you're in the canyon, scouting options are limited. You can work your way down to the top of the gorge past the bridge or rappel off the bridge. Put-in: 47.379076, -123.794283; Takeout: 47.334203, -123.828040.

**Donkey Creek into the WF Humptulips.** If you are looking for an easy waterfall to run, 16-foot Perfection Falls is about as good as it gets. Just below the put-in bridge on Donkey Creek (47.327951, -123.813296), this falls can be run multiple times with ease. Continuing down the 1.6-mile, Class IV creek stretch, another falls requires a scout downstream with more bedrock goodness down to the confluence with the WF Humptulips. It is an easy 2.2-mile, Class I float to the takeout (47.298266, -123.838938).

**The Duckabush Gorge** is worth doing once. You have two put-in options: Above the gorge (47.682951, -123.042205) where the river runs roadside, committing you to a gorge which includes a Class V+ entrance rapid; or, hiking into the gorge below the entrance rapid, enjoying the other Class IV-V rapids starting with Ranger Hole, one of the best boofs in the eastern Olympics. The 6.2-mile run ends with a long, flat paddle out to the takeout at U.S. Hwy. 101 (47.649256, -122.933378).

**The Duckabush's Big Hump and Little Hump Gorges** end where Duckabush Rd. (NF 2510) crosses the river—take out at this bridge (47.682883, -123.042151). Hike upstream 1.6 miles on river-left along the trail for the Little Hump Gorge, or a little over 4.5 miles for the Big Hump Gorge (47.693486, -123.122113). The Big Hump is full of whitewater and the Little Hump has a series of falls, the final of which is big (50ish feet), tough, and dangerous, but looks runnable. The Little Hump Gorge can be portaged with difficulty on the right. The run has been done at a minimum flow of 250 cfs, higher levels have not yet been tested. Be careful not to get gorged in above an unrunnable rapid.

**Hamma Hamma Falls** is a spectacular Class V+ cascade that has become a favorite with expert waterfall paddlers. The entry drop is about 20 feet, very challenging with some bad spots along the walled cauldron of its base, and pushes swiftly into the second, rolling 55-foot falls (47.575854, -123.260893; 4WD may be required to access).

Scott Baker

Brett Barton deep in the fifth canyon on Tshletshy Creek

**The Hamma Hamma** (Lower Bridge to Falls) is a beautiful river and gorgeous canyon! Be on your toes with this Class III (IV+) run (put-in: 47.594905, -123.128881). The toughest rapid on this 5-mile stretch, U Turn, is only about three quarters of a mile in and has a blind entrance, so approach with extreme caution at higher flows (above 600 cfs). Scout this rapid left before committing, and scout your takeout carefully; a Class VI gorge lurks just downstream, so don't miss it! (47.569207, -123.076190)
Put-in; 47.594695, -123.129020
Takeout: 47.568917, -123.076276

The Upper Hamma Hamma is for expert paddlers looking for a steep and demanding challenge. Approach this 3.5-mile, Class V-VI stretch with caution; high flows (above 250 cfs) should be considered off limits. This run is very dangerous in places with a few mandatory portages. (Put-in: 47.58434, -123.20625; Takeout: 47.597786, -123.137524.)

Scott Baker

Brett Barton working through the whitewater on Tshletshy Creek

**The Tshletshy Creek** multiday trip starts near the NF Quinault Campground (47.571288, -123.650170) at Three Lakes/Skyline Trail. Hike 7 miles up to Three Lakes then cross the low saddle into the Tshletshy's headwaters (47.602064, -123.731606), which hold some waterfalls, then five separate gorges. The top gorges are all unique, some are easy. No. 3, The Tshlasm is a class VI portage with a noteworthy bear highway on the river-right portage trail. No. 5 holds several miles of classic Class IV-V rapids climaxing just before the confluence with the Queets. Have a good attitude about exploring and charge 11.6 miles on Tshlshy and 7.5 on Queets (the gauge on which should be at 2,000-4,000 cfs in the spring) to the Sams River takeout (47.624110, -124.014179).

**The Upper Sams River** is set in a polished bedrock gorge with stunning surroundings. Small falls and chutes line this short (2.8-mile) and unforgettable (Class IV-V) section.

*Some heavy logistical issues have befallen the Sams in the last few years: Road closures have forced a hike in, while wood has blocked off some of the run's highlights. There's a high chance this run, which ideally needs 250 cfs, is still not clean. (Put-in: 47.603540, -123.822969; Takeout: 47.604537, -123.871187.)

**The Lower Sams River:** demanding, diverse, breathtaking. Old-growth forest and incredible gorges mark this Olympic Peninsula must-see-to-appreciate run (600 cfs optimal flow).

*Some heavy logistical issues have befallen the Sams in the last few years: Road closures have forced a hike in while wood has blocked off some of the run's highlights. There's a high chance this 8-mile, Class IV-V run is still not clean. (Put-in: 47.604724, -123.871177; Takeout: 47.624110, -124.014233.)

# HONORABLE MENTIONS

## OF THE OLYMPIC PENINSULA

**The Mosh Pit** is a surf wave on the Sol Duc formed by the Washington Department of Fish & Wildlife SolDuc Hatchery weir. Look for the Queets gauge to be 20K and the Hoh to be at least 5K and climbing during a period when area grounds are already saturated or when a recent heavy snow is followed by a rapidly climbing freezing level. To reach the Mosh Pit, turn south onto Mary Clark Rd. at Mile 203.5 on U.S. Hwy. 101 and then turn immediately west on Pavel Road toward the SolDuc Hatchery (48.057172, -124.309149).

Follow Pavel Road 1.3 miles to the hatchery, pull into the first parking lot on your right, and take the boat ramp down to the Mosh Pit.

**The Elwha River** from Glines Canyon Dam to U.S. Hwy 101 covers Class II-III(IV) whitewater that was historically the segment between the two dams. If you use the upper put-in at the historic powerhouse site (48.003434, -123.601776), the run starts with the last half of Glines Canyon, which includes some fun Class IIIs before arriving at a sequence of boulders and ledges creating a fun Class IV rapid (with a fairly easy portage) about 0.5 miles in. You can scout some of this canyon section from the road (look for a set of wooden steps leading down to the river about 250 yards up the road from the bridge; the Class IV rapid is just upstream). Shortly after this rapid you cross under the bridge at Altair Campground that serves as the lower, alternate put-in. Ideal flow is 500-2,000 cfs (Takeout: 48.065640, -123.577996.)

Tom O'Keefe

Helge Klockow

**The Elwha River** from U.S. Hwy. 101 to the Pacific Ocean is still developing. With the Elwha Dam gone, a new river channel routes through the sediment layers of the historic Aldwell Reservoir beginning at the put-in from the U.S. Hwy. 101 bridge (48.065669, -123.578050). Use caution through this section as wood hazards are constantly shifting and the channel is in a state of flux. This Class II-III(IV) section is a fascinating landscape of old tree stumps from when the forest was cleared a century ago prior to the Elwha Dam construction. While the whitewater is not difficult the wood hazards demand respect and this section is no place for inexperienced paddlers. You can easily scout the upper section of the old reservoir and explore it from its old boat launch.

After the upper section of the old reservoir, the river cuts through a short canyon at the Gooseneck before opening up into the lower section of the old reservoir. Soon you approach the Elwha Canyon that was once blocked by Elwha Dam.

The rapid at the former dam site is known as That Dam Rapid. If you are traveling downriver you can pull out on river-left and climb up the slope to get a partial view of the rapid. Although you cannot see much from this side, it is the best portage option. It's easy to get there if you drive down before your run.

That Dam Rapid starts with a short entry rapid before the river explodes below through a Class IV+ cascade of boulders and holes that is a technical drop at lower flows or a big-water rapid at higher flows.

Just downstream of the dam site, the river flows through a scenic gorge with some Class II rapids. There is a short stretch of flatwater before another Class II rapid on the upstream side of the Highway 112 bridge.

Once you pass under the old Elwha Road Bridge the character of the run changes as the gradient tapers off a bit and the channel becomes more braided. At moderate flows (500-2,000 cfs is ideal for the section) there are still a few rapids in this section, but there is also a lot of wood—both engineered and natural logjams. By continuing all the way to the ocean you can end your trip with a bit of ocean surf and experience the new beach that is forming at the river mouth (48.113968, -123.553164). Visit the historic access site made available at the base of the dam (48.094570, -123.555206), which enables you to scout That Dam Drop (recommended if you plan to portage or run it).

# EASTERN WASHINGTON

Charlie Munsey

Rafa Ortiz firing up the 189-foot beast, Palouse Falls

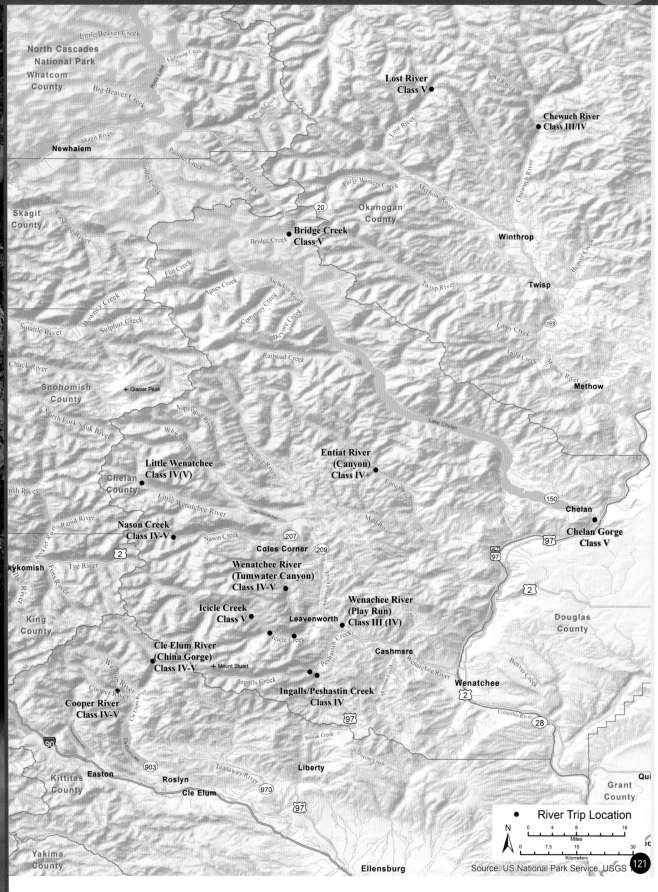

Little Beaver Creek

North Cascades
National Park
Whatcom
County

Lightning Creek

Ross Lake

Big Beaver Creek

**Lost River**
**Class V** ●

Lake Creek

Skagit River

Panther Creek

Canyon Creek

Newhalem

Early Winters Creek

**Chewuch River**
● **Class III/IV**

Skagit
County

Cascade River

Thunder Creek

Granite Creek

20

Okanogan
County

Methow River

Chewuch River

Winthrop

**Bridge Creek**
**Class V**

Bridge Creek

Flat Creek

Stehekin River

Twisp River

**Twisp**

153

Agnes Creek

Company Creek

Devore Creek

Railroad Creek

Libby Creek

Gold Creek

Methow River

**Methow**

Suiattle River

Downey Creek

Sulphur Creek

Chuck River

Snohomish
County

✛ Glacier Peak

Napeequa River

White River

Chiwawa River

Lake Chelan

**Little Wenatchee**
**Class IV(V)**

Chelan
County

Little Wenatchee River

Lake Wenatchee

**Entiat River**
**(Canyon)**
**Class IV+**

Entiat River

150

**Chelan**

nish River

Rapid River

Beckler River

**Nason Creek**
**Class IV-V** ●

Nason Creek

Mad River

207

**Chelan Gorge**
**Class V**

ALT
97

97

Coles Corner

209

kykomish

Tye River

2

Foss River

**Wenatchee River**
**(Tumwater Canyon)**
**Class IV-V** ●

Chiwaukum Creek

2

Skykomish River

**Icicle Creek**
**Class V** ●

Leavenworth

**Wenachee River**
**(Play Run)**
**Class III (IV)** ●

Peshastin Creek

Douglas
County

King
County

Icicle Creek

**Cashmere**

Wenatchee River

Beaver Creek

**Cle-Elum River**
**(China Gorge)**
**Class IV-V** ✛ Mount Stuart

Ingalls Creek

Mission Creek

**Wenatchee**

Waptus River

**Cooper River**
**Class IV-V**

Cooper River

Cle Elum River

**Ingalls/Peshastin Creek**
**Class IV**

97

2

Columbia River

28

90

Cle Elum Lake

903

Teanaway River

Swauk Creek

**Liberty**

Grant
County

Qui

**Kittitas**
**County**

**Easton**

**Roslyn**

**Cle Elum**

970

Teanaway Creek

97

**Yakima**
**County**

**Ellensburg**

● **River Trip Location**

N

0    4         16
Miles
0    7.5    15    30
Kilometers

Source: US National Park Service, USGS

# COOPER RIVER

Ahh ... the Cooper. This classic pool-drop gem runs in the summertime and has some of the best Class IV+ ledges and slides in the state. The water temp is mild and the canyon bright green with old trees arching over the river. Fed by Cooper Lake, the run starts in the pool below a sliding 50-foot falls. Walk down and scout the first slide on the right. After the first slide is a 6-foot boof that leads to a straight section with a few holes. Quickly thereafter the river bends right leading in to Norm's Resort (scout right). Norm's is a sloping pour-over ledge that you run on the FAR RIGHT to avoid the hole. From here, it's classic ledges and slides until S-Turn, which you can run anywhere. Then the last rapid finale, Wall of Voodoo. You'll know you're there by the throngs of people on the rocks, jumping in and swimming. Run the flake in the center, and stay away from the right wall at the pinch—it's undercut and the current tends to drive you right at it. Take out around the corner and rally up for more laps!

—Scott Waidelich

## THE RUNDOWN

Super clean ledges and slides. Great stepping-stone run for aspiring creekers. The opener for the '90s cult classic TV show *Northern Exposure* was shot on the main street in Roslyn.

**Difficulty:** Class IV-V

**Gauge:** US Bureau of Reclamation Cle Elum Reservoir inflow. Available at usbr.gov

**Flow Min-max:** 400-1,800 cfs

**Gradient:** 107 fpm

**Takeout:** The swimming hole near Salmon La-Sac Campground

**Put-in:** Below the 50-foot sliding falls

**Length:** 1.6 miles

**Hitchability:** Not so good, unless you have beer

**Season:** May, June, July

**Camping:** Great camping everywhere, both paid and free

**4WD Needed?** No

**Best Close Food/Beers:** Brick Saloon in Roslyn

**Quality (out of 5):** 5

**Raft Recommendations:** Small rafts OK

Jon Crain

Chris Brigman in Wall of Voodoo

## SHUTTLE DIRECTIONS

For the takeout, from Roslyn drive north on state Hwy. 903 which eventually turns into Salmon La Sac Rd. for 15 miles. Cross the Cle Elum, bear right to stay on Salmon La Sac, and follow the dirt road to its end and park. Make sure you have your Discover Pass and follow the painfully slow speed limit; they hand out tickets like candy on this section of road (47.409431, -121.106773).

Put-in: From the takeout, drive back the way you came for 2.1 miles, turn right onto NF-46 and follow for 3.3 miles. You'll pass a small road on the left and shortly thereafter, use a pull-out on the right big enough for five well-parked cars (47.418096, -121.137130).

Scott Waidelich

Mike Etger passing through Norm's Resort

# CHINA GORGE

## OF THE CLE ELUM RIVER

The run begins at Triple Drop, which is composed of two 6-foot ledges and a 10-foot slide. As the first two ledges are stacked on top of each other, many people prefer to put-in below the second drop and run the final slide. When running the final slide it is important to stay left as the right side has a turbulent pocket eddy up against the right wall.

For the next 3 miles, the whitewater is magnificent Class III-IV read-and-run boulder gardens. When you do happen to find a small eddy in the continuous Class IV boogie water, the scenery is fantastic. The gorge will only get more dramatic as the walls rise up on either side of you. At about the midpoint of the gorge you will encounter the crux section of the run: S-Turn.

S-Turn can be hard to identify amongst the continuous rapids, but the river taking a sharp bend to the left marks your approach. S-Turn is a two-sequence Class V boulder constriction in the depths of China Gorge and can be difficult to scout and arduous to portage. I have seen people try to get a glimpse from both river-right and river-left. If you can find it on the drive up, views can be had from the rim.

The typical line at S-Turn is to begin on river-right, moving back to the left off the shoulder of the first large mid-river boulder. There is a hole on the left you will punch before catching an eddy on river-right to stage for the second sequence: a similar move to the first. Heading out of the eddy on river-right, move back left for another slot on river-left, then punch a small hole at the bottom. For several years now there has been a large tree in the runout of S-Turn at river level. If you are in control, it is no issue as you can catch another eddy on river-right in front of the log.

## THE RUNDOWN

Considered to be one of the most beautiful Class IV-V runs in the state of Washington. And though remote, there is a road at the top of the gorge the entire length on river-left.

**Difficulty:** Class IV-V

**Gauge:** US Bureau of Reclamation Cle Elum Reservoir Inflow

**Flow Min-max:** 1,500-3,500 cfs

**Gradient:** 111 fpm. Put-in elevation: 3,320 feet

**Takeout:** River-right above the bridge at Salmon La Sac Campground

**Put-in:** 5.7 miles up FR 4330 at Triple Drop Rapid

**Length:** ~6 miles

**Hitchability:** Not recommended

**Season:** Snowmelt, typically mid-May through June

**Camping:** Pay camping at Salmon La Sac, plenty of free options off of FR 4330 on way to put-in

**4WD Needed?** No

**Best Close Food/Beers:** The Brick in Roslyn

**Quality (out of 5):** 4.5

**Raft Recommendations:** R-2 at the higher end of runnability

## SHUTTLE DIRECTIONS

From I-90 eastbound take Exit 80 north toward Roslyn and Salmon La Sac on state Hwy. 903. Follow 903 all the way to Salmon La Sac Campground. Cross the bridge and park upstream on river-right. This is the takeout **(47.403109, -121.097436)**.

To reach the put-in, head back across the bridge and immediately make a left onto FR 4330. Follow this ~5.5 miles to the Triple Drop put-in **(47.465237, -121.048006)**.

Below S-Turn is only more great whitewater and scenery. The next notable feature is Waptus Hole: a large hydraulic formed at the confluence of the Waptus and Cle Elum rivers just beyond the China Point footbridge. The hole takes up more than half of the river. Stay right! A little farther downriver is the last significant drop on the run, China Falls.

China Falls is a 10-foot falls/slide that can be scouted on river-right. At all flows, paddlers can grind down the far right side. At lower to moderate flows, the hero line opens on center-left (just be sure not to fall off into the left pocket). Below China Falls, the scenery remains spectacular as you exit the gorge and reach Salmon La Sac Campground. Please note that wood conditions in China Gorge can change on a week to week basis during runoff. Stay on your toes for wood—if there is an issue you can always escape to the road on river-left.

*—Jon Shelby*

Jim Good 📷

Jon Shelby hitting up China Falls 👁

# WATERSHED®

WATERPROOF BAGS | MADE IN USA 🇺🇸 DRYBAGS.COM

HANDMADE
AVL, NC

# NASON CREEK

Nason Creek canyon is awesome. If it were longer I'm sure it would get run more often. There is great camping at the canyon put-in near the railway-bridge scout and particularly at the takeout. Temperatures are also a lot cooler here if you're looking for a reprieve from the Leavenworth heat. The upper run starts with some slides that are visible from the road. If they are a little low, the canyon will be manageable; high and the canyon will be full-on. Between the slides and the canyon is mostly Class II with possible wood portages. The canyon is best scouted from the right. If you think it might be high, driving down to the railway bridge and assessing level and wood situation is advisable. The canyon itself is bedrock with chunky boulders making for some sweet boofs, a couple of bigger drops (10-12 feet), some technical pushy rapids, and some burly holes particularly at higher levels. It's mostly cliffed out on the left with generally more room to move around at river level on the right. It may be possible to take out at the end of the canyon near the railway bridge. If so it would be sweet to do laps particularly if you have a driver. If Nason is a little low, often the little Wenatchee will be at a moderate flow. Enjoy!

*—Mike Nash*

## SHUTTLE DIRECTIONS

To get to the scouting road, drive 2.7 miles heading west from Whitepine Road. (or 4.5 miles heading east from the Upper put-in). Drive about three-quarters of a mile down to railroad bridge, which crosses Nason above the canyon. The road continues up river-left to a cool camp spot on an old bridge abutment. You can scout the canyon here to check it for wood and levels, or risk it and cross the railway bridge to get a full canyon scout on river-right.

Takeout: Take Whitepine Creek Road off U.S. Hwy 2. Drive 2.7 miles, turn right and drive another half-mile. Continue past the bridge over Whitepine Creek to a camp spot at the confluence **(47.775414, -120.915750)**.

Upper (full run) put-in: Heading east on U.S. 2, drive 6.3 miles past Stevens Pass to a large pull-out on the left with some road maintenance buildings. (Creek is visible through trees below pull-out.)

Lower (canyon) put-in: Heading east on U.S. 2, drive another 2.9 miles past Upper put-in (47.769041, -120.997404), then take the small maintenance road on the right, drive 800. ft to the put-in **(47.778904, -120.941069)**. This road is 4.3 west of Whitepine Rd.

## THE RUNDOWN

Nason Creek was highlighted in the classic Twitch videos.

**Difficulty:** Class IV-V

**Gauge:** USGS #12459000—WENATCHEE RIVER AT PESHASTIN, WA; Washington DOE: Nason Cr. N Mouth

**Flow Min-max:** 5-6,000 cfs on the Wenatchee at Peshastin gauge

**Gradient:** Approx. 200 fpm. Canyon put-in elevation: 2,552 feet. Upper put-in: 2,856 feet.

**Takeout:** See shuttle directions

**Put-in:** See shuttle directions

**Length:** Short canyon run is 1.3 miles. Long run is 4.5 miles.

**Hitchability:** No

**Season:** Snowmelt, typically mid-May through June

**Camping:** Yes, lots of camping options in Leavenworth, most options are up the Icicle Creek Road and can be crowded on busy weekends so be sure that you find your spot early on Friday if you can.

**4WD Needed?** Railway scout road is marginal

**Best Close Food/Beers:** Leavenworth. Also the 59er Diner in Merritt would be the closest option.

**Quality (out of 5):** 4

**Raft Recommendations:** Not recommended

Nason Creek, Chris Ohta

Despite being a delightful creek with beautiful scenery and classic whitewater, the Little Wenatchee is an often overlooked run in the Leavenworth area, likely due to its penchant to accumulate wood. The wood situation changes every year, so paddlers need to be alert. When it's clear, this run is a true classic well worth the side-trip.

The run starts off with a fun 6- to 8-foot ledge, commonly called First Ledge. After some fun Class II/III, the walls then narrow into the First Gorge where the action picks up. The gorge leads to the Flume, which ends in a harsh left turn through a narrow slot. Be sure to scout river-left on the trail well before entering the First Gorge. Wood often accumulates in this corridor and the eddies are small. After some continuous Class IV, the next big rapid is Let's Make a Deal. Run the entrance slide and eddy out river-right to choose your slot. Generally the right slot is the drop of choice. The river corridor then opens up for a little while before the Second Gorge, where the run's largest rapid, Snaggletooth, appears shortly after the canyon walls close in. Scout or portage on river-right. The run then continues with some fun read-and-run Class III before ending at the Lake Creek Campground.

*—Ellie Wheat*

## THE RUNDOWN

Fun, continuous Class IV with a few bigger rapids sprinkled in.

**Difficulty:** IV+

**Gauge:** USGS #12459000— WENATCHEE RIVER AT PESHASTIN, WA

**Flow Min-max:** At least 6,000 cfs

**Gradient:** Average 92 fpm. Put-in elevation: 2,535 ft.

**Takeout:** Lake Creek Campground

**Put-in:** Forest Service gate 2.8 miles up FR 65 from Lake Creek Campground

**Length:** 3 miles

**Hitchability:** Poor

**Season:** Spring

**Camping:** Lake Creek Campground

**4WD Needed?** No

**Best Close Food/Beers:** The 59er Diner Leavenworth/Lake Wenatchee

**Quality (out of 5):** 4

**Raft Recommendations:** Possible, but difficult with the wood portages. Wood and blind corridors are a major problem with this run. Expect at least one portage

## SHUTTLE DIRECTIONS

From the town of Leavenworth, head west on U.S. Hwy. 2 to Coles Corner and turn right on Hwy 207 toward Lake Wenatchee. Follow the road around the north end of the lake. In 10.5 miles, the road turns into FR 65 (Little Wenatchee Rd.). Continue another 10 miles to reach Lake Creek Campground. Drop a car at the campground and make sure to walk down to the river to know your takeout **(47.873171, -121.013691)**.

The put-in is 2.8 miles up the road to a Forest Service gate. Park here and walk a few minutes down the hill to the river **(47.893892, -121.067541)**.

Kevin Cripps

# TUMWATER CANYON

## OF THE WENATCHEE RIVER

Tumwater Canyon is one of the classic roadside runs of Washington. With majestic scenery and big Idaho-style whitewater, it is not a river to miss. It runs from early spring, when the rapids are big and pushy, all the way through late summer when the levels become more friendly. It is only 5 miles long, so be ready for multiple laps for endless fun.

The Wenatchee River runs through Tumwater Canyon, fed from the snowpack of Stevens Pass. High water flows in the spring, but is most commonly run during summer at the lower levels. The friendliest level is 1,000-2,000 cfs. This is a great Class IV level, with P.O.W. and Last Exit being the only Vs, both of which are easily portaged. Many boaters will flock to the river at these levels to enjoy the steep, pool-drop rapids during the heat of the Leavenworth summer. Superboof in Chaos will leave a smile on your face for days. Above 2,000, the rapids have more Class V push. Above 5,000, be sure to scout each rapid as the big four rapids now have Class V-V+ consequences.

Since the whole run is roadside, the four major rapids can be scouted from U.S. Hwy. 2. In descending order, they are The Wall, Chaos, P.O.W. and Last Exit. The small dam after The Wall can be portaged on river-left. As the hardest rapid, most paddlers choose to take out just above Last Exit. It is an exhilarating rapid, but not one to take lightly.

—Ellie Wheat

## SHUTTLE DIRECTIONS

The put in and takeout both run along U.S. 2 up Tumwater Canyon outside of the town of Leavenworth. The takeout is 0.6 miles from the last gas station in Leavenworth up the canyon **(47.586804, -120.686446)**.

The put-in is another 4.8 miles up the canyon at a long shady pullout **(47.637959, -120.722787)**.

## THE RUNDOWN

The Tumwater Dam, in the middle of the run, once ran generators that powered part of the Great Northern Railway. The hydroelectric power helped move trains over the 4,000-foot pass to Skykomish. It was decommissioned in the early 1900s as a generator, and today serves only as a fish ladder—a resource for fisheries studies to trap and sort migratory fish species.

**Difficulty:** Class IV-V

**Gauge:** Wenatchee River at Peshastin is most commonly used, but the Wenatchee River at Plain is most accurate. USGS #12459000— WENATCHEE RIVER AT PESHASTIN, WA; USGS #12457000— WENATCHEE RIVER AT PLAIN, WA; NWRFC #PESW1— WENATCHEE AT PESHASTIN

**Flow Min-max:** 800-8,000 cfs

**Gradient:** Average 64 fpm

**Takeout:** A riverside pull-out just upstream of Last Exit. You can't miss the view of this massive rapid as you leave the town of Leavenworth on U.S. Hwy. 2. Park in the small riverside pullout just above this rapid 0.6 miles from Leavenworth.

From the river, pull into a large river-left eddy just above the frothy lip of Last Exit. Carry your boat up the bank to your car. Or, take your chances in Last Exit and take out river-left just after the rapid and scramble up the steep bank.

**Put-in:** A long pull-out above the first rapid, The Wall, 5.4 miles up the canyon from the town of Leavenworth

**Length:** 5 Miles

**Hitchability:** Good

**Season:** Spring to summer

**Camping:** Great camping up Icicle Creek

**4WD Needed?** No

**Best Close Food/Beers:** In Leavenworth, grab a burger and milkshake from Heidlburger to fight off the hanger. Then head over to Icicle Brewing to enjoy a microbrew and nice ambiance.

**Quality (out of 5):** 5

**Raft Recommendations:** Class V rafters only

Ellie Wheat
Scott Waidelich Routes Perfection of Whitewater (POW)

Chris Ohta
Sam Grafton

Mike Hagadorn

Ben Kinsella comfortable in the middle of Chaos

# HOUSE RUN

## OF THE WENATCHEE RIVER

Starting with the runout of Last Exit, the grand finale of the Class V Tumwater Canyon, boaters looking to venture into more difficult whitewater will find this section to be a perfect place to push it to the next level. If putting in at the base of Last Exit, the next quarter-mile of whitewater is the most difficult, but is read and run. After this section of splashy IV/IV+ there is a brief section of flatwater before getting to Tinley Falls, which should be run on the right through a big wave train with holes on river-left. Then it's Class III big-water fun to the takeout under the Icicle Rd. bridge. An alternate put-in can be had just up U.S. Hwy. 2 from Osprey, which allows boaters to skip the hardest part of the run, but still get some quick, quality boating. As flows increase over 5,000 cfs, the section immediately below Last Exit will provide a very big-water feel with powerful crashing waves and large hydraulics.

—Jonathan Ehlinger

### SHUTTLE DIRECTIONS

The takeout is on river-left just before crossing over the Wenatchee on Icicle Road. To get to the takeout from the west, take a right on Icicle Rd. immediately upon entering Leavenworth; from the east, take a left on Icicle Rd. on the west side of town just before entering the canyon **(47.577523, -120.674067)**.

The put-in is a gravel pull-out on river-left a quarter-mile west of Leavenworth. Make sure to ask Osprey about parking if you park there and put on below it **(47.587405, -120.685159)**.

### THE RUNDOWN

Local Hero Rob McKibbin lost his pants after swimming the bottom of Last Exit once!

**Difficulty:** Class IV-IV+ depending on put-in. The first quarter-mile is Class V- at high flows, and will feel very big and powerful.

**Gauge:** USGS #12459000—WENATCHEE RIVER AT PESHASTIN, WA

**Flow Min-max:** 1500 cfs to 10,000+ cfs

**Gradient:** N/A

**Takeout:** Icicle Road Bridge (first bridge on Icicle Rd.)

**Put-in:** Osprey Rafting or bottom of Last Exit (see takeout for Tumwater Canyon)

**Length:** 1.5 mile

**Hitchability:** Very hitchable. Also short enough to jog the shuttle.

**Season:** Late March to August

**Camping:** Plentiful camping up Icicle Rd. starting at Eight Mile Campground, 8 miles from the intersection of Icicle Rd. and U.S. Hwy. 2.

**4WD Needed?** No

**Best Close Food/Beers:** A few blocks to downtown Leavenworth with plentiful food and beer options. Icicle Brewery is highly recommended.

**Quality (out of 5):** 4

**Raft Recommendations:** Easily raftable but getting boats down to the put-in is difficult. Rafters may choose to use the alternate put-in, but will miss out on the first quarter-mile of whitewater.

Chris Ohta
Rob McKibbin in Rodeo Hole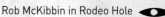

# PLAY RUN

## OF THE WENATCHEE RIVER

The Wenatchee offers up some of the best play in western U.S. when the water is up. With a multitude of put-in and takeout options, to keep things simple the best put-in during peak runoff is Rodeo Hole. At flows above 7,000 cfs, Rodeo Hole starts to form and at 10,000+ it becomes one of the country's biggest, most dynamic features with incredible eddy access.

Once you have gotten your fill of Rodeo, head a mile downstream to Drunkard's Drop, which, at flows between 10,500 and 13,000 cfs, contains Trinity Wave: another incredible feature that can support any big-wave move. At 5,000-6,500 cfs there is a nice wave on river-right as well. Another mile Downstream from Drunkard's Drop is Turkey Shoot: a calm, consistent, and beginner friendly wave perfect for those learning to surf, but which also support most hole moves for advanced boaters.

Another mile downriver, Snowblind rapid contains an almost uncountable number of catch-on-the-fly waves and retentive holes. At flows above 12,500 cfs, Snowblind is an incredible rapid with multiple retentive waves that are double overhead—worth lapping with a walk back up along the railroad tracks on river-right.

Finally, just downstream of Snowblind is Granny's, which, at flows between 6,000 and 8,500 cfs, contains one of the best and most consistent waves you will find on the river. This wave does not have eddy service, but is worth hiking via the mid-river island as multiple-minute rides are the norm, and the wave will support nearly any wave or hole move. Once you've grown tired of near-perfect kayak surfing, Cashmere and milepost 111 await just downriver, offering great post-boating food and beer options with a riverside deck.

*—Jonathan Ehlinger*

### THE RUNDOWN

**Difficulty:** Class III

**Gauge:** USGS #12459000—WENATCHEE RIVER AT PESHASTIN, WA

**Flow Min-max:** 5,000-10,000+ cfs for the main play features. Section can be run as low as 1,500 cfs

**Gradient:** N/A

**Takeout:** Cashmere River Park

**Put-in:** Rodeo Hole Fisherman Access (Requires Discover Pass)

**Length:** 5 miles

**Hitchability:** Moderately hitchable. When the waves are in, finding a shuttle at the takeout is not difficult.

**Season:** Late April to late June

**Camping:** Plentiful camping up Icicle Rd. starting at Eight Mile Campground, 8 miles from the intersection of Icicle Rd. and U.S. Hwy. 2

**4WD Needed?** No

**Best Close Food/Beers:** Milepost 111 Brewing Company offers a good selection of pub fare and craft beers at the takeout. Country Boys BBQ, also right at the takeout, is another great food option, but does not serve beer.

**Quality (out of 5):** 5 (above 7,000 cfs)

**Raft Recommendations:** This is the primary commercial raft run in the state! Great rollercoaster wave trains and fun for the whole family!

### SHUTTLE DIRECTIONS

There are many put-in/takeout options that begin in Leavenworth and end at the Columbia River. We suggest stopping at Leavenworth Mountain Sports for more beta regarding alternate river access and upstream rapids such as Boulder Bend and Rock 'n' Roll. For the Wenatchee's standard play-run, however, the takeout is located at Cashmere Riverside Park. If coming from the west on U.S. Hwy. 2, take a right onto Aplets Way and then a left onto Pleasant Ave. If coming from the east on U.S. 2, take a left on Aplets way **(47.524857, -120.468945)**.

The put-in is located along the Sunset Highway. Head back to Aplets Way/Division St. and turn left (south). Proceed through Cashmere and take the first right (Sunset Hwy.) after the railroad tracks. Continue on Sunset Hwy., which becomes Stines Hill Road after ~ 1 mile, and about 1.5 miles later, just before the road descends, look for a house with a blue metal roof followed by a dirt road. Turn right and follow to the bottom of the hill to the Rodeo Hole access parking area. Be sure you have a Discover Pass or you may be ticketed. The nearest location to purchase is at Der Sportsmann, 837 Front St. in Leavenworth **(47.530344, -120.534105)**.

# ICICLE CREEK

## INTRODUCTION

Roadside access, sweeping views of 8,000-ft. granite peaks and top quality whitewater! Aptly named it would be called the Icicle River, since many consider it low as flows approach 1,000 cfs. Icicle Creek makes the perfect full day adventure or 30-minute whitewater fix. Although many prefer to break up the run into one of three sections for convenience, running the eight-plus miles of whitewater from the Upper put-in to the Lower takeout is a great way to experience Icicle. You will have to portage a few rapids along the way, but will gain several extra miles of great whitewater.

Wood: Fires in 1994 burned much of Icicle Creek Canyon. Subsequent landslides keep depositing large amounts of wood, changing rapids and making new ones. Keep your eyes out for shifting wood—especially early spring.

A note on levels: Icicle has a huge range of flows. The Lower stretch tolerates water quite well. The Upper and Middle, on the other hand, pick up speed quickly as flows climb. Get a couple runs at low to moderate flows first and get a feel for it. The Upper is a great stretch for the Class IV kayaker looking to step it up and run a couple Class V's. Putting in at the RV access area, the action starts off fast. Hug the left bank around the first corner as recent landslides have deposited wood along the right bank. The next quarter-mile is dotted with nice Class II-III warmup rapids and beautiful crystal-clear pools.

—Darren Albright

Shane Wilder

Darren Albright running Horseshoe Rapid

The first Class V is Roadside. It's hard to miss on the shuttle and worth a look from the road. The line is obvious but the holes 100-200 yards downriver tend to catch folks off guard. Keep to the middle and boof the ones you miss.

The last Class V is Log Limbo. You'll know you're there when you see a distinct horizon line, a house-size boulder and a log perched on top of it. Limbo has a knack for collecting wood so it's a good idea to scout. Either take a look during the shuttle—since you'll likely be leaving a vehicle here anyways—or while paddling from river-right.

Below Limbo marks the common takeout for crews looking to run laps on the Upper. If you choose to continue, the next mile is pretty mellow, but be ready to catch an eddy river-left just below the bridge over Icicle Creek. Bridge Creek Rapid lurks right around the corner. Walk the dirt road a few hundred yards downstream and look for the trail that leads back to the river. Bridge Creek Rapid has been run, but the massive holes and bad sieves keep most away. When you put back in, work to the right side of the island since the left channel is blocked with wood.

Enjoy the scenery as you paddle the next few miles of Class III-IV to Eightmile Campground. Below here you tend to lose sight of the scenery and focus on the whitewater!

*—Darren Albright*

## THE RUNDOWN

Great run for Class IV boaters wanting to progress!

**Difficulty:** Class IV (V above 2000 cfs)

**Gauge:** Icicle Creek DOE. Alternate: 22 percent of Wenatchee at Peshastin (10-day forecast included).

**Flow Min-max:** 1000-2400 cfs

**Gradient:** 180 fpm

**Takeout:** Below Log Limbo

**Put-in:** RV turnout next to Icicle Creek Road, three-quarters of a mile below Johnny Creek Campground

**Length:** 1.5 miles

**Hitchability:** OK on weekends. Bad on weekdays.

**Season:** Spring runoff through April to July, plus occasional winter floods

**Camping:** Great, some free and lots of pay camping

**4WD Needed?** No

**Best Close Food/Beers:** Anything in Leavenworth

**Quality (out of 5):** 4

**Raft Recommendations:** OK, swims will be long

## SHUTTLE DIRECTIONS

To reach the takeout, follow Icicle Creek Road 9.2 miles from U.S. Hwy. 2 in Leavenworth. There is a small loop on the left to park vehicles and scout Limbo **(47.574506, -120.792546)**.

Continue 1.3 miles farther until you see a huge RV turnout on the left. There's a short trail that leads to the river **(47.588665, -120.811135)**.

Shane Wilder

Little D lacing Richochet Rapid

# MIDDLE ICICLE CREEK

There is no real way to warm up for Ricochet, but putting in at Eightmile Campground allows a few minutes of paddling to ease the tension. Anyone who's seen or paddled Ricochet before knows what I mean. When you hop out on the right bank to scout, it's an overwhelming sight. Not to mention you're only looking at the top half of the rapid. Depending on the level, it's either a quarter-mile maze of giant boulders or giant holes. The general line is to start right then work left to the distinct eddy 200 yards downstream. First-timers can scout again from here to see the move at Ricochet Rock and the bottom half of the rapid.

After several great Class IV rapids is House Drop. You can sneak it down the right or go for the boof off the pyramid shaped rock midstream. Below here the rapids get steeper and more challenging as you go.

If you don't have a guide, plan on spending some time scouting on your first trip. Keep your eyes out for a drop dubbed the Sieve. It's easily portaged on the left.

The first big ledge is Horseshoe. It sees more portages than descents for obvious reasons. It tends to flush if you go deep, but hold on (or don't) if you get stuck as the hole is stickier than it looks. Be sure to have a throw-bag ready! Horseshoe leads right into a long super-steep, high-quality boulder rapid.

Immediately below, the river constricts to about 15 feet wide and drops 10 feet over The Plunge. Fight your way through the wave-holes on the lead-in and get a good boof off the lip.

After two more rapids, paddle over the low-head dam and take out river left. If you're continuing on through Lower Icicle, paddle a few hundred feet downstream, take out before the next rapid, and portage left (on the dirt road again). The massive Snow Creek Rapid has yet to be run and will probably remain that way (the Forest Service does have plans to blast it for construction of a fish ladder though). Put in as high as you feel up for.

This is the most challenging stretch on Icicle Creek. It should not be taken lightly, especially at higher flows, and it's best to learn the lines at lower flows or follow someone who knows what's coming. It's probably a good idea to take a peek during the shuttle and get a feel for where both Horseshoe and the Plunge are since they tend to sneak up (~5 miles from U.S. 2 on Icicle Creek Road).

*—Darren Albright*

## THE RUNDOWN

Highly concentrated high-quality whitewater.

**Difficulty:** Class V–V+

**Gauge:** Icicle Creek DOE Alternate: 22 percent of Wenatchee at Peshastin – (10-day forecast included)

**Flow Min–max:** 800–2,200 cfs

**Gradient:** 225 fpm. Put-in elevation: 1,880 feet

**Takeout:** The big turnout a quarter-mile upstream of Snow Creek Trailhead.

**Put-in:** Eightmile Campground

**Length:** 2.5 miles

**Hitchability:** OK, better on weekends

**Season:** Spring runoff until April–July, plus occasional winter floods

**Camping:** Great, some free and lots of pay camping

**4WD Needed?** No

**Best Close Food/Beers:** Anything in Leavenworth

**Quality (out of 5):** 5

**Raft Recommendations:** It has been done. You'll know if it's for you.

## SHUTTLE DIRECTIONS

To reach the takeout, follow Icicle Creek Road 4.5 miles from U.S. 2 in Leavenworth. Park in the large turn-out on the left about a quarter-mile above Snow Creek Trailhead **(47.543534, -120.716260)**. Be sure to take out immediately below the low-head dam; you don't want to run the next rapid.

To reach the put-in, continue 2.5 miles to Eightmile Campground. Park on the shoulder of Icicle Creek Rd. and take the trail to the river. Don't leave a car inside the campground unless you pay the day-use fee—they enforce it! **(47.551892, -120.764263)**

Lower Icicle has something for everyone. You can dial in your new creeker, hone the boof, practice fighting out of holes or warm up for one of the harder runs upstream. It is one of the better Class IV entry runs around. The float and shuttle are short, about a mile, which makes it easy for multiple laps. It takes only 10-15 minutes to cruise.

From the Snow Creek Trailhead, peer over the edge and find where you want to put in. The hardest rapid on the run is immediately below the bridge: Line up middle, pull a hard one at the lip and get ready for a stern ender. It can easily be scouted by hiking down the left bank before putting on.

The difficulty gradually tapers off but the action stays constant. Stay about 30-feet off the right bank and look for a boulder to boof when you get to the low-head dam. Below the dam, a 200-yard wave train marks the ending of the run. Most take out river-left immediately below this rapid. It is possible to paddle one more rapid and another mile to the Icicle Creek Fish Hatchery, but it's hardly worth it.

What more could you ask for? A challenging, steep boulder-filled river that is only a stone's throw from the state's best Class III play run (Wenatchee River) and Tumwater Canyon, one of the best big-water Class V runs anywhere.

*—Darren Albright*

## THE RUNDOWN

Quick fix when you're rolling in late Friday evening.

**Difficulty:** Class IV

**Gauge:** Icicle Creek DOE. Alternate: 22 percent of Wenatchee at Peshastin (10-day forecast included)

**Flow Min-max:** 1,000-3,000 cfs

**Gradient:** 125 fpm. Put-in elevation: 1,300 feet

**Takeout:** 200 yards below low-head dam

**Put-in:** Snow Creek Trailhead

**Length:** 1 mile

**Hitchability:** Great, especially Friday through Sunday

**Season:** Spring runoff until April and through July, plus occasional winter floods

**Camping:** Great, some free and lots of pay camping

**4WD Needed?** No

**Best Close Food/Beers:** Anything in Leavenworth

**Quality (out of 5):** 3.5

**Raft Recommendations:** Yes. Hard to put in and take out.

## SHUTTLE DIRECTIONS

To reach the takeout, follow Icicle Creek Rd. 3.2 miles from U.S. 2 in Leavenworth. Just past the Icicle River RV Park there is a small shoulder to park three to four cars on the left **(47.547898, -120.690413)**. Look for a steep dirt slope and where the guardrail starts back up. If you see the river and a low-head dam you went too far. To reach the put-in, continue another mile to the Snow Creek Trailhead. Park on the shoulder unless you have the appropriate Discovery Pass **(47.544474, -120.710579)**. Take the trail to the bridge for an easier start. If you're feeling up to it, bite off a chunk what you see upstream.

 Shane Wilder
 Rob McKibbin and Darren Albright sauce out the rapid above the put-in.

# INGALLS CREEK

Ingalls is a narrow, eddyless flume at medium and higher flows—think of it as a mile-long Class IV rapid. Many Class IV boaters have gotten in over their heads dropping into this run, so don't let the Class IV rating fool you. Be sure that you have a manageable group size; large groups (more than four) can become challenging. If you have one, consider launching in waves about 10 minutes apart and meet at the confluence with the Peshastin.

From the put-in, cross the bridge to scout the first few drops, which are the steepest and most unique in character compared to the rest of the run. There is a long, fast boulder garden that culminates in a center-right boof (hit your boof on left or center). Below the initial boulder garden, the run cools down comparatively but is still a magic carpet of whitewater. There are only a couple viable eddies on the run for the whole group to catch its breath, so keep your eyes on your partners and watch for wood. The run is pretty shallow and sharp, so staying upright is preferred (but then again, isn't it always?).

As you approach the confluence with Peshastin Creek, the river fans out and become very manky. There is an island where wood has historically collected on the upstream side, so keep your eyes peeled for hazards. Most groups continue downstream on Peshastin Creek. If you want to run laps, pull over river-right in the trees and scramble for an eddy.

For flows: low water is 400-700 cfs; medium, 700-900 cfs; and high 900+ cfs. I have run it at 1,200 cfs—a hoot, but a class harder, and a no-swim environment.

—*Jed Hawkes*

## THE RUNDOWN

Great option when the Wenatchee is at spring peak and all other creeks in the area are too high. Ingalls is great fun when run in combination with Peshastin Creek. At high flows you can paddle 20 miles of continuous whitewater all the way to the takeout of the play-run on the Wenatchee in Cashmere. There is more whitewater upstream if you hike from the trailhead, but reports state that it's full-on, continuous Class V.

**Difficulty:** Class IV

**Gauge:** DOE #45F070—Peshastin at Green Bridge Road

**Flow Min-max:** 400-900 cfs

**Gradient:** 2,150 fpm

**Takeout:** Confluence with Peshastin Creek

**Put-in:** Ingalls Boulder Field Trailhead

**Length:** .64 miles

**Hitchability:** Yes. Bike shuttle: Yes.

**Season:** Spring and early summer

**Camping:** There is great camping all over Leavenworth, with several Forest Service campgrounds in the Icicle Creek drainage as well as up and down the Wenatchee. There is free camping near Cashmere on public land up Hay Canyon Road.

**4WD Needed?** No

**Best Close Food/Beers:** The Big Y Café is east of Peshastin on Rt. 2 and has decent diner fare, drive east on US-2 0.7 miles and turn left on Foster road and you will see it on your left.

**Quality (out of 5):** 4

**Raft Recommendations:** Yes, but only if you have confirmation that the run is recently free of wood. Also, experienced guides and crews only.

## SHUTTLE DIRECTIONS

To the takeout from Peshastin, take U.S. Route 97 south for 7.6 miles until you see a large paved pull-out on the right with a National Forest Service sign at the south end of the pull-out **(47.463167, -120.660374)**.

From the takeout drive, north on U.S. 97 for 0.8 miles, turn left onto Ingalls Creek Rd. and follow this for 1.2 miles **(47.463096, -120.673048)**.

Peshastin Creek is a great run that starts with some good boulder gardens and mellows out to more waves and holes with one bedrock Class IV rapid. Just after you peel out of the put-in eddy, you are in the thick of it—be sure you've knocked out the cobwebs that have gathered over the winter. Right below the put-in are some of the run's bigger boulder gardens. They are mostly down the middle, give or take. These rapids wax and wane for about 1.5 miles before Fresh Squeezed, the climax of the run.

Scout Fresh Squeezed on the shuttle, pulling over about 2.3 miles from the takeout bridge at a left bend with a bedrock bluff on the right. On the river, with swift-moving water leading into Fresh Squeezed, the few small eddies above the rapid won't accommodate much room for a big group to stop. Identify the rapid by the bedrock on the right: This the first time on the run that you will see it. Run the Rapid down the right through several holes before the final ledge, which you can boof on the left side of the channel or down the tongue. There is a fairly large pool at the bottom, though it is swift-moving.

From here the river mellows out and is mostly just wave trains. If you opt to paddle through to the play-run on the Wenatchee, be aware that of the weir about halfway down the run. The left of the weir has a fish ladder that makes it easy to get around the weir without portaging on private property. In years past, we have run this section at peak spring flows and it is a blast to do Ingalls, Peshastin and the Wenatchee all in one shuttle: high-water Ingalls plus Peshastin, and then big water on the Wenatchee to put a smile on anyone's face.

—Jed Hawkes

## THE RUNDOWN

Great continuous Class III+ run with one straightforward Class IV.

**Difficulty:** Class III+ (IV)

**Gauge:** DOE #45F070—Peshastin at Green Bridge Road

**Flow Min-max:** 400-1,500 cfs

**Gradient:** 107 fpm

**Takeout:** U.S. Route 97 bridge over the Peshastin

**Put-in:** See shuttle directions

**Length:** 4.1 miles

**Hitchability:** Yes. Bike shuttle: Yes.

**Season:** Spring and early summer

**Camping:** There is great camping all over Leavenworth, with several Forest Service campgrounds in the Icicle Creek drainage as well as up and down the Wenatchee. There is free camping near Cashmere on public land up Hay Canyon Road.

**4WD Needed?** No

**Best Close Food/Beers:** The Big Y café is east of Peshastin on Rt. 2 and has decent dinner fare, drive Easton on US-2 0.7 miles and turn left on Foster road and you will see it on your left.

**Quality (out of 5):** 4

**Raft Recommendations:** Yes with an experienced crew.

## SHUTTLE DIRECTIONS

To the takeout, drive south from Peshastin on U.S. Route 97 for four miles then park near where the bridge crosses over the Peshastin (**47.510724, -120.631543**).

From the takeout, drive 3.8 miles farther until you get to a large gravel pull-out on the right with a large Forest Service sign at the south end. This is the put-in (**47.463167, -120.660374**).

# BRIDGE CREEK

## OF THE STEHEKIN RIVER

Die-hard backcountry paddlers are gonna love this trip! Bridge Creek is an overnighter located deep in the Cascadian backcountry. Its headwaters begin in North Cascades National Park and once the hiking begins, logistics get easy. Before hiking, be certain of a few things: First, bring a map. Second, get ferry tickets from Stehekin to Chelan on the Lady Of The Lake Ferry (509-682-4584), making sure they have room for kayaks the day of your return back down Lake Chelan, which is nearly 55 miles long. It's about $40 for one person and kayak. Third, get a backcountry permit from the Marblemount Ranger Station (360-854-7245). They're free and if you get caught without one, it's a fat ticket. Pro tip: If you can't make it to the ranger station during normal business hours they are willing to write you a backcountry permit over the phone, but you have ask reeeeaally nice. Do not say, "The guidebook said you would." They won't. These three things are key.

Starting with the map, look for the ferry stop (Field's Point Landing) farther north than the town of Chelan that saves time later. For the drive in, hopefully you bribed a buddy or girlfriend to drive the car back to the Lady of the Lake ferry terminal: The shuttle is 3+ hours one-way. Camping at the put-in is nice for an early start, but not critical as the whitewater isn't too heavy the first day. From Chelan (47.835924, -120.038183), go back to U.S. Route 97, head north about 45 minutes to state Hwy. 153 (left, just outside the town of Pateros). Avoid U.S. 97 Alt., it's much slower. WA 153 eventually becomes state Hwy. 20. Don't turn, keep heading west on WA 20. Continue past Winthrop and every other town, up and over the pass. Keep an eye out for a small parking area 10 or 15 minutes down from Washington pass for a Bridge Creek sign (48.504957, -120.719087). This is your put-in and where the Pacific Crest Trail (PCT) turns south following Bridge Creek all the way to High Bridge! If you drive to Rainy Pass you've gone too far; turn around. Putting in at Hideaway Camp (4.5 miles in) is your best option. If it's high water, Fireweed Camp (3.5 miles in) offers easy river access (and a few more log portages). Watch for wood-jams in the first few miles, we had a half-dozen putting in at Fireweed.

On the water, paddlers will discover continuous rapids with a predictable nature, mostly Class III-IV the first day. There are many campsites along the way. North Fork Camp is a nice option for paddlers wanting a three-day tour. If you only have a weekend, High Bridge Camp offers some choice backcountry glamping (especially on night two) as well as a long day paddling through the hardest rapids. Plan for a full day of paddling if you only have the weekend. Watching this river grow before your very eyes is unique and this trip has several confluences where the flow doubles!

## THE RUNDOWN

I met a guy named Dave Wilson on my first trip down Bridge Creek. As we waited for the ferry, he told tall tales of him and his buddy rafting Bridge Creek all the way down to Lake Chelan back in the '70s and '80s. I believed him! (Also: It takes 10 years for Stehekin's waters to pass through the mouth of Lake Chelan.)

**Difficulty:** Class IV/V (P) (V (P) high water)

**Gauge:** USGS #12451000—STEHEKIN RIVER AT STEHEKIN, WA

**Flow Min-max:** 2,000-4,000 cfs

**Gradient:** 180 fpm

**Takeout:** The Lady Of The Lake ferry terminal in the city of Chelan

**Put-in:** Ingalls Boulder Field Trailhead

**Length:** 27 miles

**Hitchability:** Only hiking trails, until you get to High Bridge (end of the hard rapids) and even then questionable. There is a

daily shuttle from High Bridge to Stehekin (10 miles) if necessary.

**Season:** Summer, after Rainy Pass opens

**Camping:** Along the way

**4WD Needed?** No, shuttle bunny YES

**Best Close Food/Beers:** Stehekin store has great food and beer, bring at least $20

**Quality (out of 5):** 5 out of 5 stars for scenery, amount of work for days of whitewater, quality whitewater, "livin' it" factor.

**Raft Recommendations:** Raftable! This is a Class V self-support multi-day with a hike in.

Brett Barton

Once on the Stehekin proper, paddlers will be delighted to find a large riverbed full of more endless rapids with a classic 'east-side' boulder garden feel. There are several large crux gorges along the way with some heavy whitewater. Don't overcommit, especially if the water is high. This run can freight-train and you don't want to battle with one of Bridge Creek's notorious trolls. They're tough and even more elusive than Robe Canyon's gnomes. There are a couple portages along the way as well. The crux of the run is named Tumwater Canyon. That's right, there's more than one Tumwater Canyon in Washington, and Stehekin's is chock-full of stout whitewater. You'll know Tumwater isn't far when passing a prominent waterfall spraying down the left canyon wall: Carwash Falls, named for the old road that used to be here before the great flood of 2006 flood. From here the rapids are more solid IV-V until High Bridge. At the time of press, a poorly lodged old-growth required a portage directly above Tumwater's crux rapid—a committing, tricky triple set of ledges, though the river flattens just around the corner providing some room for error.

Pro tip: everything can be done at river level, catch your eddies.

The prearranged backcountry glamping is too choice to pass up, and at High Bridge Camp paddlers can relax knowing all the hard rapids are over. Count on two more hours of easy paddling to the ferry landing/takeout in Stehekin (48.309173, -120.657523). Arriving by noon the next day shouldn't be a problem; the ferry leaves at 2 p.m. Stehekin is a cool zone even if you leave the boat at home: The reality of a closed road network means far less people, less noise, and more of a natural rhythm. Tumwater Canyon alone is worth returning to at lower flows down to 500 cfs. You could pay a local to shuttle your laps.

At the end of my first trip, all I could think of on the ferry back to Chelan (besides all the other creeks pouring into the lake) was who to call for another lap! I had more or less stumbled upon a top-shelf backcountry paradise and, like most times, could barely find one person to go back with. The timing couldn't have been more critical because the Methow Valley was about to erupt in flames, with 2014's historic Carlton Complex Fire having already devastated 386,972 acres. We were lucky enough to pass through overnight and our shuttle driver made it out the next morning before 30 miles of Hwy 20 closed.

Paddlers will drive away from the ferry terminal in awe of what they've just experienced. The weather, the whitewater, the scenery, the wildlife: It's one of the rare trips that you'll never forget. While Elwha's Grand Canyon has a very different riverbed, and offers an equally magnificent backcountry experience. Stehekin is wild.

—*Brett Barton*

# CHELAN GORGE

## OF THE CHELAN RIVER

Thanks to Tom O'Keefe and American Whitewater, this annual release has been a long time in the making. In 2000, the first team of paddlers got to explore the inner gorges of Chelan and conducted a flow study to determine boatable flows through the gorge. In 2012, '13 and '14, AW and Chelan County Public Utility District revisited and conducted three more years of flow/feasibility studies, where we watched an obscure run turn into a classic.

First off, this is a short run. You'll likely be there with paddlers you don't know, and despite your best efforts to separate from the larger group, you'll inevitably be a part of the circus that's known as Chelanagins! Putting in, you'll immediately notice the warm water temp as you casually float down the first two miles of gentle Class II rapids. Soon the canyon walls form and you enter the Class IV zone where nicely spaced boulder rapids form for three-quarters of a mile. You have now arrived in Chelan Gorge. The first rapid is Entrance Exam (scout right). This is a three-part drop with a lead-in rapid above. The first main drop has a sloping green tongue into a hydraulic above a river-wide ledge hole. I run down the green tongue, pulling a late left stroke, then run the second ledge center, immediately eddying out against the wall. From this eddy you set up to run the third drop, the Pinch. Come out of the eddy paddling hard to the center of the river, hit the LEFT side of the entry V-wave above the pinch if possible. Set good safety at the Pinch: this is where lots of rodeos and good times will happen. The great thing about this drop is that all the swimmers and their gear float to "swimmer's rock" on the downstream wall in the pool, so go for it! Next comes the Chelan Chute; scout left above this drop. You can sneak down the far left side, or run the main right line (Meat Locker) and go deep. The boils on the right are strong, so set good safety here. Next up is Super Boof; run left and crush it! Immediately after is the Throne (run center-left with right angle), which sits directly above Pinnacle. Set good safety below Throne on both sides of the river; paddlers tend to get pushed into the Throne rock on the bottom left. Pinnacle is a huge double-drop ending in a brief pool above a giant boulder sieve. Set good overlapping safety here as the drops goes well, but the consequences are high. The line is center, avoiding the wall on the bottom right. You can also portage on river-right. After Pinnacle is the Boulder Sieve, have someone paddle river-left in the eddies above the drop and get out to assist paddlers over the sub-surface rock at the edge of the boulder sieve. Now you're in the brief lower gorge, where the rapids Extra Credit and Fat Lady await. These two boulder rapids are easier, but bumpy and sieved out; go slow, watch your crew, and run generally center-left.

—*Scott Waidelich*

## THE RUNDOWN

Class V boating in a shorty!

**Difficulty:** Class V

**Gauge:** Chelan PUD—Discharge from Lake Chelan Dam chelanpud.org/river-flows.cfm

**Flow Min-max:** 300-500 cfs

**Gradient:** 94 fpm avg., 480 max

**Takeout:** Developed boat launch at Chelan Falls Park at the confluence of the Chelan and the Columbia

**Put-in:** Just below the dam on river-left, take undeveloped road down to the river. The trail ends on a wide gravel bar just downstream of the dam.

**Length:** 3.8 miles

**Hitchability:** No

**Season:** September, weekends releases

**Camping:** Camp at the horseshoe pit/fields area near the put-in. We do this every year.

**4WD Needed?** No

**Best Close Food/Beers:** Camp and walk into town to party. Senor Frogs is awesome and the night scene in downtown Chelan is fun.

**Quality (out of 5):** 5

**Raft Recommendations:** Has been rafted several times. Everything was run.

Brett Barton

Rob McKibbin, the People's Champ on Pinnacle

Dan Patrinellis
Jeremy Bisson paddles Chelan's Super Boof

Dan Patrinellis
Fred Norquist passing Entrance Exam

## SHUTTLE DIRECTIONS

To the take out, from Wenatchee take U.S. Hwy. 97 north for 34 miles then turn left on U.S. Hwy. 150 shortly after crossing the Columbia River and follow it for .4 miles. Turn left onto Chelan Falls Rd. and follow for .8 miles, then turn right onto Powerhouse Rd., you will see Long Park on the right: Park and takeout here **(47.804278, -119.985848)**.

From the takeout, head back out to U.S. 150, take a left at the stop sign and follow U.S. 150 for 2.5 miles. Turn left onto E. Woodin Ave., and follow for 0.8 miles. Turn left onto S. Bradley St. (the road bends to the left and some ball fields will be to your left). The road ends in a parking lot for the Horseshoe pits. Park here then hike down to the river to put in **(47.834911, -120.010980)**.

Leif Embertson

Chris Tretwold getting his superboof on

## American Whitewater and River Advocacy in the Pacific Northwest
## Thomas O'Keefe, Pacific Northwest Stewardship Director, American Whitewater

American Whitewater was formed in 1954 as an affiliation of paddling clubs from across the United States with a mission to conserve and restore America's whitewater resources and to enhance opportunities to enjoy them safely. Among the founders was Wolf Bauer of the Washington Foldboat Club (today the Washington Kayak Club). Wolf was one of the first advocates for river conservation who understood the connection between river recreation and advocacy. He worked early on to highlight the recreational value of the Cowlitz River in the Seattle Times, and later to protect the Green River Gorge. He pioneered the way for the whitewater paddling community to recognize the responsibility we have for the conservation and stewardship of the places we recreate.

For many years, the efforts of American Whitewater were led by volunteers and leaders of our affiliate clubs who worked to protect and restore rivers, and secure access to rivers important to whitewater boating. Gary Korb spoke up for protecting Olympic Peninsula Rivers and removing the Elwha Dams, Brooke Drury fought for access to the Cispus River, Andrew Wulfers worked to prevent a hydro project on Canyon Creek, Fran Troje represented the interests of paddlers in the state legislature, Pat Sumption and Jay Cohen campaigned tirelessly for access and flows to the Green River, Doug North developed the foundation of a Wild and Scenic Rivers proposal that remains the blueprint for many of our conservation efforts more than two decades later, and Mike Deckert and Rick Williams joined in on flow studies on rivers impacted, or potentially impacted, by hydropower development.

The work of these passionate paddlers laid the foundation for American Whitewater's work today. We now have staff who lead projects, work as part of coalitions with other organizations, and provide technical assistance to local volunteers working to protect their river or improve access. In 2005, technology allowed us to implement a regional stewardship program (we have regional offices in Oregon and Washington today) while keeping our staff from across the country connected. The result was that we jettisoned our DC-based office and are better able to be attentive to local projects and to take local knowledge and experiences back to federal agencies and our elected officials.

Our community has achieved some impressive successes in recent years, from the removal of dams and the development of new and improved access to dozens of rivers, to newly designated Wild and Scenic Rivers and a growing recognition of the importance of whitewater recreation (and all outdoor recreation) to the state and national economies.

None of this work would be possible without the support of the regional paddling community through financial contributions and active volunteerism. With your help and continued support we can continue to fight the construction of new dams, protect more rivers for whitewater recreation, develop access points, and continue to represent the interests of whitewater paddlers in the halls of Congress and our state legislatures.

# THE LOST RIVER

The Lost is run for the adventure as much for the whitewater. It is a beautiful area and well worth the effort. After the hike, be ready to begin boat-scouting and portaging multiple logs before coming to a small lake where a large talus slide caused the backup of water and created a Class VI rapid at the outflow. The inlet of the lake offers a great spot to camp amid towering pink granite gorges. After portaging the rapid at the outflow of the lake, the Lost builds into great Class IV+ boulder slalom that seems to go on for miles with a few harder rapids sprinkled in. You will be stoked to have rallied to this far, the run is high quality with most rapids boat-scoutable. Wood is of major concern, however, so be wary of blind corners when you are routing down this fun section (after Monument Creek and before Eureka Creek). Then the gradient starts to decrease and the riverbed braids into Class II channels, many of which funnel into river-wide logjams. Be prepared to portage often in this slower bottom section. The eddies are small, so take precautions before arriving at the takeout bridge.

—*Scott Waidelich*

## SHUTTLE DIRECTIONS

Takeout: From Mazama take state Hwy. 20 to Mile 179.6 and turn north on Lost River Rd. (FR 5400). This road crosses the Methow and curves to the left, upstream. You'll reach the takeout bridge across the Lost, seven miles up this road.

Put-in: Return to WA 20, proceed east to Mile 192.6 in the town of Winthrop, and turn north on West Chewuch Rd. (next to the town ball field and across from the FS visitor center). Continue on this road for 9.5 miles and then turn left on FR 5130 (Eightmile Creek Rd.) to Billy Goat Trailhead. Follow the road 17 miles to its end at the trailhead and start hiking here. After a quarter-mile, go left at the split #477 trail to Eightmile Pass (Cougar Lake). Soon you arrive at Drake Creek. DO NOT cross Drake Creek; head down the unmaintained trail on east side of the creek. Expect the hike to take between 5-7 hours due to the poor condition of the second half of the trail. Bring good footwear as fallen trees and rocks block and slow your progress.

## THE RUNDOWN

A true wilderness run overnighter with pink granite gorges.

**Difficulty:** Class IV/V

**Gauge:** AW Virtual, est. based off METHOW NR. MANZAMA, Visual is Best

**Flow Min-max:** 800-1,200 cfs

**Gradient:** 96 fpm

**Takeout:** See shuttle directions

**Put-in:** See shuttle directions

**Length:** 12 miles

**Hitchability:** No

**Season:** June

**Raft Recommendations:** It has been rafted, but not recommended.

**Camping:** There are numerous good camping sites throughout the run, just be careful about camping at the base of the very active talus slopes. Good spots are at the lake or near Eureka Creek. For the first night there are campsites along Eightmile Creek road and some good backcountry campsites where the trail first meets Drake Creek towards the put in.

**4WD Needed?** No

**Best Close Food/Beers:** Town of Mazama

**Quality (out of 5):** 3, with beautiful scenery with a long hike-in and multiple wood portages.

Ellie Wheat

Scott Waidelich enjoys the beauty of pink granite canyon walls. A great camp is at the top of this short lake.

The Chewuch River comes to life every spring for a few weeks around peak snowmelt. The river from Andrews Creek Campground down to the Lake Creek confluence contains a Class V canyon that can collect dangerous wood. An alternate put-in at the Lake Creek confluence allows paddlers to run some Class IV rapids from the upper section down to Camp Four. From there paddlers can run a quick shuttle back up to the confluence for another lap on the Class IV or continue down to one of the many river access points. Aside from an island potential wood hazard it is a scenic Class III+ venture from Camp Four down to the Falls Creek Campground takeout. You can scout large sections of the river while driving up.

*—Jon Crain*

## SHUTTLE DIRECTIONS

On state Hwy 20 west of Winthrop at Mile 192.6, turn north on West Chewuch Road (across from the Red Barn). Continue on this road for about 17 miles to Camp Four Campground for the takeout, just downstream of the bridge **(48.634483, -120.155877)**.

Head another 5 miles up the road to the Andrews Creek Trailhead for the put-in **(48.756734, -120.134234)**.

## THE RUNDOWN

Quality whitewater with ample camping and activities (good rock climbing and mountain biking) for non-boaters in an area not frequently visited by the general population.

**Difficulty:** Class V (Upper); III+/ IV (Middle)

**Gauge:** USGS #12448000— CHEWUCH RIVER AT WINTHROP, WA

**Flow Min-max:** 550-1,100 cfs (Upper); 1,200-3,000 cfs (Middle)

**Gradient:** 53 fpm. Put-in elevation: 2,731 feet

**Takeout:** Falls Creek Campground

**Put-in:** Andrews Creek Campground (Upper); Lake Creek/Chewuch River confluence (Middle)

**Length:** 12 miles

**Hitchability:** Yes, especially on weekends

**Season:** Spring snowmelt (peak)

**Camping:** There is a ridiculous amount of pay and free camping up West Chewuch Road including several of the river access locations: Lake Creek-Chewuch confluence, Camp Four, and Falls Creek Campground.

**4WD Needed?** No

**Best Close Food/Beers:** Evergreen IGA grocery East 20 Pizza in Winthrop

**Quality (out of 5):** 4.2

**Raft Recommendations:** Yes

# CANYON SECTION

## OF THE ENTIAT RIVER

The canyon section of the Entiat is a great little run to explore when you're looking for something new. Like all runs east of the Cascades, the Entiat is a continuous tumble downstream through endless miles of whitewater. There is more above this run, but at the time of press, it was pretty choked with big wood that seemed pretty well put. That said, the canyon stretch is pretty wood-free. From the put-in, the Entiat rolls through continuous Class IVish holes and bouldery sections as it races to the short gorge at the downstream end of Lake Creek Campground. By entering the gorge, paddlers commit to the largest and most difficult drops on the run. At high water this section is full of stomping holes, laterals and screaming boiling ramps. A few of the boulder gardens are lightning fast.

Halfway through this first gorge, Tommy Creek comes in from the right adding about 25 percent to the flow. After the gorge, rapids ease back to III-IV with a few more eddies and chances to breathe.

There are certainly other sections and tributaries of the Entait worth exploring. This section, however, is the jewel of the drainage until the wood cleans up.

*—Brett Barton*

### SHUTTLE DIRECTIONS

From Wenatchee take U.S. Hwy. 97 Alt. north for 14 miles until you cross the Entiat River and take an immediate left onto Entiat River Road. Follow Entiat River Rd. for 24 miles. Park in the small pull-out just past Burns Creek next to the river. In addition to this takeout **(47.904760, -120.473910)**, downstream of the gorge are a number of other pull-outs along the road suitable for taking out. From the takeout, drive upstream on Entiat River Road for 3.2 miles until you reach Lake Creek Campground. Park in the campground; there is a turnout and bathroom on the upstream side of the campground above the trail (Middle Tommy) to the put-in **(47.936904, -120.516651)**.

### THE RUNDOWN

A quality out-of-the-way run when the Wenatchee classics start to lose their luster. Check out the Entiat Box Canyon after your run and let us know when the wood clears out!

**Difficulty:** Class IV+

**Gauge:** UUSGS #12452800— ENTIAT RIVER NEAR ARDENVOIR, WA; NWRFC #ARDW1—ENTIAT NEAR ARDENVOIR

**Flow Min-max:** 600-2,000 cfs

**Gradient:** 137 fpm. Put-in elevation: 1,750 feet. Takeout: 2,160 feet.

**Takeout:** National Forest boundary

**Put-in:** Lake Creek Campground

**Length:** 2-3 miles

**Hitchability:** There is a lot of traffic traveling up the Entiat. That said, most who are venturing into the woods would probably offer a wet straggler a ride back to the put-in.

**Season:** Spring and early summer

**Camping:** Camping in the area

**4WD Needed?** No

**Best Close Food/Beers:** Grab something in Ardenvoir or before you leave Wenatchee

**Quality (out of 5):** 4 for scenery, quality whitewater and uniqueness

**Raft Recommendations:** Raftable!

Kōkatat
into the water since 1979
WWW.KOKATAT.COM

# SULLIVAN CREEK

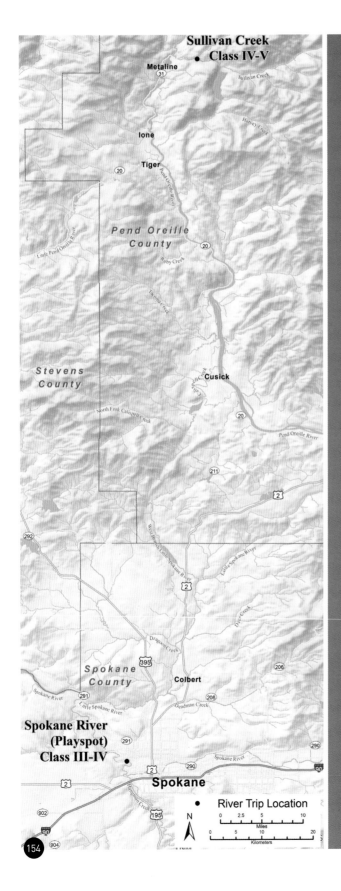

**Sullivan Creek**
**Class IV-V**

Metaline

Ione

Tiger

Pend Oreille
County

Stevens
County

Cusick

Spokane
County

Colbert

**Spokane River
(Playspot)
Class III-IV**

Spokane

River Trip Location

N

Sullivan Creek has a great section of whitewater tucked away in a dark gorge in the upper northeast corner of the state. The allure of this canyon is that it runs later in the summer with dam releases when most of the state's Class IV-V has dried up. This description is written based on runs above 320 cfs. Lower flows are still manageable, but you may have to get out and walk across some shallow sections in the creek.

Not far downstream from the put-in, the excitement starts with the first rapid, Thumper: topped with a strong diagonal wave that pushes left and pinches down with a rock in the bottom of the rapids. Not far below this is New Slide, created from a fresh landslide. Here the river drops through a set of steep chutes around large boulders, scouting options are on the right.

The next notable rapid is Two Log Plop, which starts with a ledge drop into a turbulent pool backed by a large rock. Next is Zig-Zag, another fun boat-scoutable drop. Pretty soon the walls begin to close in and you approach a short ledge known as the Plug, which leads directly into a very large logjam. Portage left and scout your next couple moves: You can see a busy section of whitewater that continues nonstop with an eddy way downstream on the left before the creek turns the corner, out of sight. Beyond that eddy the creek starts dropping through a series of 4- to 6-foot ledges and chutes known as the Squeezes until it drops over the Tooth, which had a large piece of wood in it when I saw it last; be very careful in this section.

A couple more easy rapids lead to the highlight of the run, Itchy and Scratchy. A photo of this rapid graced the pages of the Bennett book in the mid-'90s. I looked at the photo for eight years until I finally made the drive north to see this classic rapid for myself, but by the time I made it something had changed. The large rock in the middle drop had rolled downstream making the set seemingly easier with less pin potential. Afterward, the creek filters through shallow swift-moving boulder rapids then over Powerhouse Plunge, a forgiving 6-foot ledge beside the old powerhouse, visible from the takeout bridge.

—Ryan Scott

Brian Vogt

Itchy and Scratchy confined in the Sullivan Creek Gorge

## THE RUNDOWN

This is a great late-summer run!

**Difficulty:** Class IV-V (suggested portage at the Tooth, known for collecting wood)

**Gauge:** AW Virtual Gauge, see website

**Flow Min-max:** 150-500 cfs. American Whitewater has negotiated recreational paddling fall releases which have changed over the years due to the politics surrounding the removal of Mill Pond. At presstime, releases are scheduled for the first week of September Sullivan Creek runs off in the spring, and for a large part of year.

**Gradient:** 194 fpm

**Takeout:** Metaline Falls, Hwy. 31 bridge over Sullivan Creek

**Put-in:** Sullivan Lake Rd., pull-out near the creek below Mill Pond

**Length:** 1.7 miles

**Hitchability:** Easy

**Season:** Spring, fall, winter

**Camping:** Camping is available upstream of the put-in at Mill Pond Campground as well as Sullivan Lake CG.

**4WD Needed?** No

**Best Close Food/Beers:** 5th Avenue Bar & Grill in Metaline Falls

**Quality (out of 5):** 3.5

**Raft Recommendations:** Not recommended

### SHUTTLE DIRECTIONS

Take U.S. Hwy 2 north toward Newport, turn left on state Hwy. 211 toward Cusick, then follow state Hwy. 20 north to Metaline Falls. The takeout for the gorge is at the powerhouse just past Metaline Falls on state Hwy 31 **(48.860120, 117.365156)**.

To reach the put-in, continue north on WA 31 a couple miles to Sullivan Lake Rd. and turn right. The put-in for the gorge is about 3 miles ahead at the first place you see the creek near the road **(48.858794, 117.328033)**.

Grays Harbor
County

Thurston
County

121   507

Mount Rai
National

Eatonville

Mashel River

Puyallup River

+ Mount R

12

Deschutes River

Chehalis River

Grand Mound

North River

Skookumchuck River

Elbe

Paradise

Lincoln Creek

Nisqually River

706

Fall River

Centralia

Lewis
County

7

Skate Creek

5

508

North Fork Newaukum River

NF Tilton River
Class IV

6

Bunker

Chehalis

Newaukum River

Pacific
County

Pe Ell

South Fork Newaukum River

Lower Tilton River
Class III-IV

Morton

Pack

South Fork Chehalis River

Olequa Creek

Tilton River

12   Randle

Cowlitz River

Grays River
(South Fork/Main)
Class IV+ (V)

Chehalis River

505

Cowlitz River

Riffle Lake

Winston Creek

Cowlitz River

North Fork C

Cispus River

Wahkiakum
County

Grays River

Germany Creek

Toutle River

504

Green River

Hoffstadt Creek
Class IV-V(V+)

North Fork Toutle River

Hoffstadt Creek

McCoy Creek

McCoy Cr
Class V

Castle Rock

Elochoman River

Cathlamet

4

Cowlitz
County

Longview

South Fork Toutle River

+ Mount Saint Helens

NF Lewis
Class II-V+

Coweeman River

Muddy River

Clear Creek

Columbia River

Kalama River
(Park & Huck)
Class III-IV

Kalama River

Cougar

Swift Reservoir

Lewis River

Skamania
County

503

Canyon Creek
Class IV+ (V)

Wind River
(Upper)
Class IV(V)

Clark
County

Amboy

503

EF Lewis River
(Waterfalls)
Class IV

Trout Creek
Class IV-V

Wind River
(Lower)
Class IV-V

East Fork Lewis River

Battle Ground

Copper Creek

Trout Creek

Little Whi
Salmon Riv
Class

Washougal River
Class III-IV

Rock Creek
Class III-IV(V)

Rock Creek

Carson

Wind River

84

5   205

14

Vancouver

**Portland** Washougal

Washougal River

Washougal

| ● | River Trip Location |
|---|---|

0   5   10   20
Miles

0   10   20   40
Kilometers

N

American River

Bumping River

410

Pinecliff

23

anepecosh River
ass IV-V

Rattlesnake Creek

Naches River

12

Clear Fork Cowlitz
Class IV-V+

rk Cowlitz River

North Fork Tieton River

Rimrock

Tieton River

Tieton River
Class II-III

Yakima
County

Ahtanum Creek

Cispus River
(SuperSlides)
Class IV-V (V+)

Simcoe Creek

ver
oper)
7

Toppenish Creek

+ Mount Adams

Summit Creek
Class V+

Outlet Creek

Lake

White Salmon River
Class II-V

Klickitat
County

Rattlesnake Creek

142

97

141

Klickitat

Little Klickitat River

Husum

Klickitat River

te Salmon

Swale Creek

197

Columbia River

The Dalles

Dan Patrinellis

Jeremy Bisson lining up the Beast, Silver Falls

# THE OHANAPECOSH RIVER

Rolling off the slopes of the southeastern glaciers of Mount Rainier lies a majestic old valley, a wilderness protected by rugged mountains, thick with old-growth trees and backed by the Gifford Pinchot National Forest. The Ohanapecosh River drains one of the most beautiful and protected valleys in Washington. The native meaning of Ohanapecosh is "deep blue pool" and it's for good reason: with the majority of its flow originating from a glacial source just 15 miles upstream, the water is emerald blue set against florescent green moss in a purely magical gorge.

The Ohanapecosh is a tributary of the Cowlitz River and of its sister tributaries, the Ohane is by far the most classic and easily accessible. The Ohane was once runnable from Ohanapecosh Campground providing an upper canyon with very similar character as the intact section from Secret Campground downstream. A massive rain and snowstorm around 2006 flooded the river, however, choking the upper canyon with a terminal logjam and filling it with sediment and debris. Despite losing the upper canyon, the Ohane is still one of the most classic pool-drop Class IV-V playgrounds around. The river has been run from its headwaters upstream including Summit Creek, Ohanapecosh Falls, and the infamous park-and-huck Silver Falls, made famous by its daring descents from local legends.

The Ohanapecosh is primarily run in the summer after the snow melts due to its proximity to the glacier and elevation. However, it is periodically run during rain events. The USGS Cowlitz gauge for the run at Packwood is somewhat reliable taking into consideration the amount of water contributing from its sister tributaries and time of year. A good first time flow would be somewhere around 1,200-1,800 cfs in the summer months when the gauge is steady and coming down off snowmelt. Everything is runnable at these levels and the river has a fun Class IV-V pool-drop characteristic with clean ledges, waterfalls and boulder gardens. Although the river can be run up to 3,000 cfs, some of the bigger drops become portages, though the rest of the run cleans up and becomes fun, pushy Class IV-V.

The put-in for this section is down the trail from "Secret Campground" and has a nice seal launch to access the river. If you are unsure of the level there is a large tabletop granite rock, which is 15-20 yards downstream of the seal launch, that can be used as the gauge: Water at the base of the rock indicates low flow; water reaching the middle of the rock would be medium; and if it's covered, the river is at the upper levels of runnable.

From the put-in you paddle around a tight double-ledge zigzag corner to the right and back to the left that we call J.D.'s Hole. This can be scouted from the put-in before you launch, but is easily boat-scoutable from the left eddy above the drop. You'll then reach

## THE RUNDOWN

Beautiful bedrock gorges with crystal-clear, glacier-fed water. Epic camping close to Mount Rainier National Park with amazing hiking.

**Difficulty:** Class IV-V

**Gauge:** USGS Cowlitz at Packwood

**Flow Min-max:** 900-2,500 cfs

**Gradient:** 128 fpm

**Takeout:** La Wis Wis (Elevation: 1,220 feet)

**Put-in:** Secret Campground at (1,820 feet)

**Length:** 4.7 miles

**Hitchability:** During peak season it is hitchable, but otherwise tough

**Season:** Spring-summer

**Camping:** There is camping right at the put-in near the Mount Rainier National Park entrance or at La Wis Wis or

Ohanapecosh Campgrounds. The "Ohane" is a destination run attracting groups coming through the area from across the globe, so it can be a big party scene. Please be respectful. It is wise to set up camp and run multiple shuttles, for once you know the run, you can lap it several times in a day, ending with hot supper and a cold beer around the campfire, talking with old friends and new ones from around the world.

**4WD Needed?** No

**Best Close Food/Beers:** The small town of Packwood is close to resupply, get some pizza or espresso.

**Quality (out of 5):** 5

**Raft Recommendations:** Not for part-time Class V rafters

a big pool above Super Boof, a clean 6-foot ledge. Typically this drop is boofed center-right, landing with left angle to avoid the undercut wall on the right. This drop can easily be scouted by stepping out on the ledge on river-right. Next, you'll be in a pool above a slide which often collects wood; be cautious, otherwise portage or scout on river-left.

Meander downstream less than a half-mile in easy Class II until you reach Rail Slide. In larger groups, go in two or three at a time as there is only a small eddy above the drop on river-left where you can scout and set safety. Rail Slide is formed by a big tree that fell into the river years ago and notched itself in the base of the ledge

*Continued on page 160*

Tanner Sterling

Chris Totten on First Ledge

angling downstream. Rail Slide is named as such because you run this drop by getting a piece of the log and sliding off the wood to the right and away from the ledge hole. This rapid changes every year and should be scouted for wood changes. Below it you run around a big boulder to the left and are then in the midst of the walled gorge with boulders visible 20 feet down in the deep, clear blue pools. A couple of read-and-run Class III-IVs precede Chunky Monkey, a fun Class IV boulder garden rapid with a clean line on the left that is scoutable from either side of the river. Below Chunky Monkey are a few more fun read-and-runs before the first substantial sequence of drops known as Butcher's Block, which flows into Triple Drop. This rapid is marked by large boulders blocking the river with obvious logjams, wood hazards and a definite horizon line. Butcher's Block can be easily portaged on river-left. Either way, this is a good spot to get out, scout the ledge series downstream and decide if Butcher's is something to bite off. If you choose to portage, step around and put in the staging eddy directly below; from here you can scout the next series of drops or continue portaging. The next two ledges are very clean and fun with a tight exit move as the river constricts against the wall on river-right into a big pillow move you take left and into an eddy.

Below this series, the canyon winds and twists into a couple miles of fun read-and-run Class IV boofing before Summit Creek flows in from river-left: marking the eddy above Summit Creek ledge and the start of the lower canyon. Scout from the Summit Creek eddy or run the river-wide ledge center-right. Below Summit Creek, the canyon walls loom overhead as you flow down to an impressive, constricted box canyon with an obvious horizon-line as the river drops away into the Class V-V+ Elbow Room. Approach slowly and catch an eddy on river-left to scout this drop or start your portage around the canyon. Elbow Room is typically run on the lower side

due to the massive slab rock that is undercut in the middle of the river and makes a very serious hazard. At optimal levels the drop is run by boofing a 5-foot ledge on river-left and staying left through a very narrow slot between the huge overhanging canyon wall and the slab rock. This line is good to go at lower flows and cuts out a huge part of the danger factor (and portage). However, the slot is prone to collecting wood, so a scout is always advisable. If you decide to portage or the water is too high, walk back upstream on river-left from the ledge and find a trail that heads up on the canyon rim. Staying high on this trail, you traverse downstream past the canyon, finding a path back to the river-right above the Tea Cups.

Soon you reach Final Falls, and it has many options depending on water level and how hard you want to make the line. The river comes down over a broken ledge and splits into two different drops: the right is a wide, easy 15-foot falls off a rock ledge; the falls on the left constricts against the wall and plunges 18 feet off a big water spout. Both are fun and provide their own challenges, however, at high water the right sneak to right falls is preferred. If running this falls once wasn't enough, you can scramble back up on river-right and lap this falls at lower flows. Below the falls, there is one last drop paddling out of the pool that marks the canyon exit and provides plenty of excitement: Petrified, a Class V boulder garden run either far right against the wall (exiting past the boulder sieve in the middle) or far left. This rapid is worthy of a scout from river-left and is easily portaged as well. The gradient then flattens but the canyon and scenery continue through a beautiful Class II-III canyon paradise down past Blue Hole to the confluence with the Clear Fork coming in from river-left, which indicates your takeout at La Wis Wis Campground. Hike through the woods just downstream of the Clear Fork to the picnic shelters and load up for another lap.

—Chris Totten

## SHUTTLE DIRECTIONS

From Seattle, take state Hwy. 410 over Cayuse Pass to state Hwy. 123. To reach the put-in, go 100 yards from the south side of the National Park's old wooden entrance on state Hwy. 123 (three miles north from U.S. Hwy. 12) and find a dirt road that leads down to the Secret Campground. Follow the road to the right, around the tight corner and follow until it ends at a big flat camp, this is the put-in (46.715024, -121.576644).

To reach the takeout, head south on WA 123 to U.S. 12, turn right, go 1 mile then enter the La Wis Wis Campground. Park down the hill to the right of the campsites in the day-use area (46.673577, -121.587677).

Matt Kurle

Petrified Rapid and Ohane Falls stack up

# CLEAR FORK
## OF THE COWLITZ RIVER

### THE RUNDOWN

This run is stacked with drops.

**Difficulty:** Class IV-V

**Gauge:** USGS #14226500— Cowlitz at Packwood (includes water from the Clear Fork, Ohane and Muddy Fork, so use it as a guideline).

**Flow Min-max:** 1,500-3,000 cfs

**Gradient:** 230 fpm. Put-in elevation: 2,400 feet

**Takeout:** La Wis Wis Campground. If the gates are locked, go 2 miles downstream to FR1270, which will save you hiking up the hill with your boat.

**Put-in:** Below Lava Creek confluence, U.S. Hwy. 12 Mile-marker 142

**Length:** 5 miles

**Hitchability:** U.S. Hwy. 12 is next to the run, so possible on the weekends

**Season:** Pre- or post-peak snowmelt (April or June-July); or fall rains (October through November)

**Camping:** Secret Campground, state Hwy. 123 just before the park entrance. (See Ohanapecosh entry, pg 00)

**4WD Needed?** No

**Best Close Food/Beers:** Packwood, try the Blue Spruce

**Quality (out of 5):** 5

**Raft Recommendations:** Has been paddled by Class V rafters, not recommended

The Clear Fork Cowlitz is one of the most sought-after runs in Washington, as it is packed with rapids top to bottom, as well as truly breathtaking scenery. It is both a memorable and daunting experience that rewards good paddling, and being in good paddling shape. Wood is a constant concern, so take your time, and don't "bombs away" until your second or third run.

The adventure begins with a trek down into the canyon, and the decision to put in above or below Entrance Exam. With three tiers dropping 30 feet, this rapid used to be run regularly from the top, until the first drop, the Foaming Crack, became less friendly. As of 2015, most folks put in below.

Marty Smith

Seth Swallen

### SHUTTLE DIRECTIONS

Drive east of Packwood on U.S. Hwy. 12 for about 7 miles to La Wis Wis Campground on the left. Drive down and park in the day-use area **(46.674489, -121.588981)**. You can eyeball the level by driving the road to Blue Hole, which crosses the Clear Fork.

To get to the put-in, drive east from La Wis Wis on U.S. 12 until Milepost 142, where there's a big pull-out on the north side of the highway. To get to the river, cross the highway and follow the trail, which will switchback to the right. This is where you want to step off and angle down in a gully until it becomes a dry creekbed, which puts you directly below Entrance Exam. To put-in above it, simply stay on the original trail for another 200 yards, and then drop straight down the hill to the river **(46.677705, -121.526860)**.

Below Entrance Exam, the rapids roll out in quick succession. This bedrock section has some of the more memorable drops, including Furious (four drops all run on the right) and Crack Den (nice waterfall run on the left). Then a smaller rapid with a hard right turn at the bottom leads you to the unrivaled Bitch Slap (18 feet), where you can smear the right wall, or go for the left corner if it's looking good.

As you finish the top bedrock section, you'll encounter the Palisades, a columnar basalt wall rising out of sight on river-left. This is the sign to watch for a huge landslide on river-right, and means it's time to take a stroll. Put back in near the end of the landslide, wherever looks good.

After the landslide, you'll encounter Flake Falls (nice 10-footer), and a big sliding drop (15 feet) before you're greeted by Cortright Falls pouring into the canyon on river-right. This marks the start of Cortright Canyon, which has several challenging boulder gardens, including Dead Beaver (watch the sticky hole at the bottom). Pinvader is the last big drop in Cortright Canyon, and an obvious scout.

After Pinvader, there's still a bit more read-and-run, but keep an eye peeled for wood until you see the welcoming sight of the U.S. Hwy. 12 bridge. At that point it's an easy float to the takeout and a well-earned beer. Whether it's your first time, or your 20th, the Clear Fork never fails to deliver a memorable day.

—JD Gaffney

Bryon Dorr

Joe Stumfel

# UPPER UPPER

## OF THE CISPUS RIVER

### THE RUNDOWN

Behemoth was once considered a Class VI canyon and the run ended below Island Rapid.

**Difficulty:** Class IV-V+

**Gauge:** USGS #14231900—CISPUS RIVER AB YELLOWJACKET CREEK NEAR RANDLE, WA

**Flow Min-max:** 500-1,100 cfs, normally run in the summer. You can push the higher flows as long as you're comfortable with the Behemoth gorge. At really high flows, the pool turns into a powerful recirculating eddy.

**Gradient:** 130-180 fpm

**Takeout:** Bridge over the Cispus on FR-23

**Put-in:** Adams Fork Campground

**Length:** ~ 6 miles

**Hitchability:** Don't count on it.

**Season:** Mostly a summer run, but runs often in winter. Level needs to be treated according to the season. The gauge is well below this run so 1,000 cfs off rain is a lot different than 1,000 cfs off snowmelt; there is usually a little more push in the canyon during the winter. The logs in the outflow of the first falls should be duckable, if barely. Higher than that? Get ready to get awesome, or call it a day and drive one mile upstream to drool over Gail Falls (it has been run): 46.344908, -121.627483.

**Camping:** Lots of camping opportunities! Stealth camping abounds within the park and there is a campground at the takeout of the run on the south side of the Cispus River. There is also camping at the Adams Fork Campground, near the put-in.

**4WD Needed?** 4WD only needed for snow on a winter run.

**Best Close Food/Beers:** The town of Randle

**Quality (out of 5):** 4

**Raft Recommendations:** Has been done by Class V rafters, not recommended

Don't get too comfortable after snapping your spraydeck down; the first challenge of the day is right around the corner. Warmup Falls is a fun double-drop with more bark than bite. The wood in the outflow can be ducked on river-left, or center if the water level is low enough. Portage options are on the left, if you run level (level dependent).

After Warmup, the run provides more of a boulder garden feel and, similar to the rivers on this side of Rainier, the rock is volcanic, dark basalt and sharp. Many tight-spaced boulder rapids follow, one to note is Split Drop which is also referred to as Not Island by some. Scout from river-left. The left line is a fun pile-driver of a drop. Grease the wall and then hold onto your paddle. The right line is an easier, sliding dry-hair line.

Island drop is the next large horizon-line and the server of many a booty beer. The river has to force its way around a midstream rocky protrusion as it falls back together behind it. The midstream rock

Mike Hagadorn

Behemoth explored by Jim Janney

is reminiscent of a melting mushroom cap and covered in large potholes; scout from here and pick the line you like. Portage options are on the left, if you run left (level dependent).

The river then pours through a tight slot that drops about 12 feet against the right wall. This should be scouted for wood if you're unfamiliar with the run. Soon you arrive at Rapid of No Return, gatekeeper for the canyon holding Behemoth, marked by a large landslide on the right (scout from here). You can work your way down to a view of Behemoth. The rapid above Behemoth has changed from time to time due to the landslide. Scout well and keep in mind what your paddling toward, a swim here could turn serious quickly.

You have the option to scout Behemoth from river-left; the eddy is small but accommodating. The normal line is to either start river-center or from the little eddy on river-right. You can boat-scout the lead-in slope of the falls from this eddy. Just make sure you get left, square up with the curler and paddle away from the landing zone.

Behemoth is notorious for the pothole cave against the left wall at the base of the falls that captures the unsuspecting paddler. The large ledge hole below Behemoth deserves your respect. The right side is deeper and more retentive, so make it far left and you are home free down the easy line.

Below the Behemoth cauldron, a Class IV+ boulder garden packs a punch then fizzles out into Class III. Don't forget to take a look back up the canyon and check out the stacked piece of whitewater you just came down with Behemoth as the crown. About 3 miles of Class III brings you to the takeout bridge.

Forest Road 23, 12 miles south of Randle suffered heavy damage in the winter of 2015 and is washed out at two places along the Cispus River.  At publishing this access was still washed out.  FR 21 south of Packwood could be an alternate route when it's clear of snow.

—*Daniel Patrinellis*

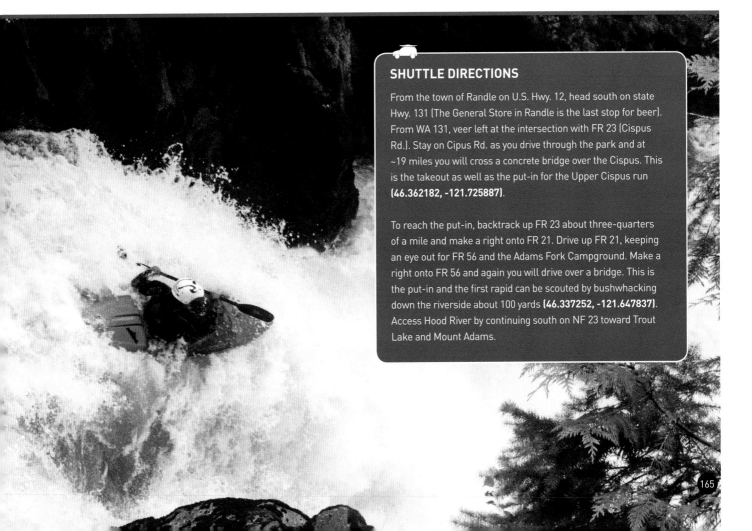

## SHUTTLE DIRECTIONS

From the town of Randle on U.S. Hwy. 12, head south on state Hwy. 131 (The General Store in Randle is the last stop for beer). From WA 131, veer left at the intersection with FR 23 (Cispus Rd.). Stay on Cipus Rd. as you drive through the park and at ~19 miles you will cross a concrete bridge over the Cispus. This is the takeout as well as the put-in for the Upper Cispus run **(46.362182, -121.725887)**.

To reach the put-in, backtrack up FR 23 about three-quarters of a mile and make a right onto FR 21. Drive up FR 21, keeping an eye out for FR 56 and the Adams Fork Campground. Make a right onto FR 56 and again you will drive over a bridge. This is the put-in and the first rapid can be scouted by bushwhacking down the riverside about 100 yards **(46.337252, -121.647837)**. Access Hood River by continuing south on NF 23 toward Trout Lake and Mount Adams.

# SUPER SLIDES

## OF THE CISPUS RIVER

This unique run is a succession of angled sliding drops on bedrock with very few eddies, some outrageous horizon-lines, strange reaction waves, water folds, rooster-tails, and sometimes extremely dangerous wood sieves that you will approach at speed. So the key is finding the right water level to match your skills: below 1,500 cfs at the gauge and the run becomes an unrunnable, not easier, "Super Scrape"; 2,000 cfs has scraping, with some speed in places but is generally a controlled Class III; 2,500 cfs transitions to minor scraping with high current speed and lack of eddies (Class IV); and above 3,000 cfs means carefully planned "into the distance" scouts around corners and to next eddies, attaining speeds of up to 35 mph!

Meanwhile, back at the put-in, the choice depends on whether you want to run the two 25-foot Goat Creek waterfalls, which are eminently runnable, especially at high flows, but have shallow rocks in places and are difficult to portage in the canyon. If so, hike straight down to Goat Creek from the car (46.456221, -121.508066), or, if not, stay high for another 150 yards heading downstream before dropping into the canyon (46.455326, -121.507661). Next is a half-mile of often, but not always, congested rocky, woody creek that can serve as an excellent warmup, or aggravator, depending on how well you can boat and push yourself over and through these obstacles.

In less than an hour, you next reach the confluence of Goat Creek with the Cispus River, and a low canyon wall appears with the river jogging right then down out of sight. Scout river-right to assess Game On, since this rapid provides a good read for the comfort (and wood) level you will experience on the rest of the run.

The run now becomes one continuous rapid that can be boat-scouted, except for the two big horizon-lines for High Five and Low Five, both 15-foot drops that are straightforward if there is no wood (scouting is necessary to determine), followed by the final three river bends which form the culmination of the run.

Scouting from river-left means running the Goal Posts, followed by a river bend right, then driving 150 yards down the Fairway to catch the side pocket on river-right. From the side pocket it's possible to scout Banzai Falls, a 40-foot-vertical, 100-yard-long monster slide that bends back to the left. For most boaters, this type of drop is completely unpredictable, thus the commitment required for the name. The speeds attained and then sustained are completely out of the realm of understanding. Angling to river-right at the bottom, you drop back to sub-light speeds and can think about catching an eddy to regroup, or walk back up to catch pictures of your friends hurtling down.

## THE RUNDOWN

Steep, non-stop cascading slides at high speed.

**Difficulty:** Class III-V (V+ above 4,000 cfs)

**Gauge:** USGS #14231900—Cispus Above Yellowjacket Creek Near Randall

**Flow Min-max:** 2,000-4,000 cfs

**Gradient:** 184 fpm

**Takeout:** River-left trail at end of canyon

**Put-in:** Goat Creek above two 25-foot falls (Elevation: 3,910 feet), or below (3,860 feet)

**Length:** 3.1 Miles

**Hitchability:** Not Recommended. (Forest Service Rd. with minimal traffic.)

**Season:** Hot late spring day with snow melted out to at least 3,500 feet

**Camping:** Gifford Pinchot National Forest

**4WD Needed?** No

**Best Close Food/Beers:** Randall or Packwood

**Quality (out of 5):** 5

**Raft Recommendations:** Not recommended

The river starts winding down, and on river left, Walupt Creek pours into the Cispus, cascading over the most spectacular Walupt Falls. It is a lot of effort to hike up the base of the cascade as far as you can get, but then probably worth the pictures taken of your descent. Mellowing further, in another half-mile the Cispus comes out of its canyon, and the takeout is the first flat treed area on the left. All that remains is a half-hour hike up the trail back to the cars where your drinks have been cooling all day in a snowbank. Let the stories begin!

* Forest Road 23, 12 miles south of Randle suffered heavy damage in the winter of 2015 and is washed out at two plaes along the Cispus River. At publishing this access was still washed out. FR 21 south of Packwood could be an alternate route when it's clear of snow.

—*Scott A. Matthews*

## SHUTTLE DIRECTIONS

To reach the takeout, head south on Cispus Road out of Randall, keeping left after one mile, then continuing on FR 23 for 17 miles, turning left onto FR 21 for 13 miles, then right onto FR 2160, crossing the river in one mile, then continuing another 2 miles to the Coleman Weedpatch Trail 121 parking area (NW Forest Pass required): **46.429050, -121.506280**. To reach the put-in, return on FR 2160, turning right onto FR 2152 just before FR 21, proceeding straight through the intersection after 2.3 miles onto FR 016, then for another 1.7 miles to just past a big rock wall on the right. Park at the first spur road on your right.

Scott Matthews

Looking down on the Goalposts with the Fairway turning out of view

Scott Matthews

The top of Banzai Falls with the bottom of the Fairway in the distance

4

# MCCOY CREEK

McCoy Creek was touted early on as classic, and this is still true despite the wood issues that periodically befall this great section of river. The first thing I noticed about this run was how low-volume it is. The canyon walls are adorned with moss and the lush green foliage bends in over you creating archways through canyon corridors. McCoy starts easy and the first real rapid has a large Pothole in the center to avoid. More great rapids continue until you reach Tom's Falls, which is a large but easy 15-foot slide that the whole crew will be stoked on. Soon after, you reach the double ledge, where a quick scout reveals a fun, narrow double ledge into a pool. Now you have reached the main event: Chinook Falls, a multi-tiered drop that can be scouted from the slippery banks on the left. We jumped in between pools to scout, and the hole at the bottom goes better than it looks with medium or lower flows. Chinook is easier to run than portage. Next is a narrow but clean 20-foot waterfall that lands in yet another pool. This is where you start thinking about how remote this place feels as it radiates an exploratory vibe. Now you have to be careful, there is a ledge just downstream of Chinook Falls and then an unrunnable 45-footer you portage on the right. The portage sucks and takes a while, but after the river ends with a few more ledges and then flows into Yellowjacket Creek. Before I gush anymore, I know this run will usually have several wood portages sprinkled in, so there is work involved. But ... it's worth the effort.

*Forest Road 23, 12 miles south of Randle suffered heavy damage in the winter of 2015 and is washed out at two places along the Cispus River. At publishing this access was still washed out. FR 21 south of Packwood could be an alternate route when it's clear of snow.

—Scott Waidelich

## THE RUNDOWN

Great falls and slides!

**Difficulty:** Class V

**Gauge:** Cispus near Randle around 2,300-3,000 cfs

**Flow Min-max:** 150-400 cfs (visual)

**Gradient:** 200 fpm (avg.)

**Takeout:** Bridge over Yellowjacket Creek

**Put-in:** FR 29 Milepost 8, walk down to the creek, or Spur Rd. 084 down a half-mile and park at U-turn area.

**Length:** 3 miles on McCoy Creek and 4.5 on Yellowjacket Creek

**Hitchability:** Not good

**Season:** Early spring/rain events

**Camping:** Everywhere!

**4WD Needed?** No

**Best Close Food/Beers:** BYOB

**Quality (out of 5):** 4

**Raft Recommendations:** Not great for rafts, shallow creek. Too many portages. Not for part-time Class V rafters.

## SHUTTLE DIRECTIONS

To reach the takeout, from U.S. Hwy 12 turn onto FR 23 at Randle, and in about a mile you reach the intersection of FR 23 and FR 25. Go left on FR 23, drive 7.8 miles to the intersection with FR 28. Turn right on FR 28, head 1.3 miles to the bridge over Yellowjacket Creek, and take out here (46.4324608, -121.8399887).

To reach the put-in go back up FR 28 to the FR 29 intersection. Go right, head 7.1 miles to Spur Rd 084, go half a mile, park at the U-turn and carry downhill to the river (46.363736, -121.80375).

Nathan Pfeifer

Roman Androsov tucking

# LOWER TILTON

There's no way around the obvious downsides to this run: a Class II two-mile warmup and another mile of flatwater across the reservoir. In between, however, is one of the most superb bedrock gorges in all of Washington, and it's chock-full of clean, powerful intermediate whitewater. A hike out here would be a chore, and only possible on river-right.

The action starts where Bear Canyon Creek comes in and the walls solidify. After a fun warmup corner is a large pool; scout or portage right, or run this first III+ down the left. Watch out for a good hole at the bottom. This drop sets the tone for the run and can be surprisingly powerful.

Be careful of swimmers, because out of sight around the corner, in slow moving water, is a large midstream outcrop of bedrock. In many years a logjam forms here. Run either side, with the usual best portage over the logs, along the shallow left cliff wall.

A series of fun Class III follows as the canyon opens up a bit. Bedrock gives way to dense cobbled cliffs, and several nice beaches appear at low water. Waterfalls abound.

There is a fun ledge best run on the right with catch-on-the-fly surf everywhere as well as a few good eddy-service spots.

The walls and rapids return below a creek entering from the right. A long-abandoned old Sevylor raft above the high-water line on the right—remnants of a local's summertime family adventure gone awry—is another landmark. A good two-part III+ rapid drops you back between solid bedrock walls so dark they seem to drink up the light.

You are immediately above Leap of Faith, a pushy Class IV drop and the crux of the run. Scout left from small eddies to clear the exit which is blind from above, out of sight around a bend right. Only the first portion can be portaged. The most common line is along the right wall, into a powerful V-wave, before moving right to exit around the corner. Other slots left and center are viable as flows and wood dictate. It's wise to set safety in the eddy on the left, halfway down, as it tends to collect boats and swimmers and cannot be accessed from downstream.

Below Leap of Faith, the canyon enters its narrowest constriction. A dangerous river-wide hydraulic can form here above 3,000 cfs and should be run with purpose. Below this constriction the walls peel back a bit. Waterfalls pour off the ink-black walls, Spanish moss drifts ethereally in the breeze, and a wonderful series of surf spots, ledges, and boulder gardens dot the next mile of canyon. Most are III or III+. This lush inner sanctum of the Tilton is supremely scenic. Linger and enjoy the surf!

## THE RUNDOWN

Superb soul surfing in the tightest row-able gorge around

**Difficulty:** Class III-IV

**Gauge:** USGS #14236200— Tilton above Bear Canyon Creek

**Flow Min-max:** 800-3,000 cfs (1,600-2,500 is pushy prime)

**Gradient:** 25 fpm

**Takeout:** Ike Kinswa State Park

**Put-in:** State Hwy. 508 Bridge in Bremer

**Length:** 8 miles

**Hitchability:** Rural highway with light traffic

**Season:** Any major rain event

**Camping:** Great options at Ike Kinswa State Park

**4WD Needed?** No

**Best Close Food/Beers:** Morton

**Quality (out of 5):** 4, secluded, scenic bedrock gorge

**Raft Recommendations:** Superb for oar and paddle crews at all but the lowest flows.

## SHUTTLE DIRECTIONS

From I-5, head west on U.S. Hwy. 12. Take state Hwy. 122 north around the lake to the takeout at Ike Kinswa State Park. There is a boat ramp, a campground, and a day-use area. The day-use area offers the shortest takeout paddle **(46.562248, -122.536484)**.

To reach the put-in, take a right leaving the day-use area. Cross the bridge and take a right at the Y intersection onto Cinnebar Road. Follow it to WA 508 and turn right. After about 7 miles, you'll see the bridge. Park and rig on the upstream eastern side. Be courteous of adjacent private property, please **(46.579948, -122.416677)**.

You are approaching the end of the run when you reach Scary Gary, a significant ledge with an easy line on the right, and several other steeper chutes center and left. Below, the river bends left and enters a long boulder garden. Scout from the corner pool, or the micro eddy at the lip of the steepest part.

Brian Vogt

Exiting Leap of Faith, the Tilton enters its narrowest constriction.

The final boulder garden is best entered left through the shallow entrance. Work center-right to line up on the biggest drop, then stay off first the left then the right walls. This is perhaps the longest drop on the run, and certainly the most congested boulder garden. Below it, a few more easy drops lead into the open valley, then the flat water. Pondering the whitewater wealth that lies slumbering beneath this placid pool is a bittersweet end to the trip.

Follow the left bank to Ike Kinswa State Park and take out when you see the lawn and picnic tables. It is a short walk to the parking lot.

The character of whitewater on the Tilton is powerful and clean, and it is very fun. This is not a technical river with myriad boulders and tons of route choices. Most rapids offer 2 or at most 3 route choices. Most all the routes are runnable if they are wood free, and, due to the bedrock character, this run holds its water very well down to 500 cfs or so. It does not need high water to become pushy. Medium flows on the Tilton are a great way to get comfortable with powerful hydraulics and canyon turbulence, but rescue is complicated by vertical or overhanging walls in many places. Friendly flows: 700-1,600 cfs. The Push Prime: 1,600-2500 cfs. Starting to wash out big water: 2,500+. Generally, 2,000 give or take is optimum.

—Brian Vogt

Brian Vogt

Even 900 cfs packs a punch! Brent Jones squares up in the first drop.

# NORTH FORK OF THE TILTON

Like many Washington Class IV runs, this is a stacked, short boulder-garden run that delivers from the put-in to the takeout and will have you itching to get back to the top for another go. From the put-in, the North Fork Tilton doesn't look like much: clear, clean flatwater flows under your feet and winds out of sight as you stand on the bridge. After you leave the put-in, this character continues for a ways with the occasional Class III rapids before you reach the confluence with Tumble/Wallanding Creek (about half a mile from the put-in) where the action starts.

Hopefully you have your Class IV reading and running skills tuned because they will be put to the test on this little gem. You can scout the first rapid on the left as you approach Tumble Creek, here the creek pinches down and increases gradient. The river pours through classic Cascade boulder gardens for the remainder of the trip; eddy-hop and scout as necessary.

About halfway through the run, the river parts around a small island. Both channels have historically been open, but is a likely pinch point for wood so be vigilant.

Continue your boogie-woogie boof-fest down to the takeout and either saddle up for a second ride or roll downstream to run the lower Tilton.

—Jed Hawkes

## THE RUNDOWN

The Tilton rivers were named in honor of James Tilton, the Surveyor General of the Washington Territory from 1854 to 1861. Great run to combine with either the upper and lower Tilton in one long trip or set a separate shuttle and run the North Fork and Lower Tilton for a great high-action combo.

**Difficulty:** Class IV

**Gauge:** USGS #14236200—TILTON RIVER AB BEAR CANYON CREEK NEAR CINEBAR, WA; NWRFC TILW1#—TILTON NEAR CINEBAR

**Flow Min-max:** 2,500-4,000 cfs (2,500-3,200 is ideal first time flow)

**Gradient:** 136 fpm

**Takeout:** First NF-73 bridge over North Fork Tilton

**Put-in:** Second NF-73 bridge over North Fork Tilton

**Length:** 2.1 miles

**Hitchability:** No

**Season:** Winter or large rain events

**Camping:** Ike Kinswa State Park has great camping and cabins. Since you'll typically be running this while it is actively raining I would recommend renting a cabin and make a weekend of it. Lap the NF on the first day, then make a long playboating day of the Lower Tilton. Open year-round with nice bathrooms, tent sites, cabins, and lake access.

**4WD Needed?** Not required, but a high clearance vehicle makes the drive down from the fork to the put-in a little less hairy. If it was really wet you might think twice about driving all the way down the road.

**Best Close Food/Beers:** Morton, Wash., has the closest amenities with beer, Mexican food and limited selection of other items.

**Quality (out of 5):** 3.5

**Raft Recommendations:** Yes

## SHUTTLE DIRECTIONS

For the takeout, from Olympia drive south on I-5 for 33 miles to Exit 71 for state Hwy. 508 east toward Napavine/Onalaska. At the end of the ramp, turn left onto WA 508 east and continue for 29 miles. Turn left onto N-73. (There is not great signage here, you will cross back over the Tilton and the river will now be on your right, and you will pass two roads on the left, Bergen Road then Maple Leaf). Your third left is NF-73; stay left at the fork shortly after turning onto NF-73 and follow for 1.4 miles until your next fork. Stay left at the fork and continue for 0.5 miles until you cross the North Fork Tilton. Park to the left but do not block the gate **(46.597624, -122.365332)**.

For the put in, drive upstream from takeout bridge on NF-73 for 1.6 miles until a fork. The right fork will steeply descend to the river; follow this for another 0.5 miles until you arrive at a bridge crossing the river. Park anywhere. Beware, the bridge is a little shady—drive across at your own risk **(46.619688, -122.388939)**.

Mike Hagadorn

Adam Griffin gets his boogie woogie on in a typical North Fork Tilton rapid

# HOFFSTADT CREEK

Hoffstadt is one of those isolated classics coming off Mount St. Helens that is just too good not to experience. It appears to be relatively unscathed by the 1980 blast on St. Helens at this point compared to the N.F. Toutle, which is in plain sight of the takeout. It is a smaller volume creek with about 250-800 cfs at the put-in. It is mostly open/jagged bedrock ledges, falls, and chutes that seem to never end. Most rapids are two and three parts, keeping the action going and keeping you alert for what's around the next corner.

At the takeout you will notice that you are now in the Mount St. Helens blast zone as well as the 370-foot-tall bridge that spans 600 feet across the takeout. At the end of the run, you earn your paddle strokes and hike up on the downstream side of the bridge, back to the parking area. If you catch Hoffstadt at a good flow, it will be well worth the effort!

Just downstream from the put-in is the first ledge drop, Bouncer. There are very few eddies above this drop, so it could be worth a short hike down from the put-in to scout for wood before you put on. The rapids then build until you arrive at Split Falls, which has an obvious horizon-line from above and offers a nice line down the right side into a small pool. The ledges then twist and turn down to Gnargasm.

Beware of the approach on Gnargasm: a set of ledges sit above it, and you want to be on the left side of the creek to scout/portage this broken piece of whitewater chaos. Gnargasm has been run with best to worst outcomes, but most take the easy portage instead of taking a ride with the river gods. Below here the creek pours over a few very fun ledges as you get deeper into the canyon.

Many small ledges and fun moves stack up one after another. Some of the bigger fun Class IV rapids are in this section, a few requiring a scout while others you can pick your way through until the action starts to fizzle out. Class III+ rapids appear as you make you way through the forested creek near the takeout bridge, but stay on your toes! You are not done until you reach the takeout. On my last trip, we were paddling nine deep and most of us swam just before the takeout due to being too close together and too excited about seeing the bridge. Lack of daylight may have played a part as well; start early.

*—Ryan Scott*

## THE RUNDOWN

You are within the blast zone of Mount St. Helens.

**Difficulty:** Class IV-V (V+, suggested portage at Gnargasm)

**Gauge:** Toutle

**Flow Min-max:** 4,000-10,000 cfs (6,000-8,000 and dropping ideal). If you put on the upper end of this scale with rising water, you could get way more than you asked for.

**Gradient:** 320 fpm in steepest mile

**Takeout:** Hoffstadt Creek Bridge just upstream of the N.F. Toutle confluence.

**Put-in:** Rd. 3100, the gate has been closed in recent years, requiring a 1.5-mile hike in (see shuttle directions).

**Length:** 4.2 Miles

**Hitchability:** Not the best due to lack of traffic, but a mountain bike could do the trick easily.

**Season:** Fall, winter, early spring

**Camping:** About a dozen pay campsites are available in Kid Valley Campground before you reach Hoffstadt Creek.

**4WD Needed?** No, unless you expect snow in the winter.

**Best Close Food/Beers:** Patty's Place at 19 Mile House (closest to Hoffstadt), also Eco Park Cafe in Toutle.

**Quality (out of 5):** 4

**Raft Recommendations:** Not for part-time Class V rafters

## SHUTTLE DIRECTIONS

Take I-5 Castle Rock exit heading east on SR 504 about 29 miles, turn left on Rd. 2900 and enter the Hoffstadt Creek Bridge scenic overlook parking area **(46.329664, -122.43715)**.

For the put-in, drive another 1.3 miles east on SR 504, turn left onto Rd. 3100. As you turn you have the option to go left or right, stay right and you will immediately see the gate. Park here and hike in about 1.5 miles (stay left at both forks in the road) and you will arrive at the put-in bridge over the creek **(46.330564, -122.391083)**.

Keel Brightman

Scott Waidelich enjoying the winter season on Hoffstadt Creek

# THE GRAYS RIVER

The Grays River is a nice run in southwest Washington that doesn't see much traffic. People tend to enjoy the run, but there just doesn't seem to be enough whitewater to justify repeat trips given the time spent in the car to get there. With the recent exploration of the South Fork Grays, the two runs can be combined, adding enough miles to easily warrant a trip.

Plan on this trip taking all day. From the bridge over the SF Grays there is a short warmup before an obvious bedrock horizon mandates a quick scout. The left side lands in a nasty pocket, a precise boof to the right lands boaters free of a beating by Step Mother. Shortly downstream are the two Step Sisters, the first is a funky chute on the right into a narrow alley with more bark than bite. The second Step Sister is a boulder garden shortly downstream that should be scouted for wood—past runs have been down the left side with a log-duck at the end.

Things keep rolling with a series of read-and-run Class IVs highlighted by Fairy Godmother, named after a poor line that graciously ended without facial reconstruction; scout right. More rapids continue, eventually reaching a Class III that ends in one of the run's best rapids: Ballroom. Boaters dance their ways down this stair-stepping rapid, preferably ending on the right. More boogie awaits between here and Stroke to Midnight, a 10-foot ledge that can be scouted left. Just around the corner is Glass Slipper, which has the highest beat-down potential since Step Mother. Slip through to the right for the final 5-foot ledge or find out if you are sized to fit. Keep an eye out below Glass Slipper for a right turn with a stream coming in from the left that has

## THE RUNDOWN

Savvy navigators can half the shuttle distance using the Pack Trail Rd. if snow is not an issue.

**Difficulty:** IV+ (V above 1,500 cfs)

**Gauge:** USGS #12010000—NASELLE RIVER NEAR NASELLE, WA

**Flow Min-max:** 500 cfs Grays, 800 cfs South Fork Grays. Max undetermined

**Gradient:** Starts at 200 fpm, drops to under 65 fpm on the Grays. Put-in elevation: 900 feet

**Takeout:** Hwy 4

**Put-in:** Logging bridge over SF Grays

**Length:** 4 miles on SF, 5.5 on Grays

**Hitchability:** Not a viable option

**Season:** Rainy

**Camping:** Primitive options available along Fossil Creek Rd.

**4WD Needed?** Mandatory for Pack Trail shuttle, recommended for Algers Truck Trail shuttle option

**Best Close Food/Beers:** Skamokawa

**Quality (out of 5):** 4

**Raft Recommendations:** Would need high water for the whole run. The main Grays is a good alternative.

## SHUTTLE DIRECTIONS

From I-5 take state Hwy. 4 heading west through Longview, traveling 42 miles to a bridge over the Grays River. There is limited parking at this takeout **(46.3591, -123.5665)**.

For those only looking to run the SF, drive up Fossil Creek Rd. along the east bank of the Grays 5.6 miles and take out at the SF Grays confluence. Paddlers have historically put in here and only run the main Grays: This course of action misses most of the whitewater. To get to the SF Grays put-in from the WA 4 bridge, drive east to the town of Skamokawa and turn left on Middle Valley Rd. Follow this road for 3.9 miles and turn right onto Oatfield Rd, taking the left fork 0.7 miles later. This is the Algers Truck Trail and it will be the most well traveled of the gravel roads. Stay on it for 3.3 miles (stay right at 1.1, then left at 2.1 and 2.9), at which point you take the right fork and follow this road 2.1 miles into the South Fork drainage where a bridge crossing the South Fork Grays marks the put-in. Bring a map **(46.3604, -123.4261)**.

Gray's River Canyon, Jacob Cruser

it is a mile of Class II-III down to the Grays. You will know you are close when gorge walls rise up again for a moment.

On the Grays there is not much respite before a bridge indicates the return of the whitewater, specifically, Class IV within a gorge where a couple of the rapids may be worth a scout. If the Naselle gauge is over 1,000 cfs, be prepared for some powerful hydraulics! Just over a mile below the bridge is the first big one: Superbowl, which has a couple powerful ledge holes. It can be scouted from either side, but paddlers have reported underestimating the size of the hole when scouting from the elevated bench on the left side. Just around the corner is Picnic, the run's largest rapid. Scout left before entering what appears to be a read-and-run boulder garden, at the bottom of which the river pinches down into a vertical walled gorge, preceded by a sieve and some powerful hydraulics. Regroup below and scout the next rapid on the right (Broken Paddle) as there is a hole-undercut combo on the left that has given paddlers trouble. Things then ease quickly, where a boulder bar runout to the State Hwy. 4 bridge is all that remains.

—*Jacob Cruser*

# KALAMA FALLS

## OF THE KALAMA RIVER

Kalama Falls is a clean waterfall set in a luscious, green forest. Described as a plunging punchbowl, it drops about 40 feet into a decent-sized boiling pool. The run is short, but the waterfall can be hucked as many times as you like. This could be described a park-and-huck if the Forest Service road reopens. For now, it requires a 1.75-mile hike in along the road to the trailhead. From there it is another half-mile hike along the trail to the falls. The lip of the falls twists slightly to the right, and there is a small Class II lead-in. Be mindful of any accumulation of wood in the pool below.

After running the falls, you can paddle half-mile down to a bridge to take out (Class II run with nice scenery), or hike back out the way you came.

*—Ellie Wheat*

## THE RUNDOWN

Beautiful waterfall in Classic PNW scenery.

**Difficulty:** Class V

**Gauge:** Visual. Good reference gauges are on the Toutle and Canyon Creek.

**Flow Min-max:** Toutle River at Tower Road: at least 3,000 cfs. Canyon Creek near Amboy: 1,000-2,500cfs

**Gradient:** Drop is about 40 feet. Put-in elevation: 1,320 feet.

**Takeout:** Hike-in, hike-out

**Put-in:** Off FR-81

**Length:** Half-mile

**Hitchability:** Poor

**Season:** Rainfed: fall, winter, spring

**Camping:** Merrill Lake Campground

**4WD Needed?** No

**Best Close Food/Beers:** Better bring your own

**Quality (out of 5):** 3

**Raft Recommendations:** Would need high water for the whole run. The main Grays is a good alternative.

## SHUTTLE DIRECTIONS

From I-5, head east on state Hwy 503, also known as the Lewis River Rd., for 26 miles. Turn left onto Forest Service Road 81 (also known as the Merrill Lake Rd.), follow this for 6.9 miles. Park at the gate on the left side of the road, grab your boat and start walking. Walk for 1.2 miles and turn left on the same forest road. The trailhead is on the right side of the road, around 1.75 miles from the gate. Follow the trail about another half-mile, crossing a tributary of the Kalama River, to reach the falls **(46.11033, -122.3586)**.

Scott Waidelich
Jeremy Bisson

liquidlogic™

GIVIN'ER FOR LIFE

PHOTO: ERIC PARKER  PADDLER: EVAN GARCIA

# EAST FORK OF THE LEWIS

The East Fork of the Lewis "Waterfall" run is a fall/winter staple for Portland-area paddlers. It is also, along with nearby Canyon Creek, part of the annual Northwest Creeking Competition. The EFL is a place where aspiring Class III-IV paddlers go to step their games up to the next level and where many indeed get their first tastes of running waterfalls. That being said, the run should be considered Class IV at most levels; despite its benign nature, it has served humble pie to some very good paddlers. It can be run at a wide range of levels (generally between 800 and 2,500 cfs at the East Fork Lewis at Hession gauge) and increases in difficulty and intensity with flow increases. Note that the gauge is very far downstream of the put-in and can be very inconsistent depending on the exact source of the water. I have been on this run at 900 when it felt like 1,500 and vice versa, so if in doubt, take a look before launching. Sunset Falls has easy access and is usually a good indicator.

While most of this run is fun read-and-run Class III+ paddling, there are five drops of note. The first and last of these are the 'waterfalls' from which this run gets its moniker. The first, Sunset Falls, is the run's opening big drop and is commonly run down the middle over an obvious boof, or left, which requires more technical timing. While forgiving at low flows, the left line can extract a penalty for a missed stroke at flows over 1,000-some cfs. (Bonus: Sunset can be lapped as many times as you can stand it.) Sky Pilot, Screaming Left/ Dragon's Back and John's Swimming Hole are downstream in the

## THE RUNDOWN

Eagles and other wildlife highlight a run that is a PNW classic. Don't miss it when paddling in the Portland area. If you are looking for another waterfall to run after your trip, check out Big Creek Falls (45.834633, -122.385275).

**Difficulty:** Class IV-IV+

**Gauge:** USGS #14222500—EAST FORK LEWIS RIVER NEAR HEISSON, WA

**Flow Min-max:** 600-2,500 cfs

**Gradient:** 80 fpm

**Takeout:** Road pull-out across from King Creek

**Put-in:** Varies. Numerous pull-outs above Sunset. If flow is adequate (visual), putting in about 2 miles above Sunset adds a fun warmup stretch.

**Length:** 4.5-6.5 miles depending on put-in

**Hitchability:** Good

**Season:** Rainy—fall through spring

**Camping:** Campground at Sunset. There are also places off the Forest Fervice road (turn left after crossing the Sunset bridge and drive a mile or two).

**4WD Needed?** No

**Best Close Food/Beers:** Battle Ground

**Quality (out of 5):** 4

**Raft Recommendations:** Expert rafters only

Sunset Falls by Paul Thompson

Adam Elliott

Evan Garcia leading the pack into Screaming Left to Dragon's Back

gorge section. Sky Pilot is a sequence of holes, the first of which can put the paddler in the pilot's seat. A bit of right angle will help keep you off the magnetic left wall.

Moving into the gorge, next is Screaming Left, named for the obvious hard left turn required for one of the possible lines. The other line, used by many in the race, goes through a slot against the right wall. This rapid is deceptive and both lines can be more difficult than they initially appear. It is always a good idea to scout this rapid if you haven't been there recently as the right slot has a tendency to collect hazardous wood. This drop is very easily scouted/portaged on the left. Screaming Left leads directly into Dragon's Back which is a fun shoulder-boof off a right-side slab. Beware of a sneaky rock in the landing that shows up at low flows.

Below Dragon's Back is a large pool good for collecting carnage flotsam and to set up for John's Swimming Hole: a paddler who misses the move here and gets intimate with the hole is likely to find out how it got named. The outflow from the hole pushes into the left-hand wall, which adds to the fun factor here. The right-side line with a boof over the corner of the hole is the most common, but as flows increase, staying right becomes more challenging. The left side also goes, but brings the wall into play; scout or portage on the right.

Next, Copper Creek comes in from the left. This is a great Class IV-V run on its own and it is possible to hike up to its bottom five drops from here. There have been landowner access problems in the past, but thanks to the contributions of long-time EFL guru, Mike "Oly" Olsen, these have been moderated. As always, be respectful of property owners if heading up there. Copper Creek has been known to greatly increase the volume of the EFL, making for some really fun III+ paddling down to Horseshoe Falls, the other waterfall that finishes the run with a bang. This drop has a couple of lines, but the first time there, no one can resist the beautifully perfect auto-boof. The falls can be portaged with some difficulty on the left side. The takeout isn't too far downriver.

—Scott Gerber

## SHUTTLE DIRECTIONS

From Exit 11 off I-5 continue on state Hwy. 502 to the town of Battle Ground, Wash. Take a left onto 10th Ave./WA 503, continue about 5.5 miles to a right turn on Rock Creek Rd. Continue straight as this will turn into NE Lucia Falls Rd. In about 8.5 miles, take a right onto NE Sunset Falls Rd.

The takeout is 4.1 miles in a small dirt pull-out on the right **(45.814353, -122.315133)**.

To reach the put-in, continue 3.4 miles upriver on NE Sunset Falls Rd.-NF 42 to Sunset Campground Falls **(45.819232, -122.249016)**.

To reach the put-in continue up Sunset Falls Rd., after another 3.3 miles past Sunset Falls Campground and continue to the desired put-in.

Paul Thompson
Trevor Sheehan droppig Sunset Falls

# COPPER CREEK

Copper Creek is a great little run! For those who put in higher on the creek at the alternate put-in, expect the upper stretch of Copper Creek to serve as the yin to the lower section's yang. Instead of mostly easy floating with a few large rapids, this section is fast-paced Class III-IV boogie-water the whole way with one rapid that is worth a look. Also, while the big drops on the lower start to become hard, Class V as flows increase, this upper stretch just gets more fun.

From the upper put-in bridge, there is a bit of technical warmup before the first notable rapid, a stair-stepping series of small holes on the left. About a half-mile in is Fishtail, a small but powerful hole best punched along the edges. Just downstream is the largest rapid on this stretch, the Weir. This is a mostly straightforward slide into a sticky hole. Safety can be set on the left where a portage route is also found. Below here, the stream gets into a rhythm for a full mile of high-quality sliding rapids with friendly and splashy hydraulics. When you pass under a bridge, get out on the right to scout/portage Certain Death.

This is the first of three main attractions on the lower section of Copper Creek. Walk down the gated road to see if you want to put-in above Certain Death or below it. Don't let the name scare you: It certainly is a challenging, tight rapid with undercuts and no clean-looking line, but I have seen several descents with various results, so scout well.

After, there's about a mile of mellow water to Triple Delight, where the creek steps abruptly down over a small ledge then pours off an 8-foot ledge into an 18-foot, plunging falls. At lower flows, after the 8-foot ledge you can run right off the spout falls; higher, you may be forced left, where you can (with luck) catch a boof flake and fly off the falls. There are a few options, but the falls' left side has been known to be shallow at lower flows. Just below Triple Delight is a Class IV ledge drop called Piton. There is a line far left and far right. Either way, keep your bow up on this one.

## SHUTTLE DIRECTIONS

The takeout is the same as the EF Lewis Waterfall Run (45.814353, -122.315133).

To reach the put-in, continue 3.4 miles upriver on NE Sunset Falls Rd.-NF 42 to Sunset Campground Falls, cross the bridge over the river and stay left on FR-41/Sunset Hemlock Rd. In 3.1 miles, take a right onto FR-4109 and continue down to the bridge over the creek. This is the first bridge. To reach the upper put-in, continue another 0.6 miles on FR-41 to a right on FR-4107 (45.796928, -122.237111).

## THE RUNDOWN

It adds an alternate, more challenging creek onto part of the EF Lewis Falls run.

**Difficulty:** Class IV-V (solid V at high flows)

**Gauge:** USGS #14222500— EAST FORK LEWIS RIVER NEAR HEISSON, WA

**Flow Min-max:** 1,000-4,000 cfs

**Gradient:** 126 fpm

**Takeout:** Below Horseshoe Falls on the EF Lewis

**Put-in:** First bridge on FR-4109. Alternative. put-in another mile up on FR-4107.

**Length:** 4 miles

**Hitchability:** No (limited traffic on Forest Service road)

**Season:** Fall through spring (best in the spring)

**Camping:** Sunset Falls Campground between the takeout and put-in

**4WD Needed?** No, unless you have to deal with snow in the winter

**Best Close Food/Beers:** Battle Ground or Vancouver

**Quality (out of 5):** 3.5

**Raft Recommendations:** The creek is a little small for that craft. Has been done by Class V rafters, not recommended.

Another long Class II section brings you to the top of the Final Five. This is a spectacular little gorge. A 6-foot sloping ledge leads into a 7-foot punchbowl pour-over directly into a sloping slide, which falls into the right wall and then drops left into a walled-in pool. The final two drops actually form a 10-foot double-drop into a turbulent hydraulic. Scout from the right, stay close to the water and obey the signs! Just downstream Copper filters into the East Fork Lewis and continues down a couple miles of Class III to Horseshoe Falls: a 22-foot dome-shaped falls with a narrow, side-crack falls on the right and a cascading falls on the left. The standard line is off the dome in the center, resulting in a perfect auto-boof. Scout on the left or from the middle of the falls if the water is low enough. The takeout isn't far downstream, opposite of King Creek.

This creek, like the EF Lewis, is highly sensitive to private property. Obey the signs and don't annoy the locals.

—Ryan Scott

**Stohlquist®**
WaterWare

LIFETIME OF INNOVATION™

TOHLQUIST.COM

4

# NORTH FORK OF THE LEWIS

This section of the North Fork Lewis is unique for the Pacific Northwest. While the area is well known for waterfalls, it is rare for a river of this size to have drops this large. Initially sought after by high-caliber boaters looking to huck large waterfalls, it has more recently gained a following of local boaters looking for something fun to do late in the season when most other rivers are too low to navigate.

The run starts with a short walk down the Lewis River Trail paralleling Quartz Creek. If flows are over 1,000 cfs, the first two waterfalls should be scouted before putting on the river via the trail. Within a quarter-mile of the put-in is the first horizon line at Taitnapum Falls. At low flows (less than 500 cfs) this 20-foot falls is scouted on the right and run in the middle, with care taken to avoid landing on a obvious shelf. At higher flows, a massive hydraulic forms in the middle. Fortunately a big, deep-water boof is available on the extreme left side. Downstream are two small bedrock slides/ledges before the next massive horizon line appears.

If flows are below 500 cfs, scout the right channel from the middle of the river (it's shallow). At these flows, the first 10-foot ledge can be run, then an eddy caught just after the 3-foot ledge and before a 20-footer that is usually portaged. After walking the 20-footer, rappel into the pothole just above the final 30-foot drop that can be run anywhere at these flows. If flows are higher, it is imperative you scout this drop from the trail before putting on. Over 1,500 cfs, a big double-drop from middle to right opens up that is hard to line up, though it has been run many times. At very high flows, yet another massive line opens up on the far left.

Downstream is a section of Class II that can be tedious at low flows until the next horizon line at Middle Falls. The left side has some tricky vertical options, while the right side is an outrageously fun and low-stress slide. It can be difficult to stop at high flows, so take caution and, if in doubt, run about 20 feet off the right bank.

Below is a long stretch of Class II to Lower Falls, another impressive waterfall in the 40- to 50-foot range that is usually run via a channel on the right. This one is more commonly run at lower flows. Be aware of the cave behind the falls, a few people have ended up back there. You can take out in the campground on the right, or continue a short way downstream to a bridge.

—Jacob Cruser

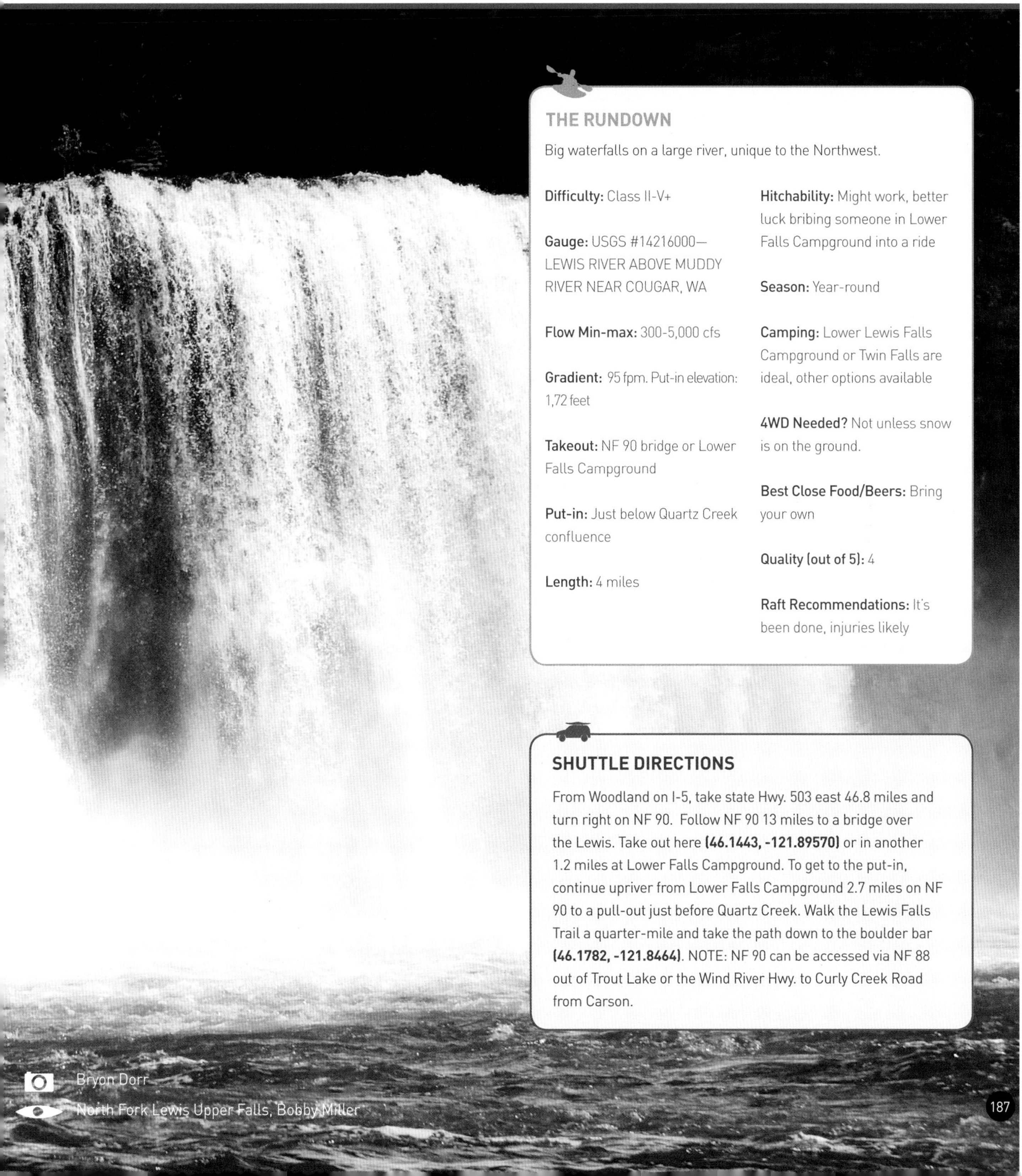

## THE RUNDOWN

Big waterfalls on a large river, unique to the Northwest.

**Difficulty:** Class II-V+

**Gauge:** USGS #14216000—
LEWIS RIVER ABOVE MUDDY
RIVER NEAR COUGAR, WA

**Flow Min-max:** 300-5,000 cfs

**Gradient:** 95 fpm. Put-in elevation:
1,72 feet

**Takeout:** NF 90 bridge or Lower
Falls Campground

**Put-in:** Just below Quartz Creek
confluence

**Length:** 4 miles

**Hitchability:** Might work, better
luck bribing someone in Lower
Falls Campground into a ride

**Season:** Year-round

**Camping:** Lower Lewis Falls
Campground or Twin Falls are
ideal, other options available

**4WD Needed?** Not unless snow
is on the ground.

**Best Close Food/Beers:** Bring
your own

**Quality (out of 5):** 4

**Raft Recommendations:** It's
been done, injuries likely

## SHUTTLE DIRECTIONS

From Woodland on I-5, take state Hwy. 503 east 46.8 miles and turn right on NF 90. Follow NF 90 13 miles to a bridge over the Lewis. Take out here **(46.1443, -121.89570)** or in another 1.2 miles at Lower Falls Campground. To get to the put-in, continue upriver from Lower Falls Campground 2.7 miles on NF 90 to a pull-out just before Quartz Creek. Walk the Lewis Falls Trail a quarter-mile and take the path down to the boulder bar **(46.1782, -121.8464)**. NOTE: NF 90 can be accessed via NF 88 out of Trout Lake or the Wind River Hwy. to Curly Creek Road from Carson.

Bryon Dorr

North Fork Lewis Upper Falls, Bobby Miller

# CANYON CREEK

## OF THE LEWIS RIVER

As you put on and float under the NE Healy Rd. bridge, keep an eye out for bungee jumpers and for spouting waterfalls entering this beauty of a canyon. After a good amount of Class II warmup the river constricts as you arrive at Swizzle Sticks. Enjoy this constriction-caused boily and raucous ride through a mini-canyon. From here each rapid stacks up one after another. At medium or low flows, recovery time is ample. As you approach the second constriction, beware of Terminator, a stout river wide hole which can be scouted and or portaged on the right. It is run always on the far left or portaged right. Below that you can run Prelude on the far right to avoid another nasty hole. Thrasher, following below prelude, will be your next opportunity to throw a glorious boof with some water separation. Directly below is the most continuous and lengthy rapid on the run, Boulder Garden. It winds down with a large whoop-de-do flume into a constricted hole on the bottom (though these last two drops have been changing a lot in nature with winter storms).

Some boogie-water brings you to the lip of the 20 foot Kahuna falls, which should be scouted from the river-right shore and eddy above. Beware of the water pushing left into an undercut wall; too far right puts you against a different wall. A center-right line, however, typically brings smiles and success. A beautiful winding section of river leads into Champagne, a delicious 10-foot boof run center-left typically. There is not much space or recovery time before Hammering Spot, another 10 foot falls where the line varies at different levels but right is usually the call. These stacked two rapids with some runout lead you to the final drop, Toby's. Scout the right line if you choose to get saucy with a potentially painful move, the left has a slab rock you can paddle up on to with speed and slide down the back of it. This is also a very precise move. The center has caused some bad pins, so be very cautious to avoid that here. Lake Merwin opens up and your flatwater paddle to the bridge commences. Thank AW for all their hard work on the new takeout stairs!

—*Nick Hinds*

Adam Mills Elliot

Greg Mallory on Big Kahuna

## THE RUNDOWN

Quality waterfall bliss in a canyon epitomizes the classic smooth-rock waterfall run that makes Pacific Northwest whitewater so famous.

**Difficulty:** Class IV+ (low), V- (medium), V (high)

**Gauge:** USGS #14219000—CANYON CREEK NEAR AMBOY, WA

**Flow Min-max:** 350-600 cfs (low), 650-1,000 cfs (medium), 1,100-2,000 (high)

**Gradient:** 120 fpm

**Takeout:** Under the bridge, at Merwin Reservoir

**Put-in:** Walk upstream of the bridge and find the trail down to the water on river-left

**Length:** 3.2 Miles

**Hitchability:** Not really, maybe run into a group from Portland

**Season:** Fall, winter, spring

**Camping:** Yes, at the put-in

**4WD Needed?** No, but watch out for ice on the road in winter

**Best Close Food/Beers:** Nick's Bar & Grill in Amboy, Burgerville in Woodland for Seattle boaters

**Quality (out of 5):** 5

**Raft Recommendations:** Sure, for experienced paddle crews!

Adam Mills Elliot

Kim Russell on Terminator Rapid

### SHUTTLE DIRECTIONS

The takeout is at the state Hwy. 503 bridge crossing Merwin Reservoir. Look for the new stairs **(45.9604034, -122.37258)**.

The putin is up NE Healy Rd. At the confluence where the put-in hits the bridge, the put-in lies upstream on river-left **(45.9401474, -122.31574)**.

Jed Hawkes on the right side of Toby's

# TIETON RIVER

Flowing east from the Cascades, the Tieton feeds into the Naches River and eventually the Yakima, which is used heavily for irrigation. In 1925, the Tieton was dammed to store water and if not for the fall releases from Rimrock Reservoir, the Tieton would be another overlooked, seldom-run stretch.

Starting Labor Day weekend, when most other rivers in the state are dried up, the Tieton experiences its spring runoff and comes to life! Although the whitewater isn't spectacular, the action stays busy from put-in to takeout. I've always thought of the Tieton as a better rafting trip than kayak float. When flows top 1,800 cfs it becomes very swift and hard to clean up swims. Though mostly Class II with a few Class IIIs, above 2,000 cfs, you'll want to be a Class III boater. Otherwise, wear pads, top off your float bags and be ready for long swims.

Islands and wood are worth noting. Wood collects easily in the small riverbed, and though seldom a major problem, the banks are full of it. There are also countless islands and some channels to avoid. If you're not sure, just pull in behind one of the countless commercial rafters.

There is a runnable low-head dam about 5.5 miles in. Keep your eyes out for the signs and stay anywhere center to the left bank. A mile downstream is High Noon. Above 2,000 it forms a massive hole in the center. When you spot some houses, just work toward the right bank.

Below High Noon is a great park-and-play wave underneath the bridge. Between 1,700-2,000 cfs, it has a nice left shoulder, retentive enough for loops. The last notable rapid is Waffle Wall, a half-mile below the Bridge Wave, which pushes you far right into the wall. If you want a shorter run, Waffle Wall makes a great alternative takeout, otherwise float the last 4 miles to Windy Point Campground.

The scenery is top notch and the camping is great, making the Tieton a perfect weekend trip to break up the long dry spell between spring runoff and winter rains—well worth the trip.

—*Darren Albright*

"River Booty"
Darren Guiding customers

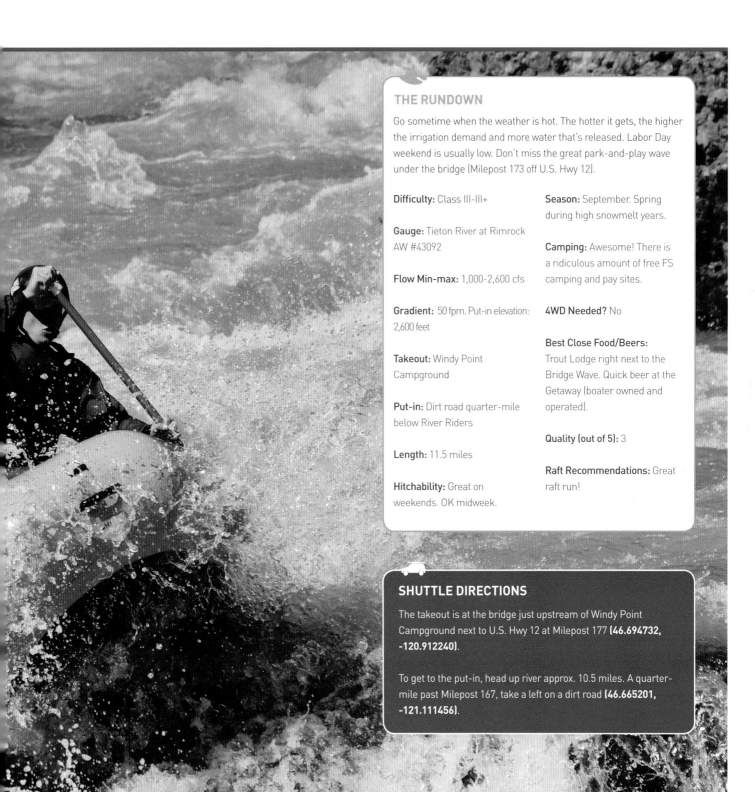

## THE RUNDOWN

Go sometime when the weather is hot. The hotter it gets, the higher the irrigation demand and more water that's released. Labor Day weekend is usually low. Don't miss the great park-and-play wave under the bridge (Milepost 173 off U.S. Hwy 12).

**Difficulty:** Class III-III+

**Gauge:** Tieton River at Rimrock AW #43092

**Flow Min-max:** 1,000-2,600 cfs

**Gradient:** 50 fpm. Put-in elevation: 2,600 feet

**Takeout:** Windy Point Campground

**Put-in:** Dirt road quarter-mile below River Riders

**Length:** 11.5 miles

**Hitchability:** Great on weekends. OK midweek.

**Season:** September. Spring during high snowmelt years.

**Camping:** Awesome! There is a ridiculous amount of free FS camping and pay sites.

**4WD Needed?** No

**Best Close Food/Beers:** Trout Lodge right next to the Bridge Wave. Quick beer at the Getaway (boater owned and operated).

**Quality (out of 5):** 3

**Raft Recommendations:** Great raft run!

## SHUTTLE DIRECTIONS

The takeout is at the bridge just upstream of Windy Point Campground next to U.S. Hwy 12 at Milepost 177 **(46.694732, -120.912240)**.

To get to the put-in, head up river approx. 10.5 miles. A quarter-mile past Milepost 167, take a left on a dirt road **(46.665201, -121.111456)**.

# HONORABLE MENTIONS

**The North Fork Cispus,** once a great run, filled with wood and became a nightmare. Hopefully one day paddlers will again enjoy the quality boulder gardens this run possesses.

**The Upper Siouxon** offers some quality Class IV ledges and boulder gardens with a couple large falls thrown in the mix, flowing through a beautiful old-growth forest. The best access is via the takeout at West Creek Campground, hiking about 5 miles up the trail to Upper Siouxon Falls. This gives you a chance to scout as you go (and to avoid the long shuttle that climbs over 3,500 feet and usually complicates winter runs). Class IV paddlers will have a blast, with a couple portages, while adventurous Class V paddlers can enjoy Middle Siouxon Falls if it looks enticing, or take a long look at the intriguing Lower Siouxon. This section is located past the put-in of Canyon Creek in the EF Lewis drainage and usually runs best in the fall and winter at flows over 1,600 cfs on the EF Lewis gauge.

Takeout: **45.946653, -122.177381**.
Put-in: **45.960014, -122.117428**.

**The North Fork Siouxon** is a neat run that has enough water when the Canyon Creek gauge is 1,000 cfs or higher. Hike into Black Hole Falls, a beautiful 60-footer with a tough lead-in. Most people will put in at the base and paddle 4 miles of Class IV whitewater with ledges and canyons abound. There is one portage around a tough gorge halfway through, and the last quarter-mile (Smokin' Aces) is Class V.

Takeout: **45.970872, -122.258275**
Put-in: **46.008375, -122.196765**

**The Middle/Lower Lewis:** This is a nice, scenic run starting at the takeout bridge of the Falls section of the North Fork Lewis. It is very pretty with mostly Class II-III rapids and a tougher Class IV just below Big Creek. Ambitious boaters can walk a short way up Big Creek to run Habitat Falls, a narrow 20-foot double drop. The lower section below the Curly Creek Bridge is known for the large waterfalls cascading in from river-left. This run is mostly enjoyable Class II with big scenery points. Take out at Eagle Cliffs.

Access: **46.062227, -121.966648**
Put-in: **46.144276, -121.895677**
Takeout: **46.065264, -122.020292**

Vaughn Johannes
Brett Barton on Paradise Slides, draining Rainier

**Muddy River:** This run has water when other area runs start to drop out, so can be a nice backup run. Most of the run is easy floating, with a Class IV gorge near the end. From here to the confluence with the Lewis is scenic with a couple small wave trains once on the Lewis. Take out at Eagle Cliffs.

Put-in: **46.121407, -122.014982**
Takeout: **46.065264, -122.020292**

**The Upper North Fork Lewis:** This run is often overlooked by many of the area's local paddlers. This is unfortunate as it is a nice run that flows later into the summer (with a decent snowpack). There are two Class V+ drops, one of which requires some effort to portage. Otherwise, the run is a Class II-IV+ playground with many small ledges and boulder gardens to keep paddlers entertained. Put in at the NF 88 bridge and take out at the Roadside Rapids, a short way upstream of Quartz Creek. A runnable, friendly level is 1,000 cfs on the Lewis River at Muddy, from snowmelt.

Put-in: **46.196326, -121.729213**
Takeout: **46.182239, -121.803489**

**Lewis River Tributaries:** There are many small creeks feeding the North Fork Lewis River that have enough water to boat and enough gradient to make you think twice. Many of these have fantastic rapids, but also some dangerous gorges. Watch out for wood! These streams usually have water when the Lewis is running over 2,000 cfs.

4

Ryan Scott

Nate Herbeck , Twin Falls, NF Lewis Tributary

The Columbia River Gorge is a place of beauty—a place where you can see a rainbow touch down to a pot of gold on each end. The mighty 1,243-mile Columbia River, on its last push from the Canadian Rockies to the Pacific Ocean, enters the eastern end of the Gorge near the Deschutes River, where only about 10 inches of rain fall per year. The west end of the Gorge, however, receives an average of 100 inches in a temperate rainforest. That spectrum of precipitation on this 80-mile stretch of the Columbia gives every river and creek in the Gorge its own distinct character and attitude.

The Washington side holds wider valleys for gradual, longer runs. With the main rivers and many smaller, steeper creeks descending out of the foothills of 12,280-foot Mount Adams and 11,250-foot Mount Hood, any single drainage holds miles and miles of whitewater of varying difficulty. Meanwhile, with the exception of the

Hood River, much of the Oregon side consists of tall basalt cliffs and abrupt waterfalls that pour into the Columbia like icing over a layered cake that climbs up to 4,000 feet.

To give you an idea of how much accessible whitewater drains just into the Columbia River Gorge, within 50 miles of the 80-mile long gorge, there are 35 runs listed in the previous guidebook on its tributaries on the Oregon and Washington sides.

Since that book's publication, 13 more runs (mostly steep Class V creeks) have been found and run, as well as six waterfalls over 60 feet tall. And the list is still growing. Some of this whitewater runs year-round and, if you're ambitious enough with a little luck in the weather, you could run them all in a single year due to the winter/glacial snowpack in the higher elevations, and rain in the

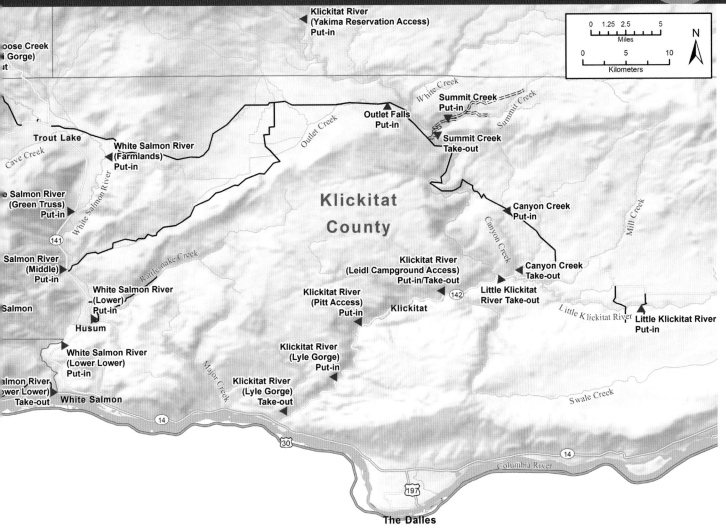

lower valley. No other region in the world has the ingredients that the Columbia River Gorge has, generating an unheard of variety of runnable whitewater in such a condensed area.

For a beginner's float, the Klickitat and Lower White Salmon rivers offer great Class II-III options. For intermediate whitewater, the Washougal, Hood, Middle White Salmon, and Sandy rivers are great Class III-IV runs. Sharpen your skills and head into the Upper Wind, Rock Creek, East Fork Hood, or Hagen Gorge for some quality Class IV+. Experts are overjoyed with the Green Truss, Stebbins Creek, and the Little White ... and with that comes the waterfall bug. Metlako and Outlet falls can scratch that itch. And for those who don't mind hiking in to get the Class V goods, Tanner Creek, the Salmon River Gorge, and the Top Rock can exhaust even the most ambitious adventure paddler.

Paddlers have found a wonderland here throughout the decades as kayaking has evolved to fit the surrounding landscape well. Like most beautiful places, you can watch the contrast in the winter season with harsh conditions. So be ready: When summer comes to an end, you start to feel the chill in the air, gray clouds return, and the rains come. The rivers fill, the cliffs stream with water, and it's time. It's time to get excited, the season has started again.

—Ryan Scott

# COLUMBIA RIVER GORGE

Paul Thompson

The beauty of Spirit Falls

5

📷 Adam Elliott

👁 Chris McTaggart on S-Turn

199

The Lower Wind's character is a bit different from the Upper. As a narrower canyon that's more intimate in places, the rapids are mellower aside from the few larger drops. Once you put on above High Bridge, the section starts with less than a half-mile of bouncy Class II warmup. As you approach a right-hand bend, look up to the impressive High Bridge on the Wind River Hwy. This signifies the start of High Bridge rapid, a couple hundred yards of fun Class IV boulder-garden action, easily boat-scouted with good eddies at normal flows, and a big, punchy wave train at higher flows.

After floating through a beautiful basalt gorge, Panther Creek comes in on the left, boosting the flow with its clear water. The next 1.5 miles consist of fun Class II-III boulder gardens with a few small ledges sprinkled in. Right after the second 3-foot ledge, the river pools up to a tall horizon line: This is the Flume, a good IV+ at most levels (scout from river-right). Generally there is a line down the center, and you blast through on a wild ride. At very low summer flows, some choose to walk this rapid. After the Flume, there is another fun chute, also generally run center.

The next horizon is Beyond Limits, a 6-foot ledge into a powerful hole. At higher flows this drop is often portaged, while at lower flows it's more forgiving; scout from the shelf in the center of the river at low flows, or from the left bank at winter flows. Be careful not to enter the fish ladder on the river-left. Scouting options on the left. From here it is about .75 miles of fun pool-drop Class III boulder gardens until you approach Shipherds Falls. From the pool above the falls you will see the concrete fish ladder structure, which has water flowing in through a hazardous open door—it's not difficult to avoid, just pay attention as you come through the entry rapid. From there, Shipherds is a series of two waterfalls and a slide into a weir. The first waterfall can be scouted from the right or the left, but the rest must be scouted from river-left. The bottom weir becomes very retentive at flows above 4 feet and as flows increase much higher than this, the whole series of drops requires a portage. Portaging can require a throw-and-go from higher up on the river-left cliff—not so bad as a fun 25-foot jump into a big, deep pool. After, it's about a half-mile of Class II boulder gardens to the takeout unless you continue to the Columbia, which adds another mile of flatwater.

If you want to enjoy the natural hot springs, you'll see them about .2 miles below the falls on river-left. There is usually a pile of rocks piled up keeping the warm water from seeping out.

—*Paul Meier*

## THE RUNDOWN

Fantastic summer run. When the upper section drops out there are waterfalls and hot springs to enjoy. (2.6-3.2 feet on the Stabler gauge)

**Difficulty:** Class IV-IV+ at all levels, minus Shipherds Falls at the end of the run (V above 3.5 feet, V+ above 5 feet)

**Gauge:** DOE— #29C100 Wind R. at Stabler

**Flow Min-max:** 2.6-8 fpm (the falls can be run as low as 2.2 feet, but getting there can be a pain)

**Gradient:** 956 fpm avg.

**Takeout:** Columbia River confluence, or one mile upstream at a gravel pull-out (see shuttle)

**Put-in:** Bottom of Old Detour Rd., just upstream of High Bridge

**Length:** 5 miles to the Columbia, about 4 miles to the first gravel takeout on the right.

**Hitchability:** Not good, bring a bicycle

**Season:** Mainly the spring and summer, but can be paddled year-round

**Camping:** You can usually camp for free at the takeout, nice little forested lot

**4WD Needed?** No, unless there is a ton of snow on the ground, which happens occasionally in the winter

**Best Close Food/Beers:** Backwoods Brewing Co. in Carson, Walking Man Brewing in Stevenson, or Andrew's Pizza in Stevenson (right on SR 14)

**Quality (out of 5):** 4

**Raft Recommendations:** Possible above 3.5', but if you don't run the waterfalls, lining the raft could be tricky

Bryce Jenkinson

Looking downstream on the last three drops in Shipherds Falls

## SHUTTLE DIRECTIONS

To reach the takeout, head to the confluence of the Wind River and the Columbia right on state Hwy. 14 in Washington, about 5 miles east of Stevenson. Head north up Hot Springs Ave., and near the crest of the hill, hang a right on Saint Martins Springs Rd. Take the immediate first right turn as you go down the hill, which turns to gravel and dead-ends at the takeout, **45.726306, -121.794869**. (Note: If this access is ever closed, return to the mouth of the Wind and take out near the Columbia, adding another mile of flatwater to the end of your trip.)

To reach the put-in (Same directions as Upper Wind takeout), take the Wind River Hwy. north to Carson off state Hwy. 14. Continue north out of Carson to High Bridge Road. Take a left, then a quick right on Old Detour Road. Don't make any more turns, continue down Old Detour after it turns to gravel, and follow it to the bottom of the hill and an open parking area by the river **(45.753581, -121.841397)**.

Bryce Jenkinson

Ryan Scott on the first waterfall
in Shipheard Falls

# UPPER WIND RIVER

The Upper Wind River Canyon is big, powerful, and has proven to challenge and excite the most experienced paddlers. Another one of the Gorge classics with its own unique character, the Upper Wind Canyon provides the bigger water Class V feel at high flows and great, challenging Class IV boulder gardens at medium-low flows.

From the put-in, the river gently drifts downstream with a nice warmup then increases tempo as you approach Trout Creek on the right about 1.4 miles in. Trout adds a little flow and greets you with one of the five notable rapids in the canyon, Initiation (scouting option on the right just after the creek). Initiation is a long and continuous boulder garden that appears to ease up before it builds again to descend on Ram's Horn, identified by a large rock in the middle of the river with an obvious horizon line. Ram's Horn forms some very large holes at higher flows and packs a healthy punch on the right side. The runout below Ram's Horn pushes through more chutes and boulders then into a flat pool.

The whitewater picks up again at Balls to the Wall Right: a Class IV boulder garden where much of the water pushes fast down the right side through a series of holes and diagonals. Around the corner is Balls to the Wall Left, another fun Class IV. Steady Class III+ leads down to the final big challenge, Climax: a classic 6-foot horizon line that splits into a few different channels. Most people run down the middle, some run it right, my favorite is down the left. Scout if needed and choose the line you like best.

The canyon eases a little as you paddle down many Class III+ to IV-rapids on your way to the takeout. Look out for the occasional surf-wave on the lower stretch to add to the fun. A large eye-opening waterfall pouring in the right side of the river adds to the beauty before you reach the takeout. The phenomenal scenery will entice you to return to the excitement of the Upper Wind River Canyon.

*—Ryan Scott*

## THE RUNDOWN

Surf waves on the lower section at medium flows and the occasional bald eagle sighting in the canyon.

**Difficulty:** IV (V above 7 feet, V+ above 8 feet)

**Gauge:** DOE #29C100— Wind R. at Stabler

**Flow Min-max:** 35.1-6 fpm

**Gradient:** 87 fpm. Put-in elevation: 890 feet

**Takeout:** At the end of Old Detour Rd., upstream of High Bridge.

**Put-in:** Stabler. (Alternate put-in listed below)

**Length:** 5 miles

**Hitchability:** Not the best, bike shuttle recommended

**Season:** Spring, fall, winter.

**Camping:** Pay camping is available north of Stabler in the Gifford Pinchot National Forest

**4WD Needed?** No

**Best Close Food/Beers:** Backwoods Brewing in Carson or Walking Man Brewery in Stevenson

**Quality (out of 5):** 4.5

**Raft Recommendations:** Yes by expert rafters above 5.2 feet and below 6.2 feet

Keel Brightman

Ram's Horn rapid in the heart of the upper canyon at higher flows

## SHUTTLE DIRECTIONS

To reach the takeout, take the Wind River Hwy. north from Carson off state Hwy. 14. Continue north out of Carson to High Bridge Road. Take a left and then a quick right on Old Detour Rd. Don't make any more turns, continue down Old Detour after it turns to gravel, and follow it to the bottom of the hill and to an open parking area by the river **(45.753581, -121.841397)**.

To reach the put-in, go back to the Wind River Hwy. and continue north, upriver until you reach Stabler. Take a left toward Stabler/Hemlock. You will cross over the river, then take your next right and proceed to the small parking area by the river on the upstream side of the bridge you just crossed **(45.808667, -121.909597)**.

Alternate put-in: At medium to medium-high flows, you can also put in on Lower Trout Creek. Take the left off Wind River Hwy. as stated above and continue until you cross Trout Creek (Old Hemlock dam site). If you are feeling more adventurous, put in to add some quality Class IV+, smaller volume rapids to the beginning of your Upper Wind run. If Trout Creek is high, this will be a fast, Class V white-knuckle boogie that drops you into the Wind just above Initiation.

Keel Brightman

Too Little To Late on the Upper Wind

# TROUT CREEK

Trout Creek's beautiful upper canyon is lined with some of the best low-volume boulder gardens in the state. This upper run wasn't paddled until the early 1990s, another little gem tucked away in the hills above the Wind River Canyon.

On a mild winter, you will have many options to run Upper Trout. On a heavy winter, you won't be able to access it until spring. The fall and spring are usually the best times to catch this action-packed run. From the put-in, the gradient starts out as a drifting stream gradually building into Class III until you see the first set of rapids below. Scout on the right.

The creek then drops into the first set of rapids and keeps a consistent pace through two more obvious, steep boulder-garden sections consisting of multiple drops. As the run builds in the middle of the canyon, it gradually tapers off after the creek splits an island and coasts down to the takeout bridge. I have run this creek at all flows and, notably at lower boatable flows, the steep rapids close out into sieves. At high flows, the eddies disappear and the drops build in power and succession.

Flows are a little tricky as it is best to look at the takeout, specifically for the 'cup rock' on the river-left side (closest to,

Bryon Dorr

Jesse Becker navigating one move after another on Upper Trout

and directly in front of, where you park), just upstream of the PCT footbridge. There is a large boulder not far off the bank, with a cup about halfway down the boulder. If you don't see it and the creek looks full of water, it is covered and flows will be on the high side. If you see the cup and there is water pouring into it, flows will be a manageable medium flow. Lower than the cup, flows will start to get pinny and much less enjoyable. Beware of wood on this creek. It is a small Northwest creek with logging operations in the area and frequent high water in the winter and spring.

—*Ryan Scott*

## THE RUNDOWN

Action-packed continuous boulder gardens.

**Difficulty:** Class IV-V (V+ above 700 cfs)

**Gauge:** PCT footbridge (visual). Check when the Wind River is running above 7 feet.

**Flow Min-max:** 300-700 cfs

**Gradient:** 194 fpm

**Takeout:** PCT bridge over Trout Creek, 2 miles from Hemlock

**Put-in:** Forest Road 43 north of Hemlock

**Length:** 3.5 Miles

**Hitchability:** Not Recommended (Forest Service Rd. with minimal traffic)

**Season:** Spring, fall, winter

**Camping:** Pay camping is available north of Stabler in the Gifford Pinchot National Forest. Or there is great camping all along Trout Creek—find a good spot if weather permits.

**4WD Needed?** Only if you have to deal with snow in the winter.

**Best Close Food/Beers:** Backwoods Brewery in Carson

**Quality (out of 5):** 4

**Raft Recommendations:** Has been done by Class V rafters, not recommended

## SHUTTLE DIRECTIONS

To reach the takeout, turn off state Hwy. 14 onto the Wind River Hwy. north to Carson. Continue north out of Carson 7.2 miles to Stabler. Take a left toward Hemlock 1.3 miles, then take a right on FR 43. In less than 2 miles, use the small pull-out and footbridge on the left: This is the takeout and best visual for the water level **(45.811255, -121.956594)**.

To reach the put-in, continue up FR 43 to the bridge that crosses Trout Creek **(45.822277, -122.016458)**. Put in here and enjoy the run!

There is a lower run on Trout Creek as well: Drive from the takeout back down to the end of FR 43, put on at the old Hemlock dam site, and paddle down into the Wind River (see Upper Wind description).

# UPPER LITTLE WHITE SALMON

The Upper LWS is arguably one of the highest quality miles of Class V whitewater in the state of Washington. When it is flowing at a good level (at least 3.7 feet) it is generally a notch faster, tighter and more rowdy than the Lower LWS. If you paddle the Lower LWS and want more, head upriver a little higher. The Upper starts with a bang. About 125 yards below the put-in bridge is a great rapid called the Flume: about 50 yards long and winding through a bedrock constriction. There are no major holes in this rapid, but it is steep and fast (possible to scout from the road on river-left where a pipe crosses the river). About 150 yards below the Flume, a large rapid called Shroom Tripper lurks below a couple blind corners; scout on river-left. The Shroom Tripper boof itself is the easy part of the rapid.

Right below the boof, the river turns right, then left and divides in a fast boulder garden that ends with two large holes on river-right. Be sure to boof or avoid these holes as getting locked in either one could end very poorly. Below Shroom Tripper, the river mellows out and is boat-scoutable for a few hundred yards until the Dam Drop. Once you arrive at the Dam, you need to scout the next 100 yards all the way to Simon Says. The Dam Drop is the lead-in to Simon Says, which can just be seen from the Dam. In recent years the line has been right on the Dam and to the left of the large rooster tail in the middle of Simon Says. This left line pushes you down the extremely fast and tight Pinball Slot. (Getting pushed right before the rooster tail, at the time of press, would be into a lethal logjam.) Willard Falls is about 75 yards below Simon Says and can be seen from the Cook-Underwood bridge.

This section of whitewater from the Dam to Willard Falls is the most technical on the entire LWS. Scout very carefully; over the years, there is lethal wood in this section more often than not. Also, understand that you are TRESPASSING if you scout or portage on river-right. This is a very sensitive area for kayakers. Please use good judgment and do not jeopardize the river access for the rest of the kayaking community. The Upper LWS is a true gem of whitewater in the Pacific Northwest. As with any river, the wood situation changes annually and the Upper is no different. Source out local knowledge as this section is so tight and fast that accidents can happen very quickly.

—Lane Jacobs

## THE RUNDOWN

One of the best miles of Class V whitewater on the West Coast is often overlooked because of the Lower LWS! If it is running, don't pass this one up!

**Difficulty:** Class V–V+

**Gauge:** Master Blaster on the Lower Little White, although many refer to the gauge at the Lower Little White put-in, which generally 'reads' about 0.2 feet higher than the actual level (at Master Blaster). Call the Kayak Shed in Hood River (541-386-4286) or check the Little White Salmon Facebook page for a level.

**Flow Min-max:** Low 3–5.1 cfs, 3.8 feet ideal for first time down, 3.7–4.3 feet ideal for a solid Class V paddler. Below 3.7 is doable, though many sharp, nasty rocks exposed.

**Gradient:** 315 feet from Willard Road bridge to Cook-Underwood Road bridge.

**Length:** 1.25 miles

**Hitchability:** Possible. Also runnable if you just paddle the Upper.

**Season:** December through May, depending on the season.

**Takeout:** Willard National Fish Hatchery, or Drano Lake if you would like to add on the Lower Little White

**Put-in:** The Willard Road bridge in Willard, Wash. (Alt. put-in: north of Willard where the river is viewable for the first time from Oklahoma Road, which provides a couple hundred yards of warmup before the entrance drop below the bridge.

**Camping:** Great campsites located directly above Willard: Big Cedars and Oklahoma Campgrounds are the two most popular.

**4WD Needed?** No

**Best Close Food/Beers:** Everybody's Brewing in White Salmon

**Quality (out of 5):** 5

**Raft Recommendations:** Has been done by Class V rafters, not recommended

## SHUTTLE DIRECTIONS

From the Willard Road bridge put-in **(45.779925, -121.628744)**, or town of Willard, head south on Oklahoma Rd. until you intersect Cook-Underwood Rd. Take a left and you will arrive at the Upper LWS takeout/Lower put-in very shortly **(45.764180, -121.629755)**. If you want to add the Lower LWS follow directions for the Lower LWS shuttle to Drano Lake.

The Lower Little White Salmon offers the best variety of Class V whitewater stacked into one run: long, technical boulder rapids, stacked pool-drop ledges and powerful waterfalls up to 30 feet high. For expert paddlers, the Little White can be what you make of it and you can get creative with your paddling. You may be in paddling shape, but the Little White demands that you be in Little White shape. Only running this river will do justice to the run. Paddlers have traveled from all over the world with the intent purpose of running this river as often as possible. With this much action packed into a canyon that is runnable more days a year than salaried workers spend at their desks, there is no question as to why many paddlers refer to this run as their Church.

From the Willard National Fish Hatchery you have a gentle three-quarters of a mile of Class III warmup until the rapids start at the wood-choked Oregon Slot at the top of Gettin Busy. This is my favorite spot on the river; the action starts right here! The river turns on end and the next mile continues nonstop through steep boulder-garden chutes testing your quickness and endurance before blending into Boulder Sluice Rapid. Boulder Sluice can be scouted on the left and offers one of the best lines on the river. Downstream around the corner, the river widens before splitting at Island Rapid. (This section is well-known for catching drifting high-water debris.)

Island can be scouted from the island or on the left above the main drop. After Island, the character adds ledge/pool-drop, but there is no shortage of boulder-on-bedrock rapids in between the bigger drops. Sacriledge (dangerous cave on left side), Double Drop, and S-Turn (dangerous cave on left side) are all ledges ranging from 6 to 10 feet with varying degrees of difficulty and character.

Backender is the next big horizon line that drops into a forgiving double-ledge set followed a half-mile later by Bowey's Hotel. Bowey's (named after the late, great Bill Bowey) is a stout ledge that can be more retentive than in looks! This is where the falls start to concentrate. Just downstream, Wishbone Falls drops about 25 feet into a large emerald pool, committing you to a section known as the Gorge. The Gorge consists of four separate drops with Horseshoe (a very retentive hydraulic at higher flows) as the fourth. Safety is highly recommended here: Stovepipe is just downstream with little recovery time before it. A swim over it would not be pretty! As with Sacriledge and S-Turn, Stovepipe has a dangerous undercut against the left wall as well as other hazards unique to this falls. And like most rapids on this river, there are a couple different lines to choose from based on your comfort and skill level. Below Stovepipe is the

*Continued on page 212*

## THE RUNDOWN

Once you get over the hype of this river, it screams fun with a variety of action-packed Class V moves!

**Difficulty:** Class V-V+, higher flows greatly intensify this run. Approach higher flows with caution.

**Gauge:** Visual. The most accurate gauge is at Master Blaster, although many refer to the put-in stick gauge on the upstream side of the bridge, which generally reads about 0.2 feet higher. Call the Kayak Shed in Hood River (541-386-4286) or ask on the Little White Salmon Facebook page. The Little White is unique in that it is fueled by underground aquifers in its headwaters. Rainfall will not immediately affect it like other rivers in the Gorge. Be patient in the fall; once the aquifers are charged, the river will run strong and hold water longer.

**Flow Min-max:** 2.7-4.5 cfs. If the river is above 3.5 feet, it will feel full. As the flow approaches 4 feet it gets very pushy. Above 4 feet, the rapids offer no recovery time. The best manageable flows are between 3-3.5 feet. (If the Little White is too high you can also go explore Class IV options on Lava Creek near the Upper LW run.)

**Gradient:** 250 fpm avg. Put-in elevation: 961 feet.

**Takeout:** Drano Lake (NOTE: Access here is sensitive, please use good judgement so we can keep our river access)

**Put-in:** On the opposite side of the bridge from the Willard National Fish Hatchery

**Length:** 4 miles

**Hitchability:** No good

**Season:** Spring, fall, winter, early summer

**Camping:** Moss Creek Campground about 3 miles above the put-in

**4WD Needed?** Not unless snow is on the ground

**Best Close Food/Beers:** Everybody's Brewing in White Salmon if you head east or Everybody's Brewing in Stevenson if you head west

**Quality (out of 5):** 5+

**Raft Recommendations:** Has been done by Class V rafters, not recommended

Jason Rackley

Steve Stuckmeyer running the Flume drop on the Upper Little White

Adam Elliott

Boaters below Island Drop

Keel Brightman 📷

Jay Gifford greases S-turn 👁

# LOWER LITTLE WHITE SALMON

only "flat" section on the river, referred to as Contemplation Canyon. If you have been here before, this gives you about 300 feet of slow-moving water to consider how you feel about running Spirit.

Originally referred to as the Altar until Jen Mullen ran the falls in 1994, aptly naming it Spirit Falls, Spirit pours about 33 feet into a powerful pool. The exit to the pool is well guarded by Chaos, a turbulent hydraulic which usually requires rope-assisted rescues if something goes wrong. Setting safety at Chaos is highly recommended if you plan on running Spirit.

Boulder gardens (and the backwards ledge) continue down to Master Blaster, a short and steep boulder-jumble rapid just above the Fish Hatchery. Below Master Blaster is a river-wide fish weir that is very retentive at higher flows. The rapids start to fade away and a couple more fish weirs drop you into Drano Lake and a three-quarter-mile paddle out to your car.

I would recommend paddling with someone who knows this run on your first few trips or taking a full day (about seven hours) scouting and working your way down the river. Everything can be scouted. Local paddlers who know it can do a run in 45 minutes or less, but if you don't know where you are going, put on early and scout well!

*Editor's note: It takes many trips down to remember where you are going on this run. There are 13 major rapids and they all have a lead-in rapid. Learn the lead-in rapids. And if you want more action, head up to Willard and put on the Upper Little White.*

—*Ryan Scott*

## SHUTTLE DIRECTIONS

Take state Hwy. 14 east of Stevenson. Turn into the Little White Salmon National Fish Hatchery and continue about a half-mile around the lake. You will see your parking area on the left and a concrete walkway down to the water on your right **(45.715433, -121.645094)**.

To reach the put-in, go back to WA 14, driving west (toward Portland/Vancouver) and take a right on Cook-Underwood Rd. Continue 5 miles to the Willard National Fish Hatchery. The put-in is on the opposite side of the bridge **(45.764180, -121.629755)**.

Paul Thompson

Jacob Cruser getting Spiritual

Kayaker: Justin Teague - A Kayak Shed Wednesday Night Happy Hour Trip Leader

Keel Brightman
Rob Bart taking flight at Boulder Sluice Rapid

# FARMLANDS

## OF THE WHITE SALMON RIVER

The Farmlands section of the White Salmon River carves its way through a narrow basaltic canyon, and gives first-time paddlers a feeling of wonder as you pass through its claustrophobic corridors. At low flows this is a technical run with small ledges and tight, technical drops. At higher flows the eddies disappear and the holes grow. The run begins with a seal-launch into the river. Paddle a few small drops before you reach the initial rapid above Sidewinder, the run's first major rapid. This narrow plunge sets the tone and is 100 feet above Sidewinder, a Class IV+ drop that looks clean until a scout of the left wall reveals an undercut hook into which much of the current flows. Many paddlers run this rapid, but many opt to portage. Bedrock ledges and holes continue until you reach Doorbell, a long rapid with a rock that sits in the center at the bottom—try to avoid ringing the doorbell. At high flows you won't even see it. More Class IV rapids push through the narrow gorge until you arrive at Lava Dam (scout right). This river-wide, 10-foot falls is generally run on the center-right flake. It's an easy

## THE RUNDOWN

Stunning basalt gorge with narrow canyons on a classic, quality section of the White Salmon River.

**Difficulty:** Class IV-V (Lava Falls)

**Gauge:** Visual, Husum stick gauge (just upstream of Husum Bridge—not the highway bridge). If it's not possible to get the most accurate reading by viewing in person, or asking a local who has, divide the White Salmon at Underwood gauge by 400. The result is a ballpark estimate of what the foot gauge is reading.

**Flow Min-max:** 2.7-5 cfs Springs below that feed the run in the summer are dry in the winter, so 3 feet in winter has more water than 3 feet in the summer.

**Gradient:** 60 fpm avg.

**Takeout:** Green Truss put-in (Green Truss Bridge). Hike up or keep paddling the Truss for a full day on the water.

**Put-in:** Sunnyside Rd.

**Length:** 5 miles

**Hitchability:** Not good

**Season:** Fall, winter, spring

**Camping:** North in Trout Lake, Trout Lake Campground

**4WD Needed?** No

**Best Close Food/Beers:** Everybody's Brewing in White Salmon or Big Man's Rotisserie in Husum

**Quality (out of 5):** 4

**Raft Recommendations:** Raftable by expert rafters, though the takeout can be a lot of work

Mike Hagadorn
Dave Fusilli lining up Lava

boof, but be weary of the cave behind the falls; set good safety here! BE AWARE OF HIGH WATER: This drop gets very retentive with a dangerous kickback behind the falls. A couple action-packed rapids follow Lava, before a long mellow section. At about Mile Four, Off Ramp is the next major rapid (scout left). This chunky rapid has a nice boof on the right, avoid the river-left side. There are a few more ledges—watch out for Toaster—before you reach the takeout, just after passing under a bridge on the right. This is also the put-in for the Green Truss section. If you have time and energy, step it up a notch and keep paddling down through the Truss, which makes for a great day of paddling!

—*Scott Waidelich*

## SHUTTLE DIRECTIONS

Driving from Hood River, Ore., cross the Hood River Bridge, take a left onto state Hwy. 14 (heading west). Just before the White Salmon River turn right onto state Hwy. 141-Alt. heading north, and follow approximately 5 miles past the town of BZ to the Farmlands takeout/Green Truss put-in, which is upriver on the right-hand side of WA 141 at Winegartner Road **(45.909938, -121.502255)**. Parking is very minimal at this location, two to four vehicles can fit on the north side of the driveway by the mailboxes. Additional parking is a quarter-mile up WA 141 on the left-hand side at Carr Road. Please be aware that they DO NOT want parking at the put-in other then next to the mailboxes! To reach the put-in, continue north on WA 141 for 3.8 miles and take a right on Glenwood Rd. Continue for 1 mile, cross the river and use a dirt pull-out on the left side of the road for the put-in **(45.964244, -121.468897)**.

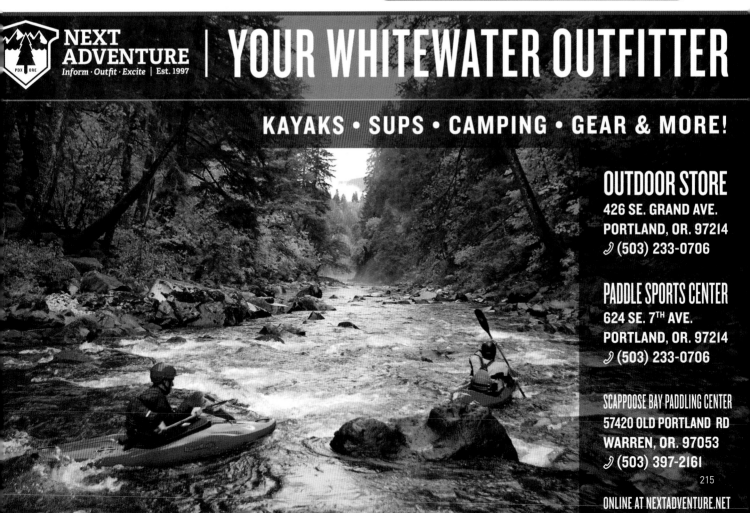

# GREEN TRUSS

## OF THE WHITE SALMON RIVER

The Green Truss of the White Salmon River is one of the most beautiful and action-packed sections of whitewater in the Northwest. If you are anywhere near the Columbia River Gorge, the Green Truss is a must-hit! It offers a variety of rapids from 22-foot Big Brother to the ultra-committing rapids Upper and Lower Zigzag. At most flows (3.5 feet and lower) the Green Truss is considered a pool-drop run with easy-to-scout rapids.

The Green Truss starts with some fun Class III-IV rapids, which are a great read-and-run warmup. The first significant drop is Meatball, typically run far left around the large meatball-looking rock mid-river. This drop consists of an 8-foot slide into a small pool that leads around the left side of the Meatball rock and through another twisty drop. You can eddy out on river-left to scout and or hold safety. Right after Meatball is Bob's Falls, an 8-foot drop with a nasty hole in the center of the river. Scout this drop on either side, the typical line is either far right or left with a boof. After Bob's is the highlight of the run: Big Brother.

Big Brother is a 22-foot waterfall with a very thin line at the entrance. The landing is shallow on river-left with has a cave at the bottom on river-right. At medium to low flows, the cave is usually quite forgiving and fairly easy to paddle out of, safety can also be held right at the point of the cave and from the far side on river-left, where the drop can be scouted and portaged. Just below is

## THE RUNDOWN

White Salmon runs year-round and is great for Class IV-V paddlers depending on water levels.

**Difficulty:** Class IV-V

**Length:** 5 miles

**Gauge:** Visual, Husum stick gauge (just upstream of Husum Bridge—not the highway bridge). If it's not possible to get the most accurate reading by viewing in person, or asking a local who has, divide the White Salmon at Underwood gauge by 400. The result is a ballpark estimate of what the foot gauge is reading.

**Hitchability:** easy

**Season:** Summer, spring, fall, winter

**Camping:** Difficult to find, logging roads

**4WD Needed?** No

**Best Close Food/Beers:** Everybody's Brewing in White Salmon, Big Man's Rotisserie in Husum

**Flow Min-max:** 1-6 feet

**Gradient:** 130 fpm

**Quality (out of 5):** 5

**Takeout:** 130 fpm

**Raft Recommendations:** Not for part-time Class V rafters

**Put-in:** Green Truss (Just before Carr Road)

Ryan Scott

Early morning winter run down the Truss with Jason Schroeder

Little Brother, a perfect 12-foot waterfall normally run on river-left with a boof. This is one of the run's most fun drops, so if you portage Big Brother, you can still put in between the drops just and run Little Brother!

Next is the run's most nerve-wracking drop: Double Drop, a 16-foot feature with almost no recovery between the two tiers. It's also the most exciting drop to watch! Paddlers will typically run the second drop sideways, backwards, stern-squirted, upside down and every so often right-side up! The river then mellows out for a while with some really fun Class III-IVs and amazing PNW beauty, highlighted by Cheese Grater, a 6-foot drop with a stick hole on river-right. Then the entire river narrows to about 10-foot-wide canyon for an unnamed and exciting rapid. It starts with a small boof into the canyon where it's boiling nonstop and difficult to get through smoothly! If you flip, it's extremely difficult to roll up in the huge boils.

The next challenge are the run's hardest rapids: Upper and Lower Zigzag. Both are Class V and extremely committing. You can scout Upper Zigzag on river-right, but portaging is not an agreeable option! The main thing to remember on Upper Zigzag is to stay in the current. Typically you enter the canyon to Upper ZZ just right of center, where there is a large diagonal wave that you want to break through. Just after is a large wave-hole to squirt through that will typically push you river-right. Start working back to the left to avoid a large hole on the right, then ride the river-left wall and it will shoot you far back river-right where you will avoid a hole on the left. After that you are in the runout of the rapid.

As you come down from your high on Upper, you are right above Lower Zigzag. Eddy out river-left, where it can be scouted and or portaged (note that the portage is almost more difficult than running the actual rapid!). Lower ZZ starts out with a Class III lead-in to a 3-foot ledge with a sticky hole. Boof this hole and prepare for the crux of the rapid as Lower ZZ steepens with large waves and holes the entire way through. The best line is the one that keeps you upright! At the bottom of the rapid are two large holes in the center of the river; try to get either far right or left.

Past the Zigzags is the top of the Orletta section full of fun Class III-IV boofs, sticky holes and exciting rapids! This section starts with two exciting Class IVs, the first being short and sweet, and the second extending for quite a ways; both are read-and-run. The next rapid is Sticky Hole, Class III with its namesake sticky hole at the bottom; go either hard right to avoid it, or test your boof and run

*Continued on page 191*

Bryan Dorr

Deek Heykamp on Big Brother

# GREEN TRUSS

## OF THE WHITE SALMON RIVER

the center (it's possible to escape this hole, though it has caused a tremendous amount of swim for even some of paddling's best)! Next up are the Orletta section's two most significant rapids: Triple Drop and The Flume. Triple Drop consists of three drops through a short canyon; make things easy and run all of them on the left. The Flume is an exciting Class IV during and after the drop, typically run down the center. At higher flows there is a large eddy at the bottom on river-left where it's easy to get pushed and may take a few attempts to get out.

Don't put your guard down yet! The biggest drop on the Orletta section is BZ Falls, a technical 12-foot drop with a Class IV lead-in that ends in a massive hole! If you clear the hydraulic at the base you'll come out smiling! Should it decide to hold on, be prepared for a ride and a likely deep swim (scout and portage on river-right). Another couple of rapids gets you to the put-in for the Middle Section of the White Salmon! Take out river-right and enjoy an ice-cold beverage in the sun!

**HIGH WATER:** At higher flows, the Truss turns into a solid Class V–V+ run where a swim can be very dangerous! All of the warmup rapids feel like a big-water Class IV and the pools disappear in between. The first Class V, Elbow Basher, is a narrow twisting rapid that suddenly turns into a large, sliding drop with a massive hole at the bottom; fine with a good boof. Around the corner is a large boulder-garden rapid—notice that the boulders you typically maneuver around are suddenly under water, creating large holes. The top line at Meatball is the same, but the bottom line is far river-left where you normally scout from. What was a slow pool after is a fast-moving boil straight over Bob's Falls., which is run farther left off of an 8-foot ledge to avoid the main hole. At high water, Big Brother and Lower Brother are typically portaged. But if you fire them up, Big Brother is run left where the 22-foot drop cascades into a boily mess that flows directly into Little Brother, which is run more center, off of a flake rock at the lip of the falls to help avoid the main flow—and a beating!

The once small recovery time between falls at Double Drop is completely gone. The first drop turns into a funnel that shoots you straight through the bottom hole, so don't worry about getting stuck in any hole, they are all blown out. Unfortunately, the exit drop from the rapid is Karen's Box, which becomes a river-wide 6-foot ledge that is a must-boof! It's run just right of center with a lot of speed

and a good solid boof. After the flow mellows for a bit, at Cheese Grater your best bet is to eddy out river-right above the drop to look at the far river-left line (normally it's run right). Next is Upper Zigzag. The line is the same, but you are just in it for the ride. The river will take you where it wants. Try to stay upright, as most of the time you won't be able to see what is in front of you. The current between Upper and Lower ZZ moves extremely fast. Eddy out river-left to check out your line (most portage the lead-in ledge, as it becomes large with a devastating swim out of it), which is the same, though the main concern is getting left or right of the large central holes at the bottom.

In the Orletta section, the rapids are all the same as lower flows, but much pushier with larger waves and holes, until you reach BZ Falls. BZ is almost always portaged at higher flows. If you decide to run it, it's a roll of the dice whether or not you make it through. Normally at high water, it's run right down the center and tucking forward, hoping to go under the hole and come out the backside. While a lot have made it, it's still a gamble and the beating may not be worth the risk; portage BZ on river-right and paddle to the takeout!

—Nate Herbeck

### SHUTTLE DIRECTIONS

From the north end of Hood River White Salmon Bridge, head west on state Hwy 14. Just before the White Salmon River, turn right onto state Hwy. 141 heading north. Follow WA 141 to the town of BZ Corner and a large parking area where rafts launch for the Middle White Salmon: This is your takeout **(45.851097, -121.510150)**.

For the put-in, drive north on WA 141 for approximately 5 miles to the right-hand side at Winegartner Road **(45.909687, -121.501834)**. Parking is minimal, as only two to four vehicles fit on the north side of the driveway by the mailboxes. Additional parking is a quarter-mile up WA 141 on the left-hand side at Carr Road. Please be aware that they DO NOT want parking at the put-in other than next to the mailboxes!

The Middle White Salmon is one of the Gorge's staple runs and provides an excellent Class III-IV boating experience all year long, except for a few days when the water is high. Because of its sheer beauty and pristine water, the middle and lower sections of the river are designated Wild and Scenic river. Most of the water flows from the White Salmon Glacier off of Mount Adams or from deep underground springs, so expect the water temps to be around 40 degrees or lower. Dress for the water as well as the air temp.

Beginning at the BZ Corner launch site, after filling out a river survey card, you switchback down the trail to the river between two metal railings (rafters use the metal bars by placing a paddle under their rafts to reduce friction and wear). On the river you get one of the largest rapids of the trip first, Class IV Maytag, which is a set of drops. Access the whole rapid by taking a left at the break in the railing three-quarters of the way down the trail, then continuing 100 feet until you see rough stairs down to the river. The most common put-in is the river-right pool directly below the railing.

Just downstream you pass under High Bridge, marking the start of Class II boogie-water that continues for a half-mile until it runs into an UnderCut Cave on the river-right wall; approach with caution. At flows around 3.5 feet, a sneak opens on river-left, but at most flows you need to start a little right of center, moving left. For the next half-mile, the river continues through more Class II and III+ including rapids Grasshopper and Shark's Tooth. More Class II boogie continues for about a half-mile until the river turns sharp right and enters Corkscrew, a steep longish rapid that is run on river-right with a half-exposed rock at the bottom, depending on flows. Downriver about a quarter-mile is another really fun rapid known as Waterspout, or Granny Snatcher by raft guides, which is a

Adam Elliott
Oregon Rafting Team approaching Maytag

## THE RUNDOWN

This is a beautiful and fun intermediate run, probably the most-run Class III section in this book, with lots of Class II in between.

**Difficulty:** Class III-IV (IV-IV+ at high flows)

**Gauge:** Visual, Husum stick gauge (just upstream of Husum Bridge—not the highway bridge). If it's not possible to get the most accurate reading by viewing in person, or asking a local who has, divide the White Salmon at Underwood gauge by 400. The result is a ballpark estimate of what the foot gauge is reading.

**Flow Min-max:** 2-6 cfs

**Gradient:** 2-6 fpm

**Takeout:** Husum

**Put-in:** BZ

**Length:** 4 miles

**Hitchability:** Pretty good

**Season:** Year-round

**Camping:** North in Trout Lake

**4WD Needed?** No

**Best Close Food/Beers:** Big Man's Rotisserie in Husum or the Logs in BZ

**Quality (out of 5):** 4.5

**Raft Recommendations:** Great raft run! Commercially guided during the summer.

©Charlie Munsey / adventurelightphoto.com

# MIDDLE WHITE SALMON RIVER

diagonal 4-foot sloping ledge. Your choices: Take the easy left line or move from right to left and take the plunge.

For the next few miles, the river mellows out with a few Class II rapids. One notable feature is Barge Wave, which is a beautiful Pipeline-style curler just below Waterspout. At flows over 5 feet this becomes a river-wide monster hole that grows with more water. The last big rapid on the journey down to Husum is Stairstep—standard lines are center or right down the three ledges that get smaller as you go. After Stairstep are about a half-dozen Class II's until you hit the main attraction for waterfall lovers: Husum Falls, a powerful 10-foot falls that can pummel boaters above 2.5 feet (the commercial rafting cutoff), and gets friendlier as the river drops. You will know you are getting close when you see the powerlines and hear the road. Keep your eyes peeled; there is a warning sign just upstream of the river-right scout/portage eddy. Set safety because the best chance of you getting bagged out is from river-right under the bridge. The river-left eddy above the falls is the best portage for a kayak and the easiest way to line your raft if you are continuing downriver. Any more questions? Search "Husum carnage."

Except for the Under-Cut Cave, all named rapids on this section can be portaged on river-right. If you have to exit the river, your best option is hiking out river-right to state Hwy. 141. Enjoy and show respect. At the time of press, the boating community is welcome by the people who live along this pristine river.

*—Hans Hoomans*

## SHUTTLE DIRECTIONS

From state Hwy. 14, turn up WA 141-Alt. at the mouth of the White Salmon. Continue 2.1 miles. Take a left at the stop sign and continue 3.9 miles to the town of Husum. This is the takeout **(45.79769, -121.485291)**. There is parking below the bridge on the left or past the bridge on the right.

To reach the put-in, continue north on WA 141 to the town of BZ and the BZ Boat Launch area, just past the Logs restaurant **(45.851725, -121.509983)**.

Brian Vogt
Robert Bartholomew in Grasshopper

Brian Vogt
Joe Sauve running the left side of Husum Falls

The Lower White Salmon is a great Class II-III run: It's short, has easy access and can be paddled every day of the year. The first and biggest rapid of the run is Rattlesnake (assuming you're not quite ready for Husum Falls yet, just upstream of the put-in). Access the put-in with a short scramble at the north end of the parking lot, or kayakers have the option to follow a path at the lot's south end that leads to just below this drop. Rattlesnake is a 2- to 3-foot river-wide ledge that is typically run right down the middle with a slight sneak for kayakers moving right to left. This rapid is the best play-hole in the gorge between 3.75 and 4.5 feet. You access the wave by using a fixed rope attached to the river-left bank. Continuing downriver provides a few warmups before Deadman's Corner, marked by a 90-degree right turn with a boulder on the left side (easily avoided by catching the eddy on the right, inside of the turn). The next rapid comes quick and is also marked by a center boulder that you also want to be right of. This rapid is a wave-filled fun-fest for the beginner paddler.

A few more Class II rapids run through a scenic valley until you reach the Cave Wave, a Class II surf-wave that is in at lower flows and has good eddy access from river-left, under the cave. This is a good spot to chill out, practice ferries, eddying out, or surfing. After this, the river starts to change, and continues to do so as a hundred years of sediment works its way downriver following 2012's historic Condit Dam removal. The most dramatic changes are first noticed at a cinder block castle on river-left where, as of 2015, a fair amount of wood has collected. Expect this to continue upriver through the years: This is all Class I with the chance of wood. When you see some newer exposed bedrock you enter some fun, deeper splashy wave trains. The takeout is just after the Northwestern Lake Bridge on the right. Just under the bridge you get one last rapid before the takeout. Follow the ramp up to the original boat ramp.

—Hans Hoomans

## THE RUNDOWN

Rattlesnake packs a punch at higher flows! You can surf all day long at the Cave Wave!

**Difficulty:** Class III (Husum Falls Class IV+ at normal flows, Rattlesnake and Deadman's Class IV at higher flows)

**Gauge:** Visual, Husum stick gauge (just upstream of Husum Bridge—not the highway bridge). If it's not possible to get the most accurate reading by viewing in person, or asking a local who has, divide the White Salmon at Underwood gauge by 400. The result is a ballpark estimate of what the foot gauge is reading.

**Flow Min-max:** 1-6 cfs

**Gradient:** 30 fpm

**Takeout:** Northwestern Lake Recreational Area

**Put-in:** Husum. Above or below Husum Falls

**Length:** 3 miles

**Hitchability:** Pretty good

**Season:** Year-round

**Camping:** Limited, but there are a couple spots up Buck Creek near the takeout

**4WD Needed?** No

**Best Close Food/Beers:** Big Man's Rotisserie in Husum

**Quality (out of 5):** 4

**Raft Recommendations:** Very fun raft run!

## SHUTTLE DIRECTIONS

From state Hwy. 14, turn up state 141-Al.t at the mouth of the White Salmon. Continue 2.1 miles. Take a left at the stop sign and continue 1.9 miles up WA 141 north and take a left at the Northwestern Lake sign. Drive down .3 miles to the recreation area (**45.779836, -121.516619**).

To reach the put-in go back out to 141-N and continue 2 miles to Husum. There is parking below the bridge on the left or past the bridge on the right (**45.797694, -121.485291**).

Keel Brightman

Surfing at the cave wave on the Lower White Salmon

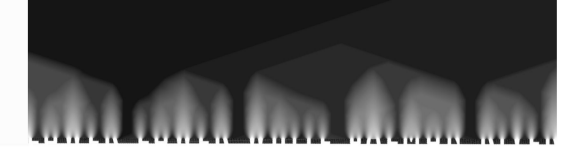

## THE RUNDOWN

Half of this run was buried behind the 120-foot Condit Dam for nearly 100 years. For the most part, this run gets better with higher flows, minus Steelhead Falls.

**Difficulty:** Class III (IV+, Steelhead Falls turns into V at high water)

**Gauge:** Visual, Husum stick gauge (just upstream of Husum Bridge—not the highway bridge). If it's not possible to get the most accurate reading by viewing in person, or asking a local who has, divide the White Salmon at Underwood gauge by 400. The result is a ballpark estimate of what the foot gauge is reading.

**Flow Min-max:** 1-6 cfs

**Gradient:** 50 fpm

**Takeout:** Confluence with Columbia, upstream of state Hwy. 14

**Put-in:** Old Northwestern Lake Recreational Area

**Length:** 4 miles

**Hitchability:** Pretty good

**Season:** Year-round

**Camping:** Limited, but there are a couple spots up Buck Creek near the put-in

**4WD Needed?** No

**Best Close Food/Beers:** Big Man's Rotisserie in Husum

**Quality (out of 5):** 4

**Raft Recommendations:** Fun raft run, beware of Class IV+ Steelhead Falls

## SHUTTLE DIRECTIONS

The takeout is located just off state Hwy. 14, west of Bingen, WA at the mouth of the White Salmon River **(45.728966, -121.520738)**.

To reach the put-in, continue 2.1 miles up state Hwy 141-Alt. Take a left at the stop sign and continue 1.9 miles up WA 141 north and take a left at the Northwestern Lake sign. Drive down .3 miles to the recreation area **(45.779836, -121.516619)**.

The Lower Lower, aka Bottom Big White to some locals, is a new run so to speak. The first half used to be buried under Northwestern Lake, and the lower half (the narrows) was a rarely run (due to access) dewatered section just below Condit Dam. Nowadays it's a continuous Class II+ sediment-dodging wave train through a continuously changing environment. Above the dam the river has begun to work its way down to the bedrock, while below the dam it will take years in many places to hit bedrock due to the enormous amount of sediment that was deposited during the dam blasting.

Begin your run at Northwestern Recreational Park (aka Northwestern Lake Park) by heading down the old boat ramp to the river. The first few miles is a continuous, building Class II that climaxes where a waterfall (Church Falls) comes in at river-right.. Then it is pretty chill floating down to the dam site, which is hard to recognize due to the thorough concrete removal by the decommissioners. After the dam site, the river gorges up quite a bit and much older trees mark the bank. The next half-mile has some fun Class II until you get to a giant left bend in the river; get out on river-left to scout/portage. Just below here the Class II lead-in ends with the river-wide Steelhead Falls, a Class IV with Class V consequences that has sent many folks on a half-mile swim due to the walled-in narrows section below. This rapid is not the same falls of years past and will continue to change as sediment is pushed downriver. Typically this rapid is run on river-left. Below the falls, the narrow stretch goes for about a half-mile, where there are no big rapids but every couple of years produces some nasty river-wide logs to proceed with caution.

From this stretch down to the Columbia, the rapids are mostly sediment-filled Class II with the occasional dam debris. The one exception is a boulder-filled picket fence right below the old powerhouse. At lower water, rafts have a hard time fitting through and may be forced to portage. It is then pretty chill floating down to the slack waters of the Columbia River, where on hot summer days the headwinds can be tremendous. The takeout is on river-left just before the state Hwy. 14 bridge. This stretch of river has become a popular playboat run recently and will continue to get better as the river finds the natural bedrock again. Flags have begun to appear along the shore and in the river, placed by biologists to mark salmon spawning beds, and they have asked that paddlers don't walk in the river on the lower half of this run.

—*Hans Hoomans*

David Spiegel
The gorge on the Lower Lower

# WASHOUGAL RIVER

If you've ever spent much time boating in Portland or around Hood River you may have heard the claim that "all the best paddling in Oregon is in Washington." While that may very well be the case with this run, I can assure you that there is plenty of good whitewater in Oregon. This southwest Washington classic is barely an hour's drive from Portland near the town of Washougal. Situated at the west end of the Columbia River Gorge, abundant winter rain and spring runoff feed the Washougal through much of the fall, winter and spring. Draining into the Columbia, the Washougal and its steep tributaries offer wonderful Class III-V boating. The Big Eddy section is easy to find with simple logistics—the entire run winds its way roadside next to Washougal River Road.

The highlight of the run is Big Eddy Rapid through Retaining Wall Rapid. Both these rapids stand out above the rest with a large-volume pushy feel. When the water's pumping, kayakers will be maneuvering through huge holes, tall exploding waves, surging currents and boiling eddylines. The rapids are closely spaced but offer a small section between the two for recovery. Big Eddy is an exciting run and moves very quickly at higher flows and can easily be completed in under two hours barring incidents. The Washougal is renowned by the locals for having some of the best rainy season playboating in the Northwest.

The play-spot known as "the Washougal Hole," or Wave as it should be more appropriately called, is a spectacular spot! When it's in, water pours over two low-angle ledges forming off the river right wall. The first wave is better at medium to lower flows (2,000-5,000), while the lower feature is best from approx. 4,000-8,000 cfs. Remember however, like most rivers seasonal, high-water events can change features; always check with the locals for current info.

Unfortunately the play-spot is not on the Big Eddy stretch. Paddlers must put in at the Fish Hatchery on the North Fork Washougal and paddle down through the confluence to the waves. Beware of the weir and Class IV rapid that awaits right below the put-in. Run the weir river-right and scout or run the next drop river-left. No matter what you come to the Washougal for if you catch things at the right flows, paddlers won't leave disappointed.

*—Luke Spencer*

## THE RUNDOWN

It has been suggested that D. B. Cooper, who hijacked a Boeing 727 in 1971 then parachuted from the plane with ransom money, may have landed in the Washougal River Basin.

**Difficulty:** Class III-IV

**Gauge:** Washougal at Washougal AW #34960 NWS location ID #WASW1

**Flow Min-max:** 500-10,000 cfs

**Gradient:** 35 fpm. Put-in elevation: 304 feet.

**Takeout:** Lower Fishing access site on Washougal River Rd. MP 2.5-3

**Put-in:** End of the short gravel road marked "Public Fishing" at approx. MP 8.5

**Length:** 7 miles

**Hitchability:** Yes

**Season:** Rainy season / November to May

**Camping:** Yes, in the hills above the "Falls Section"

**4WD Needed?** No

**Best Close Food/Beers:** Amnesia Brewing / Washougal

**Quality (out of 5):** 4.5

**Raft Recommendations:** All rafts!

## SHUTTLE DIRECTIONS

To get to the takeout, from state Hwy. 14 turn left onto Washougal River Rd. Follow the signs to "Washougal River Recreation Area." At Mile Marker 3.0 there is a pull-out and ramp down to the river used by driftboat fishermen **(45.616138,-122.341947)**.

To get to the put-in: Continue upstream to MP 8.5 and look for the sign that says "Public Fishing Access." Take a right at the gravel road and park near the river **(1,45.618112,-122.255172)**.

# HAGEN GORGE

## OF HAGEN CREEK

Hagen Gorge is a relatively new run first discovered by Jason Rackley, Pete Giordano and friends in January 2006. Its close proximity to Vancouver, easy access, clean bedrock rapids and short, but action-packed nature quickly made it a local favorite. Only about a mile in length, it boasts a manageable 260-fpm pool-drop gradient all the way into the falls run on the NF Washougal.

This creek has one very unique feature. Using the normal put-in, you end up above a sloping 8-foot ledge drop where the left headwall hooks around and most of the water pushes. Stay far right and you'll soon arrive at the Big Log Jam. This collection of propitiously placed old-growth has acted as a strainer, keeping the gorge free of wood by holding it all in place here. Using the alternate put-in, you end up just downstream of this logjam—Either way it is an awesome feature that keeps the gorge clean and clear of wood.

The main canyon steps its way down multiple 4- to 8-foot ledge drops. It starts with a single ledge, builds into a triple set of ledges then keeps up that pace until you reach Hagen Daaz Falls: a 20-foot bedrock sliding falls with a split on the left-center. Scout right; you can run the falls almost anywhere on the right entry. A couple rapids later the creek gets rocky again, quickly making a right-left

bend in the middle of Class III rapids. Eddy-hop throughout this section. Before the creek bends left, there is a single eddy (under the tributary on the right), that is the last to scout Euphoria, a beautiful cascading double-falls. The creek twists and turns before fanning out over the top falls. Below Euphoria, the creek drops off one final 6-foot ledge before blending into Teakettle Falls and the North Fork Washougal River. Scout on the right as Teakettle can pack a healthy punch at high water.

On the NF, flows double and the river cruises downstream. A Class IV rapid accelerates and pinches down at the bottom of the rapid; stay clear of the left wall at the bottom. Soon after is Double Falls. Be alert, this one sneaks up. Scout/portage on the left as this falls can go really good or really bad—I witnessed a paddler disappear behind the unassuming top 12-foot falls for an uncomfortably long period of time. Be sure to clear the landing zone if you decide to run it.

The bottom drop folds to the right, dropping about 6 feet off an angled ledge with the downstream point on the left. The canyon pinches off the exit, creating a pocket against the right wall and an

*Continued on page 230*

Hagen Gorge, Bryon Dorr

5

Scott Baker

Charging Double Falls on the North Fork Washougal near Hagen Gorge takeout

# HAGEN GORGE

## OF HAGEN CREEK

agitated pool of water pushing downstream. It runs easier than it looks, but scout it well. The portage is down the left through the crack in the creekbed, which high water will fill, to a perch over the falls' runout requiring an 8-foot seal-launch back into the water. Take the long hike around if the water is too high. The next mile is gradual Class III to the takeout bridge.

Add on another 3.5 miles of the Classic NF run down to the Fish Hatchery. Beware of Bowey Falls (you'll know when you see it, portage recommended). The rest of the run filters through a beautiful gorge with many fun rapids to keep you alert and smiling once you reach the takeout.

*—Ryan Scott*

## THE RUNDOWN

Continuous, fun bedrock rapids, pool-drop ledges and sliding falls in a short action-packed run.

**Difficulty:** Class IV-V

**Gauge:** Pinpoint the flow on Hagen using the Washougal River gauge at Washougal (the better to use as the Washougal reacts faster on rainfall), and the East Fork Lewis gauge at Heisson

**Flow Min-max:** 3,000 cfs or 8.5 feet on the Washougal River at Washougal (if lower than 2,000 cfs, the flow you expect could still be frozen upriver); 2,500 cfs on EF Lewis at Heisson. The upper flood-level limit has yet to be explored. Fun at higher flows.

**Gradient:** 260 fpm

**Takeout:** Bridge over the NF Washougal

**Put-in:** Short hike in off 1200 Rd. above the gorge on Hagen Creek

**Length:** 2.5 miles

**Hitchability:** Limited traffic, but short 2.5-mile shuttle (mountain bike recommended)

**Season:** Spring, fall, winter

**Camping:** Dougan Creek Campground up the main Washougal. Less private land above and more chances for a camp above Stebbins Creek on the main Washougal.

**4WD Needed?** No

**Best Close Food/Beers:** Amnesia Brewing in Washougal

**Quality (out of 5):** 4.5

**Raft Recommendations:** Not for part time Class V rafters

## SHUTTLE DIRECTIONS

From Vancouver, Wash., to the takeout, drive state Hwy. 14 east to Washougal River Rd. Follow this 10.7 miles then take a slight left on Skye Rd. Continue 3.7 miles then turn right onto NE 412th Ave. In 0.2 miles, stay right as the road turns into Skamania Mines Rd. Go another 1.1 miles to the takeout bridge over the NF Washougal. From Bridge of the Gods to the takeout, drive 15 miles west on state Hwy. 14 to Salmon Falls Rd. Take a right and drive 0.6 miles then left onto Canyon Creek Rd. Continue 3.1 miles to a right turn onto Washougal River Rd. Go 0.5 miles to a slight left onto Skye Rd. In 3.7 miles, turn right onto NE 412th Ave., and 0.2 miles later, stay right as the road turns into Skamania Mines Rd. Proceed another 1.1 miles to the takeout bridge over the NF Washougal **(45.6634222, -122.2394500)**.

Alternate takeout: To add on the extra 3.5 miles, park a shuttle vehicle at the Fish Hatchery. Before you make the slight right onto Skye Rd, continue on Washougal River Rd., and after it crosses the NF, take the next left up to Steelhead Rd., and into the hatchery parking area near the river **(45.6218472, -122.2178222)**.

Put-in: Continue up Skamania Mines Rd. another 1.4 miles and turn left onto 1200 Rd./Skamania Mines Rd. In 0.1 miles, stay left on 1200 Rd., and drive another 1.2 miles to the sharp right-hand uphill bend in the road. There's a pull-off on the right to park **(45.6942639, -122.2463389)**. Toward the creek, just upstream in the distance is a cluster of tall fir trees (above the new growth in front of you). Start hiking for those trees and with luck you will find the trail under the canopy. The put-in is on the other side.

Alternate put-in: Just before you reach the put-in, note the spur road (blocked off) to your left **(45.6935389, -122.2452583)**. Park here, walk down a couple hundred feet and stay right (another spur forks to the left). Walk another hundred yards and find your way down to the creek following what is becoming a nicely worn path. You will enter the creek just below the large log deck **(45.6913750°, -122.2479667)**.

Stebbins Creek pours through Brice Canyon on its descent into the Washougal River over multiple cascades down bedrock ledges with the occasional boulder-choked rapid, climaxing at the spectacular 40-foot Tsunami Falls. John Whaley and Jason Rackley were among the first to descend the canyon back in 2000. Since then, Stebbins has grown popular among local paddlers, but there's a catch: It doesn't run at a good flow often. Catch it in the fall after the hard rains and before dropping snow levels lock out the put-in access. After my first run at higher flows, this fast-paced, action-packed creek run quickly became a favorite.

From the trailhead it takes about 35 minutes to hike down to the confluence with the North and South forks. The trail parallels the SF (to your left) for the last half-mile or so with two other runnable waterfalls on the SF just before the confluence. Below the confluence, the creek offers a short warmup section down to the first 8-foot ledge drop, which lands in a nice pool. The creek then takes off toward JetBoat Falls, which drops about 10 feet to a nice bedrock transition and is normally run against the right wall.

The next couple rapids, Get in My Belly and Boulder Chute will require a quick scout with safety recommended. Just downstream is an ever-changing hazard called Lethal Injection. Large old-growth logs used to block the exit of this falls, forcing a portage on the left. The wood has shifted in recent years, making this drop a little more user-friendly, but scout with care. Tsunami Falls sits just downstream pouring off an impressive stacked series of runnable ledges and ending in a cascading veil of whitewater.

After the awe of Tsunami wears off, head to the next major obstacle, Zoom Flume. This tight boulder-choked rapid has a big overhanging wall on the left and a nice portage option on the right for those who don't like it. Downstream, Bongo Furry keeps you on your toes until you reach the takeout bridge and Mad Dog Falls.

*—Ryan Scott*

## THE RUNDOWN

Tsunami Falls!

**Difficulty:** Class IV-V+ (suggested portages at Lethal Injection, if the wood is still in play, and Zoom Flume)

**Gauge:** Washougal River - 5,000-14,000 cfs

**Flow Min-max:** Takeout estimate on Stebbins Creek, 300-800 cfs

**Gradient:** Steep

**Takeout:** Bridge over Stebbins Creek just above the confluence with the Washougal

**Put-in:** North Fork-South Fork confluence

**Length:** 2.9 miles

**Hitchability:** Not recommended

**Season:** Fall and winter, though shuttle access is usually closed in the winter due to snow levels. Catch this run in the fall during big rain events before the freezing level drops.

**Camping:** Dougan Creek Campground. Less private land above and more chances for a camp above Stebbins Creek.

**4WD Needed?** No, unless you have to deal with snow in the winter

**Best Close Food/Beers:** Amnesia Brewing Pub in Washougal

**Quality (out of 5):** 4

**Raft Recommendations:** Has been done by Class V rafters, not recommended

## SHUTTLE DIRECTIONS

To reach the takeout from Washougal, head east on state Hwy. 14 about 10 miles to a left on Salmon Falls Rd., go 3.4 miles and turn right on Washougal River Rd. Proceed another 5.7 miles to a right turn on Rd W-2000. Go 2.5 miles to the bridge that crosses Stebbins Creek **(45.6910750, -122.1220250)**.

To reach the put-in, continue up Rd W-2000 another 1.9 miles and turn right, drive another 2.3 miles and turn right again. Go 1.1 miles and turn left, go 0.5 miles and turn right, then 2.1 miles later, take a right. In about 2.5 miles, before you reach Milepost 12, the put-in trail is on the side of the road along a slight right-hand bend, marked by a deteriorating sign—keep your eyes peeled. This trail will lead you down to the confluence **(45.7155722, -122.0855056)**.

# ROCK CREEK

This stream is mostly busy Class II-IV with the most action in the first and last mile. There are two Class V rapids that can be easily portaged, making this a good run for groups with mixed ability levels. When the water is up, this is one of the more convenient adventures in the Columbia River Gorge.

The run begins immediately with Class III-IV boulder rapids and slides, eventually culminating in a difficult-to-scout 7-foot ledge. This is usually runnable down the middle, and worth the effort to scout on the left for wood. A short way downstream, the river bends to the right and roars over Heaven and Hell, the first Class V rapid. The first tier is a twisting chute into a dynamic hole followed by a short pool before the crux, where paddlers must punch a big hole to get left for a 10-foot auto-boof. Paddlers who fail to get left of the hole will either get a beating they won't soon forget, or encounter a rock they may very well not remember, or both. Both tiers can be portaged left, the second via a wildly fun seal-launch following a groove in the bedrock.

Things keep rolling, easing off a Class past the Steep Creek bridge just downstream of the unmistakable Steep Creek Falls (shallow landing, but has been kayaked). This middle section is less interesting than the beginning and the end, but it moves along at high flows and has a couple Class IV rapids in the mix to keep paddlers honest. After a couple miles of easier floating, Three Swims Falls can sneak up on the lackadaisical. Here the river pinches slightly between rock walls with a small hole at the bottom of a Class III rapid. Scouting this lead-in rapid isn't a bad idea as an immediate eddy on the left is required to scout/portage the Class V Three Swims Falls. Catch an eddy as high as possible; paddlers have missed and run the falls blind, usually with poor results. This rapid starts with a tough 15-foot drop into a narrow landing and numerous hazards. This empties straight into a Class V boulder garden with numerous moves and a sticky hole at the bottom. Safety can be set along the portage route on the left, but this drop does not get run very often in its entirety. Below are a few more boulder gardens and a long sliding rapid before the bridge at the takeout.

The section from the takeout to Ryan Allen road is mostly Class II-III with a couple of log hazards. Below the Ryan Allen bridge are two small ledges before a 30-foot falls, usually run in the center. Downstream are a couple of small slides before Money Drop, a fast slide into a big vertical drop (45.6992, -121.8959). The banks here are unstable, routinely changing the scale of the drop. It has been measured as low as 10 feet just after a major mass wasting event, and as tall as 70. Just downstream is a boulder garden followed by a Class IV ledge drop, then Rock Creek is all Class II-III boulder bars with some wood down to the confluence with the Columbia.

## THE RUNDOWN

The fabled Bridge of the Gods land bridge was created by a mass wasting event 500-1,000 years ago, originating on Table Mountain, a feature visible from the area.

**Difficulty:** Class III-IV (V)

**Gauge:** East Fork Lewis

**Flow Min-max:** 1,000-4,000 cfs (3k max if gauge is rising)

**Gradient:** 140 fpm. Put-in elevation: 1,000 feet.

**Takeout:** Bridge upstream of Spring Creek

**Put-in:** Rock Creek Campground

**Length:** 4.6 miles

**Hitchability:** Poor

**Season:** Rainy

**Camping:** No

**4WD Needed?** No, but the shuttle is on a gravel road

**Best Close Food/Beers:** Andrews in Stevenson

**Quality (out of 5):** 3.5

**Raft Recommendations:** It is doable in a raft

## SHUTTLE DIRECTIONS

From state Hwy. 14 in the town of Stevenson, turn onto SW Rock Creek Dr., then Ryan-Allen Rd, staying right at the T. In half a mile, turn left onto Red Bluff Rd., and drive 2.5 miles, where you turn right. Follow this road a short ways down to the takeout bridge **(45.724, -121.9344)**.

To get to the put-in, return to Red Bluff Rd., and turn right. In 3.2 miles, cross the Steep Creek Bridge over Rock Creek, and continue past this bridge 1.5 miles to another bridge over Rock Creek where you can put in **(45.756, -122.0103)**.

*—Jacob Cruser*

5

This run may be the biggest adventure available to paddlers in the Columbia River Gorge. Each phase of the trip ranks in the epic category. The first trick is getting enough rain without having too much water in the creek. Next is getting the two-hour shuttle set early enough to give you a shot at completing the run before dark. Add a short hike in and many hours will have elapsed before you take your first stroke. Once on the creek, paddlers face numerous waterfalls of varying difficulty, with the majority being in the 30- to 40-foot range. Throw in a plethora of Class III-V rapids, shifting wood hazards, exposed portaging, weather issues plus the likelihood of minimal daylight and it's possible to see why this creek is rarely paddled. Regardless of the level of success, this is sure to be a memorable trip to all who attempt it.

With the shuttle complete, a short walk along a berry path is necessary to reach the stream. The trail peters out in places, but no one has gotten lost yet. A falls marks the put-in (Bree), then a mile of Class II is broken up by a 25-foot falls (Weathertop) and a couple of wood portages. When you get to the first IV/V rapid, things are about to kick off. After running/portaging this rapid, you

## SHUTTLE DIRECTIONS

From state Hwy. 14 in the town of Stevenson, turn onto SW Rock Creek Dr., then Ryan-Allen Rd, staying right at the T. A half-mile later, turn left onto Red Bluff Rd., and drive 8.1 miles (stay right at miles 7.3 and 8.0 ) to the takeout at a bridge of Rock Creek (45.7623, -122.0248).

To get to the put-in, return to Stevenson, then follow WA 14 east to the Wind River Hwy., and head north 8.6 miles past Carson and into Stabler, where you turn left onto Hemlock Rd.  After 1.3 miles on Hemlock Rd., turn right onto NF 417, and 3.2 miles later stay left onto NF 43. In 1.8 miles (5 miles after turning off Hemlock Rd.), cross Trout Creek and immediately stay right, noting your mileage. In 1.4 miles, stay left, and 2.7 miles past the Trout Creek bridge is a painted marker and tree (orange) indicating the parallel elevation as the head of the gorge, helpful in determining whether you will encounter snow in the canyon or not. From the left turn, NF 43 climbs for about 2.6 miles until it Ts at NF 41/Sunset Hemlock Rd., where you turn left. Go about a quarter of a mile, there will be a berry picker path on the right marked by an orange square painted on a tree.

**Trailhead:** Approximately 45.8015, -122.0722
**Put-in:** (45.7943, -122.0813)

## THE RUNDOWN

Paddlers familiar with the Lord of the Rings trilogy can track downstream progress using the parallels in the rapid naming scheme to the story by J.R.R. Tolkein. Get an early start and bring plenty of snacks, this is a tough section of river.

**Difficulty:** Class V-V+

**Gauge:** There is a foot gauge near Ryan Allen Bridge in Stevenson. Or estimate using the EF Lewis gauge at Heisson, Washougal at Washougal, and Wind River

**Flow Min-max:** 2 feet is a runnable flow on the staff gauge, full range not yet determined. 2,000-4,500 cfs(EF Lewis), 5,000-6,000 cfs Washougal, and 1,200-2,000 cfsWind River can be used to ballpark runnable flows.

**Gradient:** 400 fpm, one quarter-mile span drops 200 feet. Put-in elevation: 2,400 feet, shuttle over 3,000 feet

**Takeout:** Road bridge near North Fork Snag Creek

**Put-in:** Berry Path

**Length:** 4.5 miles

**Hitchability:** Not a viable option

**Season:** Rainy, often gets snowed in

**Camping:** Trout Creek Campground

**4WD Needed?** Helpful, especially if there is snow on the shuttle road. Lots of gravel driving.

**Best Close Food/Beers:** Stevenson or Carson

**Quality (out of 5):** 3 or 5 depending on your disposition for adventure.

**Raft Recommendations:** Has been done by Class V rafters, not recommended! This adds another level of adventure.

Ryan Scott
Put in on the Top Rock

Keel Brightman

Jacob Cruser below 'Rivendell' working through the Top Rock on the first successful descent

have about a hundred yards before the waterfalls start in earnest. First is Rivendell, a section with three waterfalls. Portage the first on the right by lowering boats, the last two can be scouted/portaged on the left. The next horizon line marks Moria, a 20-foot slide into an alleyway between boulders. Scout/portage right being careful of the unstable terrain. The next hundred yards is a bit manky; proceed with caution.

Shortly below here the barren river-right wall soars 400 feet overhead at Helms Deep, with an easy slide at the base of this wall. A small stream enters on the left just downstream, signaling two of the least friendly waterfalls on the run: The Two Towers. Tower 1 must be portaged on the right, followed by a scary-ferry to river-left just above Tower 2, which is favorably shaped, though the landing appears too shallow for a descent. After a few rapids and another horizon is Gondor, a set of three waterfalls ending in the double-drop Minas Tirith. Not too far downstream is the Black Gate, which can be portaged with difficulty on either side if you do not wish to run this 40-foot falls. The next mile contains numerous obstacles (one of the portages even required a short swim on the first successful descent). This section of the river is known as Shelob's Layer, where most of the rapids are boulder gardens. The final whitewater hurdle is Crack of Doom, a 10- to 15-foot drop into a narrow landing, which was complicated by a woody lip in 2013. Once downstream, the going gets easier, but efficiency is still advised if one wishes to avoid finishing in the dark. As things wind down, a green cliff on the left and shortly after The Pacific Crest Trail mark The Shire. The creek is benign below here, and while it is possible to hike out on the PCT, most will choose to finish the mile of Class I-II down to the road bridge.

—Jacob Cruser

# OUTLET FALLS

## OF OUTLET CREEK

Nestled in southwest Washington's steep canyons surrounding the Klickitat River, Outlet Falls plunges off the high farmlands below Glenwood, Wash. Tucked back in an unlikely spot, the falls sit hidden just a short distance off the Glenwood Highway. As Outlet Creek enters the steep Klickitat River Canyon, it falls dramatically off a 70-foot plunge into a huge bowl. The falls lived in relative obscurity to most of the public with the exception of the adventurous waterfall hunters looking for their next scenic photograph. In January 2009 with kayakers actively hunting for the next big drop, Erik Boomer was the driving force behind Outlet Falls. Followed by Boomer's first descent, two more kayakers descended the waterfall followed the next day by two others. Shortly after the descents Outlet Falls was featured in videos, on the Web, and in adventure magazines across the world. The descent was so dramatic that it was even featured on NBC's *Today* show. Today it's a classic destination for expert waterfall paddlers.

Approaching the viewpoint from the highway, a thunderous roar fills the canyon, sending all but the most mentally prepared paddlers back to their cars. Most paddlers will be content with this amazing view alone before proceeding on to one of the many standby runs in the area. Those prepared will have the chance to bomb over one of the PNW's truly classic waterfalls! This drop is no gimme, as a sketchy 15-foot seal-launch lands at the bottom of a Class IV-V rapid and into a pool where paddlers can collect themselves and prepare for the large drop below. In the pool, there's no going back as the only reasonable way out requires descending the falls. From the pool, a giant horizon line appears with a treetop view that one won't soon forget. A junky Class III rapid then requires confidence and expert boat-handling as the water speeds toward the lip. A turbulent yet airy landing zone sits 70 feet below. A short but steep climb back up and out of the canyon to the car will seem quick after all the excitement of the plunge. Dropping a waterfall of this size and caliber isn't for the average paddler, plus the potential for serious injury is possible for even the best kayakers. However, for those up to the challenge, the reward is impossible to describe.

*—Luke Spencer*

Keel Brightman

Erik Boomer charging down Outlet Falls in 2009 on the first descent of the falls

Paul Thompson

Kory Kellum braces for impact January 8, 2015

## THE RUNDOWN

Wait until you see it!

**Difficulty:** Class V+

**Gauge:** Klickitat at Pitt

**Flow Min-max:** 4,000-7,000 cfs. Keep in mind that Outlet is at 1,900 feet in elevation and a sudden drop in the freezing level can lock up the water flow, making winter flows tricky to catch. When everything is on the rise and the Klickitat is at the levels stated, it's worth taking a look to see if Outlet is flowing strong.

**Gradient:** 70 feet of free-fall

**Takeout:** Below the falls

**Put-in:** Seal-launch upstream of the falls or tackle the mini-gorge upstream before the free-fall.

**Length:** Park and huck

**Hitchability:** No need

**Season:** Winter (typically January to February)

**Camping:** Great camping all around. Downstream on the Klickitat is best

**4WD Needed?** No

**Best Close Food/Beers:** Glenwood Store, The Logs in BZ.

**Quality (out of 5):** About as good as it gets for a clean 70-foot waterfall

**Raft Recommendations:** No

## SHUTTLE DIRECTIONS

No shuttle needed. The falls is located 6 miles east of the town of Glenwood at a small dirt pull-out near the creek **(46.017422, -121.172609)**.

# SUMMIT CREEK

This run is a ridiculous anomaly. At the takeout, the creek looks too small and rocky to even consider paddling. However, not far upstream, the bedrock creek slopes into a kicker falls with a very unique quarter-pipe-like transition. As the story goes, the Wells brothers located Summit from the air and let the cat out of the bag.

In 2009, several of the sport's top paddlers descended on Summit Creek for four exploratory days working out the logistics of the creek's waterfalls and two distinct canyons. If you can access the upper one, it holds some quality whitewater.

For this lower run, the put-in is similar to the takeout. Bump your way down about a mile until a mess of jumbled rocks forces you out of your boat. On the other side is your first drop, which backed by the bottomless horizon line of the Skate Park Drop. This lead-in 20-foot slide sends you into the pool where you can get out and scout the main attraction.

The Skate Park drops around 60 feet with a natural transition more than halfway down. This is the highlight of the run and the reason you're here. Scout well beyond the pool. You basically have one eddy on the left and a small eddy on the right before you enter The Well just downstream.

The Skate Park has been run at various flows, and though higher water seems to be better, the two rapids will start blending together. Scout well and enjoy the flight! The Well starts as a bumpy, sloping 20-foot falls that constricts to about a boat width in the landing zone and then accelerates down the final 20 feet of the slide. If you portage the Well, you can seal-launch in halfway, finish the drop and run the next 30-foot slide around the corner, or keep hiking down and put on at water level.. This slide drops you back into the familiar small rocky creek you would imagine Summit to be. The takeout is about a mile downstream through the bumpy Class III+ creekbed.

*—Ryan Scott*

## THE RUNDOWN

Ride your kayak off of a natural bedrock quarter-pipe and fly into the pool.

**Difficulty:** Class V+

**Gauge:** Visual

**Flow Min-max:** 200-800 cfs, worth a look when the Klickitat at Pitt is over 2,000 cfs

**Gradient:** 300 fpm. Put-in elevation: 1,500 feet

**Takeout:** Just above the confluence with Klickitat River

**Put-in:** 2 miles upstream, see shuttle directions

**Length:** 2 miles

**Hitchability:** Not recommended

**Season:** Spring, winter

**Camping:** Camping is abundant, best on the other side of the Klickitat near Outlet Creek

**4WD Needed?** No, but could come in handy

**Best Close Food/Beers:** Glenwood Inn or Everybody's Brewing in White Salmon

**Quality (out of 5):** 3.5

**Raft Recommendations:** Has been done by Class V rafters, not recommended

## SHUTTLE DIRECTIONS

From state Hwy. 14, take state Hwy. 142 north to Glenwood Hwy. Continue on Glenwood Hwy until Trout Creek Rd., on the right (opposite an old mill). Take Trout Creek Rd. down until you cross over the Klickitat River, where the road splits. Stay right and look for the creek on your right. This is the takeout. Yes, that really is Summit Creek **(45.9877972, -121.1252278)**.

To reach the put-in, continue up the road to the first obvious road on the right (it is dirt/mud, not even gravel, as you head up the hill). Take this right, and in about a quarter-mile you will come to a trench in the middle of the road. From here, either hike to the bottom of the road and put on the creek, or hike straight down the hill to the Skate Park Drop **(45.9987500, -121.1098556)**.

(NOTE: You are on the very edge of the Yakima Indian Reservation. Obey all signs pertaining to reservation laws.)

**5**

# HONORABLE MENTIONS

**Klickitat River—Yakima Reservation to Leidl Campground:**
The Klickitat is an excellent fishing river, as well as offering over 20 miles of intermediate whitewater. It is possible to overnight this trip, with the best camping lower in the river away from the road. The run begins near the Yakama Reservation boundary. This first section is fast, with many islands. Check with local guides for recent wood beta as many side channels are dangerous and fatalities have occurred on the logjams that change yearly. The upper canyon features some immense columnar basalt walls, several fun Class III rapids, and a few small camps. The canyon character changes to grassy hills and oak trees as you move lower and whitewater mellows. The lower canyon is more open with large benches and fun easy whitewater continues at a slower pace. Flows 1400 - 3000 Klickitat at Pitt.

Put-in: 46.025891, -121.160608
Takeout: 45.824848, -121.115409 OR 45.824848, -121.115409

**Klickitat River—Pitt to Fishing Access:**
This is the Columbia Gorge best beginners run with easy access, large eddies, Class II whitewater down to the takeout where Class III Ishy Pishy waits the brave. Even if you're just looking for a mellow and low stress paddle, this is the perfect run. Flows 700-3,000cfs Klickitat at Pitt.

Put-in: 45.794256, -121.202383
Takeout: 45.739982, -121.228853

**Klickitat Rive—Lyle Gorge:**
The alter ego to the upper section, this ornery little canyon Class IV+ (VI) should only be explored by experienced boaters. The upper drop in the canyon, at the top of the concrete fish ladder, looks like it will actually eat you and never looks good at any level. Beware this is a favorite native fishing spot so go when there are no fisherman. There is also fishing debri, undercut walls, tight pinches in the canyon and yearly wood, approach this run with caution. Flows 330-1,000 cfs Klickitat at Pitt

Put-in: 45.739944, -121.228831
Takeout: 45.703628, -121.280766

**Little Klickitat:**
The Little Klickitat rarely runs with enough water for paddlers to enjoy it's arid placement of Class IV+ whitewater, but when the conditions are right don't miss out on this one. Approach the first rapid with caution, scout on the left, as a dangerous sieve hides mid rapid. The rest of the whitewater is action packed Class IV down to the big falls. The falls is a clean 15-foot vertical falls on the left side and a cascading stair step on the right. The rest of the run is fun Class III+ down to the take out, with the occasional epic surf wave on the way. When the Klickitat at Pitt is at 3,500-10,000 the Little Klickitat is in. Class V at high water.

Put-in: 45.810760, -120.925792
Alternate put-in: 45.813455, -120.909450
Takeout: 45.843091, -121.059834

**Canyon Creek (Little Klickitat Tributary)** - Class IV - V
Canyon Creek is an overgrown low volume creek that rarely runs. At the put-in you won't believe that is your creek, but hike down and put on where you see fit. It has a couple short sections of great whitewater, one spectacular waterfall a lot of overgrown brush in between, and an impressive canyon on the lower section of the creek. Take your swimming goggles for the over growth. Flows 7,000-12,000 cfs Klickitat at Pitt.

Put-in: 45.905499, -121.055274
Takeout: 45.848328, -121.042116

**W.F. Major Creek** - Class IV - V (VI)
This is more of an exploratory adventure than a paddling trip, but believe it or not all the falls (with the exception of the lower 40-foot falls and the upper hundred footer) were run in April 2010 by Dan Laham. The WF Gorge has several falls from 10-100 feet on this minute creek that rarely runs. Portaging is possible with difficulty. The main fork of major has several Class IV rapids, most are in the few miles above the take-out. Everything needs to be flooding for this creek to have enough water to run.

Put-in (Be very nice and ask for permission to access):
45.790254, -121.409065
Takeout: 45.714766, -121.351092

# HONORABLE MENTIONS

### Upper Trout Lake Creek:

This stream has been run from the confluence with Mosquito Creek down to the confluence with the White Salmon. The stretch above Cultus Creek is not well documented, but the word is that it has whitewater and wood. The stretch below Cultus has a number of Class IV-V rapids within a good sized creek bed. There are some powerful rapids, some wood issues, a number of boulder gardens and at least one gorged in rapid. Scout often and enjoy. The take out is at the bridge a couple of miles below the confluence with Little Goose Creek. Look for a minimum of 4 feet on the White Salmon foot gauge.

Put-in: 46.078870, -121.682181
Takeout: 46.059056, -121.618257

### Cultus Creek:

The put in for Class IV-V (V+) Cultus Creek is just after it passes under NF-88 via a culvert. The run starts off with some interesting rapids in between log ducks and portages. When the bedrock and a short ledge appear, get out of the river quick! Just downstream is a beautiful 40 footer with a shallow landing, scout and portage left. Shortly below this drop the creek enters a gorge full of tough slides and ledges with some wood hazards. It is easiest to deal with these obstacles at river level down to the confluence with Trout Lake Creek (described above). The best time for this creek is usually in the spring after the snow melts, when the White Salmon is running over 4 feet, and you are able to access the creek again.

Put-in: 46.075270, -121.705973
Takeout: 46.059071, -121.618300

### Lower Trout Lake Creek:

The put-in in for this Class III-IV run is next to Trout Lake Country Inn off Guler Road. It is mostly class III bedrock rapids through the backyards of the residence of Trout Lake. There is one long ledgy Class IV rapid just above the Mt Adams Rd bridge. Below the confluence with the White Salmon the run is splashy down to a low head dam where most people take out. Between here and the Farmlands put in is Holstein Falls, a tough Class V rapid. Look for a minimum of 4 feet on the White Salmon foot gauge.

Put-in: 46.002336, -121.538689
Takeout: 45.988597, -121.492143

### Kenobi Gorge on Little Goose Creek:

The Class V+ Kenobi may hold the steepest runnable mile of whitewater in the Columbia Gorge Region. Less than a mile drops nearly 700 feet over a variety of steep sliding falls and congested boulder gardens. The best put-in is well below Little Goose Creek Falls above the 40-foot Kessel Run Slide. Beggar's Canyon, just before Little Goose creek drops into Trout Lake Creek is an impressive sight! Landslides in this canyon have caused minor problems in the past few years. I'd recommend scouting the run in its entirety before planning to put on this creek. The best time for this creek is usually in the spring after the snow melts, when the White Salmon is running over 4 feet, and you are able to access the creek again.

Put-in: 46.057979, -121.671813
Takeout: 46.059079, -121.618289

### Wind River—Mineral Springs Rd. to Stabler - 5 miles - Class II-III

The Upper Wind is an interesting little float through alternating sections of class II roadside river bed and III bedrock canyon sections. Most of the run is straightforward with the biggest obstacles being wood and overhanging branches. When bank full it can be continuous and difficult to stop. There are a couple of standout rapids, the hardest of which is in a mini gorge. Several routes between boulders are available. Watch out for a left hand bend that leads quickly into a blind and narrow bedrock chute that can gather wood.

Put-in: 45.926426, -121.944845
Takeout: 45.808645, -121.909406

### Panther Creek—PC Campground to Wind River:

Many boulder drops with tight chutes and fast paced action on a small volume creek before dropping into the full flowing lower Wind River. A must-see Class IV-IV+ in the Wind River drainage.

Put-in: 45.771545, -121.849159
Takeout: 45.726336, -121.794902

### Falls Creek—Upper run (Wind River Tributary):

Bring your elbow pads for this Class IV-V+ run. It starts, 1.7 miles up the trail on the slides below the breathtaking Falls Creek Falls and continues through steep boulder gardens down to the foot bridge where the Class IV gorge awaits. The take out is after the gorge, before the trailhead. Or continue down the lower run to the Wind River.

Trailhead: 45.905823, -121.939908
Put-in: 45.910943, -121.918430

### Falls Creek—Lower Run:

A short run with a handful of Class IV rapids set in a mini gorge. The put-in is where the trail crosses the creek less than a half mile after leaving the parking area. Take out where the Wind River crosses under Meadow Creek Rd.

Put-in trailhead: 45.905823, -121.939898
Takeout: 45.902666, -121.952375

### Lava Creek (Little White Tributary):

Lava Creek is a fun little Class III - IV creek that drains into the Little White Salmon in Willard. There are several Class IV drops that only get better with more water.

Put-in: 45.795212, -121.666415
Takeout: 45.779925, -121.628319

### Hamilton Creek (North Bonneville):

Hamilton Creek has seen a limited amount of descents due to the challenging access. There are access roads, but they are usually snowed in. So generally you must hike up the abandoned road and much of it has been washed out making the hike much more difficult. However, for those brave explorers, just over 4 miles up you can put in at a challenging and steep boulder garden set down in a beautiful canyon. The gradient stays consistent and fast with several steeper rapids and a very impressive side falls pouring in on river right about halfway down. There are rumors of more bedrock rapids farther upstream. The upper reaches are yet to be explored for runnable whitewater. It takes a lot of water for this Class IV+ creek to run good. Make sure the creek has a comfortably amount of water in it at the take-out before you hike up.

Put In: 45.645924, -121.985041
Take-out (Hike-up) 45.645924, -121.985041

### White Salmon—Mount Adams Section:

The many wood portages have kept paddlers away, but those who have made the trip report many ledgy Class II-IV (V) rapids between portages in yet another White Salmon River Gorge.

Put-in: 46.105826, -121.605234
Takeout: 45.964237, -121.468886

### Washougal Falls Run:

This is a Class III (V) run that is equally as fun in a raft as a kayak. This section really hits its prime when the Washougal gauge is over 3,000 cfs, and becomes more exciting as flows approach 10,000 cfs. Use good judgement. The run consists of easy floating broken up by four bedrock rapids that are somewhere between large ledges and true waterfalls. There are also a number of logs set in the river for fish habitat that create serious hazards for boaters and resemble low head dams at higher flows. The run can be done without portages, but be cautious. Scout each of the four ledge/falls before putting on, and if in doubt, run far right. The put in is just upstream of the confluence with Stebbins Creek at the obvious Doc's Drop. The take out is at the bridge just below the equally obvious Dougan Falls.

Put-in: 45.693218, -122.124224
Takeout: 45.672933, -122.153854

### Lacamas Creek (Camas):

The Class IV-V Lacamas falls are more of a novelty than anything else and the final slide (Little Norway) is impressive! Up on the hill in the town of Camas (just east of Vancouver), Lacamas Lake drains out of a dam on the south side of the lake on its' final push down to the Columbia River. Flow depends on how much water is coming out of the dam and it changes daily in the winter due to heavy rainfall. But when everything else is running high, check out Lacamas. A popular trail follows the creek from the dam down to below the final falls. The ledge below the dam, Potholes falls, and Little Norway make the run short, sweet, and action packed. You can hike back up to the put-in at the end of the run or continue down to the bridge that crossed the creek. Best season for this creek is in the winter after heavy rain events.

Put-in: 45.603773, -122.406888
Takeout: 45.589303, -122.391526

# OREGON

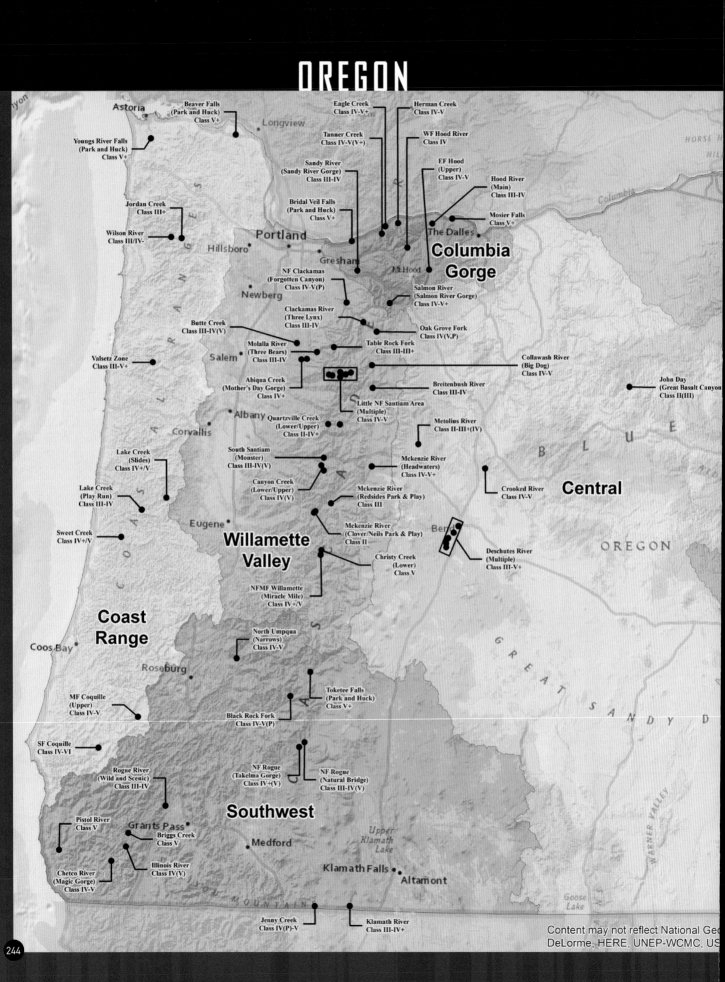

Astoria

Longview

Beaver Falls
(Park and Huck)
Class V+

Eagle Creek
Class IV-V+

Herman Creek
Class IV-V

Youngs River Falls
(Park and Huck)
Class V+

Tanner Creek
Class IV-V(V+)

WF Hood River
Class IV

Sandy River
(Sandy River Gorge)
Class III-IV

EF Hood
(Upper)
Class IV-V

Hood River
(Main)
Class III-IV

Jordan Creek
Class III+

Bridal Veil Falls
(Park and Huck)
Class V+

Mosier Falls
Class V+

Wilson River
Class III/IV-

Portland

Hillsboro

The Dalles

Columbia

Gresham

Columbia
Gorge

Mt.Hood

NF Clackamas
(Forgotten Canyon)
Class IV-V(P)

Salmon River
(Salmon River Gorge)
Class IV-V+

Newberg

Clackamas River
(Three Lynx)
Class III-IV

Oak Grove Fork
Class IV(V,P)

Butte Creek
Class III-IV(V)

Table Rock Fork
Class III-III+

Valsetz Zone
Class III-V+

Molalla River
(Three Bears)
Class III-IV

Collawash River
(Big Dog)
Class IV-V

Salem

John Day
(Great Basalt Canyon)
Class II(III)

Abiqua Creek
(Mother's Day Gorge)
Class IV+

Breitenbush River
Class III-IV

Little NF Santiam Area
(Multiple)
Class IV-V

Albany

Quartzville Creek
(Lower/Upper)
Class II-IV+

Metolius River
Class II-III+(IV)

Corvallis

B  L  U  E

South Santiam
(Monster)
Class III-IV(V)

Mckenzie River
(Headwaters)
Class IV-V+

Lake Creek
(Slides)
Class IV+/V

Canyon Creek
(Lower/Upper)
Class IV(V)

Crooked River
Class IV-V

Central

Lake Creek
(Play Run)
Class III-IV

Mckenzie River
(Redsides Park & Play)
Class III

Eugene

Mckenzie River
(Clover/Neils Park & Play)
Class II

Bend

OREGON

Sweet Creek
Class IV+/V

Willamette
Valley

Christy Creek
(Lower)
Class V

Deschutes River
(Multiple)
Class III-V+

NFMF Willamette
(Miracle Mile)
Class IV+/V

Coast
Range

North Umpqua
(Narrows)
Class IV-V

G  R  E  A  T

S  A  N  D  Y

Coos Bay

Roseburg

MF Coquille
(Upper)
Class IV-V

Toketee Falls
(Park and Huck)
Class V+

Black Rock Fork
Class IV-V(P)

SF Coquille
Class IV-VI

WARNER VALLEY

Rogue River
(Wild and Scenic)
Class III-IV

NF Rogue
(Takelma Gorge)
Class IV+(V)

NF Rogue
(Natural Bridge)
Class III-IV(V)

Pistol River
Class V

Grants Pass

Briggs Creek
Class V

Southwest

Upper
Klamath
Lake

Medford

Chetco River
(Magic Gorge)
Class IV-V

Illinois River
Class IV(V)

Klamath Falls

Altamont

Goose
Lake

Jenny Creek
Class IV(P)-V

Klamath River
Class III-IV+

HORSE
HILL

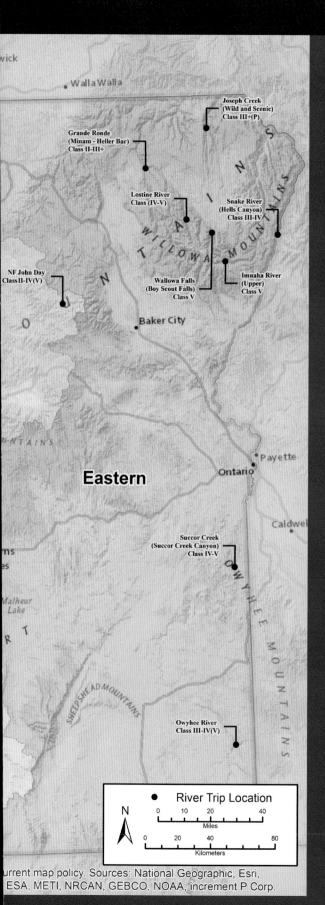

Walla Walla

Joseph Creek
(Wild and Scenic)
Class III+(P)

Grande Ronde
(Minam - Heller Bar)
Class II-III+

Lostine River
Class (IV-V)

Snake River
(Hells Canyon)
Class III-IV

NF John Day
Class II-IV(V)

Wallowa Falls
(Boy Scout Falls)
Class V

Imnaha River
(Upper)
Class V

Baker City

Payette

Ontario

Caldwel

**Eastern**

Succor Creek
(Succor Creek Canyon)
Class IV-V

Malheur
Lake

Owyhee River
Class III-IV(V)

● River Trip Location

N

0   10   20        40
Miles

0      20      40              80
Kilometers

urrent map policy. Sources: National Geographic, Esri,
ESA, METI, NRCAN, GEBCO, NOAA, increment P Corp.

# INTRODUCTION

Oregon is blessed with abundant rain, mild winter weather and a plethora of rivers throughout the state. From classic desert multi-day trips in eastern Oregon to waterfalls in the Gorge, Oregon has a breathtaking diversity of boating opportunities any time of the year. Long known for classic beginner and intermediate rivers, kayakers and rafters have, over the past 15 years, pioneered runs down more advanced river sections, particularly the abundant waterfalls found throughout Oregon. With all the quality boating found within the state, it is still amazing that, except for a few of the more popular trips on certain days, the rivers remain uncrowded and pristine.

There are ample rivers to choose from in any part of the state. Portland or Hood River are usually the bases for waterfall hucking in the Columbia River Gorge or classic Class V trips on the Little White Salmon or the Green Truss section of the White Salmon, as well as intermediate trips like the forks of Hood River. For Oregon options, Portland locals usually focus on the stalwart intermediate trips in the mid–Willamette Valley including Opal Creek and the Breitenbush as well as others to the north like the Sandy, Clackamas, and Molalla Rivers. Some of the best playboating in the state is also within easy reach of Portland. The big waterfalls on the upper McKenzie River as well as classic Class V runs like the North Fork of the Middle Fork of the Willamette are conveniently close to Eugene.

For wild, isolated multi-day trips, the Owyhee River is the crown jewel in Oregon with amazing desert scenery, hot springs, and camping as well as enough whitewater to keep things interesting. If you can catch the snowmelt season right, most trips you won't see hardly anyone there. A different but also Classic trip down the Rogue River in southern Oregon should be on anyone's Oregon list of boating destinations.

With the incredible progression in boating equipment, skill and culture in the past 10-15 years, there is a need for a new kind of guidebook for Oregon that captures the spirit of boating in Oregon. *Paddling Pacific Northwest Whitewater* is that guidebook. While including most of the true classic trips in Oregon, *Paddling Pacific Northwest Whitewater* extensively describes many new, cutting-edge trips and waterfalls that have never been consistently documented in the past. Included are trips that require a large amount of planning and logistics as well as considerable effort to get to the river. Also included is an amazing collection of the biggest waterfalls currently being run in Oregon.

*—Pete Giordano*

# COLUMBIA RIVER GORGE

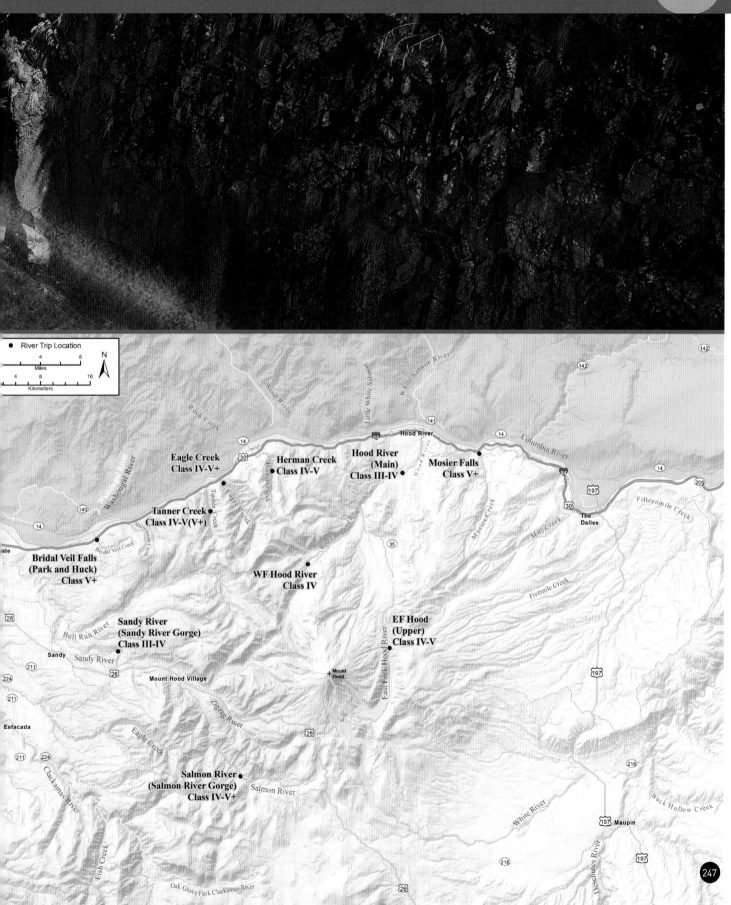

**6**

Eagle Creek
Class IV-V+

Herman Creek
Class IV-V

Hood River
(Main)
Class III-IV

Mosier Falls
Class V+

Tanner Creek
Class IV-V(V+)

Bridal Veil Falls
(Park and Huck)
Class V+

WF Hood River
Class IV

Sandy River
(Sandy River Gorge)
Class III-IV

EF Hood
(Upper)
Class IV-V

Salmon River
(Salmon River Gorge)
Class IV-V+

● River Trip Location

N

Miles

Kilometers

# SANDY RIVER GORGE

Less than an hour east of Portland, just outside of the town of Sandy, the Sandy River originates from Mount Hood's Sandy Glacier. As it descends toward the Columbia River Gorge near Troutdale, Ore., it picks up water from many tributaries including the Zig Zag and Salmon River. A longtime classic for local paddlers, the Sandy has quality Class II-IV sections, stunning scenery, and reliable flows. The gorge section of the Sandy is the best whitewater it offers with great pool-drop Class III-IV.

Toward the old Marmot Dam site, the geology changes, the canyon steepens, large boulders appear frequently in the riverbed, and the rapids increase in size. Not far past the old dam site, paddlers run into their first obstacle. Logs stacked up like pick-up sticks plug the majority of the river, creating a dangerous rapid which most paddlers portage. Shortly downstream of the portage the river canyon starts, with a nice Class II-III called Warm Up. The pool above Warm Up has also been used as an alternate put-in, but the old dam site is recommended for easier access. Paddling downstream in fun Class III rapids, keep your eyes open for play-waves above Boulder Drop, the first of the run's big Class IVs. The rapids down to Boulder Drop can easily be boat-scouted and are less consequential than the Big Four. Sieves, blind slots, shifting wood, sticky holes, and powerful hydraulics make the Big Four (Boulder Drop, Rasp Rock, Drain Hole and Revenue Bridge) more hazardous to paddlers. Scouting these rapids or following someone who knows the run is recommended. Boulder Drop is the first of the Big Four with house-sized boulders creating three blind slots that often catch debris; scout from river-left to check for wood. For Rasp Rock, scout river-left or right and run right or left depending on flow. Drain Hole follows shortly and can be scouted river-right. Here the river makes a dramatic S-turn as the current accelerates then slams into three house-sized boulders then back to the left through a narrow slot against the right wall. This rapid can be scouted and partially portaged on the right. After Drain Hole, the walls peel back and the canyon opens. Don't let your guard down as one of the biggest rapids, Revenue Bridge, awaits just before the takeout. This two-part rapid can be pushy and has the reputation of handing out some beatings. Take out underneath or just after the bridge on river-left and find the trail leading up to the road.

—*Luke Spencer*

## THE RUNDOWN

Represented by local volunteer Keith Jensen, American Whitewater joined the settlement agreement to remove Marmot Dam in 2007. Now paddlers and salmon can both enjoy one of the few free-flowing rivers in the area.

**Difficulty:** Class III-IV

**Gauge:** USGS #14137000—Sandy River near Marmot

**Flow Min-max:** 600-8,000 cfs (can be run down to 200 cfs if desperate)

**Gradient:** 40 fpm. Put-in Elevation: approx. 700 feet

**Takeout:** Revenue Bridge. Park at the small pull-out up the hill back toward Sandy. Room for about 4-5 cars so be sure to carpool.

**Put-in:** By the old Marmot Dam site, look for the abandoned road that leads to the river

**Length:** 6.5 miles

**Hitchability:** Low chances

**Season:** Rainy season and spring/summer runoff

**Camping:** Not close by

**4WD Needed?** No

**Best Close Food/Beers:** Tamale Factory in Sandy

**Quality (out of 5):** 4

**Raft Recommendations:** Yes, smaller boats advised, oar frames not recommended

## SHUTTLE DIRECTIONS

To get to the takeout, follow U.S. Hwy 26 through the town of Sandy. At the east end of town, take a left at the light immediately after the Arco gas station onto SE Ten Eyck Rd., and continue to the Sandy River-Revenue Bridge. Backtrack back up and around the corner to the small gravel pull-out at Ten Eyck & Kubitz **(45.399881, -122.133091)**.

To find the put-in, cross the Sandy and take the first right up SE Marmot Rd., and continue on Marmot Rd. approx. 5.5 miles and look for a gravel road on the right (has an open gate): This is Big Sandy Dam Rd., and it leads down to the old dam site. **(45.407512, -122.235009)**.

# BRIDAL VEIL FALLS

## OF BRIDAL VEIL CREEK

Bridal Veil is a beautiful creek pouring through a tight V-shaped canyon descending over several large falls and complex rapids on the last leg of its push down to the Columbia River. There are a couple things you need to know before running here to put on this creek. Like Eagle Creek, this is another hotspot for tourists. Be as discreet as possible. Only experts paddlers with a good waterfall resume should consider these falls.

From the parking area you can hike down the paved trail to a viewpoint facing the falls. Lower Bridal Veil drops around 125 feet in two spectacular tiers. The first drops 85 feet off a shallow fanned-out veil that tapers in a little toward the bottom and lands in a nice pool. This drop was first run by David Grove in 2001. The left wall wraps around a little, causing a lot of the current to push into the wall and downstream. About 150 feet from the base of this falls, the second tier drops off about 40 feet into a small pool with a narrow exit to the left.

*Continued on page 250*

Keel Brightman

Tony Skrivanek sending Middle Bridal Veil Falls on the first descent in February 2014

# BRIDAL VEIL FALLS

## OF BRIDAL VEIL CREEK

To view the Middle Falls, from the parking area, walk up to the bridge on the historic highway that crosses the creek. Proceed up the west side at water level (obey the No Trespassing signs) a half-mile until you reach the Middle Falls. It drops around 60 feet into a small and deep pool. Remnants of the old logging operation can been seen here as some of the cables that were left behind span the falls. The canyon pinches up and the walls are nearly impossible to get around to access the top of the falls. For that access, you have to drive up Palmer Rd. and hike over to the top of the canyon and down to the falls. Above the falls there has been a big log across the creek that we have used to scout the opposite side of the falls and the launch to run the falls.

The half-mile of the creek from Middle Bridal Veil to the Lower Falls is fast-moving Class IV whitewater with few eddies and a lot of small logs thrown in the mix. The middle falls is the easier of the two. I'd recommend scouting that one first then if you're still fired up consider the lower falls. The mini-gorge above the Middle Falls looks enticing, but it ends in what appears to be an unrunnable drop.

This creek has some impressive history from the late 1800s. It was the site of one of the most intense logging operations in the Northwest. Palmer Mill on the side of Larch Mountain supplied the logs for the lower mill at the base of Bridal Veil Falls. Logs were sent down a wooden flume that was build in and elevated over the creek. Remnants can still be seen along the creekbed in places and higher in the forest along Palmer Rd.

*—Ryan Scott*

### THE RUNDOWN

These waterfalls were once covered and altered by a massive logging operation from the late 1800s and early 1900s.

**Difficulty:** Class V+

**Gauge:** Visual is best. You can estimate from the USGS #14137000—Sandy River near Marmot online gauge or, USGS #14138850 Bull Run River near Multnomah Falls, OR.

**Flow Min-max:** Can be run lower if you are willing to take a hit, but 4,000-8,000 cfs on the Sandy at Marmot gauge or, 1,000 cfs or more on the Bull Run gauge is best.

**Gradient:** Middle Falls drops about 60 feet, Lower Falls drops about 125 feet in two tiers

**Takeout:** Bridal Veil Falls State Park Parking area, Historic Hwy.

**Put-in:** Read description and decide from there

**Length:** .75 miles

**Hitchability:** N/A

**Season:** Spring, fall, winter

**Camping:** Pay camping sites are available east on the Historic Hwy at Ainsworth State Park

**4WD Needed?** No

**Best Close Food/Beers:** McMenamin's Edgefield in Troutdale

**Quality (out of 5):** 3.5

**Raft Recommendations:** Not recommended

### SHUTTLE DIRECTIONS

From I-84 (eastbound only) take Exit 28. Take a right at both stop signs and head back to the west on the Historic Hwy. for about a mile to the Bridal Veil State Park parking area, and start from here **(45.553403, -122.182825)**.

To make it to the top of the Middle Falls, head back west on the Historic Hwy. about a half-mile to Palmer Rd. on the right. Continue up Palmer about a mile until you see a small pull-out on the right with a semi flat section off to the right in the woods **(45.549883, -122.176231)**. From here, hike toward the creek and angle downstream before you drop into the canyon. It may take a few minutes to get your bearings on the fall: There is a very small tributary pouring in just downstream of the falls. If you reach that while hiking, you have gone a little too far.

# TANNER CREEK

anner Creek starts with tight, steep boulder gardens. It eventually transitions to bedrock with three nice falls between 10 and 40 feet. It then enters a frightening gorge with big falls guarding both the entrance and exit. Below this gorge, the stream sieves through a few questionable boulder rapids before easing down to the takeout. It is possible to hike out before this final gorge.

From the power lines at the put-in, boulder gardens start right away, continuing for a mile or so. Be on the lookout for wood, though most everything goes. If the water is low, this part won't be much fun. About a mile into the run, a small bedrock ledge/slide presents itself as the river turns right; be sure to grab an eddy on

the left to scout this unique falls. Volition Falls drops 10 feet before transitioning to flat, then ramps up and over a 5-foot ledge into a hole. The transition looks abrupt, but has been run successfully on the left. Below are more boulder gardens, including the largest non-falls rapid on the run, Coppertone, which is marked by a large vertical wall on river-left. The next hazard is a long slide ending in a logjam; be cautious and make sure to eddy-out above it on the left to scout. Just downstream is the second waterfall named Caesura Falls. This drop has two options: a picture-perfect 10-foot deep-water boof in the middle, or a narrow chute on the right.

*Continued on page 252*

Paul Thomson
Lucas Rietman running Sundance Falls deep in the Tanner Gorge

# TANNER CREEK

Shortly below Caesura is Sundance Falls, a 40-foot falls with multiple lines—take your pick! Exiting the pool below Sundance is the crux of the run. A small rapid bends left and enters Tanner Creek Gorge, a Class V-VI section of whitewater locked into a vertical-walled gorge. A confident boater will be able to find a way to stop partway down the Class III entrance rapid on the right bank, and once that first boater is out, then pull his/her buddies onto shore. The consequences of a mistake here are severe and this location is the point of egress for paddlers not interested in the gorge downstream. A portage around this 0.2-mile-long gorge may be possible, but at the time of press, it has never been done with a boat.

To hike out at the head of the gorge, walk perpendicular to the stream until reaching a cliff band. Follow it upstream until it is possible to scramble up the hill—a little over 1,000 vertical feet in a difficult third of a mile before reaching the road. If your vehicle is there, your day is over. If you hiked in, it is another two miles downhill on the road before you can relax. If running Tanner Creek Gorge is something you are capable of, a guidebook description is not something you need. What does the gorge hold? A 60-foot entrance falls (Swaawa) and an 80-foot exit falls are linked together by a boxed-in series of slots, ledges and lesser waterfalls. From the base of the final 80-footer (Wahclella Falls), there is a series of dubious boulder rapids before the stream eases to Class II-III with intermittent wood before reaching the parking lot just before Tanner Creek crosses under Interstate 84.

*—Jacob Cruser*

## THE RUNDOWN

Wachlella Falls has been run, but at the time of press, the gorge above it has not seen a descent.

**Difficulty:** Class IV-V (V+/VI or P)

**Gauge:** Visual is best, estimate based off the Bull Run gauge USGS #14138850—Bull Run River Near Multnomah Falls, OR

**Flow Min-max:** Around 1,000 cfs on the Bull Run gauge is a lower, but enjoyable flow (which was the level the photos on the adjacent pages were taken).

**Gradient:** 320 fpm above Wachlella Gorge

**Takeout:** Wachlella Gorge or trailhead parking area

**Put-in:** Power lines

**Length:** 2.5 miles (1.5 to upper takeout)

**Hitchability:** Not viable

**Season:** Rainy

**Camping:** Yes

**4WD Needed?** No

**Best Close Food/Beers:** Cascade Locks

**Quality (out of 5):** 4—could be the run of a lifetime if Wachlella Gorge is in the cards

**Raft Recommendations:** No recommendations

## SHUTTLE DIRECTIONS

Vehicle access is not usually available to paddlers. Most boaters should plan on hiking 4 miles in, with various and challenging egress options waiting at the end. From the I-84 bridge over the Sandy River in Troutdale, drive 22.4 miles east on I-84 to the Bonneville Dam exit (#40). Turn right to drop a car at the takeout **(45.630046, -121.954106)**. After leaving a vehicle, drive back toward the freeway, taking a right before the onramp onto Star Route. In less than a quarter-mile there will be a road going off to the right, next to a water tower. (The gate on it is usually locked.) Travel up this road just under 4 miles, the put-in is where the power lines cross the creek **(45.597023, -121.945299)**. The upper takeout is just upstream of the second tributary you cross traveling up the gravel access road **(45.615611, -121.951391)**.

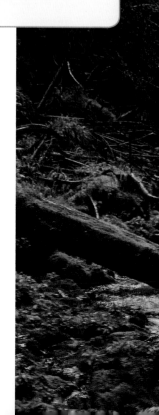

Paul Thomson

Sundance falls from the lip of Swaawa Falls

# EAGLE CREEK

Eagle Creek is a breathtakingly beautiful run! From the hike in to the unique concentration of waterfalls in this pristine gorge, it is one of the Pacific Northwest's most awe-inspiring canyons. The whitewater on the run has progressed with the local paddling scene. At first, paddlers ventured up to run Punchbowl Falls and hike back out. Later, hiking two miles up to Skoonichuck Falls was added by local boater Tim Gross. The Priestley brothers hiked another two miles up with their kayaks and found yet another large runnable waterfall (Grand Union Falls), plus two more miles of fun whitewater. In May 2004, David Grove proved Eagle Creek could be run from the put-in to the takeout at river level when he ran 80-plus-foot Metlako Falls. After several years Metlako became a destination for training on large waterfalls. Now it's not uncommon for expert paddlers to hike either four or six miles up and run all the major falls on Eagle Creek.

The Eagle Creek Trail follows the creek up, up, and up, climbing above the gorge on a narrow (very narrow and cliffed out in places) trail that has been notched into the wall in several spots on the trail. At about 1.5 miles is Metlako Falls, visible from a downstream viewpoint.

Two miles in is Punchbowl Falls. Continuing upstream, glimpses of the canyon appear below. At High Bridge, the canyon locks into bedrock walls with a rapid leading into and exiting it. Continue upstream another three-quarters of a mile to Skoonichuck Falls. This is the standard put-in. Paddlers looking for a little more action can continue up another two miles to the confluence with the East Fork and West Fork (just downstream of Tunnel Falls). Below the confluence, Eagle Creek pours over 45-foot Grand Union Falls. If you've hiked your boat this far, this is your destination. Scout well and take flight!

The next two miles downstream of Grand Union consists of great read-and-run Class III+ and IV- boulder rapids down to Skoonichuck Falls, which drops about 35 feet into a narrow landing zone. It then pushes hard off the next 15-foot falls just 30 feet from the base of the first one. This action-packed double-set is usually run down the center, then quickly moving left off the final drop. From the pool below, the creek quickly heads toward vertical walls and a semi-blind drop. These rapids have a nearly blind exit, dropping into the right wall and abruptly turning left and out of sight—good news that there's a pool just past where you can see.

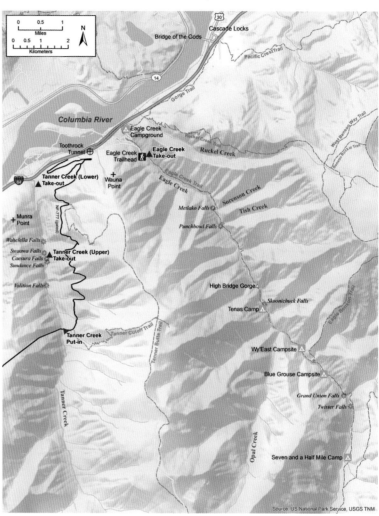

Next is the rapid you could scout upstream of High Bridge. It twists and spits you out into the narrow and deep hallway that exits above a tight pour-over against the right wall. This rapid has an undercut cave on the right that gets bad at high flows; scout on the left. The next mile or so consists of Class III+ boat-scoutable rapids with the occasional log hazard. The canyon starts to close in again and there's a tight 8-foot drop into a deep pool letting you know to scout on the left for Punchbowl Falls.

Punchbowl is one of the most picturesque waterfalls in the Columbia River Gorge (cover shot). The pool above the falls agitates the water forcing it out and into the left wall, folding the falls as it spouts 35 feet out into the large Punchbowl cauldron. The folding lip of the falls tends to pre-aerate the water before it

*Continued on page 256*

6

# EAGLE CREEK

## THE RUNDOWN

This canyon would be inaccessible if is wasn't for the Civilian Conservation Corps and the Works Progress Administration originally cutting the trail for the Pacific Crest Trail in the 1930s.

**Difficulty:** Class IV-V+

**Gauge:** Visual is best, but the USGS #14138850— BULL RUN RIVER NEAR MULTNOMAH FALLS, OR is commonly used as an estimate.

**Flow Min-max:** 400-1,000 cfs; 550-750 is ideal for connecting all the drops. It used to be that Skoonichuck did not get run at higher flows, but a new line has been opened up on the left. Also, 600- 900 is better for Metlako since at low flows the green water provides a huge hit, and at high flows the pool becomes hazardous.  However, the whole river could still be (and mostly has been) done at the entire range.

**Gradient:** 185 fpm, waterfall pool-drop

**Takeout:** Eagle Creek parking area

**Put-in:** Skoonickchuck Falls, or hike another 2 miles up to the East Fork-West Fork confluence

**Length:** 4-6 miles

**Hitchability:** No shuttle, you earn your paddle strokes by hiking to the top of this one.

**Season:** Spring, winter (beware of icy winter conditions on the trail!)

**Camping:** Eagle Creek Campground near the takeout. There is a great campsite at and above Skoonichuck Falls, if you want to hike in the night before.

**4WD Needed?** Not unless snow is on the ground.

**Best Close Food/Beers:** Thunder Island Brewing in Cascade Locks or McMenamins Edgefield in Troutdale for something closer to Portland

**Quality (out of 5):** 4.5

**Raft Recommendations:** Has been done by Class V rafters, not recommended

⬜ Charlie Munsey

👁 David Grove on the first descent of Metlako, May 2004

plunges into the pool, making the landing on this falls a harder hit than most falls around this height. Just downstream of Punchbowl, around the corner is the access trail up to the main trail. Hike out here if you don't want to get anywhere close to Metlako Falls. Little Punchbowl (15 feet) is just downstream before the canyon tightens up above Metlako.

Metlako pours out in a firehose fashion in a 90-degree turn in the canyon. The geology here is very impressive. Metlako has been called one of the easiest 80-foot waterfalls to run considering the straightforward approach, but it is very tall! Pool to pool it is about 100 feet. Downstream of Metlako, a rapid drops about 12 feet in two steps against the right wall. The scout/portage is on the left. Downstream, the creek continues through Class III+ shallow boulder rapids back to the parking area.

—*Ryan Scott*

## SHUTTLE DIRECTIONS

Take I-84 to Exit 41 (an eastbound exit only) to Eagle Creek National Fish Hatchery. Drive back to the trailhead and find a parking spot **(45.636649, -121.919735)**. The put-in is 4 miles up the trail at Sckoonichuck Falls **(45.604545, -121.880355)** or add another two miles on by hiking up to Grand Union Falls and putting on **(45.584060, -121.853508)**.

One of the last Columbia River Gorge creeks to be explored between Portland and Hood River, Herman Creek didn't see kayak exploration until 2013—and the creek has remained in relative obscurity with no known descents since. Just getting to the put-in requires good cardio fitness and unwavering determination with a dose of self-inflicted torture. For those up to the challenge, efforts will be rewarded with clean waterfalls, fun boulder gardens, pristine wilderness, and scenery matched only by other Gorge runs like Eagle Creek. After the ascent from the trailhead up to Casey Creek Junction, paddlers will find a beautiful spot to rest and refuel before making the descent down the spur trail to the East Branch-West Branch confluence put-in.

A short bushwack back up the East Branch allows kayakers to scout and run No. 1 and No. 2 of the triple falls (Lost Falls) on the East Fork. Not long after the East-West confluence, the creek changes character and Class III boulder gardens give way to bedrock basalt that signals paddlers that a scout is in order. A vertical-walled gorge lies below the intimidating horizon line created by Entrance Drop. This 35-foot double-falls drops paddlers into the heart of Abandoned Gorge. Escaping this gorge is not an option, paddlers must exit out the bottom by running Exit Drop. After the gorge the creek rushes down Class III-IV whitewater with boulder gardens and small bedrock ledges. A small but fun falls named Hijacked lies in the section below the gorge. Not far below Hijacked is a footbridge over Herman Creek signaling the final stretch above the takeout at Forest Lane Rd. Don't forget this last stretch's portage: around a boulder sieve that leads to a long Class IV boulder garden before the gradient subsides and the fish hatchery comes into view. Be advised there is a small weir at the fish hatchery (which can be run) and its operators aren't keen on paddlers running it. The takeout bridge will come into sight just past the weir.

—Luke Spencer

## THE RUNDOWN

Herman Creek has the largest surviving forest of old-growth fir, cedar, and hemlock left in the Columbia Gorge.

**Difficulty:** Class IV-V

**Gauge:** Visual, the creek should appear boatable at the bridge

**Flow Min-max:** 150-350 cfs

**Gradient:** 200 fpm. Put-in elevation: 1,125 feet

**Takeout:** Bridge over Herman Creek on Forest Lane Rd. Take out just before the bridge.

**Put-in:** Hike starts at the Herman Creek Trailhead. Ascend to Casey Creek Junction then descend on spur trail to East Branch-West Branch confluence.

**Length:** 5 miles

**Hitchability:** No

**Season:** Rainy, spring runoff

**Camping:** Yes, Herman Creek Campground if open

**4WD Needed?** No

**Best Close Food/Beers:** Thunder Island Brewing, Cascade Locks

**Quality (out of 5):** 4

**Raft Recommendations:** No Rafts

## SHUTTLE DIRECTIONS

From Portland, take I-84 east to Cascade Locks, Exit # 44. Drive under I-84 and through town 1.8 miles to the eastbound entrance ramp. From the stop sign, continue east 1.6 miles toward Oxbow Fish Hatchery, then on to Herman Creek Campground and the takeout **(45.678967, -121.860650)**. Start the demanding hike at the Herman Creek Trailhead, then ascend to Casey Creek Junction. From the junction, follow the small spur trail that leads down into the canyon and to the East Branch-West Branch confluence **(45.653995, -121.816424)**. Backtrack up the East Fork to descend the falls on the East Branch.

Keel Brightman

Willie Illingsworth dropping into the Abandoned Gorge

# THE HOOD RIVER

Along with the Middle White Salmon across the Columbia in Washington, Hood River is one of the primary intermediate river trips in the Columbia Gorge. Lacking any real amount of bedrock in the riverbed, Hood River still has an enjoyable mix of long, steep boulder gardens. The river is away from the road and other development for much of the trip, and although lacking any dramatic gorge scenery, still provides boaters with ample scenic views that make the trip very worthwhile. With lots of other, more dramatic runs in the Columbia River Gorge, it is easy to overlook Hood River. But for up-and-coming intermediate boaters, it remains one of the area's best skill-building trips.

If boaters choose to putin on the East Fork of Hood about a mile above the confluence with the West Fork, there are several really fun rapids set in a tight gorge. Recent floods have changed this section considerably by channelizing the riverbed and making the rapids much cleaner than in the past. From the confluence with the WF, the riverbed widens and flattens, so many of the rapids are easy to scout from a boat. At high water this first section still can pack a punch with a few large holes to avoid, but in general, it is a good way to get a feel for the river and work on the moves required farther downstream.

As boaters approach Tucker Park on the right, about a mile or so above Tucker Bridge, the gradient picks up considerably and several excellent, long boulder gardens challenge paddlers. The first of these rapids, Island, is one the biggest, and can be recognized by the water pipe crossing the river, a house on the right and two distinct channels to choose. Most boaters will want to stay right and run the main rapid which zigzags through some strong currents and holes. There is a brief recovery pool at the bottom before the river enters the next steep rapid around the corner. This rapid takes a sharp turn to the right while pushing into a wall, which intimidate many paddlers—it is more forgiving than it appears. There are several more long boulder gardens downstream that are difficult to scout, but generally can be run successfully by making some strong, decisive moves to avoid rocks or holes.

The river below Tucker Bridge eases off a bit, although there are still some exciting rapids to contend with until the river finally flattens completely within a half-mile of the takeout in Hood River. This section is generally more shallow than the section upstream, so most paddlers opt to only run it when the water is at a healthy high level. Still, with the removal of Powerdale Dam in 2010, this section of the river is free-flowing and it is getting more popular with beginning boaters as well as standup paddlers training for harder runs.

—*Pete Giordano*

## THE RUNDOWN

When the dam below Tucker Bridge was removed, the riverbed was reshaped to make a new rapid.

**Difficulty:** Class III+

**Gauge:** USGS #14120000— HOOD RIVER AT TUCKER BRIDGE, NEAR HOOD RIVER

**Flow Min-max:** 1,000-5,000 cfs

**Gradient:** 60 fpm

**Takeout:** Tucker Bridge or Hood River

**Put-in:** Dee

**Length:** 12.5 miles

**Hitchability:** Decent from Tucker Bridge, poor from Hood River

**Season:** November to May

**Camping:** Yes

**4WD Needed?** No

**Best Close Food/Beers:** Big Horse Brew Pub, Hood River

**Quality (out of 5):** 4

**Raft Recommendations:** Very raftable but more fun at higher water

## SHUTTLE DIRECTIONS

There are two possible takeouts for Hood River. The lowest takeout is where Hood River meets the Columbia on the north side of the town. There is an undeveloped parking area on the west side of the river off 1st Avenue **(45.714515, -121.508434)**, as well as in Port Marine Park on the east side of the river near the footbridge crossing. The upper takeout is at Tucker Bridge approximately 10 miles south of Hood River on Tucker Rd. Take 13th St., south out of town, which turns into Tucker Rd. There is limited parking here so be polite **(45.654919, -121.548767)**.

To reach the put-in, continue south on Tucker Rd. and follow the signs to Dee on the Dee Hwy. Once in Dee you'll have to decide where to access the river. Most of the land around the river is privately owned although largely undeveloped. There is access upstream and downstream of the bridge on the west side of the bridge but it's helpful to inquire locally about the current access situation **(45.589604, -121.629062)**. There is public access at the confluence of the West Fork and East Fork which is just downstream of the usual takeout for the West Fork run. The confluence can be reached by hiking down a half-mile on a trail at Punchbowl Falls.

# WEST FORK OF THE HOOD RIVER

The West Fork of Hood River is one of those special trips that brings boaters back year after year. With forgiving, fun rapids and great scenery, the WF appeals to boaters with a wide range of abilities. More experienced boaters should aim for higher water levels which increase the difficulty level and challenge. The rapids are generally wide-open boulder gardens with multiple lines except for a few rapids that develop large holes.

The run's first three miles contain two gorge sections with wonderfully fun, technical Class III-IV ledges separated by a flatter section. The scenery is top-notch. Shortly after the second gorge begins, there is a tough, Class V rapid. The only reasonable portage option is up the hill on the left at the lip of the rapid. This portage will take you to the base of the gorge at a second, easier rapid. From here the river mellows for a bit and gains water as the Lake Branch Fork enters on the left.

More boulder gardens continue as the river alternates between beautiful, basalt walls and more open canyon scenery. About three miles from the Lake Branch is a dangerous fish ladder that blocks the entire width of the river—stay on the lookout for an intake structure a few hundred yards above the fish ladder and for a small eddy on the left to portage.

The biggest rapids are below the fish ladder, particularly the first long boulder garden. Eddies can be small, and at high water the rapids run together with few places to stop. Recovering gear can be very difficult if someone has problems. Despite the increased difficulty, hazards are fairly minimal so the fun factor is pretty high. The last half-mile of the run is set in a deep gorge with several entertaining rapids, the last of which can be seen from the bridge at the takeout. Most paddlers choose to take out on the right before Punchbowl Falls unless they are continuing downstream onto the main Hood River run, though Punchbowl Falls can be a fun end of the trip for some boaters. The falls is just short of ten feet with a powerful hydraulic in the center. It has been boofed successfully on the left. There is a large pool below.

—Pete Giordano

## SHUTTLE DIRECTIONS

From the town of Hood River, travel south on 13th St., which turns into 12th St./Tucker Rd. Shortly after crossing Hood River, turn right to stay on Dee Hwy. In 6.5 miles, turn right again and follow the road across the East Fork of Hood River in Dee. Turn right on Punchbowl Rd., and travel just over a mile to a pull-out on the right. There is a trail down an old road to scout Punchbowl Falls as well as the trail up from the river **(45.601336, -121.635865)**. At one time this site was owned by PacifiCorp, but Western Rivers Conservancy helped paddlers and fishermen transfer it to public ownership. The last rapid of the run can be seen looking upstream from the bridge around the corner.

To reach the put-in, return to the junction of Punchbowl Rd. and Lost Lake Rd. and continue straight on Lost Lake Rd. Travel about 8 miles to National Forest Rd. 18 and turn left. There is access at the bridge across the river after about a mile. There is an alternate put-in trail on the left about 5.6 miles from the junction, just after crossing the Lake Branch Fork of Hood River **(45.525715, -121.742694)**.

## THE RUNDOWN

Keep paddling past the takeout and add on the main Hood run.

**Difficulty:** Class IV

**Gauge:** USGS #14120000—HOOD RIVER AT TUCKER BRIDGE, NEAR HOOD RIVER

**Flow Min-max:** 4 cfs

**Gradient:** 80 fpm

**Takeout:** Punchbowl Falls

**Put-in:** National Forest Road 18

**Length:** 8 miles

**Hitchability:** Poor

**Season:** November to May

**Camping:** Yes

**4WD Needed?** No

**Best Close Food/Beers:** Solera Brewery in Mount Hood/Parkdale

**Quality (out of 5):** 4

**Raft Recommendations:** Very raftable although higher water is more fun

A relationship with the Upper East Fork Hood is like dating twin sisters. The good sister shows up for some amazing days late in May when the spring snowpack on Mount Hood taps out from 90-degree heat. This sister is solid Class IV with moderate flows and great paddling in warm sunshine. But it is the East Fork's evil twin sister that is notorious for skyrocketing gauges and complete rebellion. The evil sister shows up when warm Pacific storms drop rain on the midwinter snowpack, and she quickly throws down miles of nonstop, rowdy Class IV+ paddling at fluctuating levels. This sister has few inhibitions and will gladly hand out pain to the unsuspecting.

There is only a vague similarity in the rapids from year to year because the riverbed is volcanic sand and boulders, all of which move around during really high water. New boulders feed into the river from scree slopes on the east bank, so the run changes often, leaving paddlers scratching their heads about the old lines. But that constant change is unique to only this run, and it is what makes the East Fork so intriguing. Each year we find a new river in some respect, and it is always as good as the year before.

For those same reasons, there are no reliable rapids to catalog. The gradient tells the story and can be seen from the road. The steep paddling starts near the Polallie Trailhead, the most popular put-in, which is just above the Cooper Spur turnoff. The first twisting rapid, called the Worm, was named for a truck-sized culvert that was twisted by a flood and wedged into the top moves of the S-turn. But even that massive culvert simply disappeared one year. From the Worm down is a matrix of continuous drops, some quite steep, in a subalpine setting. The first few miles are always the steepest, simply pounding down the valley in one long rapid.

To say the river backs off a bit is true, but misleading, since blind, steep drops continue until two-thirds of the way where paddlers head into the forest above Routson Park. The river remains consistent, but is also more prone to sweepers and wood. Portages come and go and scrambling for eddies is common.

For seasoned paddlers, this run is serious entertainment for mile after mile, and East Fork paddling is as good as it gets if you catch it just right. If you catch it wrong, however, either sister will punish you. The river is a consistently shallow blur of white as it cascades over sharp and misaligned boulders. The sisters mock the unfortunate by stealing gear and keeping runaway boats pinned until the levels drop. Consider the long boulder garden on the West Fork Hood, and then think about it lasting for miles, and you will start to understand the Upper East Fork.

*—Ron Reynier*

## THE RUNDOWN

Combines well with a morning of powder skiing.

**Difficulty:** Class IV-V

**Length:** 5-6 miles

**Gauge:** USGS #14120000— HOOD RIVER AT TUCKER BRIDGE, NEAR HOOD RIVER

**Hitchability:** OK

**Season:** Winter, late spring

**Flow Min-max:** 4.4 feet in May, 6.5 feet in winter; up to 8.5 feet (Class V)

**Camping:** Routson Park (spring only)

**Gradient:** 155+ fpm

**4WD Needed?** No

**Takeout:** State Hwy. 35 bridge, 18.5 miles south of Hood River

**Best Close Food/Beers:** Solera Brewery

**Put-in:** Sherwood Campground, lower bridge or Polallie Trailhead

**Quality (out of 5):** 5 in the sunshine

**Raft Recommendations:** Class V R-2 paddlers only at higher flows

## SHUTTLE DIRECTIONS

The takeout is roadside at the state Hwy 35 bridge upstream of the Dog River parking area, so multiple laps are easy, and, unlike many higher elevation rivers, the run is accessible all winter because OR 35 is plowed **(45.465111, -121.569273)**. To get to the putin **(45.400654, -121.570818)** travel upstream on Hwy 35 from the takeout bridge, just over 5 miles to a parking area on the right, some boaters put in at the bridge ½ mile below this parking area. The best summer levels are 4.4 feet to the maximum melt at 5 feet on the Tucker Bridge gauge. The gauge typically ramps up over a period of really hot days and the river gets surprisingly filled. A winter gauge reading of 6.5 feet and rain on the mountain is ideal, similar to 4.5 in the summer, though it gets progressively harder as the river heads to 7 and 8 feet, jumping a Class in difficulty. Higher than 8 feet is another story, and there are plenty of bad stories out there.

The Salmon River, fed by Palmer Glacier, gently flows south out of Salmon River Meadows toward a deep forest. With a westerly turn, the Salmon starts dropping over the spectacular waterfalls of the Salmon River Gorge, locked between dark vertical basalt walls. Moss-covered old-growth conifers surround the landscape, leaving much to the imagination. Be prepared: The access and terrain can be challenging.

The run starts at the takeout (see map on page 237). Choose whether to hike six miles up a gradual trail or drive for a couple hours to Linney Creek Campground before hiking in two miles. After taking both approaches many times, I prefer hiking up from the bottom. It takes about the same amount of time and you don't have a four-hour shuttle when your done.

Emerging from the forested hike gets you riverside at Split Falls, which like the name suggests, splits into two separate veils, the left unrunnable due to wood. The right split has a busy and twisting lead-in to a 20-foot spouting waterfall into a deep pool. The next rapids are usually run down the middle with an immediate portage around a small logjam. The next mile gently cruises through relaxing Class II until you approach Little Niagara. The ledge drop above is separated into four tight channels; all go with various results. Little Niagara has a fast lead-in to an abrupt 12-foot ledge. Stay left, the center to right of the falls pours onto a nasty, sharp rock slab.

Next, the river drops into a dark and ominous gorge starting with Vanishing Falls. Vanishing has a lot going on: Back-cut cave on the left, a pocket wall on the right, and no good takeoff options on the lip. Scout and portage on the right. The river pushes through vertical walls downstream and over the exit ledge. Take this mini-gorge one drop at a time and set safety as needed. Getting around this gorge also means going through it. If you don't like Vanishing Falls you need to do a throw-and-go into the pool or find a friendly place to seal-launch back in.

After you exit Vanishing Gorge, one more Class IV rapid appears before Frustration Falls. To scout Frustration, get creative on the right side as the easiest route is usually through the cave. Three tiers drop around 75 feet over dark basalt stepping and streaming down into the abyss. Frustration is the deciding factor on how high you can safely paddle this run. Once you drop in on the standard river-left, right, right line and land off the bottom 40-foot falls you are surrounded by waterfalls—a very special place to sit in your kayak! Paddling downstream, avoid the river-left shoulder falls that nearly blocks off the canyon (this is where high water can block the exit to Frustration). Just outside the veil you can eddy out on river-left to scout the next 25-foot falls, just above Final Falls.

Keel Brightman

Ryan Scott below Final Falls

*Continued on page 264*

# SALMON RIVER GORGE

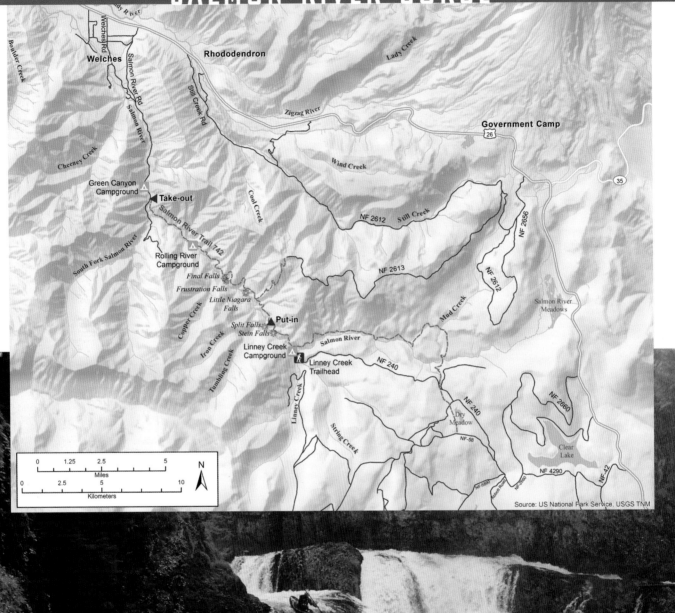

Final is completely cliffed out just downstream of the falls leaving no option to hike around and put back on at river level. So, think about running it, think about the jump, or break out the rappel gear. The pool below brings a huge sense of accomplishment! But don't let your guard down yet. Class IV boulder gardens stack up quick, creating a very tight cluster of boulders where paddlers have pinned in unexpected sieves. The river gradually tapers off and another 3 miles Class II-III whitewater carry you to the takeout bridge.

—*Ryan Scott*

Scott Baker

Paddlers descending Frustration Falls

## SHUTTLE DIRECTIONS

For the takeout, drive U.S. Hwy. 26 from Portland to Sandy and proceed 17 miles to a right turn on E. Salmon River Rd. Go 2 miles and stay straight, merging into E. Welches Rd., to the takeout bridge. The Salmon River Trail #742 is on river-left before you cross the bridge. From Hood River, drive south on state Hwy. 35 toward Mount Hood for 38.2 miles and merge onto U.S. 26 west. In 14.4 miles, turn left onto E. Salmon River Rd. In 2 miles, merge into E. Welches Rd., and head 3 miles to the takeout bridge **(45.277855, -121.939831)**.

For the put-in, drive back to U.S. 26 and head east 22.8 miles to a right turn onto NF-42/Oregon Skyline Road (check your distances as some of these turns are unmarked). Go 1.1 miles and take a right on an unmarked road (NF 4290 on the map). Go 2.5 miles and take a left onto NF-2660. In 0.9 miles, this runs into NF-58/Abbott Rd. Stay right at both junctions and go 0.6 miles to a right turn on NF-240. Proceed 2.1 miles to a split and stay right following 240. In a half-mile stay left at another split in the road, following 240 to the Linney Creek Campground, with your trail down to the Salmon, about 5 miles down the bumpy road **(45.216865, -121.856135)**.

Linney Creek Trail access: A short distance into this hike you have to ford the Salmon River and continue downstream. Then about a mile in, the trail starts to climb above the canyon. Nearing two miles you can hear Stein Falls in the canyon far below you (Stein is very large and very un-runnable, make sure you have climbing gear if you put in above this drop). Continue down the trail another half-mile until you see a small grassy meadow down to the left. Follow the trail down as it wraps around the cliffs and drops you into the forest above Split Falls. Use the sound of the falls to guide you to the put-in. There are a handful of rapids between Stein Falls and Split Falls, though many are too tight and un-runnable with little fun factor.

To the put-in via takeout trail, hike up about 6 miles to the Split Falls access trail. On the way up you hike in and out of many small tributaries. There are only a couple places with small grass meadows off to the side of the trail, but the one at Split is easy to locate because you have to hike down (right) off the trail a little to get out from under the forest canopy. Follow the trail down as it wraps around the cliffs and drops you into the forest above Split Falls. From here use the sound of the falls to guide you to the put-in **(45.228721, -121.875219)**.

Keel Brightman

Jay Gifford below Frustration

# SALMON RIVER GORGE

### THE RUNDOWN

Final Falls is the canyon's exit crux with no water-level portage option. Paddle off the falls, jump the 70-foot cliff or rappel to get out of the canyon.

**Difficulty:** Class IV-V+

**Gauge:** Visual is best. Worth a look when USGS #14137000—Sandy River near Marmot gauge reads 500-1,000 cfs during snowmelt, or 1,000-1,500 cfs when the tributaries still have a little water.

**Flow Min-max:** The flow at the takeout looks a little deceiving. The rapid upstream of the takeout bridge should look a little on the low side, but easy to paddle down. If it looks like high water, then the gorge's constriction at Frustration will likely be closed out and unrunnable. Go with a local if possible or take the time to hike in and scout the exit to Frustration Falls ahead of time.

**Gradient:** Pool-drop nature, the mile from Little Niagara to below Final Falls drops over 500 feet

**Takeout:** Bridge over the Salmon River on E. Welches Rd.

**Put-in:** Split Falls, 6 miles above the takeout

**Length:** 6 miles

**Hitchability:** No

**Season:** Spring

**Camping:** Great camping at the takeout and several hike-in sites on the hike up from the takeout. Great camping at Linney Creek Campground as well.

**4WD Needed?** Not necessary, but handy

**Best Close Food/Beers:** Mount Hood Brewing Company in Government Camp

**Quality (out of 5):** 4.5

**Raft Recommendations:** Has been done by Class V rafters, not recommended

**Upper Sandy:** Putting in at McNeil Campground, this continuous Class IV run, if it's free of wood, can be quite fun and can be paddled at higher levels (with a corresponding increase in difficulty). Below the Lolo Pass bridge (a possible takeout), it's Class II-III down to the old Marmot dam site, aside from one fun Class IV near Alder Creek. Minimum flow: 1,500 (Sandy gauge at Marmot).

Takeout: 45.399306, -122.137086
Put-n: 45.384614, -121.871902

**Bull Run:** Since this river supplies drinking water for Portland, the Class III-IV(V) stretch from the lowest reservoir to Laughing Water Creek is illegal. The stretch from the powerhouse to Dodge Park has a handful of good Class III rapids and provides a great training ground, especially when the slalom gates are set up just below the powerhouse. Looking for a longer day? Continue down the Sandy River to a boat ramp in Oxbow Park for 7 more miles of Class II-III paddling (45.497967, -122.291932). Flow minimum-max: 50-10,000 cfs; 200-3,000 cfs recommended.

Takeout: 45.444654, -122.248661
Put-in: 45.428314, -122.232972

**Salmon:** Below the mighty Salmon River Canyon is a nice Class II-III scenic float —the kind of run for people who love kayaking for the sake of kayaking. If you are looking for challenging whitewater, head elsewhere. The Salmon can be run at a wide flow range. Recommended flow: around 2,000 cfs (Sandy River gauge at Marmot).

Takeout at the Sleepy Hollow Rd. bridge: (45.383737, -122.046023)
Put-in: 45.277738, -121.940028

Ryan Scott

Keel Brightman on a tributary of the WF Hood

**Beaver Creek, Rock Creek (Clackamas) and Deep Creek** are all urban creeking options within 10 minutes of Powell Butte (within the Portland city limits). Each has their own unique features and start to flow when the Beaver Creek gauge near Troutdale passes 7.5 feet. One flows through a 50-foot-deep, vertical-walled gorge through a neighborhood, another has a 15-foot waterfall. They are silly little creeks but are fun for the right people and a pre-trip scout on foot is recommended. Take out on both Rock and Deep creeks where they cross under state Hwy. 212. The Beaver Creek takeout is Kiku City Park or just across the creek. Put-in location is wherever you can access the creeks above the takeouts and near the following coordinates:

Beaver (45.523209, -122.383653)
Rock (45.423457, -122.494993)
Deep (45.423399, -122.386626)

**Little Sandy** is now illegal, but with the removal of Marmot Dam this could change in the future, opening up a Class V run with limited eddies, more rapids than you can count and some wood hazards. The run starts at the NF-14 bridge. Be as prudent as possible until past the 20-foot Meatcleaver Falls, which has minimal stopping options above it. The takeout is at Dodge Park on the Bull Run. (Flows: 300-800 cfs.)

Takeout: 45.428119, -122.232563
Put-in: 45.403634, -122.021662

**Zigzag:** Fast-paced Class III+ rolling down the flanks of Mount Hood. The best whitewater is between the two U.S. Hwy. 26 bridges, but upper reaches have been run. Watch out for wood. Zigzag runs from both snowmelt and rain, no gauge but if you are in the area, take a look when the Sandy gauge at Marmot is over 1,500 cfs.

Takeout: 45.347132, -121.942432
Put-in: 45.311187, -121.889275

# HONORABLE MENTIONS

**Lake Branch:** This tributary to the West Fork Hood has a handful of Class IV+ rapids in a gorge. Wood can be an issue, try to get local beta before dropping in. Usually it's in when the Hood River gauge at Tucker is between 5.5 and 7 feet.

Takeout: 45.548316, -121.703055
Put-in: 45.536770, -121.767020

**Multnomah Creek:** Above Multnomah Falls, the most famous waterfall in the Pacific Northwest, are several drops from 8- to 20-foot sliding falls and a vertical, nearly perfect, 60-foot plunge (Wiesendanger Falls) that kicks off a packed Class V-V+ half-mile section. All these drops have been run, minus Multnomah—take out above its bottomless horizon line, hiking back down to the parking area. You have to really want this section of whitewater since the hike up is not fun, and you must skirt past the overly concerned workers and tourists at the Multnomah Lodge. If you're wary of the crowd, hike in from the back, up Wahkeena

Falls Trail #420: 45.575390, -122.127928
Takeout: 45.577717, -122.117732
Put-in (Wiesendanger Falls): 45.574410, -122.107601

**Middle Oneonta Falls** is one of several more waterfalls above one of Oregon's natural wonders, Lower Oneonta Gorge. It's the only one that is runnable. A three-quarter-mile hike up Trail #424 gets you to the footbridge for a perfect view of the falls upstream. Take a look downstream to see the 100-foot horizon line of the lower falls. Beware of high flows on this creek, again noting that 100-footer just downstream. Find your exit plan before committing to the 25-foot Class IV+ drop.

Trailhead: 45.588567, -122.078540

**Fifteen Mile Creek** is a fun Class IV+ novelty run near the Dalles, which really needs heavy rains to run. If Mosier Creek is flowing over 100 cfs, Fifteen Mile Creek might be in.

Takeout: 45.612091, -121.123122
Put-in: 45.610119, -121.078021

Priscilla Macy

Nick Hymel drops Mosier Falls in an inflatable kayak

**Mosier Falls** was first run in 2008 by Erik Boomer. This gnarly 60-foot step-down falls with a terrible cave on the right side of the landing zone has only been run a few times since. Right on top of the town of Mosier, on the east end of the Gorge, this little creek needs serious rain to reach a good flow. The drop has been kayaked in the 100-500+ cfs range, and even lower by expert waterfall rafters. When everything else in the gorge is running high after a big rain event, take a look at Mosier. Both sides of the falls have been run, but right is more common; where good lines have proved the transition can be smoother than it would appear. USGS 14113200 MOSIER CREEK NEAR MOSIER, OR (45.682659, -121.390568). While public access is tricky, there is more Class IV action upstream.
Takeout parking: 45.682280, -121.390890

Paul Thompson

Dan McCain and Jeff Compton
on Mosier Falls

# WILLAMETTE VALLEY

Nate Pfeifer

Chris Arnold

270

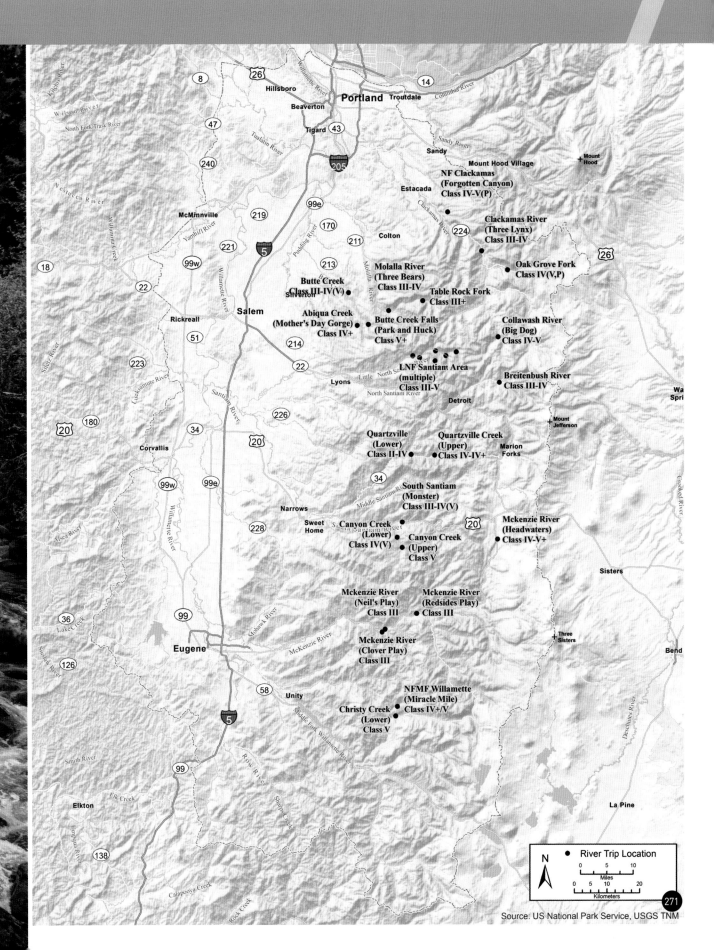

## 7

Portland
Hillsboro
Beaverton
Troutdale
Tigard
Sandy
Mount Hood Village
Mount Hood
Estacada
NF Clackamas
(Forgotten Canyon)
Class IV-V(P)
McMinnville
Colton
Clackamas River
(Three Lynx)
Class III-IV
Oak Grove Fork
Class IV(V,P)
Molalla River
(Three Bears)
Class III-IV
Butte Creek
Class III-IV(V)
Silverton
Table Rock Fork
Class III+
Salem
Abiqua Creek
(Mother's Day Gorge)
Class IV+
Butte Creek Falls
(Park and Huck)
Class V+
Collawash River
(Big Dog)
Class IV-V
Rickreall
LNF Santiam Area
(multiple)
Class III-V
Breitenbush River
Class III-IV
Lyons
Detroit
Mount Jefferson
Quartzville
(Lower)
Class II-IV
Quartzville Creek
(Upper)
Class IV-IV+
Marion Forks
Corvallis
South Santiam
(Monster)
Class III-IV(V)
Narrows
Sweet Home
Canyon Creek
(Lower)
Class IV(V)
Canyon Creek
(Upper)
Class V
Mckenzie River
(Headwaters)
Class IV-V+
Sisters
Mckenzie River
(Neil's Play)
Class III
Mckenzie River
(Redsides Play)
Class III
Three Sisters
Bend
Eugene
Mckenzie River
(Clover Play)
Class III
Unity
NFMF Willamette
(Miracle Mile)
Class IV+/V
Christy Creek
(Lower)
Class V
Elkton
La Pine

N
● River Trip Location
0  5  10
Miles
0  5  10  20
Kilometers

Source: US National Park Service, USGS TNM

# MIRACLE MILE

## NORTH FORK OF THE MIDDLE FORK WILLAMETTE RIVER

About 10 miles up from the small town of Westfir lays a mile-long stretch of whitewater known as the Miracle Mile, or simply, the Mile. Dropping around 250 feet along its short length, there are no single drops larger than 3-4 feet. Rather, this gradient is lost through a labyrinth of continuous boulder gardens. Although sections of this run have been given names, they pretty much run together and will be indistinguishable your first few times down. This run is a true classic and probably the most commonly run section of whitewater for the area's Class IV/V creekboaters. Note that wood is an ever-present hazard, and constantly shifts around from flood events.

Starting about quarter-mile up from the NF-1926 bridge (around 13 miles up from Westfir), is a little warm-up through some Class II+ rapids. After passing underneath the NF-1926 bridge, the bottom drops out as you become "Initiated" to the run. Although general beta can be helpful (especially for known hazards), your best bet is to tuck in behind someone and follow their lines. If you get a little lost, there are many alternate routes to get back in line—this is reactionary boating at its finest!

After Initiation, the boulder gardens just keep coming: starting with Ricochet (first island), followed by Confusion, Shark's Tooth, Whoop-De-Do (second island), Silly Putty, and finally Swimmer's Alley. You will know you're on the final stretch when you pass the confluence with Christy Creek and the road bridge comes into view. The takeout is just above the NF-1925 bridge, on river-left. Once you've had a chance to catch your breath and hike up to the parking area, grab a beer in celebration or head back up for another lap or two!

—Nate Pfeifer

### THE RUNDOWN

This run is short and sweet, next to the road, and easy for running multiple laps!

**Difficulty:** Class IV+/V

**Gauge:** Painted bridge gauge and USGS #14147500—NFMF Willamette near Oakridge

**Flow Min-max:** 6-24 inches (bridge gauge), or 2.6-4.4 feet (USGS gauge)

**Gradient:** 250 fpm. Put-in elevation: 1,900 feet

**Takeout:** NF-1925 road bridge (just below the Christy Creek confluence)

**Put-in:** Quarter-mile upstream from the NF-1926 road bridge

**Length:** 1 mile

**Hitchability:** Spotty, but it's only a mile

**Season:** Early December to early June (typical year)

**Camping:** Yes, a few spots at the takeout

**4WD Needed?** No, paved road

**Best Close Food/Beers:** Westfir Lodge and restaurants and pub in Oakridge

**Quality (out of 5):** 4.5

**Raft Recommendations:** Only at high water. Experts only!

Nate Pfeifer
Paddlers in the midst of Swimmers Alley on the Miracle Mile

### SHUTTLE DIRECTIONS

The road on which one drives out of Eugene is Hwy 58, reached by taking Exit 188 off I5. To reach the takeout, drive from Eugene about 40 miles east to the town of Westfir. From the red covered bridge (in Westfir), drive 12 miles north up North Fork Road (aka Aufderheide Drive) to the NF-1925 bridge over the NFMF Willamette—this is the takeout **(43.879913, -122.385449)**. To get to the put-in, get back to North Fork Road and drive another 1.2 miles, using the small pull-out between the road and the river to put on **(43.884400, -122.367526)**.

Nate Pfeifer

Classic scene on the Miracle Mile

# CHRISTY CREEK

Christy Creek is some good creeking! The first part of the trip is full of steep boulder gardens. Some are read and run, some require a shore scout and maybe a portage. There is a transition section where both boulder gardens and bedrock are present, then things get really steep with boulder gardens separated by big bedrock drops. Below the steep section there are a few more boulder gardens before a set of low-angle slides marks the end of the whitewater. The run has taken over six hours including the hike, but has also been done in half that with previous knowledge.

The hike to the put-in takes 30 to 60 minutes depending on group size and hiking ability. Things start off from the get-go with steep and fast, boat-scoutable boulder gardens. There were no mandatory wood portages in 2011, but this is not the place to let your guard down. Before long, the rapids dictate a couple of quick scouts and some may choose to portage a couple of times in the first couple of miles. The run increases in intensity as it enters the middle mile where over 400 feet of elevation is lost. The meat of this mile starts off with a large boulder garden on a left-hand turn with a tricky sieve in the middle. There is an optional portage on the left; if you get 20 feet above river-level, it's an easy, flat portage before descending back in to run the last ledge or two in the rapid. If you want to run the rapid, scout along the left bank.

Downstream is Rhinosex, an ugly rapid usually portaged on the left; though it has been run with a high rate of carnage. This is the beginning of the bedrock rapids, with Balls Falls and Snake Bite not far below. Proceed cautiously as Balls Falls has a Class III-IV rapid that wraps around a left bend into the drop. Scout left with a possible portage on the right. This rapid starts with a 20-foot kicker/ramp before quickly dropping over two difficult ledges with large hydraulics and at least one piton spot on the right. It is possible to run the first drop on the right into the eddy and portage the rest, though it requires a little effort. Snake Bite is not far below and can be scouted/portaged/run left or right. The hole at the bottom looks like it would take a bite out of you, but the speed gained in the fast slide *usually* helps boaters punch the hole's edges. Below are a number of Class IV-V boulder gardens; paddle cautiously as blind corners and limited eddies are conducive to blind descents of these rapids. The last rapid of note is a section of low-angle slides with sticky holes at higher flows. Below the slides, things cool off for the last mile down to the NFMF Willamette. Upon entering the larger river, paddle to the left side to take out just above the bridge.

*—Jacob Cruser*

## SHUTTLE DIRECTIONS

The takeout is the same as the Miracle Mile, described in the previous entry **(43.879786, -122.385355)**.

From the take out turn left onto NF-19 (the paved road you drove in on). Follow this road for 0.9 miles and turn left onto NF-1926, which immediately crosses the NFMF Willamette. Go 2.5 miles and take a left onto the gravel road. At the upcoming "Y" turn right onto NF-637. Follow this for 0.2 miles as you ignore a spur road on both the right and left. When you reach the 0.2 mile mark on NF-637 it will make a sharp left turn; after this turn continue about ¼ of a mile to a point where you will drop down to the creek on foot (In 2015 this area was forested and just beyond a clear cut). Enter the forest to the right, beginning by walking downhill until you are able to attain the ridge to the right of the first rivulet as it exits a small bog. Follow the fall-line/ridge to the creek **(43.911415, -122.365844)**.

Alternately, when you turn off NF-19 onto NF-1926, do not make any more turns. In 4.8 miles that road crosses Christy Creek (43.922381, -122.311970). While this access is easier, you will be faced with a longer day on the water due to unfriendly boulder gardens and an unhealthy dose of wood hazards. Regardless of which access you choose, bring a detailed map.

Takeout: **43.879814, -122.385410**
Put-in: **43.911427, -122.366878**

Nate Pfeifer

Shawn Haggin charms The Snake

## THE RUNDOWN

One mile drops 400 feet—it's all been run!

**Difficulty:** Class V

**Gauge:** NFMF at Westfir

**Flow Min-max:** 3.5-4.5 feet

**Gradient:** 400 fpm in steepest mile. Put-in elevation: 2,300 feet

**Takeout:** Miracle Mile takeout

**Put-in:** Downstream of Mill Creek confluence

**Length:** 3.2 miles

**Hitchability:** Not a good option

**Season:** Rainy with a snowmelt buffer

**Camping:** Yes, at the takeout

**4WD Needed?** No, but gravel shuttle road.

**Best Close Food/Beers:** Eugene

**Quality (out of 5):** 4

**Raft Recommendations:** Has been done by Class V rafters, not recommended

Nate Pfeifer

Roman Androsov drops into Balls Falls

# UPPER LITTLE NORTH FORK SANTIAM

This may be Oregon's most classic stream. Starting at Jawbone Flats and ending 25 miles downstream at its confluence with the North Santiam, this gorgeous stream is a paradise. The upper sections are largely unmolested by man, protected in part by mining claims and maintained by the Friends of Opal Creek. To get to Jawbone Flats requires 3 miles of easy hiking along an old logging road. Ambitious boaters can hike an additional mile or two past Jawbone Flats to run either Battle Axe Creek or Opal proper. Battle Axe has numerous 5- to 15-foot bedrock ledges, while Opal has some of the best rapids in the entire drainage mixed in with some portages. Battle Axe Creek and Opal proper merge in Jawbone, creating the Little North Santiam.

Once on the Little North Santiam, the stream rolls along with numerous Class III-IV rapids and gin-clear water. There are only a few ledges before the first rapid of note, Cascadas De Los Ninos. This 15-foot waterfall can be scouted from either side of the river; if you find yourself on river-right, check out the vestiges of an old Sawmill. The lines off the waterfall are obvious, but beware of rocks in the landing of the far right and far left side of the falls, especially at low water. People who tire of hiking sometimes put in at this falls.

Below are a couple of blind rapids before Harvey Wallbanger appears around a right-hand turn. Catch one of the eddies on the left before the turn to scout this near mandatory rapid. Harvey Wallbanger looks intimidating from above, but it tends to go smoother than it appears. This rapid funnels through a few soft holes on the right before regrouping and plunging over a narrow ledge into a sticky hole. It is possible to eddy out before the final ledge to take a peek and set safety.

There are a couple more good rapids below and before Coyle's Boil, the most commonly portaged rapid on this stretch. Attentive boaters will see the road supports above on river-right, just below here the river enters a Class III boulder garden which bends to the right through a couple of small holes. This lead-in rapid is not particularly difficult, but it does push directly into Coyle's Boil. There are eddies on both the right and left immediately below the lead-in, with the portage/scout on the left. Coyle's is a small, but intimidating rapid. Look around the cliff walls in the pool below Coyle's Boil, there is a mineshaft along both walls. The river-left entrance allows access for paddlers who do not mind small dark places! Just downstream is a ledge with a pin spot on the right, and a variety of viable routes center and left. The final obstacle is a ledge above the mine put-in that is safest to run by scraping down the right side. Strong paddlers sometimes run the left-side Hypoxia Hole with mixed results. From the pool below this ledge, get out on the right and walk a half-mile back to your car or continue through the next section (Classic Opal).

*—Jacob Cruser*

Nate Pfeifer 📷
Anna Herring on the ledge below Coyle's Boil. 👁

## SHUTTLE DIRECTIONS

Follow I-5 to Salem, then take the Detroit Lake exit, heading east on state Hwy. 22. Travel just under 22 miles before taking a left on North Fork Road SE, moments before OR 22 crosses the Little North Fork of the Santiam. Follow this road for 20.7 miles until it ends at a gate. Walk past the gate 3.3 miles to the put-in at Jawbone Flats. Use either the footbridge just below the town, or the bridge over Battle Axe just above the confluence **(44.846894, -122.208361)**. Ambitious boaters can hike an additional mile or two up either Battle Axe Creek or Opal Proper for more bedrock action.

The upper section can be done by itself by taking out below the mine at the put-in for Classic Opal **(44.858472, -122.252535)**. If this is what you do, you will hike back up the road you hiked in on about a mile to where you left the cars by the gate (Classic Opal put-in, just in reverse). Most paddlers choose to take out at Three Pools (directions in the Classic Opal description) and add the classic section of Opal to the trip.

## THE RUNDOWN

Running Battle Axe Creek through Salmon Falls is probably the best day of paddling in Oregon.

**Difficulty:** Class IV(V)

**Gauge:** USGS #14182500— LITTLE NORTH SANTIAM RIVER NEAR MEHAMA, OR

**Flow Min-max:** 700-2,500 cfs

**Gradient:** 110 fpm. Put-in elevation: 2,100 feet

**Takeout:** Salmon Falls

**Put-in:** Jawbone Flats

**Length:** 2.6 miles

**Hitchability:** No shuttle needed unless you add Classic Opal, then you will want to set your own shuttle

**Season:** Rainy, some snowmelt

**Camping:** Yes

**4WD Needed?** No

**Best Close Food/Beers:** Little North Fork Restaurant, Gingerbread House

**Quality (out of 5):** 4 (5 if you add one of the tributaries)

**Raft Recommendations:** Doable, not recommended. The hike will keep most away.

Roman Androsov

Nate Pfeifer paddling over Cascadas De Los Ninos

# CLASSIC OPAL

## OF THE LITTLE NORTH FORK SANTIAM

This is one of Oregon's best stretches of river. The many Class III-IV rapids broken up by a couple of harder ones, combined with truly breathtakingly water quality within a dark but friendly gorge makes this run must-do. It starts with a walk along a gravel road down to the put-in at an old mineshaft below a small ledge. The stream rolls along with pool-drop Class II-III rapids to warm up on, quickly building to easy Class IV. At flows over 2,000 cfs, the run starts to feel like solid Class IV. At all but the highest flows, there is just the right mix of entertaining whitewater and scenic floating to make people really appreciate that they are boaters.

Keep an eye out for wood, though it is rare to make any portages for strainers. There are a couple tricky spots that are best run at the edges of the main flow, but the consequences are typically low. Most paddlers follow a veteran down the first time to avoid having to scout the many Class IV rapids, while prudent boaters can still have a stress-free trip if they are competent at boat-scouting or willing to shore-scout some of the rapids.

The two standout rapids are Big Ugly and Big Fluffy. Big Ugly is marked by the river turning 90 degrees to the right before entering a straightaway and then dropping through some boulders into Big Ugly itself. Be mindful of the left wall at the bottom, it has caused some pins and pitons in the past. Drive left-to-right in the chute just below Big Ugly. A short distance downstream at the next horizon line is the lead-in to Big Fluffy. Get out on the right just before a river-wide 5-foot ledge to scout this tricky drop. Many paddlers follow the main current through an S-turn at the lip, which sometimes causes boaters to end up uncomfortably close to the left wall. After running the lead-in wherever's clever, there will be a pinch along the left wall about 30 yards above the falls. A line that starts a foot off the left wall, coming through this pinch and maintaining proximity until the last moment, allows paddlers to counter the tricky current by driving back to middle just in time for a strong stoke at the lip. If you wish to portage Big Fluffy, it can be done via seal-launch on the right, or by crossing the logs bridging the canyon below the falls.

The river then eases a bit with more Class II-IV rapids and longer pools. Cedar Creek enters on the left just above a bridge and signals that you have entered the home stretch. Less than a mile downstream is an innocuous Class IV rapid with a pin spot in the middle at lower flows. The rapids ease off below here until the finale at Thor's Playroom. Thor's is a three-part rapid with a variety of routes starting with a series of doors. The most common route is to use the door second from the right, dropping over two small ledges. Next is a splashy middle section before eddying out on the

### THE RUNDOWN

This may be Oregon's most classic intermediate kayak run.

**Difficulty:** Class IV-V

**Gauge:** USGS 14182500 LITTLE NORTH SANTIAM RIVER NEAR MEHAMA, OR

**Flow Min-max:** 700-2,500 cfs

**Gradient:** 100 fpm

**Takeout:** Three Pools

**Put-in:** Mine

**Length:** 4 miles

**Hitchability:** Not a good option

**Season:** Rainy, with some snowmelt

**Camping:** Cedar Creek Campground, various undeveloped spots throughout the Opal Creek Wilderness, and cabin camping at Jawbone Flats

**4WD Needed?** No, but a gravel shuttle road.

**Best Close Food/Beers:** North Fork Crossing Restaurant in Lyons

**Quality (out of 5):** 4.8

**Raft Recommendations:** Rafts are fine over 1,000 cfs if you don't mind carrying your boat to the put-in

### SHUTTLE DIRECTIONS

Follow I-5 to Salem and take the Detroit Lake exit, heading east on state Hwy. 22. Travel just under 22 miles before taking a left on North Fork Road SE, moments before OR 22 crosses the Little North Fork of the Santiam. Follow this road for 16.5 miles, where you will turn right and drive another 0.8 miles before turning right into a paved parking area, which is the takeout **(44.838674, -122.310773)**. Take a left coming back out of the parking lot, and 0.8 miles later turn right on the road that you came in on. Follow it for 4.2 miles to a locked gate. Park here and walk upstream, in a half-mile you cross Gold Creek (yes it has been run). A hundred or so yards farther, take a decommissioned road to the right. This will lead you down to an old mine site and the put-in **(44.858503, -122.252427)**.

right above the final portion, a slide into a ledge. Take out in the pool below this rapid at a convenient boulder bar on the right. There are some steps leading back up to the parking lot.

—*Jacob Cruser*

# The Best on All White Water.

# OPAL GORGE

## OF THE LITTLE NORTH FORK SANTIAM

This stretch of the Little North Santiam is more committing than any other on this stream. It starts with a mile or two of Class II before the walls rise up to present boaters with a boulder garden at the head of the gorge. Run the top anywhere, then boof left or right of the rock in the center at the bottom (left is more common). The pool below is committing, forcing paddlers to run an unscoutable/unportageable ledge (UnUn/Mystery). This can be run far left or right (or middle over 1,000 cfs). The most common line is to be a foot off the left bank, pointed slightly right, letting your nose drop for a reconnect. There is a small ledge just downstream and then you are in the pool above the Undertaker.

Be sure to take in the location—this is the heart of Opal Gorge. Flows below 1,500 cfs allow for a shorter, but exposed portage of the Undertaker on the left. Higher flows mean a must-do portage on the right. At normal flows this rapid ends in a river-wide sieve, but has been run at flows around 5,000 cfs. If you portage left, the Tombstone rock is your next obstacle. Most paddlers run the left side driving back right, but the rock can sometimes be boofed on the right side. Be wary of pin/piton potential on both sides. Just downstream is Unicorn, a large boulder garden that is run down the middle with the majority of the current, avoiding the pushy left side. Below, a large waterfall cascades in from river-right via Henline

Creek. At the base of this waterfall is Henline Rapid, which can be run right or left; be ready to compensate for the current sloping to the middle from both sides.

The next rapid, Sierra Slot, releases paddlers from the gorge. It's a narrow ledge that can clear your sinuses if you plug. This drop can be boat-scouted from a river-right eddy at the lip, or from shore on the right. A short stretch of Class II-III follows before a horizon line appears for Fish Ladder aka Elkhorn Falls. This is usually portaged on the left, though it has been run with a variety of lines. If you plan to paddle this rapid, take a good look at the rock finger in the exit. Nearly the entire river goes under this block of rock before entering the calm pool below. Below 2,000 cfs there is an easy portage on the left; over that level paddlers may need to portage from higher up. At very high flows this rapid fills in and becomes more appealing. It's then another mile or two to Salmon Falls. Scout on the left along the retaining wall—some people run the lead-in far left while others seal-launch above the main drop. At flows over 1,500 cfs, paddlers can take a center-to-left line that lands in the left channel just above the main drop. Take out on the right in the pool below the falls.

*—Jacob Cruser*

Nate Pfeifer

Shawn Haggins paddling through the walls of Opal Gorge

## THE RUNDOWN

Has been run near 5,000 cfs and holds its water well. Some of the drops are more runnable, while most of the run gets MUCH harder.

**Difficulty:** Class IV+ (P)

**Gauge:** USGS #14182500—LITTLE NORTH SANTIAM RIVER NEAR MEHAMA, OR

**Flow Min-max:** 500-2,000 cfs

**Gradient:** 150 fpm through the gorge. Put-in elevation: 1400 feet

**Takeout:** Salmon Falls

**Put-in:** Three Pools recreation area

**Length:** 3.5 miles

**Hitchability:** Possible, bike is better

**Season:** Rainy, some snowmelt

**Camping:** Yes

**4WD Needed?** No

**Best Close Food/Beers:** Little North Fork Restaurant, Gingerbread House

**Quality (out of 5):** 5

**Raft Recommendations:** Has been done by class V rafters, technical rope-work is needed for rafts to make one of the portages. Not recommended.

## SHUTTLE DIRECTIONS

Follow I-5 to Salem, then take the Detroit Lake exit, heading east on state Hwy. 22. Travel just under 22 miles before taking a left on North Fork Road SE, moments before OR 22 crosses the Little North Fork of the Santiam. Follow this road for 13.8 miles to Salmon Falls County Park—this is the takeout **(44.831540, -122.370554)**. To get to the put-in, head upstream (NE) on the same road 2.7 miles and turn right. Drive down this road 0.8 miles and turn right into a large, paved parking lot. The put-in is down some stairs at the far end of this parking lot. This area is known as Three Pools **(44.838694, -122.310736)**.

 Nate Pfeifer
 The entrance to Opal Gorge

281

# SOUTH SANTIAM RIVER

This is a cool run that can be enjoyed by intermediate boaters and experts alike—mostly easy floating with a good amount of Class III-IV and two Class V rapids. Near the end of the run is the Hobbit Gorge, the type of place that makes boaters love our sport. The run tends to get overlooked when it is running from a rain event as there are other good area creeks with more whitewater. The South Santiam does serve a niche for the area's boating community though: It is sometimes run as a backup when paddlers are shut down trying to run one of its tributaries (often occurring with gates being closed), and it also runs from snowmelt for a couple of weeks once everything else in the area has dropped out. It really is a nice run that deserves more traffic, sure to leave paddlers satisfied.

The first two miles from the Half Bridge to the U.S. Hwy 20 bridge offer a warmup section with one ledge (Longbow Falls) and a nice boulder garden or two. Below the bridge the action picks up with a long series of fun Class III-IV rapids. Downstream of this stretch of rapids, a 4-foot ledge on a slight right bend warns paddles of the upcoming Monster (the ledge is usually run right). The next hundred yards leading into Monster is moving flatwater, which is fortunate

## THE RUNDOWN

Some of the oldest rock in the Cascades.

**Difficulty:** Class III-IV (V)

**Gauge:** USGS #14185000—South Santiam River Below Cascadia, OR

**Flow Min-max:** 700-3,000 cfs

**Gradient:** 55 fpm. Put-in elevation: 1,150 feet

**Takeout:** Cascadia State Park

**Put-in:** Half Bridge

**Length:** 6.5 miles

**Hitchability:** A viable option

**Season:** Rainy and snowmelt

**Camping:** Yes, but limited

**4WD Needed?** No

**Best Close Food/Beers:** Sweet Home

**Quality (out of 5):** 3.5

**Raft Recommendations:** It is raftable, the Monster may be a challenging portage.

Nate Pfeifer

Entrance to the Hobbit Gorge on the South Santiam River

because eddies can be a little tricky. Scout or portage from either side, each having their pros and cons. The Monster is a wild flume that crashes off undercut walls. A short pool separates the Monster from Crawdad, a small but malicious rapid that can be hard to style. The general consensus is that this drop gets more difficult at lower water levels.

The river opens up below a narrow pinch just downstream of Crawdad. There is easy floating and a rapid or two between here and Tomco, a tricky rapid with deceptive hydraulics. Crossing under a bridge, be ready to eddy out on the right above an obvious horizon line for a scout. The scout requires wading through Moose Creek, which can make things difficult at high water. A benefit to higher flows, however, is a shallow sneak route that opens up on the right. Tomco can be run down the meat, or paddlers can seal-launch in wherever's clever.

Downstream is the entrance to the Hobbit Gorge. A small ledge and dynamic hydraulic guard the entrance, which can be difficult to scout. Once this obstacle is cleared it is smooth sailing for the remainder of the run. The Hobbit Gorge is an incredible place where

## SHUTTLE DIRECTIONS

From I-5, take U.S. Hwy 20 about 40 miles east through the towns of Lebanon and Sweet Home, then 14 miles past Sweet Home a left turn will take you over the South Santiam. Turn right immediately after the bridge into Cascadia State Park and a trail leads down to the river takeout **(44.401198, -122.363817)**. Return to U.S. 20 and continue upstream (east) for 6.5 miles to the Half Bridge site where you can put in **(44.398296, -122.480416)**.

small waterfalls pour in from the sides and easy floating allows one to take in the beauty. Once below this Gorge, it is a short float down to Cascadia State Park where a couple of small rapids and playspots keep paddlers engaged.

—*Jacob Cruser*

# QUARTZVILLE CREEK

This run is all about having a fun day on the river. There are no waterfalls or large boof lines, but many steep rapids and ledges stack up to a great time. The recommended routine is to scout for wood the first trip down, then once the lines are known, go for another lap without leaving the comfort of your boat!

From the put-in, there is a short warmup. Historically there has been a log feature just before things pick up that can be negotiated on the right. The river turns right not far below and enters Technical Difficulties (TD), a fun boulder garden with a pin spot in the middle of a 3-foot ledge partway down; scouting from the road beforehand is common practice. TD finishes off with a fun slide that gets more exciting the farther right it is run. Just around the corner is Grocker, with a nice ledge on the left or a slide on the right.

Downstream, Quartzville gets into a rhythm of read-and-run Class III-IV. The next named rapid is Wooden Wall, which has an easy lead-in to a ledge. The outflow from this ledge pushes right and into a log—not too hazardous, but good to know it's there. More boogie leads to David From Behind, marked by a large log propped from the left bank into the middle of the rapid. There is a sneak route to the left and under this log, or a wild airplane turn on the right into a strong hydraulic. The next obstacle is a river-wide log around a right-hand turn. This log allows enough room underneath for a boater to pass through on far river-left with a duck as you punch a small hole, with the center and right being very dangerous. A short way downstream is Corkscrew: one of the signature drops on Quartzville that will paste a smile on your face every time! Run the ramp on the left. The next rapid is Movie-Star, which has one of the more noteworthy holes on the river. If you do not wish to fully engage the hole, a boof exists on the far right. The next quarter-mile is a series of fun boulder gardens that are generally run following the main flow. The stream eases just before the end, with a final ledge in view of the takeout that can become sticky at higher levels. There is also a good ender spot on the river-left side of this ledge. Some boaters will choose to continue another mile down to the next bridge. There are two rapids in this section that will need to be scouted and probably portaged: Pick-Up-Sticks and Double Dip. Most boaters will choose to do another lap on the classic section instead!

If you are into marathon-style boating, consider continuing down 14 miles to Green Peter Reservoir. This stretch has plenty of rapids but also long Class II stretches. There are a few ledges between the normal takeout and Yellowbottom Recreational Site

## THE RUNDOWN

Expert local boaters love the stretch from Yellowbottom to the reservoir at flows over 6,000 cfs. Do not leave gear unattended in the area, as thefts are disappointingly common.

**Difficulty:** IV-IV+

**Gauge:** USGS #14185900—QUARTZVILLE CREEK NEAR CASCADIA, OR

**Flow Min-max:** 1,000-4,000 cfs

**Gradient:** 100 fpm. Put-in elevation: 2,200 feet

**Takeout:** Wrapped Bridge

**Put-in:** NF 11 bridge below Minniece Creek

**Length:** 3.2 miles

**Hitchability:** It is likely you could catch a ride if the weather is nice, better to set your own shuttle though

**Season:** Rain or snowmelt

**Camping:** It's everywhere, but usually roadside

**4WD Needed?** No

**Best Close Food/Beers:** Sweet Home

**Quality (out of 5):** 4.5

**Raft Recommendations:** It has been done, Class V skills recommended.

## SHUTTLE DIRECTIONS

From Sweet Home, drive about 6 miles to Quartzville Rd., and turn left over the reservoir. Take this road for about 28 miles (you are getting close when you see signs for Yellowbottom) to the takeout bridge **(44.576778, -122.299089)**. Looking downstream you will see the "wrapped bridge" on river-right. Continue upstream on Quartzville Rd., 3.2 miles to another bridge, the put-in **(44.580580, -122.245458)**.

that are larger than anything on the upper run, a couple of which are recommended portages. If flows are really high (6K+ cfs), Yellowbottom to the reservoir is a hoot for high-water enthusiasts.

—Jacob Cruser

Nate Pfeifer
Andy Janoski finishes off David From Behind

Nate Pfeifer
Eric Emerson at the end of Technical Difficulties

This section is sometimes paddled by locals when nothing else is running, but is most commonly done by people wanting to run large waterfalls. There are a number of tributaries feeding Clear Lake that run dry once the rains ceases. However, large underground aquifers keep the water flowing late into the summer. Waterfall runners often shoot for late spring when the USGS gauge shows 400-600 cfs exiting Clear Lake. Be wary that on rare occasions this gauge can read low as the groundwater system can add significantly to the flow downstream of the gauges. Regardless of aspiration and river level, it is wise to scout the eddies above the major rapids before putting on.

The McKenzie exits Clear Lake via a set of splashy Class II-III rapids. These whisk paddlers around corners that have been known to collect wood. Throughout the rest of this stretch aquifers sometimes bolster the flow. Before long, the river enters a bedrock section between short gorge walls with a number of ledges, culminating in an 8-foot ledge. The pool below exits into the lead-in for Sahalie Falls (80 feet), where a series of ledges with odd currents and intermittent log hazards flush straight over the falls with a last-chance eddy on the right. The usual route is to run the 8-foot ledge, then portage the lead-in to Sahalie. At higher flows, some may wish to start their portage above the ledge. Sahalie has been run a number of times, with paddlers usually forgoing its lead-in and peeling out of the river-right eddy just above the lip. Good safety is recommended here as aside from the massive drop, the runout is a difficult Class V rapid complete with log hazard. The falls, along with the subsequent Class V rapid, can be portaged along trails on either the left or the right.

More ledges and corners are present below, once again culminating in a drop. This one is about 20 feet tall and has a logjam at the base, dictating a portage. From here, walk downstream to scout Koosah Falls (70 feet). This waterfall lands in a large pool, with a tricky lip that has sent many paddlers off-kilter. If you do not wish to run this drop it can be portaged left. The trip can also be ended here if paddlers so choose. The stream exits the Koosah pool and enters a Class III gorge. The first rapid downstream has must-portage wood that can act as a gear catchment when paddlers part from their boats at Koosah. It is a short way to the reservoir; keep an eye out for wood throughout the entire run.

The run is pretty short, so some paddlers bring their playboats and check out some of the roadside playspots farther down the river. The most well known are Neil's, Redside, and Clover. The entire

## THE RUNDOWN

Three miles below Carmen Reservoir is Blue Pool. Here a 50-foot falls is dry most of the year. However when the McKenzie gets very high, this waterfall sometimes springs to life.

**Difficulty:** Class IV-V+

**Gauge:** USGS #14158500—MCKENZIE RIVER AT OUTLET OF CLEAR LAKE

**Flow Min-max:** If there is 400-600 cfs on the USGS gauge the waterfalls are probably at a good flow, though they can be run both higher and lower (Koosah more often). The section can be paddled down to 200 cfs.

**Gradient:** 250 fpm. Put-in elevation: 3,000 feet

**Takeout:** Carmen Reservoir

**Put-in:** Clear Lake

**Length:** 1.5 miles

**Hitchability:** Plenty of cars, but it's a highway. Hiking the trail back to your car is more enjoyable.

**Season:** Year-round

**Camping:** Many sites along lower river and near lakes, also primitive sites can be found via spur roads.

**4WD Needed?** No

**Best Close Food/Beers:** Sisters, McKenzie Bridge, Eugene

**Quality (out of 5):** 3, unless you are there for the waterfalls, then 5+

**Raft Recommendations:** It could be done, work-to-reward ratio is low. A raft decent of the waterfalls would likely result in injury or worse.

river from Olallie Campground to Hayden Bridge offers year-round Class II-III whitewater, providing good raft runs. The farther downriver you paddle, the easier and less continuous the rapids become. The most commonly run section is from Finn Rock to Leaburg Dam where the Class III Brown's Hole and Marten Rapid provide entertainment for novice boaters.

—Jacob Cruser

7 (top corner)

## SHUTTLE DIRECTIONS

Follow Interstate 5 to Eugene, then take state Hwy. 126 east about 72 miles to National Forest road 750. Turn left and find a takeout along the reservoir, NF 750 has a bridge over the McKenzie on the north (upstream) edge of this reservoir that works nicely **(44.340873, -122.002979)**. To get to the put-in, return to OR 126 and drive upstream (north) 1 mile, then turn right onto NF 770 and follow it for a half-mile to a point where the road gets close to the lake—put in here **(44.361126, -121.990429)**. Paddle left along the bank to reach the outlet into the McKenzie. During the shuttle you will see signs for Sahalie and Koosah Falls, and it is a short walk from either of these parking areas to scout the meat of the run.

Emile Elliott

McKenzie River Headwaters, Koosah Falls

# MCKENZIE RIVER (PLAY RUN)

**Redsides** (44.159576, -122.301877) is about 2 miles upstream of the town of Blue River. It's a great summertime wave-hole enabling fun blunts, cartwheels, and big loops. The best levels are between 1.4-1.6 feet on the Vida gauge. Park at the trucker turn-out (don't leave valuables in your car) and walk across the road. The wave is about a hundred feet downstream, and there are rumors this spot forms a good wave at flood.

**Clover** (44.115492, -122.420910) consists of three play-features. Look for 4-6 feet at Vida, though you can go a little higher or lower depending on which feature you like best. Drive into the small town of Nimrod along Hwy 126 and park at what used to be Mom's Pies about a quarter-mile upstream of the waves and float down to the features on river right. You can take out a quarter-mile downstream at the old bridge. The top feature is a fast, bouncy wave. About 30 feet downriver is a bigger, glassier wave with a foam pile. The corners flush, but if you catch it right, this is the best feature. On river-left is a small, friendly hole that is good for cartwheels and loops. There is a large eddy on river-right and you can even work your way up river-left for the small hole.

**Neil's** (44.108419, -122.432556) is a great medium-sized wave just shy of 1 mile downstream of the NF-805 bridge in the town of Nimrod. The best access is to float downstream from Clover, eventually taking out at the Silver Creek boat ramp.

—*Emile Elliott*

## THE RUNDOWN

The McKenzie River has a handful of fun play features. Redsides is one of Oregon's best summertime play-spots and during the winter months, Clover and Neil's offer decent waves.

**Difficulty:** Park and Play

**Gauge:** McKenzie River at Vida

**Best Close Food/Beers:** There is a small store and a diner in the town of Vida, plus a few more small towns upstream for more options

Emile Elliott

Ben Mckenzie playing at Neil's

Emile Elliott
Surfing at Redsides

# HENLINE CREEK

 Henline is an exciting run when streams in the area are running high. It is a very short, nonstop bedrock run that could be done in under 10 minutes if paddlers are familiar with it. However, plan on being there for a few hours as scouting your first lap takes time and boaters usually like to do a few laps. The first thing to do is look upstream from the bridge to assess the level: If it looks good, suit up and give the section a go! The portion of the creek from the put-in to just below this bridge is the best part. The rapids below the bridge are also good, but tend to have more issues. Some boaters choose to scout the entire run before putting on, while others scout from river level. To access the put-in, walk upstream from the bridge on river-right until the terrain guides you to river level. Scout out the entry rapid, then hold on for a wild ride! The first lap can be overwhelming, but with a lap or two under your belt, the run seems to lose a half-class of difficulty. Scout the section below the bridge carefully to assess the rapids but also to locate egress before Henline Falls, a 70-foot unrunnable drop. Finish the run on river-right, walk a few yards away from the stream to the trail, then walk back up and do it again!

## SHUTTLE DIRECTIONS

Follow I-5 to Salem, take the Detroit Lake exit, heading east on state Hwy. 22. Travel just under 22 miles to a left on North Fork Road SE moments before OR 22 crosses the Little NF Santiam. Follow this road 15.9 miles to a bridge over Henline Creek. To reach the put-in, walk upstream a few hundred yards on river-right until the terrain guides you down to the creek **(44.844634, -122.337708)**. The takeout is anywhere before Henline Falls on river-right **(44.840603, -122.336798)**. Henline Falls is just over a quarter-mile below the bridge. There is a trail you can follow back upstream to the road your car is on. Some boaters choose to portage Henline Falls and continue through Salmon Falls. See Opal Gorge entry for directions to the Salmon Falls takeout.

## THE RUNDOWN

Henline Falls can be portaged down into the Little North Santiam in order to add the last portion of Opal Gorge to the trip.

**Difficulty:** Class V-

**Gauge:** USGS #14182500— Little North Santiam River near Mehama, OR

**Flow Min-max:** 2,500-5,000 cfs

**Gradient:** 650 fpm. Put-in elevation: 1,500 feet

**Takeout:** Above Henline Falls

**Put-in:** 200 yards above the NF 2207 bridge

**Length:** 0.3 miles

**Hitchability:** Unnecessary

**Season:** Rainy

**Camping:** Yes

**4WD Needed?** No, gravel road driving required

**Best Close Food/Beers:** North Fork Crossing Restaurant, Lyons

**Quality (out of 5):** 4.5

**Raft Recommendations:** Has been done by Class V rafters, not recommended

Nate Pfeifer

Chris Tretwold on First Drop

Hilary Neevel running the Bridge Drop on Henline

# CEDAR CREEK

Most of this run is fast and steep class IV, with four stand-out rapids and some wood hazards. The biggest deterrent to this fun run seems to be the small eddies above the larger rapids. Fortunately, the run is roadside, so it is not difficult to scout out the eddy situation above the big drops beforehand. The most obvious put-in is the NF 2207 bridge, three miles upstream of the take out, but some may choose to put in one mile below this bridge and just above a sloping falls. The section above the bridge has seen some boating, but no documentation exists. There are at least three waterfalls in the 20-foot range up there, one of which has been run with certainty.

From the regular put-in bridge, the creek starts with some bedrock, but slows down for a bit, picking back up in the form of steep boulder rapids. When the road becomes visible on the left, you are just above the first notable challenge. This sloping, 10-foot falls lands in a pool with a rock under the surface. Run right, and keep that nose up. There is a series of boulder gardens leading right into the next and largest rapid on the run, Hellevator. Be sure to scout both of these rapids and the corresponding scouting eddies before putting on. Hellevator starts with a shallow twenty foot falls, feeding a slide that whips around a tight corner. This rapid is a harder version of the infamous "Gorilla" on the other side of the country. Hellevator can be portaged on the left via the road, paddlers put in a short distance downstream near the confluence with Sullivan Creek. The next horizon line below Sullivan Creek is a fun slide that is worth a scout.

Just around the corner from this slide is "Coombs", a tough 20-foot double drop with a number of hazards. Scout/portage left, and definitely check out the eddy situation beforehand as they are extremely limited. There are a number of steep class IV rapids between here and a hundred yard straight-away section of class II that ends when the creek bends right and drops over "The Impaler," a nasty rapid with limited eddies on the left where the portage is found. The run out of this rapid is a nice ledge, ending the Hard Knocks section and entering the less heinous lower portion of the creek. Paddlers will quickly encounter "Box Drop," stick to the theme and scout/portage left. The creek continues to rip along with a series of boulder gardens that are steeper than glimpses from the road would suggest. These boulder gardens continue to the confluence with Opal Creek, with a couple of ledges thrown in for good measure. As always, keep an eye out for wood. This is especially important on Cedar Creek, as this steep run is less conducive to amiable eddies than most. Take out just upstream of the "One Lane Bridge" sign 100 yards above the confluence with the Little North Santiam or continue another mile down to Three Pools.

—Jacob Cruser

## THE RUNDOWN

Every drop has been run, but it has been over a decade since that occurred.

**Difficulty:** Class V

**Gauge:** USGS #14182500—Little North Santiam near Mehama

**Flow Min-max:** Visual, worth a look between 1,000-3,000 cfs. The creek should look floatable, but there should still be plenty of rocks showing.

**Gradient:** 260 fpm. Put-in elevation: 2,200 feet

**Takeout:** Little North Santiam Confluence or Three Pools

**Put-in:** First Bridge over Cedar Creek, NF 2207

**Length:** 3 miles

**Hitchability:** Not a good option, mountain bike is possible alternative

**Season:** Rainy, buffered by snowmelt

**Camping:** Yes, throughout the area. Cedar Creek Campground is close.

**4WD Needed?** Helpful if there is snow on the ground (gravel shuttle road).

**Best Close Food/Beers:** North Santiam Crossing Restaurant

**Quality (out of 5):** 3.5

**Raft Recommendations:** No recommendations.

## SHUTTLE DIRECTIONS

Follow I-5 to Salem and take the Detroit Lake exit, heading east on state Hwy. 22. Travel just under 22 miles to a left on North Fork Road SE moments before OR 22 crosses the Little NF Santiam. Follow this road for 16.5 miles then turn right onto NF 2207 and continue 1.9 miles to a bridge over the Little North Santiam, which is the takeout **(44.846103, -122.298599)**. To reach the put-in, continue heading east on NF 2207 (paralleling Cedar Creek) 2.9 miles to the put-in bridge **(44.831389, -122.251099)**. At a minimum, it's advised to scout the eddy situations at 0.8, 1.7 and 1.9 miles above the takeout.

7

Jacob Cruser

Brian Butcher slides down Cedar Creek

293

# CANYON CREEK

This is a true Oregon classic, housing 7.5 miles of boulder gardens and ledges with some scenic floating through the lower portions. The upper two miles is high-quality, high-octane Class V, with a lower section allowing intermediate boaters to enjoy the creek. Once a hot commodity for Willamette Valley boaters, this run is no longer paddled nearly as often. The attrition could be credited to a landslide changing the largest rapid on the run (Day of Judgment), or perhaps to the lack of waterfalls to entice media-savvy boaters.

Using the uppermost put-in near the Owl Creek confluence, paddlers have about a half-mile of loggy boulder-bar floating to warm up on. When boulders start to appear, be ready to get out on river-right to scout the first rapid, Chocolate Chips. This two-part drop is one of the trickier rapids to style, but is less hazardous than some of the run's other standout rapids. There is a short Class IV boulder garden below here before the river bends right and enters Chicken Little, which has some large boulders and can be scouted/portaged left. Exiting this rapid, the creek keeps rolling with many Class IV-IV+ rapids that can be boat- or shore-scouted as necessary. One of the ledges, Demon Seed, sends much of the water under the right wall, making it nastier than the rest and often portaged on the right.

When the road becomes visible on the right, the run's two biggest rapids are not far. Scout both Terminator and Day of Judgement on the right. Terminator is usually run, but mind the sieve on the left and pocket on the right. Day of Judgment starts just downstream

📷 Nate Pfeifer

👁 Chris Arnold running Terminator on Upper Canyon Creek

## SHUTTLE DIRECTIONS

From I-5, take U.S. Hwy. 20 east through the towns of Lebanon and Sweet Home, then 15-16 miles past Sweet Home to the takeout at a bridge over Canyon Creek (44.396710, -122.447680). Just past the U.S. 20 bridge over Canyon Creek, turn right on NF 2022/Canyon Creek Rd and drive upstream 5 miles to the lower put-in trail, just short of the Black Creek bridge, or 7.2 miles where a right turn takes you to a bridge at the upper put-in (44.333984, -122.361904).

with a large ledge; catch an eddy below here on the right to scout/portage the rest. This rapid is less friendly since a landslide rearranged things and is most commonly portaged right these days. The next quarter-mile has a few Class IV-IV+ rapids, including a log move that can be difficult to scout. Fortunately it goes better than it looks from upstream (drive left).

Below this log move, the trail for the lower section meets the river. The first set of rapids is the most entertaining, with some nice ledges and sticky holes at higher flows. Less than a half-mile below the put-in, the lower run settles into a rhythm of Class II paddling separated by interesting bedrock ledges and chutes. The exception to the rule is the largest rapid on this lower section, Osprey. This rapid can sneak up on paddlers, feeding the current down the right channel through a series of ever more menacing holes between large boulders. There is a portage route on the right that is used more often than not. Nearing the end of the run is the Constrictor, a rapid that looks similar to the rest with the addition of a terminal hole at the base. Constrictor is an easy portage on the right at the end of a long and straight stretch of Class II. For boaters only running the lower portion of the creek, the last mile will be the best, possessing a high concentration of fun Class IV ledges in a gorge. Take out below the bridge on river-right, or continue onto the South Santiam to paddle the beautiful Hobbit Gorge.

*—Jacob Cruser*

## THE RUNDOWN

An abandoned classic in the Willamette Valley.

**Difficulty:** Class V (Class IV if using lower put-in)

**Gauge:** Estimate on Pat Welch's website (levels.wkcc.org); USGS #14185000— South Santiam River below Cascadia, OR

**Flow Min-max:** 300-800 cfs; 1,000-4,000 cfs

**Gradient:** 90 fpm, upper section has one mile at 200 fpm. Put-in elevation: 1,600 ft.

**Takeout:** U.S. Hwy. 20 bridge or Cascadia State Park

**Put-in:** Bridge near Owl Creek confluence

**Length:** 7.5 miles

**Hitchability:** Not a good option

**Season:** Rainy

**Camping:** Cascadia State Park

**4WD Needed?** No, gravel shuttle road though

**Best Close Food/Beers:** Sweet Home

**Quality (out of 5):** 4

**Raft Recommendations:** Not for part-time Class V rafters

# BATTLE AXE CREEK

I first heard about Battle Axe Creek in the early 2000s when my paddling crew started looking for adventure higher up several popular river basins. The regular, classic runs on Opal Creek were just starting to gain more traction as more paddlers heard stories of the fun, accessible rapids and flow information became available online. The Little North Santiam drainage can be particularly flashy with big rain storms, so even with a gauge it was often hard to predict whether the boating experience would be terrifying, fun, or too low.

The rumors about Battle Axe were that it had been run several times in the past, was very high quality but as hard to paddle as it was to dial in access and flows. All of these facts remain unchanged. There is still little beta about the run, though I'm sure there have been several descents since mine in 2004. That lack of reliable beta, however, only adds to the mystique and enjoyment for boaters who do make the effort and successfully complete a descent, so I won't spoil the surprise. Suffice it to say that Battle Axe is at least 5 miles upriver from the nearest road access, is snowed in early in the winter season some years, and contains many waterfalls and ledges up to 18 feet in a beautiful gorge setting. The creek at the suggested put-in is tiny and a bit claustrophobic. It was mostly clean when I was there, but wood is a constant concern and one misplaced piece could make for an exceptionally bad day. About halfway, things open up a bit but the rapids are harder in places. The big waterfall about a quarter-mile above the takeout is the perfect finale to a truly special trip

—*Pete Giordano*

## THE RUNDOWN

At the end of your trip, continue downstream of Jawbone Flats for another few miles and run a few more rapids including Cascada De Los Ninos.

**Difficulty:** Class IV+-V

**Gauge:** USGS #14182500—Little North Santiam River near Mehama

**Flow Min-max:** This gauge is far downstream, so it only gives a rough flow estimate. Expect maybe 10 percent of the flow at the takeout for Battle Axe, which generally has enough water when the gauge is 2,000 cfs or higher, although it's been run as low as 1,100 cfs during snowmelt. High water would create some very tough spots to stop and scout or portage.

**Gradient:** 235 fpm

**Takeout:** Jawbone Flats

**Put-in:** Trail 3369

**Length:** 2.2 miles

**Hitchability:** No

**Season:** Nov.-May

**Camping:** Yes

**4WD Needed?** No

**Best Close Food/Beers:** BYO, this is almost an hour from civilization

**Quality (out of 5):** 5

**Raft Recommendations:** No

## SHUTTLE DIRECTIONS

From the Willamette Valley, take state Hwy. 22 east from I-5. After 22 miles, turn left on North Fork Rd. After about 14 miles, the road turns to gravel and becomes NF-2209. Continue until it ends at the Opal Creek Trailhead. Jawbone Flats is about 3 miles upriver from here. Once at the Jawbone takeout **(44.846905, -122.208353)**, cross Battle Axe Creek and turn left, following the trail up along the creek until it intersects the an old road that continues upriver. From here, look for a sign for the Whetstone Mount Trail #3369 on the left which descends to the river. If you miss the trail there are a few other access points in the area **(44.856566, -122.169790)**.

Jason Rackley

No swimming allowed on Battle Axe, best bring your boof stroke!

The Clackamas River just outside of Estacada, Ore., offers great intermediate rafting and kayaking. The classic intermediate section begins just above the Three Lynx power station and ends at Moore Creek access site. The stretch from Hole in the Wall to Moore Creek is a go-to run for local and out-of-town boaters alike. Although it lacks some of the steep, narrow rapids found in the Columbia River Gorge, year-round flows, mild winter weather, and great whitewater make this run a classic!

The river section upstream of Hole in the Wall consists of several great rapids separated by longer stretches of quiet water. This section is farther from the road so boaters get a nice sense of isolation. Powerhouse Rapid is just downstream from the put-in, while the Narrows is about a mile farther downstream and Roaring River another mile below that. Carter Bridge and Toilet Bowl are the two signature rapids downstream of the lower put-in and push Class IV at high water levels. Both have multiple lines to choose from and can be scouted from the road at MP 38.5 and 37.5, respectively.

Every May, whitewater enthusiasts from around the Northwest come to celebrate the river and compete in fun, competitive events that take place at the Carter Bridge site on the Upper Clackamas. Slalom, downriver, and head-to-head races, plus boat demos, music, food and great camping have brought hundreds of people to celebrate the Clackamas for over 30 years. The charm of the Clackamas lies not only in its whitewater but also in the community that calls the river home. The welcoming attitude of paddlers and the river's logistic ease make it the perfect after-work summer run. If you happen to be in the area during the hot months you might even be lucky enough to catch the weekly Carnage/Confidence Run—a Wednesday evening weekly gathering of paddlers that has been a tradition for over 15 years and runs from June–Sept. (visit upperclackamasfestival.org)

—Luke Spencer

## THE RUNDOWN

At flows above 7,000 cfs, the river develops features similar to rapids on much bigger rivers like the Grand Canyon. Waves are huge in places and the current is close to 15 mph.

**Difficulty:** Class III-IV

**Gauge:** USGS #14209500—Clackamas River above Three Lynx Creek, OR

**Flow Min-max:** 400-10,000 cfs

**Gradient:** 33 fpm

**Takeout:** Moore Creek

**Put-in:** Sandstone Bridge

**Length:** 12 miles

**Hitchability:** Yes

**Season:** Year-round

**Camping:** Yes, multiple Forest Service campsites and unimproved camping available

**4WD Needed?** No

**Best Close Food/Beers:** El Pepe taco truck/stand on state Highway 224 in Estacada ($1.50 tacos!), Cazadero Bar on the corner of OR 224 and 211

**Quality (out of 5):** 4-

**Raft Recommendations:** This stretch is friendly for all type of craft at appropriate water levels

Jacob Cruser

A calm spot on the Clackamas

## SHUTTLE DIRECTIONS

Moore Creek is roughly a one-hour drive from downtown Portland. Take state Hwy. 205 to Exit 12. Head east to the OR 212-224 junction, then turn right to follow OR 224. Continue through the town of Estacada, then beyond it an additional 11 miles. Moore Creek will be on your right (45.195172, -122.189746). To get to Fish Creek, continue approximately 3 miles to Milepost 39, turn right on Forest Road 54, cross the bridge, and take the first right into the Fish Creek Trailhead parking lot **(45.157451, -122.151213)**. To get to Three Lynx, continue up OR 224 for 6.6 miles past the Fish Creek turnoff to the Sandstone bridge. **(45.115471, -122.075229)**

# NORTH FORK OF THE CLACKAMAS

Bryon Dorr 📷
NF Falls after the recent landslide change 👁

Often overlooked by Portland-area boaters, the North Fork Clackamas is one of the closet Class IV-V runs near Portland. A great winter and spring run, the NF drains into the NF Reservoir below the Wild & Scenic section of the Upper Clackamas. Although relatively short, the NF can dish out a nasty lesson to those in over their head. This small, steep tributary offers boaters a secluded canyon, tight boulder gardens, blind ledges, twisting narrow drops, and waterfalls. Hazards and a continually changing creekbed demand kayakers' attention and skill as they descend toward the reservoir.

From the put-in, where the old abandoned road meets the creek, boaters get a nice warmup as the gradient steepens and rapids increase in difficulty. One or two easy portages are likely before the fun Class III-IV mini-gorge sweeps boaters into the heart of the canyon! Paddlers can scout the top part of the gorge from river-left, but more often, boat-scouting is in order. Fun Class IV continues as kayakers approach the crux of the gorge, where they must decide whether to portage the falls known as Speed Bump, making the portage around the next 50-foot falls substantially easier, or run Speed Bump. The latter choice forces paddlers to make the grueling walk through the clear-cut followed by a muddy rope-assisted descent back to the river just below the falls. The easier route above Speed Bump historically follows a logging road then drops back down to the top of Stairway to Heaven—thought clear-cutting may have altered that route.

Stairway to Heaven, the run's biggest rapid, sits just downstream of the 50-foot falls. This 30-foot slide has a stout hole at medium to high flows, so having a kayaker with a throw-rope placed below the drop is recommended. Below S.T.H., the river starts to change in character. The falls and basalt bedrock give way to continuous Class III and a couple of rocky Class IV+s. The potential for pins and increased wood make this run a true Oregon creeking experience. Just above the reservoir, logjams become frequent. Luckily, just when the portaging grows old, the lake appears. A short paddle across the North Fork arm of the reservoir gets you to the takeout.

—Luke Spencer

# NORTH FORK OF THE CLACKAMAS

**7**

Luke Spencer

## THE RUNDOWN

The canyon is named after the 50-footer that has yet to be run. It filled in with rubble after a 2014 landslide.

**Difficulty:** Class IV-V (P)

**Gauge:** Estimate from USGS #14209500—Clackamas River above Three Lynx Creek, with good flows at 3,500 cfs and rising, or preferably 5-6,000 cfs and dropping. It has been run down as low as 2,500 cfs on this gauge, but the run's quality decreases. Beware that spring and winter levels may not correlate.

**Flow Min-max:** 250-1,000 cfs

**Gradient:** 200 fpm. Put-in elevation: 1,400 feet

**Takeout:** Next to closed gate on state Hwy 224, North Fork Clackamas arm of NF Reservoir

**Put-in:** A spur road descends close to the creek and provides access

**Length:** 3.5 miles

**Hitchability:** No

**Season:** When it rains heavily

**Camping:** Up the main stem of the Clackamas, closest campground is Lazy Bend

**4WD Needed?** No

**Best Close Food/Beers:** Cazadero Restaurant & Bar, Estacada

**Quality (out of 5):** 3.5

**Raft Recommendations:** Not recommended, but it has been done a couple times.

## SHUTTLE DIRECTIONS

Take out where state Hwy. 224 crosses the NF arm of the North Fork Reservoir **(45.233280, -122.253177)**. To reach the North Fork put-in, continue SE on OR 224 and turn left at the sign marked "Clackamas River RV Park" across the highway from Promontory Park. Stay left, turning onto FS-4160 continue the uphill drive for a little over 3 miles. Look for an abandoned road on the left designating OHV use. This is the road you use to hike down into the canyon for about 10 minutes, or until the old road parallels the creek at river level. Find an easy spot here to put in **(45.227664, -122.212575)**.

Luke Spencer

301

# OAK GROVE FORK

## OF THE CLACKAMAS RIVER

The Oak Grove Fork winds through a beautiful, forested gorge with large, mossy boulders that form technical, interesting rapids. This section rarely runs, as most of the water is diverted for hydropower at Lake Harriet. Rarely, during high-water events, there is enough water spilling over the dam to paddle the river.

The first view of the river from the put-in at the dam looks serious, as the river twists away into a tight, vertical-walled gorge. Paddlers should exercise caution working their ways downstream, as the river never gets high enough to flush out wood. Dangerous logs are an ever-present threat.

Below the first constriction are several bouldery Class IV drops and some logs in tight places that can be avoided with precise eddy-hopping. The river maintains a continuous character, but the difficulty eases as paddlers arrive at the first large drop on the river, Crack Falls. You will hear the falls long before you get to it, and stopping above it is easy. Crack is a fascinating cascade that drops into a narrow rock channel, then turns left and falls 15 feet into the actual crack, which is about 10 feet wide. Just downstream, the exit from the crack is guarded by another 10-foot drop that falls into a powerful hole with a couple of logs mixed in just for fun.

Portaging Crack Falls is relatively easy, and below the falls the difficulty decreases as the river approaches the finale, Barrier Falls. This runnable 25-foot waterfall was named by the fisheries biologists, as it prevents migrating fish from getting upstream. Portaging Barrier is also relatively easy, for those who choose not to run it.

After Barrier, the difficulty eases but the logs remain, though most can be avoided.

*—Jason Rackley*

## THE RUNDOWN

Rarely run, but a new online gauge may make boating opportunities more abundant.

**Difficulty:** Class IV ( V, P)

**Gauge:** USGS #14209250—Oak Grove Fork at Ripplebrook Campground, OR

**Flow Min-max:** 300 cfs is a runnable flow, upper limits unknown. Be careful of wood.

**Gradient:** 130 fpm, almost 200 fpm in the first gorge

**Takeout:** 224 bridge over the Oak Grove Fork

**Put-in:** Below the dam that forms Lake Harriet, on FR 4630.

**Length:** 6 miles

**Hitchability:** Not the best

**Season:** Fall/winter rains or high water events

**Camping:** Yes, it's everywhere in the Clackamas drainage

**4WD Needed?** No, but some gravel roads

**Best Close Food/Beers:** Old Mill Saloon or the Safari Club in Estacada are local favorites

**Quality (out of 5):** 3

**Raft Recommendations:** Lots of work cut out for rafters

## SHUTTLE DIRECTIONS

There are two different ways to access the put-in, which is important given that gates may be closed when attempting to access this run. Route 1: From Estacada, take state Hwy. 224 for 25 miles until you cross the Oak Grove Fork bridge (which is the takeout). Immediately turn left onto Oak Grove Fork Rd. (NF-57), which is paved. Drive 6.3 miles until you cross the Oak Grove Fork again. Immediately turn left on NF-4630 and drive 1.5 miles along Lake Harriet until you get to the dam. Route 2: From Estacada, take state Hwy. 224 for 24.4 miles until you reach Ripplebrook Road. Turn left on Ripplebrook and follow it approximately 2.4 miles until it intersects with NF-4630. Turn right on NF-4630 for approximately 3 miles until you reach the dam at Lake Harriet, and put in at the base of the dam **(45.075237, -121.970139)**. The takeout is where OR 224 crosses the Oak Grove Fork near the Ripplebrook Ranger Station **(45.079656, -122.042770)**.

Jason Rackley

Josh Knapp working through the Oak Grove Fork at 300 cfs

# COLLAWASH RIVER

The first few miles of the run are easy Class II floating, with classic Oregon scenery to help this first hour fly pleasantly by. There is one small bedrock rapid to break up the Class II and a large logjam that signals the end of the float-in. The logjam is one of the largest in Oregon—a cool thing to see! The logs are mostly stable, making portaging easier than it may appear at first glance. Below the logjam is a couple hundred yards of flatwater with dead trees standing as sentinels, guarding the entrance to the whitewater section which starts in earnest just around the corner. The first rapid is a nice Class IV along the left wall to get your balance under you. Eddy out immediately after on the left to scout Big Dog. Here boulders have forced the river onto the left wall, creating a large rapid. This rapid has been run, but can be portaged on the right. After Big Dog, the river bends left, then right and over the Churn. This rapid is ever changing and can be scouted/portaged with minimal difficulty on the right. Rapids continue for two miles before reaching the takeout bridge. One rapid about a half-mile above the bridge, called The Cave, has a number of hazards to be assessed before running. Paddlers can take out at the bridge or continue as far as they wish into the next section, which is mostly Class II-III aside from two larger rapids (Boulderdash and Chute to Kill).

## THE RUNDOWN

Hiking upstream of the put in area on river left along a trail for about 1 mile adds a Class V gorge (though an unportageable rapid often collects wood so the whole gorge should be scouted before putting on).

**Difficulty:** Class IV-V

**Gauge:** USGS #14209500—Clackams River above Three Lynx Creek

**Flow Min-max:** 2,000 cfs (max unknown, 4,000 cfs is not too high)

**Gradient:** 80 fpm, steepest section is 150 fpm. Put-in elevation: 2,500 ft.

**Takeout:** Peat Creek

**Put-in:** Near East Fork Collawash-Elk Lake Creek confluence

**Length:** 6 miles

**Hitchability:** Not a viable option

**Season:** Rainy and snowmelt

**Camping:** Yes, throughout the entire Clackamas drainage. Try Little Fan Campground near the Hot Springs Fork confluence.

**4WD Needed?** No, but gravel roads need to be driven

**Best Close Food/Beers:** Estacada

**Quality (out of 5):** 4

**Raft Recommendations:** Would be fun if not for the log jam portage, so can't really be recommended.

## SHUTTLE DIRECTIONS

From the intersection of state highways 212 and 224 in Estacada, drive east on OR 224 for 28.8 miles. Turn right onto National Forest Road 63 and follow it for 5.9 miles to a bridge over the Collawash marking the takeout **(44.966558, -122.045241)**. Park cars a quarter-mile downstream for a bonus Class IV rapid. From the takeout bridge, continue driving upstream 8.8 miles on NF 63 (stay right at Mile 6.5) to reach the put-in bridge **(44.897741, -122.006247)**.

Pete Giordano

Beginning of the Class V gorge above the standard put-in

# BUTTE CREEK

This is a nice intermediate run in the middle Willamette Valley area. Only a half-hour off I-5 near Salem, this run sees plenty of action from boaters looking for something a bit different: long Class II stretches punctuated by action-packed sections of bedrock Class III-IV. The biggest rapids are at the put-in and takeout, both of which can be skipped.

The put-in is just short of a Boy Scout camp. Signs along the gravel road read "No Trespassing," but boaters have historically been granted access. Be sure to park in the open area at the put-in and not along the gravel road on the way there.

Scout the first rapid before putting on; the Butte Crack is a flume that bounces between narrow walls as it incises through a fault line. Boaters can seal-launch in below, or find a way to scramble down to the water if this drop (not commonly run) is contrary to their liking. Downstream is a warmup stretch leading into a set of Class III slides. Take note of Coal Creek entering in on the right via a slide of its own. (Access to this run has been made via that creek as well.) Below the Coal Creek confluence is some mellow floating with a couple of surf waves at higher flows. The next named rapid, Splittin' Hairs, is a small ledge just above a private bridge, where the creek splits around a small rock outcrop and both sides become problematic at lower flows.

More mellow floating leads to a good stretch of a couple bedrock rapids, both of which can be scouted from the river-right bank. The first is run along the right-hand side, with the crux move occurring at the end, where a ledge-hole should be run on the left. Between this drop and the next rapid, Knuckle Buster, is a small hole just above the scouting eddy. Knuckle Buster has a variety of lines at higher flows, but the line seems to become less obvious at lower levels. Following this set of rapids, the creek continues along with stretches of Class II broken up here and there by a bedrock rapid or ledge. As the run nears its end, a final bedrock section with basalt walls appears and offers a quarter-mile of fun rapids.

Not long after this gorge, the stream pools up above a hybrid falls-dam combo. This is the Scotts Mills Dam, confident boaters can take the fun plunge over the drop. If this drop is too intimidating, boaters can take out in the grassy park on the left. If the drop is run, there is a short set of fun ledges below to be negotiated before the takeout. Take note that the closer one gets to the bridge, the more difficult it is to find egress to the road.

Another 10-15 miles upstream of this run are a set of fun waterfalls that can be park-and-hucked. The first is 25 feet, the second 80 feet, and the third is 30 feet. There are nice trails to these falls, but the access road is sometimes gated. (These falls are described in the next entry.)

—Jacob Cruser

## THE RUNDOWN

The mile above the put-in has some nice Class IV action if you can get access figured out.

**Difficulty:** Class III-IV (V)

**Gauge:** USGS #14201500—Butte Creek at Monitor

**Flow Min-max:** 250-1,000 cfs (higher by people who know the run)

**Gradient:** 70 fpm. Put-in elevation: 775 feet

**Takeout:** Scotts Mills Park

**Put-in:** Fault Line

**Length:** 5 miles

**Hitchability:** Could be done, a bike is a better option here

**Season:** Rainy

**Camping:** Silver Falls Park is about a half-hour away

**4WD Needed?** No

**Best Close Food/Beers:** Silverton

**Quality (out of 5):** 3

**Raft Recommendations:** Can be rafted on the upper end of recommended flows

## SHUTTLE DIRECTIONS

Drive to Scotts Mills, 20 miles northeast of Salem. The main road through town (Nowlens Bridge/3rd/Mount Angel Scotts Mills Rd.) crosses over Butte Creek just east of the main part of town. The best parking is 100 yards upstream of this bridge along Crooked Finger Rd. on river-left at Scotts Mills Park (45.043164, -122.665822). If the gate is open, leave your vehicle within the park. If the gate is closed, there is a pull-out just uphill from the park entrance. For the put-in, return to and cross over the bridge over Butte Creek. Take your first right onto Maple Grove Rd., then take the very next right within a hundred feet onto Butte Creek Rd. Follow it 4.6 miles to a gravel road and turn right. Follow this gravel road for 0.7 miles where a parking area on the left can be used by boaters (45.006868, -122.593448). There are No Trespassing signs, but historically paddlers have been allowed to park here. Alternately, put in on Coal Creek (which you cross seconds after turning onto the gravel road). Coal Creek enters Butte Creek via a 10-foot slide best run on the right.

# BUTTE CREEK FALLS

Butte Creek is along forest road CF400 southeast of Portland. Crisscrossed with logging roads and trails, the area is well known and access is easy. The upper falls is about 20 feet tall and is fairly straightforward. It is a wide, even ledge falls with multiple line options and lands into a large pool.

The middle falls is about 80 feet tall and should be considered by waterfall experts only. There is a tight slot rapid just above the large falls that is often jammed with wood. The Big Boy itself is clean on the left and cascades down the rock shelf on the right. The left wall at the base of the falls is a bit overhung, and can develop a dangerous boil and recirculation at some water levels.

The pool is large, but empties over another difficult and dangerous falls that splits around a tall finger of rock before falling around 30 feet to a somewhat questionable landing. There is a ledge that extends near the base of the falls, but might not be an issue. As with any big falls, scout carefully before making a decision.

Access is easy, but consequences could be great. The main falls has had limited descents and should be considered by WATERFALL EXPERTS ONLY.

*—Chris Korbulic*

## THE RUNDOWN

While the upper drop is a local go-to park and huck, the lower two drops are for expert waterfall runners only.

**Difficulty:** Class IV, V+, V

**Gauge:** USGS #14201500— Butte Creek at Monitor

**Flow Min-max:** 200-2,000 cfs (over 1,000 cfs is optimal for the Middle Falls)

**Gradient:** 20 ft. + 80 ft. + 30 ft. in approx. 0.5 miles

**Takeout:** Above or below falls of your choice

**Put-in:** Above upper falls

**Length:** .20 miles

**Hitchability:** N/A

**Season:** Spring, winter, fall

**Camping:** In surrounding National Forest

**4WD Needed?** No

**Best Close Food/Beers:** Silverton

**Quality (out of 5):** 5+

**Raft Recommendations:** Not recommended, injury probability is high.

## SHUTTLE DIRECTIONS

From the town of Scotts Mills, turn onto Crooked Finger Road. After about 11.5 miles on Crooked Finger Rd., turn left onto road CF400. Continue on CF400 for 1.9 miles to the trailhead **(44.920889, -122.511075)**.

Cade Waud
Kory Kellum running the Upper 20-foot falls

# BREITENBUSH RIVER

With crystal-clear water, numerous quality Class III-IV rapids, wonderful scenery and a long season, the Breitenbush River is, for many paddlers (particularly those living in the mid-Willamette valley), their first taste of creeking. Because it's often a paddler's first foray into the world of small creeks, the Breitenbush either has a punishing or playful reputation depending on how the day went. Either way, many experienced paddlers come back to the Breitenbush for an entertaining and relaxing trip, yet still tell stories of their misadventures as they ride to the put-in or connect at the takeout after the run.

There are easy options to put in at the bridge above Cleator Bend Campground. But if the first turn just downstream of the bridge is blocked by wood, there is usually a good put-in option at the entrance of the campground. Just downstream is the first rapid where boaters get a taste of what the Breitenbush has to offer with some fun moves past or through holes and stepping down over small ledges. If boaters have trouble here, it might be better on a different day as the rapids only get harder downstream and egress to the road is difficult in places. Generally considered the hardest rapid on the run, the Slot is less than a half-mile from the put-in and contains a near river-wide ledge with a very sticky hole at most levels, followed by a narrow, twisty flume that ends in a good pool. Many boaters do just fine on the ledge only to relax and have trouble with the slot just downstream. Either way, it's a great rapid to start your run.

The rest of the first 6 miles contains lots of rapids and small ledges, almost all of which can be boat-scouted, though it is difficult to see the bottom of some of the rapids without getting out of your boat. Experienced paddlers will find this entertaining while the less experienced could be intimidated. When in doubt, scout for wood that crops up in different places every year.

After crossing under the road bridge below Humbug Creek Campground, the river widens and gains volume and push, making for a fun change of pace compared to the upper section. Barbell Rapid isn't very far downstream of the bridge and has a fun ledge-line on the right of the large rock in the middle of the river, plus an interesting line on the left. Woo Man Chew Rapid is the run's last significant rapid, where the short plunge through a hole on the left or an airplane-turn plunge on the right (if the water is high enough) makes for an exciting, satisfying finish.

*—Pete Giordano*

## THE RUNDOWN

The Bretitenbush Hot Springs Resort makes for an interesting visit if in the area.

**Difficulty:** Class III-IV

**Gauge:** USGS #14179000—Breitenbush River above French Creek near Detroit

**Flow Min-max:** 400-2,000 cfs

**Gradient:** 62 fpm

**Takeout:** Gauging Station

**Put-in:** Bridge upstream of Cleator Bend Campground

**Length:** 8 miles

**Hitchability:** Fair

**Season:** November to June

**Camping:** Yes

**4WD Needed?** No

**Best Close Food/Beers:** BYO, although there are some local places in Detroit

**Quality (out of 5):** 4

**Raft Recommendations:** Above 800 cfs

## SHUTTLE DIRECTIONS

The Breitenbush River is located just outside the small town of Detroit, Ore., accessible from the Willamette Valley and Bend along state Hwy 22. From town, travel east on NF-46 or follow signs to Breitenbush Hot Springs Resort. The takeout is only a few miles from town and is located along the road just downstream of a gate on the road to the gauging station **(44.750180, -122.133570)**. Reach the put-in by continuing upstream on NF-46 until the junction of NF-2231 just past Cleator Bend Campground **(44.778452, -121.999585)**.

Pete Giordano 📷

Scott Gerber entering Entry Ledge on the Slot 👁

# ABIQUA CREEK

This run is a hike-and-huck special. Scout the first falls, Momma Duke's, before putting in. It can then be lapped easily on the left. Once you have had your fill, it is only 40 yards to the next falls, Peony Falls, which is a clean 20-foot waterfall that lands in a friendly pool. It can be lapped with a little effort on the right. Downstream, the creek enters the Mother's Day Gorge, which contains a handful of Class III bedrock rapids before the creek funnels down into the Cattle Ramp. To avoid getting swept into Cattle Ramp (which sometimes collects wood), don't commit to going downstream anywhere on the run unless you are sure you see the next eddy to stop in. If you can't see the next eddy, you are probably at Cattle Ramp, so utilize the slow moving water to hop out on the creek-left bench to scout and/or portage. Here the creek funnels down to a tight corner and over a 5 foot ledge. Take out immediately below this rapid on the right above the horizon line that is Abiqua Falls. If you are paddling the creek too high, you will not be able to take out and will be forced to run the falls. Currently 500 cfs is the highest this section has been run and taking out was not a problem.. From the lip of the falls, a scramble and some rope work is required to get up the initial cliff band before a short walk out along a trail. If you want some more waterfall practice check out Butte Creek Falls, which is found in the next drainage over.

## SHUTTLE DIRECTIONS

From the town of Scotts Mills, turn onto Crooked Finger Road near the bridge over Butte Creek heading south. After 9.5 miles, the road turns to gravel. Drive another 1.4 miles before turning right onto a poorly marked spur road. Follow the route shown on the map 1.6 miles to the put-in, where a decommissioned road heads upstream (you should be able to see the creek through the brush from where you park). From here, walk upstream a couple hundred yards before dropping down to the creek via a short but steep trail, slippery if it has been raining **(44.922103, -122.559576)**. The easiest way to do shuttle is to walk the half-mile from the end of the takeout trail. If you are using a vehicle for shuttle, drive downstream about 0.5 miles from where the vehicles get left near the put-in to a barely noticeable pull-out on the creek-side of the road. There will be a small trail heading upstream from this pull-out that you will use to exit the creek **(44.926404, -122.567634)**. Look for a painted square on trees at both the put-in and takeout parking areas.

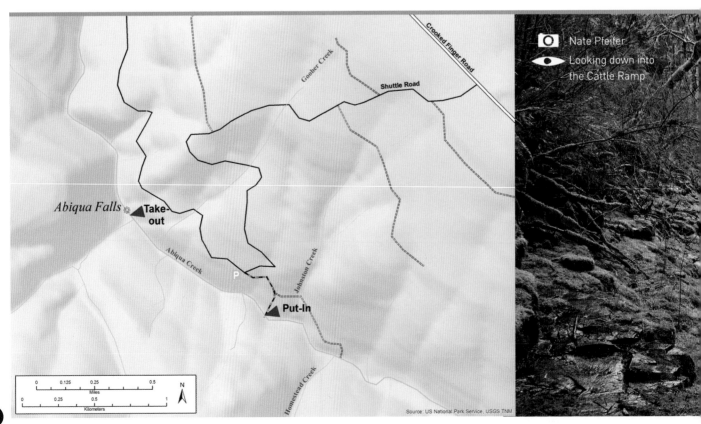

Nate Pfeifer

Looking down into the Cattle Ramp

## THE RUNDOWN

The massive waterfall at the takeout has been run successfully at flows over 1,000 cfs on the Butte Creek gauge.

**Difficulty:** Class IV+

**Gauge:** USGS #14201500—Butte Creek at Monitor

**Flow Min-max:** 200-500 cfs

**Gradient:** 120 feet in a half-mile. Put-in elevation: 1,360 feet

**Takeout:** Pool above Abiqua Falls

**Put-in:** Roadside pull-out

**Length:** 0.5 miles

**Hitchability:** No need, easiest to walk

**Season:** Rainy, often in when other stuff has just dropped out

**Camping:** No

**4WD Needed?** It reduces stress, but can be done in most vehicles.

**Best Close Food/Beers:** Salem

**Quality (out of 5):** 3.5

**Raft Recommendations:** Likely not worth the effort. An IK would be a better option.

Nate Pfeifer

Andrew Bradley running Peony Falls on Abiqua Creek

# THREE BEARS RUN

## OF THE MOLALLA RIVER

The Three Bears section of the Molalla is a fantastic intermediate run with high-quality technical pool-drop rapids. Boulder gardens, small ledges, and a narrow steep-walled canyon await paddlers on the descent! The most challenging rapids on the run are named after the children's story "Goldilocks and the Three Bears." Papa Bear, Mamma Bear, Baby Bear, and Goldilocks are enjoyable for both intermediate and advanced boaters. Great roadside access, superb scenery, and a general lack of crowds make this an instant river-running classic. High flows (over 5,000 cfs) deliver fun playboating and exciting downriver action with powerful holes, exploding waves, and surging hydraulics! Mamma Bear, the largest rapid, starts with a right-to-left bend as water pours through a solid Class III-IV boulder garden terminating in a vertical-walled mini-canyon with spectacular columnar basalt formations that spiral high on the canyon wall. While flows are up, take the time to explore the Upper and Lower Table Rock Sections as well as the Nasty Fork. But don't be lured upstream unless the Three Bears section is feeling pushy and high or you'll be wondering how you allowed yourself to be talked into a boney, slow Class II-III run. On the contrary, if flows are below 3000 cfs and you;re looking for a quick Class IV-V fix, the short, scenic gorge section of the Table Rock Fork should be just what the doctor ordered. This superb run is often overlooked with so many options available in the area, so make sure to put it on your short list of must-do rivers!

—Luke Spencer

## THE RUNDOWN

In the 1840s, mining became popular in the area near the headwaters of Ogle Creek on the Molalla River.

**Difficulty:** Class III-IV

**Gauge:** USGS #14200000—Mollala near Canby

**Flow Min-max:** 1,000-10,000 cfs

**Gradient:** 55 fpm. Put-in elevation: 1,000 ft.

**Takeout:** Roadside pull-out just upstream of Glen Avon Bridge (do not cross bridge)

**Put-in:** Roadside pull-out just upstream of Tucker Bridge

**Length:** 5 miles

**Hitchability:** Moderately easy, but don't expect many cars on the road during the rainy season

**Season:** Fall, winter, spring, early summer

**Camping:** Yes, great camping up and down the river!

**4WD Needed?** No

**Best Close Food/Beers:** Best to bring your own.

**Quality (out of 5):** 5

**Raft Recommendations:** Good to go!

## SHUTTLE DIRECTIONS

Head to Molalla, continue southeast through town and turning right toward Feyrer Park Road. Continue past the park, over the bridge and the Molalla River, and take a right on Dickey Prairie Rd. Go past the Dickey Prairie Store, veering right at the three-way intersection and continue upstream until you cross the NF Molalla. Glen Avon Bridge will be about a quarter-mile on the left. Continue another quarter-mile and park on your right (river left) where there's a car-width pull-out next to the river **(45.080965, -122.485447)**. To find the put-in, go back downstream the short distance, turn left at the first road, cross the bridge, and continue upstream approx. 9 miles on South Molalla Forest Rd. After crossing the Turner Bridge, find the large gravel pull-out next to the river a quarter-mile upstream **(44.980119, -122.482162)**.

Brian Vogt
Chris Vogt enjoying the scenic Molalla River

Priscilla Macy
Molalla Panorama

# TABLE ROCK FORK

## OF THE MOLALLA RIVER

The Molalla River has long been an intermediate classic for Portland mid-Willamette Valley boaters. It is a bit surprising that the Table Rock Fork only got popular in the late '90s. Perhaps the fact that it lacks the classic scenery of other parts of the Molalla kept it off boaters' radars. What it lacks in scenery, however, it more than makes up for with continuous, steep Class III-IV whitewater. The most popular section is located just downstream of a short section with several Class IV-V drops and just above a difficult Class V gorge. Pick your put-in and takeout carefully!

The nature of this run changes dramatically with water levels. At low water, be prepared for a steep, rock-bashing trip with constant maneuvering. At high flows, most of the rocks get covered, and the river becomes a freight train with very few eddies and some surprisingly powerful holes throughout. The run almost always has some wood to contend with so best not to jump on unwittingly at high water.

From the put-in bridge, the river immediately drops through a long series of steep, fun boulder gardens. These are typical of much of the run and make for a good start to the trip. After a brief break, be prepared for the Pinch, the trickiest rapid on the run. The Pinch can be scouted from either side of the river but is best portaged on the left. It contains several tight lines at the top leading into a narrow slot with a powerful diagonal wave which flips boats into the right wall. After a very short pool there is another steep drop into a river-wide hole. There is very little recovery time below as the river continues to rip downstream.

After miles of great, fun rapids, the river again picks up steam in the last mile descending though several great rapids. At high water this section is solid Class IV with big waves and powerful holes—all very visible from the road so you can plan ahead. At high water, I usually like to come back up and just run the last mile a second time. So fun!

—Pete Giordano

## THE RUNDOWN

The Class V gorge below the takeout can easily be seen from the road on the drive. Well worth a stop, particularly at high water.

**Difficulty:** Class III-III+

**Gauge:** USGS #14200000—Molalla River near Canby

**Flow Min-max:** 2,500-6,000 cfs on the Canby gauge. Judge actual river level visually along the shuttle.

**Gradient:** 120 fpm. Put-in elevation: 2088 ft.

**Takeout:** Roadside pull-out about 1.5 miles upstream of the lowest bridge over the Table Rock Fork (Rooster Rock Rd. bridge).

**Put-in:** Bridge across from Quarry, 6.7 miles upstream of Rooster Rock Rd. bridge.

**Length:** 5 miles

**Hitchability:** Poor

**Season:** November to May

**Camping:** Yes

**4WD Needed?** No

**Best Close Food/Beers:** Molalla is pretty hit or miss for food or drink

**Quality (out of 5):** 4

**Raft Recommendations:** Marginal but could be done at high water

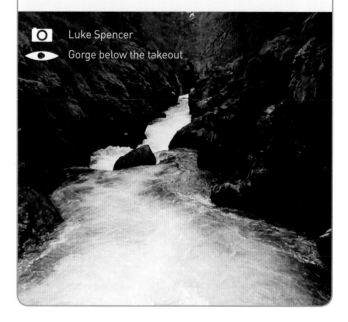

Luke Spencer

Gorge below the takeout

Michael Freeman

Anna Herring in The Pinch

## SHUTTLE DIRECTIONS

From the junction of state Hwy. 211 and Mathias Rd. east of downtown Molalla, travel south on Mathias Rd. Stay left on S. Feyrer Park Rd. Turn right on Dickey Prairie Rd. after crossing the Molalla River and continue upstream about 5.5 miles. Turn right on Molalla River Rd., crossing the Molalla River and continue upstream about another 12.5 miles to where the Table Rock Fork Rd. begins on the left. This is a gravel road. Travel about 2.5 miles to the large pullout on the right near the river **(44.980715, -122.386815)**.

To reach the put-in, continue upstream on the Table Fork Rd. another 5 miles and look for a gated bridge crossing the river on the right. Access the river around the bridge unless you want to tackle the harder rapids just upstream, if so, continue upstream to the next bridge over the stream or to a gate. Do not block any of the gates in the area **(44.990492, -122.303124)**.

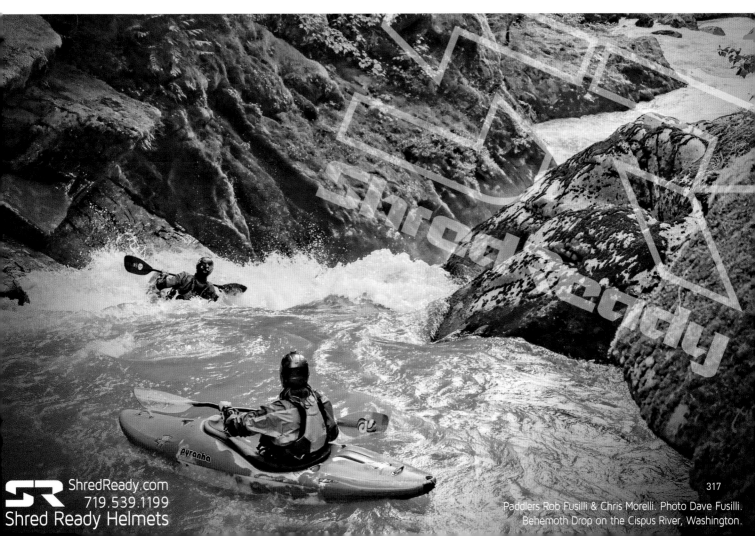

Paddlers Rob Fusilli & Chris Morelli. Photo Dave Fusilli.
Behemoth Drop on the Cispus River, Washington.

# HONORABLE MENTIONS

## OF THE WILLAMETTE VALLEY

**The Killer Fang stretch of the Clackamas** is characterized by easy floating through a rugged landscape interrupted by rapids created by landslides. These rapids tend to have large boulders creating sieves, but also channels with safe passage for intermediate/advanced boaters. While not much more difficult overall than the Classic Three Lynx section of the Clackamas, this run is more adventurous and consequential. The run's Killer Fang namesake is an extremely hazardous rapid ending in a near river-wide sieve about halfway through the run. This rapid is preceded by the Class III-IV Prelude, which ends in a moving pool (at higher flows) from which you can portage on the right. Put in near the confluence with the Collawash and take out at the turnoff to Indian Henry Campground, also the put-in for the Three Lynx run. (Flows: 1,000 cfs at Three Lynx is low but runnable.) Takeout: 45.114401, -122.074086. Put-in: 45.031985, -122.060817.

**Brice Creek** is a Class IV-IV+ roadside classic near Eugene. Look for 5.25 to 6.5 feet in the Row River. The upper put-in is either just above, or at a bridge a quarter-mile below Parker Falls depending on the wood situation. The lower put-in is at a bridge just below the Champion Creek confluence (also runnable). The takeout is at the Cedar Creek Camp (43.671151, -122.707775). Lower Put-in: 43.641905, -122.658481. Upper Put-in: 43.637028, -122.616891.

**The Roaring River** is a fun mission in the Clackamas drainage: high-quality Class IV boating with a clean 30-footer. Access is challenging and requires navigation of logging roads and a hike in. Shoot for 2,500-3500 cfs in the Clackamas gauge at Three Lynx, be wary of high flows. Check oregonkayaking.net for directions and other info. Takeout: 45.158884, -122.117408. Put-in: 45.178694, -122.064358.

**Staley Creek** is a roadside classic high in the Middle Fork Willamette drainage. Mostly Class III-IV with two Vs. Look for between 2,500 and 5,000 cfs at the inflow to Hills Creek Reservoir. Put in near the confluence with Davey Creek and take out at a bridge just above the Dome Creek confluence. Check wheelsandwater.blogspot.com for more info. Takeout: 43.452318, -122.365703. Put-in: 43.409210, -122.356806.

**The North Santiam River** is a summertime classic that never gets too low. The run from Big Cliff dam to Packsaddle Park is Class III (IV+) with a dam to negotiate. Packsaddle to Mill City is a beginner's run with one of the best play-spots in Oregon at Spencer's Hole (44.7542, -122.4305), which is prime at summer flows and about two-thirds of the way through the run. Takeout: 44.755560, -122.477859. Put-in: 44.753396, -122.288604.

**Middle Santiam** (Concussion) is a summertime fix for locals. This run has reliable releases in the afternoon throughout most of the summer months. Starting as Class II with dynamic eddies and surf waves, the run builds to a series of fun Class III-IV rapids. Check the Green Peter Discharge to see when they are releasing each day. (There is usually a pattern and the run is in if they are releasing water.) Put in just below the Green Peter Dam and take out about 2 miles downstream where the road is close to the river. Takeout: 44.437796, -122.588038. Put-in: 44.448996, -122.549322.

**Eagle Creek** is a fun, intermediate run in the Clackamas drainage. There are two 10- to 15-foot waterfalls between the fish hatchery and Eagle Creek Road as well as a number of fun Class III+ boulder gardens. The upper waterfall is clean and the lower one is more challenging. There is also a more adventurous upper section with yet another 10-foot waterfall. Minimum flow is 2500 cfs in the Clackamas at Three Lynx; 10K cfs is pretty high but runnable. Access is also possible at Eagle Fern Park (45.320792, -122.287329). Takeout: 45.341462, -122.345576. Put-in: 45.276139, -122.205455.

**Thomas Creek** is a classic intermediate stream with a runnable 30-foot waterfall a short distance above the standard put-in. Historically only accessible during hunting season, logging roads coming from Rock Creek allow access to navigationally savvy boaters. Look for 500-1,500 cfs on Pat Welch's Thomas Creek gauge USGS #14188800—Thomas Creek near Scio, OR. Takeout: 44.702558, -122.567309. Put-in: 44.682982, -122.503160. Falls put-in: 44.682997, -122.483964.

**The Middle Santiam** wilderness section is the best overnight run in Oregon's portion of the Cascade Range. Put in at the Sheep Creek Road bridge and take out just before Green Peter Reservoir or at Whitney Creek Park. There are two Class V rapids, the O.K. Corral just below the put-in and Shelter Falls an hour or two later. The rest of the run is Class II-IV. The Quartzville gauge should read 1,500 cfs or higher. Takeout: 44.504228, -122.388528. Second takeout option: 44.469067, -122.439527. Third takeout option: 44.477798, -122.507539. Put-in: 44.466549, -122.147259.

**June Creek** of the Clackamas is a local favorite for intermediate paddlers who want something a little different than the Three Lynx section. Most of the run is Class II-III whitewater with three evenly spread-out stretches pushing Class IV. The run's big bonus is the riverside hot springs a couple bends downstream of Granite Creek. Put in at the NF 4651 bridge and take out at a bridge just before the confluence with the Collawash. This run can be paddled with as little as 1,000 cfs on the Three Lynx gauge, but has also been done as high as 10,000 cfs by expert local paddlers. About 4,000 cfs or less is suggested for your first trip. Takeout: 45.032235, -122.059107. Put-in: 45.016770, -121.920501

**The North Fork Molalla** was once a local classic before a gate requiring about a 4-mile hike now keeps most paddlers away. A similar number of miles of Class IV-IV+ whitewater reward those who make the trip. Optimal flow is 2,500 cfs in the Molalla River at the Canby gauge. Most boaters put in near the confluence with Dead Horse Canyon Creek. Takeout: 45.083720, -122.488775. Put-in: 45.073290, -122.370079

**Sardine Creek** is a tough Class V run flowing into Big Cliff Reservoir. Flows of 2,000 cfs and rising on the Breitenbush River are the minimum. There are two V+ rapids (Superboof and Chasm), otherwise the rest of the run is mostly difficult boulder gardens with a couple of slides. Everything from Superboof down has been run. Driving up the road from the takeout (44.746687, -122.276325), you will eventually see a small sliding double-falls, the road then gets steep. When the road gets flat again ~1.3 miles above the takeout you are at Chasm Falls. Paddlers looking for a Class V day can put in at the base of this drop (44.761138, -122.267357). Superboof is a short ways upstream, where people looking for more spice can start

(44.763775, -122.266670). There is also an unrun falls with a shallow landing a half-mile above Chasm.

**Opal Creek** requires a hike upstream about a mile and a half from Jawbone Flats on the Kopetski Trail until you are at creek level and all you can see upstream is Class II. Many good bedrock rapids and small falls are scoutable on the hike up. Optimal flows are from 1,500-2,000 cfs in the Little North Santiam gauge at Mehama with no snow on the ground. Takeout: 44.845692, -122.208211. Put-in: 44.828417, -122.201155.

**The Blue River** is a classic intermediate run flowing into the McKenzie. The Blue River gauge should be above 300 cfs, and 1,500 cfs is not too high. Put in near Cook Creek and take out in the Blue River Reservoir (44.207183, -122.262505). Put-in: 44.251317, -122.232379.

**French Creek**, a sister drainage to the Breitenbush, is a mostly Class IV-IV+ run minus a tough gorge near the end. Look for 2,000-3,000 cfs in the Breitenbush and also look out for wood as the situation changes year to year. Takeout: 44.744143, -122.156565. Put-in: 44.760202, -122.168297.

Priscilla Macy
North Santiam River

# HONORABLE MENTIONS

## OF THE WILLAMETTE VALLEY

**Wiley Creek** is a fun intermediate whitewater with a gated logging road requiring a 3.5-mile hike in most of the year. Look for the South Santiam to be over 1,000 cfs. Takeout: 44.363554, -122.610375. Put-in: 44.316696, -122.518175

**Tire Creek** is a silly little run flowing into the North Fork of the Middle Fork Willamette just above Dexter Reservoir. The last quarter-mile of this creek has some bedrock action that has been paddled a couple of times. Look to this run when everything else in the area is too high. Staging Area: 43.796798, -122.553748.

**Salmon Creek** is a nice run near Oakridge with reliable flows during the winter and spring. The crux is a mile-long gorge with Class IV+ water. There is also a small falls a ways downstream of the gorge. Put in near Wall Creek and take out at Salmon Falls. This run is usually in at the same time as the Miracle Mile. Takeout: 43.778884, -122.358128. Put-in: 43.787778, -122.335225.

**Nohorn Creek** is a fun intermediate run high in the Clackamas drainage. Snow is often an issue; when access is possible 5,000 cfs at Three Lynx is a good medium. Put in in the short falls 2.5 miles above the Hot Springs Fork confluence and take out at Pegleg Falls. Watch out for Cookie Monster, a large sliding rapid toward the end of the run. Takeout: 44.956813, -122.162316. Put-in: 44.935134, -122.211703.

**Canal Creek** is a fun tributary to Quartzville Creek beginning at the confluence of Elk Creek and the Canal Creek Fork. It's Class III-IV with a blind 10-foot slide best run center/left. Look for high water in Quartzville. Check out either Elk Creek or the Canal Creek Fork for more III-V action. Takeout: 44.587773, -122.347462. Put-in: 44.619241, -122.320773.

**Elk Lake Creek** has been run from the lake itself down to the confluence with the Collawash, though the large shuttle and high workload keep most paddlers from ever seeing the upper stretch. From Battle Creek down, the stream builds slowly and by the time you pass Welcome Creek, the whitewater is pretty consistent and quality. The main event is in the last mile, where the creek enters a gorge with a ledge-waterfall combo entrance, then some locked-in boulder rapids before a 10-foot ledge that often collects wood. It is imperative that you scout this rapid before dropping into the gorge as the portage is incredibly difficult and dangerous. This ledge can be scouted pretty easily by veering off the trail paralleling the creek on river-left. Some paddlers hike up from the takeout bridge to run just this gorge. Look for a minimum of 2,000 cfs in the Clackamas at Three Lynx for the final gorge to be in, and over 4,000 cfs for the top section. Takeout: 44.897614, -122.006458. Put-in: 44.827394, -122.088891.

**Silver Creek** features many runnable waterfalls and many unrunnable waterfalls. Paddling was illegal for a while in the State Park, but that seems to have changed. The biggest runnable drop is a 60-footer upstream of state Hwy 214 (put-in access road) on the North Fork. If you plan to run any of the falls on the NF, scout the run carefully before attempting as it would be easy to get swept over an unrunnable falls. It is also possible to just hike down to the South Fork confluence, below which there is lots of easy floating separated by drops in the 10-foot range. Takeout is on the Silverton Reservoir (44.983250, -122.744753). Flow range is 500-1,500 cfs in Butte Creek at Monitor. Check signs before putting in to make sure paddling has not been re-banned. Put-in: 44.885144, -122.628171.

**Crabtree Creek** is a fun intermediate run accessible during hunting season east of Albany. Pat Welch's Thomas Creek flow should be around 1,000 cfs. Put in at the bridge just upstream of the South Fork confluence. USGS 14188800 THOMAS CREEK NEAR SCIO, OR. The first mile to the South Fork Confluence sometimes collects wood, there is an alternate putin right at this confluence via a spur road off the main shuttle route. The next 4.5 miles down to the take out at the Now Peak bridge are class II-III with a couple of rapids some might call class IV. Every few years floods rearrange the riverbed, so be ready for new features year to year. Adventurous boaters will find a class V run upstream of the standard section, beginning at the confluence with Bonnie Creek is ideal for that run. There are two bridges downstream of Bonnie Creek that provide options for taking out. Standard Takeout: 44.630248, -122.740761 Standard Put-in: 44.578735, -122.585021

**North Fork of the Middle Fork Willamette:** This gnarly run flowing out of Waldo Lake can be run late in the season but has never been completed in a day. Many large waterfalls, some of which have been run, plus tons of wood. Takeout: 43.871705, -122.171452. Put-in: 43.768332, -122.052992.

**Boulder Creek:** The 1.5 miles above Highway 22 near the town of Idanha is nearly pure bedrock, with a larger 15 foot double drop called The Venue. Look for scrapy flows of 1,000 cfs in the Breitenbush USGS 14179000 BREITENBUSH R ABV FRENCH CR NR DETROIT with 2,000 cfs being more fun but it becomes difficult to stop. At all flows be careful of blind corners and wood hazards. In 2016 there was a trail to the put in marked by flagging, starting where Boulder Ridge Rd makes a 180 degree turn to the left (trail goes right) 1.3 miles east of Hwy 22. Takeout: 44.704310, -122.089749 Put-in: 44.709991, -122.069664

Priscilla Macy

Lucas Rietmann on a rare descent of Tamolitch Falls

# COAST RANGE

Nate Pfeifer

The map contains the following labels:

Astoria
Youngs River Falls (Park and Huck) Class V+
Olney
Beaver Creek (Park & Huck) Class V+
Cannon Beach
Wilson River Class III/IV-
Buxton
Jordan Creek Class III+
Jordan Creek
Portland
Oceanside
North Fork Trask River
Beaverton
Nestucca River
McMinnville
Oretown
Salem
Valsetz Zone Class III-V+
Rickreall
Newport
Corvallis
Seal Rock
Marys Peak
Alsea River
Lake Creek (Slides) IV+/V
Lake Creek (Play) III-IV
Lake Creek
Eugene
Mapleton
Sweet Creek Class IV+/V
Dunes City
Siuslaw River
McKenzie River
Unity
Elkton
Hauser
Coos Bay
South Fork Coos River
South Umpqua River
North Umpqua River
Roseburg
East Fork Coquille River
Middle Fork
MF Coquille (Upper) IV-V
Coquille River
SF Coquille IV-VI
Iron Mountain
Rogue River

N
River Trip Location
0 5 10 20 Miles
0 12.5 25 50 Kilometers

Source: US National Park Service, USGS TNM

323

# WILSON RIVER

The Wilson River, known by whitewater enthusiasts for fun intermediate rapids and good play-waves, drains out of northern Oregon's Coast Range down to the Pacific Ocean. The range's highest point, Rogers Peak, rises over 3,700 feet near the headwaters of the Wilson River. With a moderate climate that sees an average annual rainfall between 60-180 inches and consistent storms that bring heavy rains, the coastal mountains' ample water supply creates reliable flows feeding the Wilson River and its tributaries throughout the rainy season. With almost 30 miles of whitewater between the Upper Devil's Lake Fork and MP 12, there's plenty of quality boating to be had. Between Jordan Creek and MP 12, paddlers enjoy mainly fun Class III rapids with two approaching Class IV at high flows: the Ledges and the Narrows. Be aware that the Narrows above 7.5 feet should be scouted from the left bank. A powerful surging eddy feeding back into a narrow slot creates a recirculating trap that can hold multiple boaters at once. The Ledges, which lies below the Narrows, is formed as the river slides over solid low-angle bedrock that creates fun hydraulics, large standing waves and spectacular surf spots at the right flows. The rest of the run is fun Class III with play-spots interspersed along the way. Cedar Butte Wave, the MP 16 Wave and a few other bonus spots will keep kayakers entertained throughout the run. Save some energy for the takeout, as MP 12 offers multiple spots to play and is often some of the best surf on the run. Upstream sections above Jordan Creek include Jones Creek (Class III), Lower Devil's Lake Fork (Class III to IV-), and Upper Devil's Lake Fork (Class IV-V).

—Luke Spencer

## THE RUNDOWN

For a bit more adventure, take a look at the South Fork's "Prison Camp" stretch and the North Fork Wilson.

**Difficulty:** Class III to IV-

**Gauge:** Wilson River at Tillamook

**Flow Min-max:** 4.5-10 feet

**Gradient:** 35 fpm. Put-in elevation: 487 feet.

**Takeout:** Bridge and Gravel pull-out on state Hwy. 6 at MP 12

**Put-in:** Gravel pull-out on OR 6 at Jordan Creek-Wilson River confluence

**Length:** 5-6 miles depending on whether paddlers hike or not

**Hitchability:** Yes, easy

**Season:** Rainy

**Camping:** Yes

**4WD Needed?** No

**Best Close Food/Beers:** Rogue Brewery/Banks

**Quality (out of 5):** 5

**Raft Recommendations:** Yes to all

Luke Spencer

Leif Anderson shredding the Cedar Butte Wave

## SHUTTLE DIRECTIONS

To reach the put-in, follow U.S. Hwy 26 west out of Portland for about 20 miles to the Banks/Tillamook exit where you will follow state Hwy. 6 west for about 33 miles to the bridge over Jordan Creek **(45.547096, -123.603491)**. To reach the Milepost 12 takeout, from Jordan Creek follow the OR 6 another 6.5 miles until you hit the Bridge over the Wilson and MP 12 **(45.490770, -123.635276)**.

Luke Spencer

# JORDAN CREEK

Jordan Creek is one of the main tributaries of the Wilson. For some reason, Jordan Creek only started being boated consistently in the late '90s. It was immensely popular until many paddlers replaced the run with more difficult creeks in southwest Washington. It remains popular and is still one of the closest creek runs to the Portland metro area and the variety of rapids offer great training for other more difficult rivers. The run used to start 7.5 miles above the confluence with the Wilson but heavy winter rains washed out a road bridge so most start the trip where the road ends or hike up a half-mile and start just above an interesting rapid.

If you decide to hike up a half-mile from the end of the road, you'll get a chance to run a gorge ending in a rapid with a narrow, twisting slot on the left and a double-ledge on the right. There is only a small eddy above this rapid. Below it, the run continues through several scenic, small gorges interspersed with flatter sections. There is a great variety of rapids through the run including several tight slots, ledges and big boulder gardens. There are several more difficult drops spread throughout the run which are usually scouted from the road on the drive up to the put-in. First timers will generally be more comfortable at lower water levels as several of these rapids are solid Class IV at higher flows and regularly punish Class III boaters who aren't prepared. The two biggest of these rapids are located where side-roads cross the river with their bridges as good landmarks.

—*Pete Giordano*

## THE RUNDOWN

Intermediate classic within an hour of Portland.

**Difficulty:** Class III+

**Gauge:** USGS #14301500—Wilson River near Tillamook

**Flow Min-max:** 5-10 feet (6-8 feet is medium range)

**Gradient:** 90 fpm

**Takeout:** Confluence with Wilson River

**Put-in:** End of Jordan Creek Rd.

**Length:** TK

**Hitchability:** Poor

**Season:** November to May

**Camping:** Yes

**4WD Needed?** No

**Best Close Food/Beers:** Might be a roadside tackle shop

**Quality (out of 5):** 3

**Raft Recommendations:** Not done very often, although possible

## SHUTTLE DIRECTIONS

The takeout is on the Wilson, just downstream of where Jordan Creek crosses under state Hwy. 6, about 17.5 miles east of Tillamook **(45.546367, -123.604535)**. If you are coming from Portland, travel U.S. Hwy 26 west for about 20 miles to the Banks/Tillamook exit where you will follow OR 6 for about 33 miles west to the bridge over Jordan Creek. To get to the put-in, drive up Jordan Creek Rd., 5 miles to the end of the drivable portion of the road **(45.543889, -123.520629)**. Either put-in here, or hike up the abandoned road as far as you like, it is less than a mile to the put-in above the gorge.

Clean 50-foot waterfall near Portland? Yes please! It takes a lot of rain to bring 'The Beaver' in, but when it's running, drive an hour west of Portland for one of the cleanest park-and-hucks in the area. Beaver Creek has a small drainage and tends to rise and fall quickly so try to catch Beaver Falls after a few days of heavy rain - or preferably a torrential downpour. From the parking area it's a short walk back up the road to where you can view the falls. If you decide to drop the falls, there is easy access upstream with good opportunities for spectators and safety on river-right. Running the falls on river-right provides the deepest and softest landing.

At medium to low flows, the lip can be shallow and can make for some dynamic lines. The lip is more of an abrupt ledge than a rolling plug. Stay in control and drive your craft until you're safely over the lip and you've spotted your landing. Having a paddler in the short recovery pool is a good idea as paddles and gear may disappear into the swiftly moving, wood-filled creek downstream. There is a trail back up on river-left, so if you want to perfect your new waterfall technique or make the most of the drive, grab your boat and take another lap. If you want to step it up a notch, drive over to Youngs Falls which is also in the area.

—Tony Skrivanek

## THE RUNDOWN

Good waterfall to practice your plug technique.

**Difficulty:** Class V

**Gauge:** Visual—drainage is small and rain-dependent. 2,000 cfs on the Nehalem gauge at Vernonia (USGS #14299800) was a minimally runnable flow. When the Wilson is over 10K cfs, the rest of the Northern Coast Range is running really high as well, a perfect time to check out this falls.

**Flow Min-max:** Visual and personal estimate

**Gradient:** 50 feet in one drop

**Takeout:** Just below the falls

**Put-in:** Just above the falls

**Length:** 100 yards and 50 vertical feet

**Hitchability:** Park and huck

**Season:** Fall-winter after heavy rains

**Camping:** No

**4WD Needed?** No

**Best Close Food/Beers:** Colvins Pub & Grill in Clatskanie

**Quality (out of 5):** 5

**Raft Recommendations:** Not recommended

## SHUTTLE DIRECTIONS

Take U.S. Hwy 30 west out of Portland. About 6 miles past Rainier and 0.7 miles past Milepost 53, turn right onto a road signed for Delena. In about 3.2 miles there is a small parking area on the left side of the road **(46.104379, -123.122015)**.

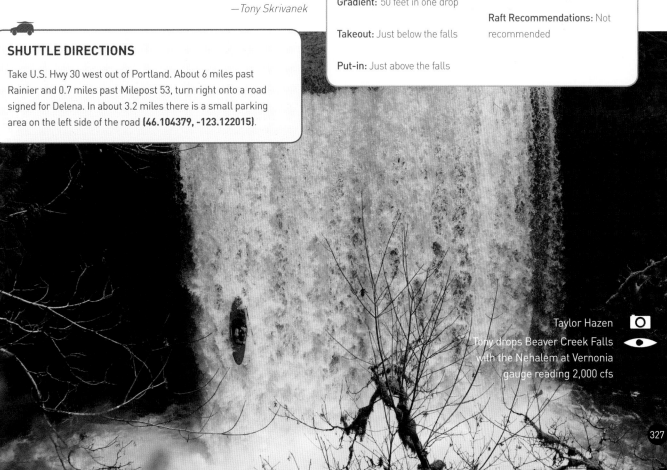

Taylor Hazen

Tony drops Beaver Creek Falls with the Nehalem at Vernonia gauge reading 2,000 cfs

# YOUNGS RIVER FALLS

Youngs River Falls is a glorious waterfall that falls 60 to 70 feet depending on water levels. This waterfall is no joke and is not a gimme. There is a solid, demanding lead-in that is intimidating and AWESOME. There are multiple close options for scouting the falls. While scouting, you will see that there is a hole or massive wave with a foam pile and cross-currents that you need to punch through to get on the river-left side of the falls.

The right side is a no-go. There has been a massive log in it for some time and it is shallow. The best line is to be center-left off the fall's major flake. If you fall off too far left, get ready for a potential beatdown on the left wall. The center line has been run, but I don't recommend it; there is a large pool below and no runout rapids. Safety is a must and it is easy to set up at the base of the falls. Scout well. If you're looking for something with a little less bite, check out Beaver Creek Falls nearby.

*—Johnny Ott*

## THE RUNDOWN

The waterfall lands in a pool only 30 feet above sea level and only six people have run it at the time of press.

**Difficulty:** Class V+

**Gauge:** Give this drop a look when all coastal rivers are flooding. I have four personal descents, all when the Wilson River gauge was at 10,000 cfs or higher, which correlated to good flows in Young. USGS #14299800—(Nehalem River at Vernonia) should also be over 2,000 cfs

**Flow Min-max:** Slightly flooding to full-on flooding

**Gradient:** 60-70 feet in a single drop

**Takeout:** Swim out or paddle out at the base of the waterfall

**Put-in:** A micro-eddy before the falls

**Length:** Park and huck, short and sweet

**Hitchability:** No need for that

**Season:** Any major rain event

**Camping:** No

**4WD Needed?** No

**Best Close Food/Beers:** A nice cold beer from your personal cooler

**Quality (out of 5):** 5 freakin' stars

**Raft Recommendations:** No recommendations

## SHUTTLE DIRECTIONS

From Portland, head six miles north on U.S. Hwy. 26 from the Sunset Rest Area and look for a road to Jewell. From Jewell, take state Hwy. 202 and head north for about 15 miles until you reach a sign for Lewis and Clark Trail. Turn left and look for a Y in the road. Stay right and Youngs Falls will be about 4 miles away. Look for the Lewis and Clark sign **(46.067558, -123.788707)**.

Dave Brigg

Johnny charging Youngs River Falls

8

# SWEET CREEK

This perfectly named creek is found in the Oregon Coast Range, near the small town of Mapleton. The run itself is very short at about a mile long, starting at Sweet Creek Falls and ending at the Homestead Trailhead/parking lot. By Oregon standards, this creek is a very unique run, combining extremely steep gradient and very low volume. Most boaters concentrate exclusively on the bottom half of the run, foregoing the top stuff and instead running multiple laps on the crux gorge section and the drops that lie below. This can be easily done by utilizing the convenient hiking trail that's built into the rocks and parallels the entire length of the run.

The gorge contains five main drops that are stacked right on top of each other. The first one is a small double-tiered drop with a sticky pocket on the left. On the other end of the short runout, the creek splits around a large stream boulder, with the right side dropping off one of the finest 8-foot boofs anywhere. A short boulder garden follows this boof and leads to the edge of the steepest part of the run, which contains three notable ledges separated by shallow slides. Scouting from the hiking trail will provide the appropriate beta, but there is one hidden danger that should be noted. This hazard, which is located on the second of the three ledges, comes in the form of an underwater undercut, edged into the rock slab on the right side of the landing zone. This spot has desperately pinned a few boaters, including myself, so take it seriously.

Below the gorge are the final three drops: a 12-foot falls with a shallow lead-in and a narrow landing; a fast, steep slide; and finally, a fun 6-foot boof. As with the gorge above, all of these can be easily scouted from the trail on the hike up.

Predicting flows for this run can be tricky and a bit of a crapshoot. That said, if the Siuslaw gauge (at Mapleton) is at least 7 feet and it's had a 2-foot spike in the previous few days, there's a good chance it's in. Even if it's not, you'll get to enjoy a pretty cool hike.

—Nate Pfeifer

## THE RUNDOWN

The run lives up to its name!

**Difficulty:** Class IV+ -V

**Gauge:** USGS #14307620— Siuslaw River near Mapleton, OR

**Flow Min-max:** At least 7 feet on the gauge and 2 ft. spike within the last few days.

**Gradient:** 500 fpm (from gorge down). Put-in elevation: approximately 400 feet

**Takeout:** Homestead Trailhead

**Put-in:** Anywhere between Sweet Creek Falls and the top of the gorge

**Length:** 1 mile from Sweet Creek Falls or 0.3 miles from the top of the gorge

**Hitchability:** Not necessary. You hike up from the takeout on this run.

**Season:** December to May (after heavy rain event)

**Camping:** A few Forest Service / BLM campgrounds and plenty of National Forest Land to bivouac.

**4WD Needed?** No

**Best Close Food/Beers:** A few choices in Mapleton

**Quality (out of 5):** 3.5

**Raft Recommendations:** Has been done by class V rafters, not recommended.

## SHUTTLE DIRECTIONS

From Eugene, drive about 45 miles west on state Hwy 126 to Sweet Creek Road, just before the bridge over the Siuslaw River and going into Mapleton. Turn left and drive 4.6 miles south on Sweet Creek Road and then turn left to stay on Sweet Creek Road — you will now be on the road that parallels Sweet Creek. From here, drive another 5.6 miles to the takeout, at the Homestead Trailhead/parking lot **(43.957976, -123.901946)**. From the parking lot, hike up the trail and put on wherever you want **(43.946409, -123.903183)**.

8

Nate Pfeifer
Brian Walsh on Sweet Creek

Joe Bushyhead
The beauty and challenge
of Sweet Creek

331

# LAKE CREEK (SLIDES)

Lake Creek, located in the Oregon Coast Range, is best known for its amazing playboating when levels are high. Although far less known or run, Lake Creek also offers up some solid creekboating near its headwaters, just below Triangle Lake, where it tumbles over a waterfall and down a series of large slides and congested boulder gardens.

The creek exits Triangle Lake and begins to tilt on edge over a series of low-angle slides. The run really kicks off when these slides get vertical at Lake Creek Falls. If this drop is not to your liking you can start your day just below. Run it center, or use the line down the far right that also provides plenty of excitement, especially when the water level is high.

Just below the falls, the creek drops over a couple more large slides. The first of which is next to an obvious fish ladder and is a straight shot down the left side, finishing with a fun boof. The third slide has rapid leading up to it that funnels water left toward a guard hole at the lip of the slide. This hole must be punched or surfed to the right in order to run the final slide on the right (and away from a tree on the left at the base). This move gets more difficult as flows increase.

Below the slides are a series of boulder gardens—the first is the toughest. Note that there is a sieve about halfway down the first boulder garden. Between that and the possibility of wood, it is highly recommended that you pre-scout from the bank, as boat-scouting would be difficult due to the lack of eddies. After a couple more rock gardens, you'll come to the run's last significant drop: an airplane move down the right that it is quite tricky to run clean. This is also a good one to scout ahead of time, to check for wood and to determine your approach. After the airplane move, the creek runs through a couple of smaller boulder gardens before eventually mellowing out to slack water. You'll eventually reach the takeout at a road bridge over the creek, about a mile and a half from the start.

—Nate Pfeifer

## THE RUNDOWN

This is NOT the Lake Creek you were thinking of.

**Difficulty:** Class IV-IV+ (V at high water above 10 ft. on the gauge.)

**Gauge:** Siuslaw near Mapleton

**Flow Min-max:** 6-13 feet (has been run higher)

**Gradient:** 200 fpm. Put-in elevation: 675 ft.

**Takeout:** Road bridge, near the Fish Creek confluence.

**Put-in:** Just downstream of Triangle Lake

**Length:** 1.5 miles

**Hitchability:** Lots of traffic on this road, so pretty good

**Season:** Rainy season, early December to May (typical year)

**Camping:** Yes, an established campground at Triangle Lake, but not a good area for dispersed camping

**4WD Needed?** No, paved road.

**Best Close Food/Beers:** Nothing close, Junction City or Eugene are your best bet

**Quality (out of 5):** 3.5

**Raft Recommendations:** May be possible, but only at high water—experts only!

Nate Pfeifer
Jacob Cruser working through the boulder gardens

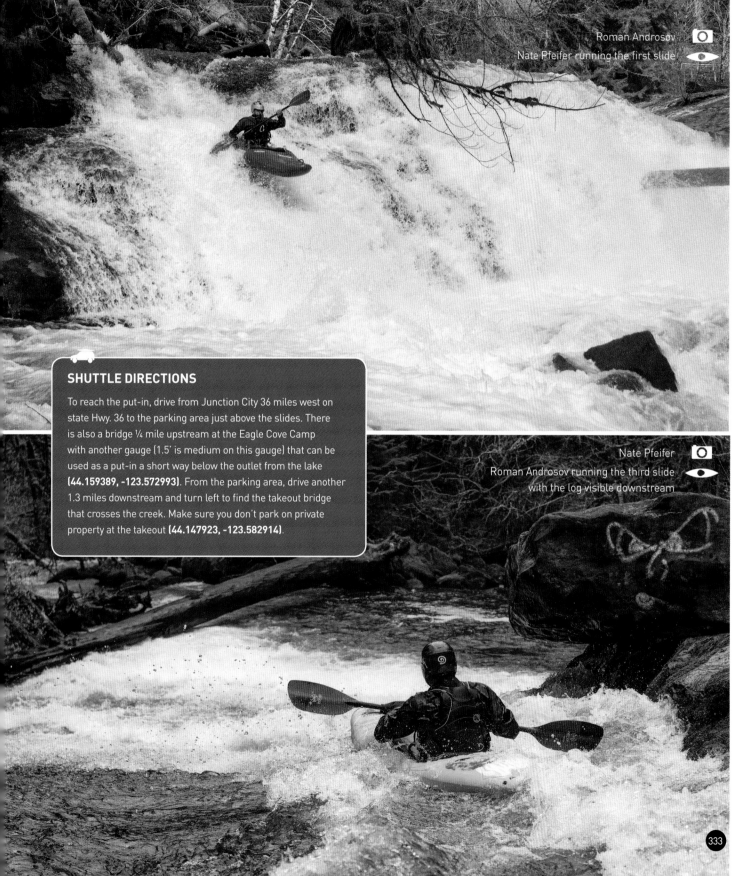

Roman Androsov 📷
Nate Pfeifer running the first slide 👁

## SHUTTLE DIRECTIONS

To reach the put-in, drive from Junction City 36 miles west on state Hwy. 36 to the parking area just above the slides. There is also a bridge ¼ mile upstream at the Eagle Cove Camp with another gauge (1.5' is medium on this gauge) that can be used as a put-in a short way below the outlet from the lake **(44.159389, -123.572993)**. From the parking area, drive another 1.3 miles downstream and turn left to find the takeout bridge that crosses the creek. Make sure you don't park on private property at the takeout **(44.147923, -123.582914)**.

Nate Pfeifer 📷
Roman Androsov running the third slide 👁
with the log visible downstream

# LAKE CREEK (PLAY RUN)

It comes in after heavy rains and is loaded with a variety of play-features. Since it is flood-stage kayaking, having a solid roll is essential. The water is moving swiftly and the eddies are often in the trees and shrubs. At the main put-in, the action starts off immediately with the Ledges. Some people put in a mile or two upstream — only do this if you need a warmup because it doesn't offer many play-spots. The ledges are a series of relatively shallow catch-on-the-fly ledge holes. A small hole forms at medium flows near the top that is good for looping but you have to react quick to catch the eddy. At 20+ feet, the Ledges turn into massive wave holes; avoid them or be very careful which ones you choose to surf.

Just downstream is the Horn, Lake Creek's biggest rapid. Run it left and get ready for some big waves and a few easily punched holes. There is a large pour-over rock on the right that creates the main hazard on the right side. Catch your breath and get ready for Mini Bus Stop or Upper Bus Stop, a series of ledge holes with small eddies on river-left that can be pretty sticky and powerful at the right levels. Expert playboaters will have fun throwing a few tricks and getting a little beatdown here. Everyone else should run river-right.

Next up is Bus Stop. Between 9 and 15 feet, the river-left side of the hole can be VERY sticky. Expert playboaters might 'enjoy' a rough

## THE RUNDOWN

Lake Creek arguably offers Oregon's best playboating.

**Difficulty:** Class III-IV

**Gauge:** Siuslaw/Lake Creek at Mapleton

**Flow Min-max:** 9-20+ feet

**Gradient:** 30 fpm avg.

**Takeout:** Tide County Park

**Put-in:** Large gravel pull-out 3.5 miles above Tide County Park

**Length:** 3.5 miles

**Hitchability:** Medium to low

**Season:** Fall and winter high-water events

**Camping:** I wouldn't, but I'm sure you could find a turnout

**4WD Needed?** No

**Best Close Food/Beers:** A few small stores in Mapleton

**Quality (out of 5):** 5 stars

**Raft Recommendations:** I guess you could, but why?

Nate Pfeifer

Kim Russell throwing down at Grassy Lawn

beatdown, but everyone else should run far river-left (if you're feeling confident, sneak past the hole on far river-right). Above 15 feet, Bus Stop forms some amazing waves that expert boaters will love. There are a few different waves that form in the rapids at slightly different levels with very small optimal windows. Eddy access consists of pulling yourself up through the bushes, but it's worth it if you like getting air.

About 300 feet downstream is one of the main play-features called Grassy Lawn. Good eddy access with park-and-play options. At 10-12 feet, it's a nice retentive-chunky hole. Around 14-16 feet, it gets a little green wave on surfer's left. Blunts, backstabs, and clean 360s are all possible.

Downstream of Grassy Lawn is the confluence of Lake Creek and the Siuslaw. A half-mile past Grassy Lawn, look out for a pour-over ledge on river-left that should be avoided. It forms a hydraulic similar to a low-head dam and it's the only hole on Lake Creek that I have never been in. Stay away.

After about a mile of fun wave trains is the next main play-feature —actually two waves with eddy access called MTV Wave and Mill

Wave. MTV is a fast diagonal wave and Mill is a nice, fast medium-sized wave. Try these waves between 10 and 11 feet.

The last play-spot on the run is called Red Hill. At 9 feet, this wave is great for getting a lot of air. It isn't very retentive so think of it as just a launching pad for one big trick. It has a nice big, easy eddy. It's worth a look around 17-18 feet too. Below here, especially at higher flows are a few fun catch-on-the-fly waves before the takeout at the Tide boat ramp.

*-Darren Dangerdeeds*

### SHUTTLE DIRECTIONS

From Eugene; take Exit 195A-195B for Randy Pape Belitine/ Oregon 569 W. Less than a mile later, merge with OR 569 W/ Randy Pape Belitine. In 9.1 miles, turn right onto OR 126 W/ W 11th Ave for 41.2 miles. Just after you cross the Siuslaw River, turn right onto state Hwy. 36 east and continue 6 miles to the Tide County Park **(44.071063, -123.788541)**. To reach the put-in, continue on OR 36 another 3.5 miles to a dirt pull-out on the right side of the road **(44.066334, -123.839625)**.

Nate Pfeifer

Bobby Brown paddling into the Horn

# SOUTH FORK OF THE COQUILLE

The South Fork Coquille is a neat Coast Range stream with quality boating opportunities in a part of Oregon that doesn't see much paddling traffic during the portions of the year when this stream has water. The upper reaches of the river are full of both runnable and unrunnable waterfalls, challenging boulder gardens and large cataracts. One of these sections is currently viewed as unrunnable at over 600 fpm, though each year boating boundaries are breached; maybe one day this section will be within grasp for whitewater's elite.

With miles of Class II-IV (V) whitewater, the reaches below Coquille Falls are a more favorable destination for the everyday boater. The entire South Fork Coquille is roadside, making access points easy to find. The stretches described below are grouped by difficulty of whitewater, so bring a map to choose your own put-ins and takeouts. This drainage tends to hold its water for a couple of days after a rain event, and a couple of the sections are runnable even after that. With the multitude of camping opportunities in the area, a great way to explore this drainage is to make a weekend of it, running different stretches on different days based on water flow and the level of challenge desired by the group. Upstream of Panther Creek the river is pretty flat, though a couple of the upper tributaries have diamonds in the rough.

Panther Creek to Upper Coquille River Falls: Mostly Class III-IV boulder gardens with a few ledges, ending in a clean 30-foot waterfall (can be park-and-hucked). Take out immediately below this drop on the left. Downstream the river enters the Cataracts.

Cataracts: Starts with a clean 30-foot waterfall (Upper Coquille River Falls) before entering a mile of steep cataracts, topping out over 600 fpm. This section ends with a potentially runnable 40-foot waterfall that promptly flushes over an unrunnable 80-foot waterfall (Coquille River Falls).

The Gem: A trail leading to the base of Coquille Falls is used as a put-in for this section. Ending at the NF 33 bridge a short way above the confluence with Rock Creek, this section has a handful of Class V boulder gardens. Look for a minimum of 1,000 cfs on the Powers gauge with knowledge that this high in the drainage, the gauge should be taken with a grain of salt (2,000 cfs is a more desirable flow).

Rock Creek to Kelly Creek: This section is mostly Class III-IV with one larger rapid that is worth a scout.

Kelly Creek to Myrtle Grove: This section is Class II with strainers present.

## THE RUNDOWN

The Cataracts ending with Coquille Falls have yet to be run.

**Difficulty:** Class IV-VI

**Gauge:** USGS #14325000— South Fork Coquille at Powers

**Flow Min-max:** 1,000-3,000 cfs (some sections can be run lower during snowmelt).

**Gradient:** Runs the range from less than 50 fpm to over 600 fpm. Put-in elevation: 2100 feet for highest whitewater option.

**Takeout:** User's choice

**Put-in:** User's choice

**Length:** Over 20 miles of runnable whitewater

**Hitchability:** Not recommended

**Season:** Rainy

**Camping:** Yes

**4WD Needed?** No

**Best Close Food/Beers:** If you're bold, try Powers

**Quality (out of 5):** 4

**Raft Recommendations:** Some sections would go in an R-2 when the water is up, other sections listed below the National Forest boundary would go fine with passengers.

Myrtle Grove to Coal Creek: This section has numerous Class IV rapids mixed with easy floating, a couple of the rapids warrant a scout.

Coal Creek to National Forest boundary: This is Coal Creek Canyon, likely the most notorious stretch on the river. The large boulders on this run are prone to creating sieve hazards; scout carefully. The run is mostly IV with a couple of Class V features, including Lost Paddle where a tough move past a sieve has nearly taken the life of at least one paddler.

National Forest Boundary to Baker Creek Road: The rest of the SF Coquille is mostly Class II that fades to flatwater. This transition occurs with a short jump in difficulty as some bedrock action occurs within and downstream of the town of Powers. The bedrock rapids are mostly Class III with one larger drop.

## SHUTTLE DIRECTIONS

From the town of Powers, drive upstream 17 miles along NF 33/219, then turn left onto NF 3348. Follow this road 22.6 miles to the uppermost put-in **(42.777810, -123.950756)**. Everything between here to the Baker Creek Rd. bridge just below the town of Powers **(42.907630, -124.111151)** has whitewater worth checking. All has been run aside from the very steep/very dangerous section ending at Coquille Falls and beginning 1 mile upstream at the base of Upper Coquille River Falls (a runnable 30-footer). Read the descriptions to determine which section sounds the most appealing to you. Our best advice is to bring a map, then mix and match to choose your own adventure!

Jordan Kourupes

Hunter Conolly below one of the clean ones on the SF Coquille

# MIDDLE FORK OF THE COQUILLE

This run has minimal glory boating. It is a difficult run with difficult rapids. Paddlers who like running hard whitewater will enjoy the challenge, all others be wary about attempting this stretch of river. Water collects upstream of the run within Camas Valley, slowly moving downstream until it reaches a geographic pinch point. From here down to the confluence with the south fork, the Middle Fork Coquille is not ever long from sight for travellers using highway 42. The run starts below one of the many Hwy 42 bridges, just below the geographic pinch. There is some time to warm up with a short section of flat water and a couple of lesser rapids before paddlers encounter the signature drop of the run (Shot in the Dark). Shot in the Dark has a sliding, twisting lead in before dropping ten or so feet into a narrow landing. This drop has been successfully paddled by running the left side of the final ledge. Below here the river works its way through more non-descript boulder rapids and a few ledges. Most of the run can be scouted beforehand by poking around along highway 42. Below the gauge at the Twelvemile Rd Bridge Handful of Hell begins. This is a series of hard class V rapids that will be a portage for many. These ease to flatwater down to the next bridge, below which are a final set of rapids before the take out.

—Jacob Cruser

Priscilla Macy 📷
'Shot in the Dark' on the MF Coquille River 👁

## THE RUNDOWN

A class V run hiding in obscurity under a highway.

**Difficulty:** Class IV-V

**Gauge:** Visual inspection needed, but the WF Cow Creek near Glendale can give you a ballpark. USGS #14309500— There is a foot gauge at the Twelvemile Creek road bridge. Lots of water is needed in the area for this section to run.

**Flow Min-max:** WF Cow Creek should be between 500 and 2,000 cfs. For the staff gauge 6 inches is minimum, with some portaging.  Upper runnable levels are not known, 1.5 feet would be a reasonable first time flow.

**Gradient:** 170 fpm. Put-in elevation: 1,000 ft.

**Takeout:** State Hwy. 42 bridge near Bear Creek Campground

**Put-in:** Near Mystic Creek

**Length:** 3.3 miles

**Hitchability:** A viable option

**Season:** Rainy

**Camping:** Yes

**4WD Needed?** No

**Best Close Food/Beers:** Roseburg

**Quality (out of 5):** 3

**Raft Recommendations:** Not for part-time Class V rafters.

## SHUTTLE DIRECTIONS

Follow Interstate 5 to Hwy 99 (about 5-15 minutes south of Roseburg). Take Hwy 99 to Hwy 42 (the turn is near Winston). Drive Hwy 42 for 25.5 miles west, passing through Camas Valley to a left turn onto Slater Creek road. This crosses over the MF Coquille shortly, this bridge is the takeout.  To reach the put-in, return to Hwy 42 and drive upstream 4.7 miles (passing Twelvemile Creek Rd where the gauge is located at 3.1 miles) along Hwy 42 to a bridge near Mystic Creek marking the put-in **(42.994960, -123.724758)**. Paddlers will find access and parking on the downstream river right side. There are many other bridges over the MF Coquille that can be used as alternate takeouts or put-ins for a longer, or shorter day. The whitewater below the takeout never surpasses class IV short of flood **(42.963521, -123.796170)**.

# VALSETZ AREA

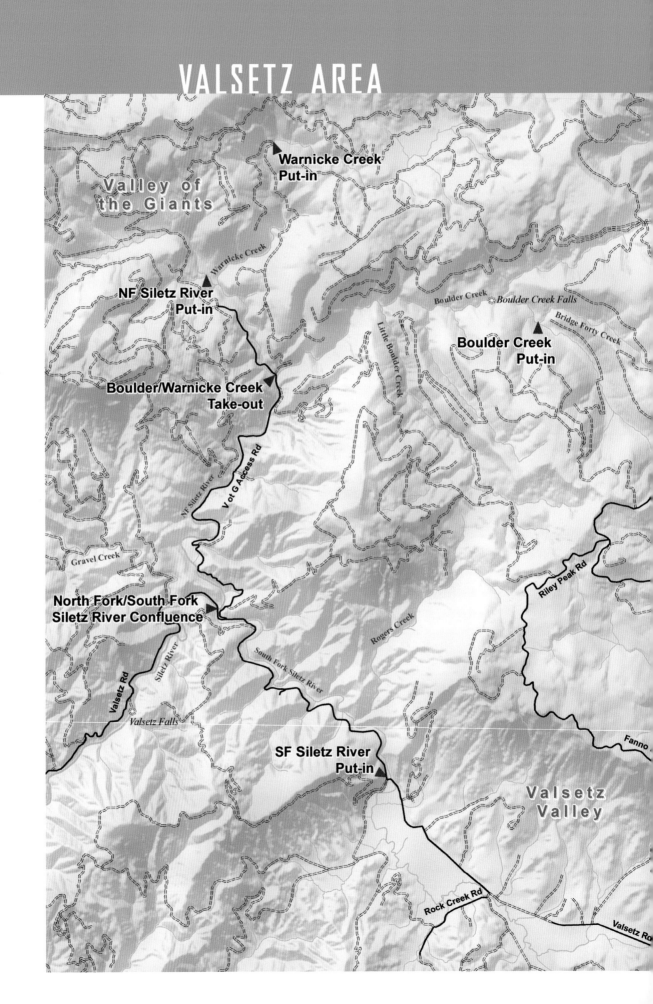

Valley of
the Giants

Warnicke Creek
Put-in

NF Siletz River
Put-in

Boulder/Warnicke Creek
Take-out

Warnicke Creek

Boulder Creek

*Boulder Creek Falls

Bridge Forty Creek

Boulder Creek
Put-in

Little Boulder Creek

NF Siletz River

V of G Access Rd

Gravel Creek

North Fork/South Fork
Siletz River Confluence

Rogers Creek

Riley Peak Rd

South Fork Siletz River

Siletz River

Valsetz Rd

Valsetz Falls

Fanno

SF Siletz River
Put-in

Valsetz
Valley

Rock Creek Rd

Valsetz Rd

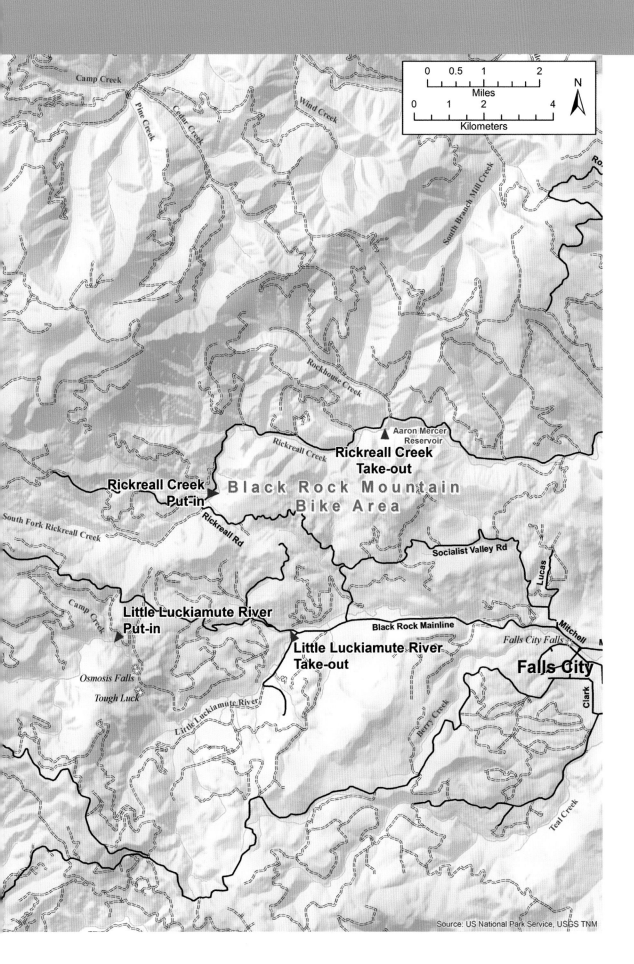

Camp Creek

Pine Creek

Cedar Creek

Wind Creek

South Branch Mill Creek

Ro

Rockhouse Creek

Aaron Mercer
Reservoir

**Rickreall Creek
Take-out**

Rickreall Creek

**B l a c k   R o c k   M o u n t a i n
B i k e   A r e a**

**Rickreall Creek
Put-in**

South Fork Rickreall Creek

Rickreall Rd

Socialist Valley Rd

Lucas

Camp Creek

**Little Luckiamute River
Put-in**

Black Rock Mainline

Mitchell

*Falls City Falls*

M

**Little Luckiamute River
Take-out**

**Falls City**

*Osmosis Falls*

*Tough Luck*

Little Luckiamute River

Clark

Berry Creek

Teal Creek

Source: US National Park Service, USGS TNM

# VALSETZ AREA

This area is for the adventurous; everyone of these runs is on private logging land and the myriad gravel roads/gates may seem a labyrinth to the layman. A number of groups have run out of light before reaching the takeout on these runs, so it's not a bad idea to consider a summer scouting trip to the area before bringing in a boat. At best the roads are open during hunting season and sometimes on weekends, while many are gated year-round. Learn the rules and consider investing in a CB radio, those logging trucks stop for no one. That said, there is some good kayaking to be found in this area. If you have what it takes to complete these runs you will be amply rewarded. Get an early start, coordinates are for put-ins only.

**North Fork Siletz** (44.937235, -123.712577): This is the most straightforward run on this list, reached via Valsetz Rd., then a private road accessing the Valley of the Giants where boaters can put in via a short walk. It is mostly beautiful roadside Class II-III with three larger bedrock rapids.

**Warnicke** (44.961837, -123.696723): This III-IV(V) run is near the Valley of the Giants (a worthy hiking destination) and is accessible nearly any weekend. It requires an easy hike in and has quality whitewater. The largest drop (Golden Goose) is near the beginning of the run and should be scouted/portaged on the right,

**South Fork Siletz** (44.850319, -123.667073): If everything else is too high, this one will usually still go. There is some serious surf potential for the bold. It is also roadside and generally accessible each weekend via Valsetz Rd.

**Little Luckiamute** (44.867549, -123.556613): This unique run has a gorge with four waterfalls ranging from 15-40 feet tall. The names of the drops in order are Catalyst, Osmosis Falls, Tough Luck and Little Lucky. Logging in the area makes the wood situation dynamic. Tough Luck is the most unfriendly waterfall and can be portaged via a slippery climb up the left wall before pulling the boats up after. Your best bet is to drive in during hunting season, though year-round access is available for those willing to hike.

**Rickreall** (44.903061, -123.526413): The creek is split by Aaron Mercer Reservoir, where the town of Dallas gets its drinking water. The stretch above the reservoir is fun Class III (IV+). The IV+ is a gorge that can be scouted on the left. The outflow of the reservoir is a wild ride of questionable legality. The stretch from here to the rock quarry is Class II-III with wood. The area above the rock

## THE RUNDOWN

A special place for those with an acute sense of adventure.

**Difficulty:** Class IV-V(V+)

**Gauge:** USGS # 14305500— Siletz River at Siletz

**Flow Min-max:** 4,000 cfs (8,000 cfs is not too high)

**Gradient:** Low to around 200 fpm. Put-in elevation: Some roads top out near 3,000 feet.

**Takeout:** User's choice

**Put-in:** User's choice

**Length:** Variable

**Hitchability:** Not a valid option

**Season:** Rainy

**Camping:** No

**4WD Needed?** Helpful, sturdy tires and a spare are paramount

**Best Close Food/Beers:** Falls City

**Quality (out of 5):** 3-5 depending on your disposition

**Raft Recommendations:** All could be run in an R-2, with varying degrees of effort output.

quarry is only accessible during the month of November (the signs don't apply during that month). Below the rock quarry into the heart of Dallas is an interesting Class II-III run that locals might be interested in doing. The Luckiamute should have more than 2,000 cfs at Suver (USGS #14190500) to consider Rickreall Creek.

**Boulder Creek** (44.929879, -123.628796): A long run with miles and miles of Class III-IV+ whitewater and a tough 50-footer near the beginning. The best put-in option is near the Bridge Forty Creek confluence. Plan on an extra long day.

**Valsetz Falls** (44.862845, -123.733045): An unrun mega-rapid on the main fork of the Siletz. The section from here to Moonshine Park is a nice, long intermediate run that can be run down to 500 cfs.

—*Jacob Cruser*

Nate Pfeifer
Jacob Cruser enjoying some rarely run
whitewater in the Valsetz Zone of the
Oregon Coast Range

## SHUTTLE DIRECTIONS

Valsetz Road out of Falls City is the mainline to get you into
this area of the Coast Range. This gravel road is open to the
public on weekends, but can be closed by logging companies for
various reasons, with the most common being fire danger. Most
of the other roads in the area are gated year-round, but a few
of them are open during hunting season (Black Rock Mainline
being one of these). Expect to spend a lot of time on gravel
roads away from cell reception. A GPS and map are nearly
mandatory, with a CB radio recommended.

# HONORABLE MENTIONS

## OF THE COAST RANGE

**The Salmonberry River** is a neat Coast Range run following abandoned train tracks that have become a part of the riverbank. Enjoy Class III (IV, V) if you use the North Fork access, or bring your 4WD for access via the Beaver Slide Road, which makes the run Class III (IV). Best to bring a map for either shuttle. The Nehalem near Vernonia (USGS #14299800) at 700 cfs is an enjoyable flow, though it has been run at over double this flow. Takeout: 45.701119, -123.752065. Put-in: 45.705864, -123.495025; North Fork put-in: 45.745640, -123.489470.

**The D River** stakes a claim to the world's second shortest river and flows into the Pacific Ocean within the town of Lincoln City. Access this total novelty, Class I run from D River State Park, and be careful crossing the street. D River State Park: 44.967704, -124.016809

**Drift Creek** is an intermediate adventure for intermediate boaters. The run is a classic when the Siletz gauge is at 4,000 cfs, and highly recommended at those flows. Put in near the Mennonite Camp and take out at the County Park near U.S. Hwy. 101. Takeout: 44.916626, -123.981418. Put-in: 44.898586, -123.907600.

**Gladiator Creek:** Routinely shifting ownership means that legality and accessibility here is in flux year to year. At the time of press, access was possible via a 6-mile hike along a gravel road alongside the creek from the bottom up. Paddlers who find it are rewarded with arguably the best whitewater run in the state, the main event of which is an ultra-clean 40-footer named Vesuvius Falls. Paddlers who leave this Rock unturned can still treat themselves to a feast at the nearby Spirit Mountain Casino. A good flow was 1,500 cfs and stable in the S. Yamhill at Willamina (USGS # 14192500). Check out mthoodh2o.blogspot.com for details.

**The East Fork Coquille (Brewster Canyon):** Approach this run from the upstream side and only scout the upper portion of the canyon; the bottom section of the canyon (below where OregonKayaking took out) is so gnarly that once you see it, you won't want to touch your boat. (We mistakenly drove up the narrow road following the lower canyon, scouting what we thought was the run and then bailed without knowing about the runnable section above.) There is indeed more whitewater and a couple of small waterfalls below the takeout. Brewster Canyon flows when the other Coquille runs are in. Takeout: 43.147853, -123.893393. Put-in: 43.147186, -123.885006.

**The Elk River** is a south coast classic. Call the Elk River fish hatchery (541-332-0405) for flows—3 feet is the minimum. The roadside run alternates between Class II stretches and fun Class IV gorges. Takeout: 42.739257, -124.410961. Put-in: 42.726318, -124.270740.

**Little Nestucca** is a good training run between Pacific City and Grand Ronde. The Nestucca at 2,000 cfs is a friendly flow in the Little Nestucca. The first rapid is a long, fun boulder garden that is conducive to lapping. Easy floating is broken up twice more by Class IV+ bedrock rapids before the stream hits the tidal flow. Takeout: 45.139043, -123.900468. Put-in: 45.110857, -123.852685

**NF Smith (Reedsport):** Hike into Kentucky Falls, there is a nice Class IV run below the confluence with the NF ending at the first road bridge. There are some fun bedrock rapids. The Siuslaw at 12 feet was a good flow. Takeout: 43.876096, -123.828768. Put In: 43.928829, -123.816148

**Mill Creek** offers an intimate little Class II-III (IV) run a half-hour west of Salem that is accessible during hunting season. The S. Yamhill gauge at Willamina (USGS #14192500) needs at least 1,000 cfs, though 2,000 is better. Be sure to take out above the V+ gorge below the park. Takeout: 44.988924, -123.423086. Put In: 44.973071, -123.522621.

Lucas Rietmann

Coast Range creeking

Priscilla Macy 📷
Coast Range beauty 👁

**North Fork Alsea River:** A half hour shuttle on gravel roads grants paddlers access to a rarely run stream complete with a clean 20-foot falls and a 10-foot ledge. Aside from those two drops, the whitewater is mostly class III-IV with some mellow floating. Get an early start and have your route picked out beforehand via BLM Mgmt Rd 10. Rack's Creek has a runnable falls below its bridge as well. The Alsea gauge at Tidewater (USGS #14306500) needs at least 2,000 cfs. Takeout: 44.415730, -123.562605. Put-in: 44.455063, -123.609934.

**The Smith River**, near Reedsport, offers a play-run overshadowed by the incredible Lake Creek to the north. Look for similar flows on the same gauge as Lake Creek. Smith Falls at the put-in is a pretty serious drop when the level is high. Takeout: 43.788417, -123.864064. Put-in: 43.788337, -123.818095.

**The Luckiamute River** is a fun high-water run for the area's paddlers. There is a mile of fun intermediate whitewater below Rock Pit Creek that is runnable at 1,000 cfs or higher at Suver (USGS #14190500). Around 5K cfs was a nice Class IV flow. The final Class III rapid is upstream of the Wildwood Rd. bridge. There are often log issues in the last mile above this bridge and it is possible to find takeouts upstream. Downstream is pleasant Class I-II. Takeout: 44.728781, -123.518623. Put-in: 44.772896, -123.585079

# SOUTHWEST OREGON

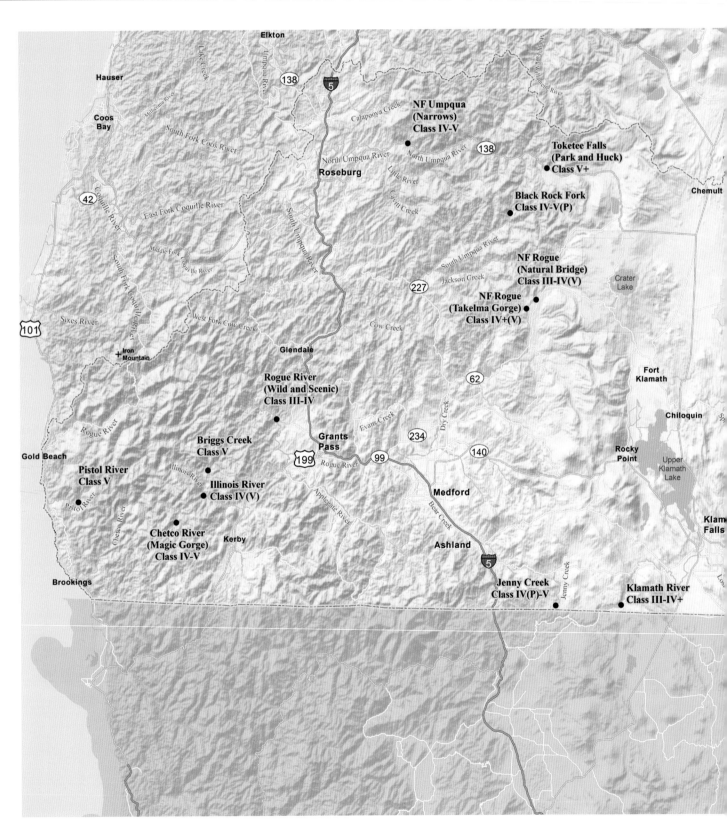

Elkton

Hauser

Coos
Bay

Lake Creek

Umpqua River

138

5

South Fork Coos River

Millicoma River

Calapooya Creek

**NF Umpqua
(Narrows)
Class IV-V**

North Umpqua River

138

**Toketee Falls
(Park and Huck)
Class V+**

Chemult

42

Coquille River

East Fork Coquille River

North Umpqua River

Little River

**Roseburg**

Cavitt Creek

North Umpqua River

**Black Rock Fork
Class IV-V(P)**

Middle Fork Coquille River

South Umpqua River

South Umpqua River

Jackson Creek

227

**NF Rogue
(Natural Bridge)
Class III-IV(V)**

Crater
Lake

101

Sixes River

South Fork Coquille River

West Fork Cow Creek

Cow Creek

**NF Rogue
(Takelma Gorge)
Class IV+(V)**

Iron
Mountain

**Glendale**

62

Fort
Klamath

**Rogue River
(Wild and Scenic)
Class III-IV**

Evans Creek

Dry Creek

Chiloquin

Rogue River

**Briggs Creek
Class V**

**Grants
Pass**

234

140

Rocky
Point

Upper
Klamath
Lake

**Gold Beach**

Illinois River

199

Rogue River

99

**Pistol River
Class V**

**Illinois River
Class IV(V)**

Applegate River

**Medford**

Bear Creek

Klam
Falls

Pistol River

Chetco River

**Chetco River
(Magic Gorge)
Class IV-V**

Kerby

**Ashland**

5

Klam

**Brookings**

**Jenny Creek
Class IV(P)-V**

Jenny Creek

**Klamath River
Class III-IV+**

River Trip Location

N

0    3.75   7.5           15
              Miles
0      7.5      15              30
          Kilometers

Fort
Rock

Christr
Valle

Silver
Lake

Beatty

Bly

Priscilla Macy

Source: US National Park Service, USGS TNM

# THE CHETCO RIVER

The Wild and Scenic Chetco is a highly sought after, but rarely accomplished, late-season multi-day wilderness adventure. The trip logistics keep most paddlers from boating this incredible stretch of river. There are a number of ways to access the upper stretch with the Babyfoot Lake Trail being the most straightforward. Another common access route enters from the Illinois River and crosses Chetco Pass. This run is exploratory in nature due to low traffic; do your research, pick your route carefully, and be aware of trail changes due to forest fires or other issues. The Siskiyou Mountain Club does a lot of maintenance work and usually has info on recent trail conditions.

For Day One, camping is available at the put-in, at the end of the trail, and in a couple of locations along the trail. Bring your map, in the past there have been a couple places where the direction of travel is unclear. Also note that most structures marked on the map were burned down in 2002's Biscuit Fire. Once on the river, camping is available, but don't hold out for a picture-perfect beach. The best first-night camp options are before launching at the Chetco's confluence with Carter Creek, or river-left below Slide Creek on a small beach that can hold three or four tents at low water.

The section starts in good form with many Class II-III rapids. Shortly thereafter, the Chetco cuts the dramatic bedrock Magic Gorge through serpentine walls. The whitewater is not difficult at recommended flows, though it captures the full beauty that the Chetco is known for. The rapids move along nicely this high in the drainage, broken up by deep pools with water often clear enough to see the river bottom. Some rapids may be barely passable at 500 cfs, but Slide Creek, 3 miles below Carter Creek adds enough flow to smooth things out.

Below Slide Creek, the action picks up to Class IV and a few larger rapids that begin to appear. Some can be boat-scouted while at least one warrants a shore-scout. Be cautious as wood is sometimes present in blind spots. One standout rapid offers a clean leading to a powerful, steep chute. The character is boulder gardens occasionally shaped by small bedrock ledges. This section is the crux of the run and features the steepest gradient and most stacked-up action. There are few good camps for a long section of canyon through here with Taggart Bar as the best option.

The most notable rapid has an undercut on the left that should be avoided, and can be scouted and portaged right. Most simply refer to this as "The Class V." Whether or not the rapid actually rates as a Class V (a subjective call), it does take a good amount of water for this drop to clean up and it may be unrunnable at the lower end

## THE RUNDOWN

A 2010 proposal threatened to permanently close almost half the length of the river for gold mining, though there is currently a temporary ban on mining imposed in rebuttal.

**Difficulty:** Class IV-V

**Gauge:** USGS #14400000— Chetco at Brookings

**Flow Min-max:** 500-6,000 cfs (upper limits to be truly tested)

**Gradient:** Up to 120 fpm, or as low as 30 fpm near the end

**Takeout:** South Fork Chetco Confluence

**Put-in:** Carter Creek

**Length:** 40 miles

**Hitchability:** Not recommended

**Season:** Year-round, but gets snowed in

**Camping:** Yes

**4WD Needed?** No, plenty of driving on gravel roads though

**Best Close Food/Beers:** Brookings

**Quality (out of 5):** 4.5

**Raft Recommendations:** If you can handle the hike, the river is raftable over 4,000 cfs. An IK is a better option. The final gorge could be rafted with road access by Class V boaters.

of flows. The run continues with miles of intermediate whitewater through a lush forested canyon, eventually slowing down, but not getting flat until near the end of the trip.

The Boulder Creek confluence provides a good camp site for paddlers doing three-day trips (one hiking, two paddling). Below Boulder Creek the pace slows, but a few more fun rapids await. Some boaters choose to take out at the NF 1376 bridge, while others continue down through the lower section to run a couple more challenging rapids. The first rapid in this lower section is Candy Cane; scout from the right. The next, larger rapid, Conehead, is a short way downstream. This Class V rapid is dominated by a large cone-shaped rock at the bottom of the rapid. Much of the river pushes into this rock, but routes past the feature exist. Once again, scout this rapid from the right. Below, the river softens to pool-and-riffle as it meanders through gravel bars until the takeout at the South Fork Chetco confluence.

*—Jacob Cruser and Brian Vogt*

## SHUTTLE DIRECTIONS

The best way to do shuttle is to track down "Bearfoot Brad" out of Gasquet, (707) 457-3365. If you insist on setting shuttle for yourself, drive to the town of Brookings and head upstream along N Bank Chetco River Rd. (784). Just under 16 miles up this road, make a left on a gravel road just before the S Fork Chetco River Rd. crosses the South Fork Chetco. This spur road ends shortly at the confluence of the South Fork and main Chetco rivers, which is the takeout **(42.186306, -124.134767)**. Reach an alternate takeout that avoids the final two challenging rapids by crossing the bridge over the South Fork Chetco and taking an immediate left. Follow this road for 4.2 miles to a bridge over the Chetco River.

To reach the put-in, return to the town of Brookings, then traverse the Coast Range an hour and a half to the east via U.S. Hwy. 101 to California Hwy. 197 to U.S. Hwy. 199 into the town of Cave Junction. From Cave Junction, drive north on U.S. 199 for 5.4 miles. Turn left onto 8 Dollar Rd/NF 4201 and follow for 7.2 miles. Then turn left as the name changes to NF 4201 and follow for 7.4 miles. Turn left at the Y and continue 0.7 miles along the main gravel road to reach the Babyfoot Lake Trailhead.

Hike about 10 miles along the Babyfoot Lake Trail and a series of decommissioned roads to reach the Chetco River. Reaching Babyfoot Lake, the trail may disappear for a short while. Start by following the rivulet exiting the lake downstream, but staying at roughly the same elevation as the lake as you wrap around the hill on the rivulet-left side of the lake, taking care not to get too far downstream, until you meet a decommissioned road that you follow (uphill) for 5 miles. Follow this as it gains, then traverses, the ridgeline. After 5 miles, turn right and follow this trail/road 4 more miles down to the put-in at the confluence of the Chetco River and Carter Creek **(42.225659, -123.884780)**. The trail can be difficult to follow near the Bailey cabin site, but it is there if you poke around a bit.

Alternately, boaters experienced in exploratory style boating and cross-country navigation will find less strenuous access and a shorter shuttle via Vulcan Peak. Enter the Chetco using Box Canyon Creek (class V) or Fresno Creek (difficulty unknown). Regardless of your access choice, prior research of your route should be conducted and a detailed map covering shuttle, hike and river should be brought along for any Chetco trip.

Brian Vogt
Shaun Riedinger finds the gradient below Slide Creek

Brian Vogt
Bill Tuthill boat scouting in the Chetco Gorge at 500 cfs

# THE PISTOL RIVER

This run is created entirely from landslides depositing many large boulders in the river. There is a half-mile downhill walk on a decommissioned road to get to the put-in, followed by a stretch of pleasant, easy floating with a couple of small warmup rapids. Just as you begin to wonder if you are on the right river, a Class III rapid with a house-sized boulder in the middle gives you a feel for the style of rapids you will face in the crux section. After a short section of boulder bars and sand riffles, the river abruptly changes character and enters the Pistol, a half-mile-long section of whitewater amongst large boulders. When viewed from satellite imagery, this section of whitewater appears roughly in the shape of a pistol, complete with grip and barrel. Beginning at the Grip, room-sized boulders choke off the channel creating tough rapids and big hydraulics. All the rapids are scouted and portaged by crawling under and over the large boulders. Watch out for a couple of big holes within the Barrel. There is a short pool (at low flows) as the river exits the Barrel. Below it is one more rapid worth scouting before things ease to riffles. Less than a quarter-mile later an overgrown road offers legal egress. There are a few more rapids downstream, but it can be challenging finding a legal takeout before the long Class I float to U.S. Hwy. 101.

—*Jacob Cruser*

## SHUTTLE DIRECTIONS

Consult a map and use online resources beforehand. To replicate our route, start at the U.S. Hwy. 101 bridge over the Pistol River, 10 miles south of Gold Beach or 18 miles north of Brookings, and travel 0.6 miles south on U.S. 101, turning east onto Frontage Rd. Shortly after, merge left onto Carpenterville Rd. In another half-mile, turn right onto N. Bank Pistol River Rd. In 5.2 miles, there is an overgrown road that heads toward the river. However, finding a takeout farther downstream will yield some bonus rapids. From the takeout road mentioned, continue 1.5 miles upstream before turning right onto NF 070. Drive about 1.5 miles to where a decommissioned road veers off to the left. Walk down this road about three-quarters of a mile to the put-in **(42.272329, -124.276374)**. There are more whitewater sections upstream, but private land makes access difficult **(42.279853, -124.324125)**.

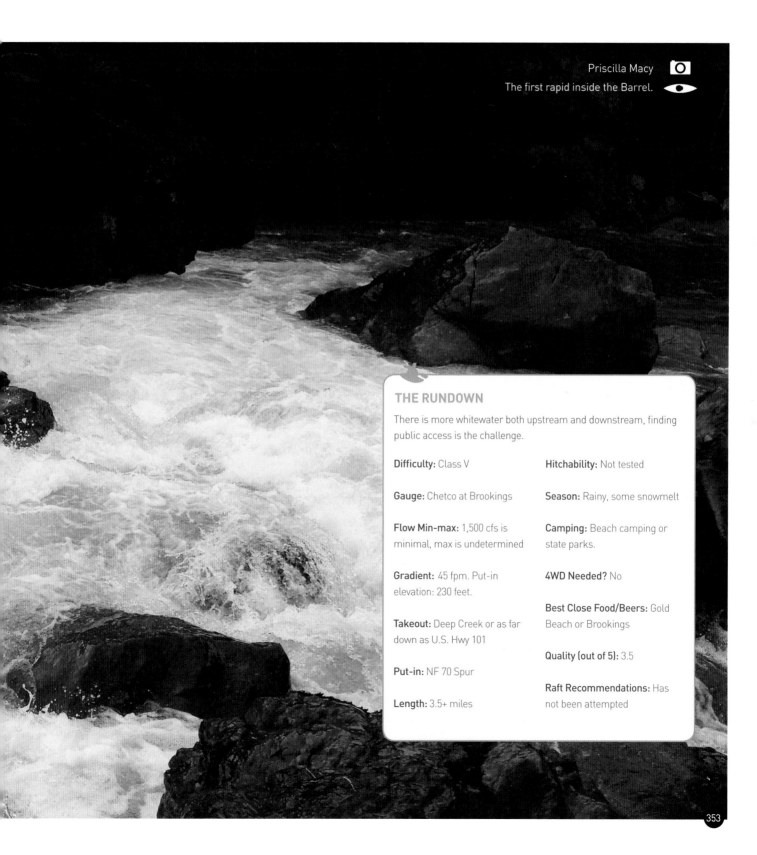

Priscilla Macy

The first rapid inside the Barrel.

## THE RUNDOWN

There is more whitewater both upstream and downstream, finding public access is the challenge.

**Difficulty:** Class V

**Gauge:** Chetco at Brookings

**Flow Min-max:** 1,500 cfs is minimal, max is undetermined

**Gradient:** 45 fpm. Put-in elevation: 230 feet.

**Takeout:** Deep Creek or as far down as U.S. Hwy 101

**Put-in:** NF 70 Spur

**Length:** 3.5+ miles

**Hitchability:** Not tested

**Season:** Rainy, some snowmelt

**Camping:** Beach camping or state parks.

**4WD Needed?** No

**Best Close Food/Beers:** Gold Beach or Brookings

**Quality (out of 5):** 3.5

**Raft Recommendations:** Has not been attempted

# THE ILLINOIS RIVER

The Wild and Scenic Illinois River carves a deep canyon through the rugged Kalmiopsis Wilderness and offers fantastic wilderness whitewater set amidst scenic splendor. Her rewards, however, come with a price: volatility. The thin soil and steep hills conspire to make this a flashy river that can spike to dangerous Class V high water conditions quickly. No trip plan is complete without a thorough weather review before launch.

The Illinois begins below Illinois Falls with a gentle float past a few cabins. The first section of whitewater runs from Panther Creek to Pine Flat. There are a number of fun rapids through this section, usually at confluences with tributaries. Panther, Labrador, and Nome creeks all have rapids. Rocky Top, one-third of a mile below Nome Creek, can be tricky at higher flows and is best scouted from river-right.

## SHUTTLE DIRECTIONS

To reach the putin, follow US-199 to Selma, Oregon. Stop at the Selma Market on Highway 199 to get your free Forest Service permit at the self-issue station outside the store. Then drive west on Illinois River road, USFS 3504. About 7 miles from Selma, bear left and downhill and proceed 9 more miles to Miami Bar.

To reach the takeout, you can go north over Bear Camp road, which is shorter but can be closed by snow, or south to Gold Beach, which works in winter but is longer.

**North:** Drive north on U.S. Hwy. 199. Go left on OR-260 E. Take a left on Robertson Bridge Road and follow it to Galice Rd. Next, turn left on Galice Creek Road. Follow BLM Rd 34-8-36 and NF-23 to Agness Rd/NF-33. Drive downriver 1.5 miles along Rogue River, then turn left on NF-450 and drive 4 miles to Oak Flat **(42.516842, -124.039974)**.

**South:** Drive southwest on U.S. 199, taking the Highway 197 shortcut (North Bank Road) to Crescent City and then turning north up U.S. 101. Drive up the south bank of the Rogue River 34 miles, cross the Illinois, and turn right on NF-450.

Class IV York Creek, at Mile 4.7, forces the flow against the left wall and has a large feature at the bottom. Clear Creek is a long two-part Class IV- drop that is most difficult at the bottom. Pine Creek Rapid, Mile 8, offers a big boat-stopping hole right, or a sneak left of the midstream boulder. There are camps near Panther, Nome, and Clear creeks. The largest camp on the river, Pine Flat, is on river-left after Pine Creek rapid. Klondike Creek is also a lovely camp but can be quite cold. Camps will become limited in the canyon, and quite scarce at high flows. Deadman Bar at Mile 12.5 and South Bend at Mile 17 are the last high-water camps above the whitewater, with more camping below Collier Creek.

The second whitewater stretch runs from Prelude to Submarine Hole and is locked in an inaccessible gorge. Camps are unavailable in this section, especially at high water. If weather conditions warrant concern about flow, a high-water camp will let you wait out the flows.

Prelude, a IV- drop at Mile 17.8, is steepest on the left and indicates the approach of Green Wall, which is a long Class V rapid at Mile 18 that is most safely scouted from the calm pool well above the rapid. You may also scout after running a III+ entry rapid. Catch a two-raft eddy 30 yards above the horizon line on the left, and be prepared to read and run if it's full. The rapid itself occurs where the river bends right and huge boulders stud the left bank. Large hydraulics form along the wall on the right. The crux of the rapid is a boulder fence extending across the channel, and roiling whitewater rebounding off the cliff. This drop can be portaged with effort on the left amidst large boulders. At lower flows it may ease a half-Class in rating.

*Continued on page 356*

Bill Tuthill
Green Wall Rapid, paddler Brian Vogt

# THE ILLINOIS RIVER

Little Green Wall, Class IV, follows after a brief calm and can be quite powerful along the right wall. Scout left. Several more III-IV rapids dot the canyon down to IV+ Submarine Hole, where the river is constricted by bedrock and a large hole forms at the bottom of the rapid; the best route ends left at the bottom. The lower canyon slows to Class II and is lovely and steep, with a few small camps between Collier Creek and Oak Flat. Buzzard's Roost, near the mouth of Indigo Creek, was a proposed dam site. This is a great area for exploring the unique flora and fauna of the Kalmiopsis.

It is possible to run the section between Selma and Miami Bar, but beware two portages. The first at Illinois Falls, a V+ bedrock drop, and an extremely low bridge at the McCaleb Ranch, which is an alternate access point.

Shuttle: To reach the put-in, follow U.S. Hwy. 199 to Selma, Ore. Stop at the Selma Market on U.S. 199 to get your free Forest Service permit at the self-issue station outside the store. Then drive west on Illinois River road, USFS 3504. About 7 miles from Selma, bear left (downhill) and proceed 9 more miles to Miami Bar (42.365960, -123.792047). To reach the takeout, you can go north over Bear Camp road, which is shorter but can be closed by snow, or south to Gold Beach, which works in winter but is longer.

—*Brian Vogt*

## THE RUNDOWN

*Handbook to the Illinois River Canyon* (Quinn et. al) features aerial photos of 100 rapids. Check out some of the tributaries for adventure creeking opportunities.

**Difficulty:** Class IV (V)

**Gauge:** USGS #14377100—Illinois near Kerby

**Flow Min-max:** 500-4,000 cfs

**Gradient:** 24 fpm. Put-in elevation: 870 feet

**Takeout:** Miami Bar

**Put-in:** Oak Flat

**Length:** 32 miles

**Hitchability:** Low

**Season:** Primarily rain-driven. Best in late spring with more daylight.

**Camping:** Camps are limited but well established.

**4WD Needed?** No

**Best Close Food/Beers:** Agness, Ore.

**Quality (out of 5):** 5

**Raft Recommendations:** Powerful features at high water. Rig to flip.

Brian Vogt

Bill Tuthill threads the technical left line through the lower half of Green Wall at 1,900 cfs

9

Eric Michelson
Hillary on Green Wall

Eric Michelson
Chris Tretwold

357

# THE ROGUE RIVER

Pristine natural surroundings, abundant wildlife, quality rapids, easy accessibility and year-round character combine to make this 35-mile Wild and Scenic section on the Rogue one of the most popular multi-day wilderness runs in the United States. Because of its Wild and Scenic designation, this run does require a permit to float. The permits are selected by annual lottery for launches in the peak season (May 15-Oct. 15), although leftover or returned permit spaces can usually be acquired should you miss in the lottery (excepting some busy summer weekends). Outside of peak season, permits are self-issued by dropping in at the Smullin Visitor Center at Rand.

The run is characterized by mostly Class II and III pool-and-drop rapids, with average to middle-high flows (1,200-10,000 cfs). It's an altogether friendly and forgiving section of river. Special attention should be given to the Class V Rainie Falls as well as to Mule Creek Canyon and Blossom Bar (IV).

The most consistent—though by no means continuous—section of whitewater on this run comes in the first 13 miles, the fun beginning right at the outset with Upper and Lower Grave Creek leading to arguably the largest single drop on the Rogue River: Rainie Falls. This drop has three doors (from left to right) offering respective gradations of difficulty/consequence. Door One, on river-left, is the Main Chute. Formed by a persistent metamorphic jut and considered Class IV+ - V at flows up to ~10,000 cfs, the Main Chute of Rainie Falls drops 10-12 feet into a mixed bag with an impressive boil on the left, a steep ledge on the right, and a narrow tongue of outflow in between. Door Two offers a good and fun alternative, with a rock-dodging entry into a two-tired 8- to 10-foot drop, though it can be hard for the unfamiliar to find and tricky to navigate in a raft. Door Three (the Fish Ladder) is an entertaining bump-and-scoot alternative along river-right and is the most common choice.

After the falls, the action continues with Tyee, Wildcat, Russian, Howard Creek Chutes, Slim Pickin's, Upper Washboard, Lower Washboard (Class IV at →15,000 cfs), Upper and Lower Blackbar Falls, Horseshoe Bend (Class III+ - IV between 10,000-20,000 cfs), Dulog, Quiz Show and Kelsey Falls.

For the next 8 miles, the river slows down and stretches out some, with rapids spaced farther apart, punctuated by more extended sections for serene floating.

## THE RUNDOWN

Runs have been made upwards of 100,000 cfs at Agness by experts familiar with the Rogue.

**Difficulty:** Class III-IV-

**Gauge:** USGS #14361500—Rogue River at Grants Pass (USGS #14372300—Rogue River at Agness when flow is greater then 10,000 cfs at Grants pass)

**Flow Min-max:** 800-25,000 cfs

**Gradient:** 13 fpm. Put-in elevation: 636 feet.

**Takeout:** Foster Bar

**Put-in:** Grave Creek

**Length:** 35 miles

**Hitchability:** Possible but not great—and leaving a car at Grave Creek overnight nearly ensures you car will be stolen or at least broken into. Use one of the local shuttle companies.

**Season:** Year-round

**Camping:** There is excellent camping all along the Wild and Scenic section of the Rogue, but as this is a roadless wilderness area, all gear must be boated-in and all sites are primitive or wholly undeveloped. In addition, you are required to carry a toilet.

**4WD Needed?** No

**Best Close Food/Beers:** For pre-trip, The Riffle or Baldini's in Merlin; post-trip, Cougar Lane Store & Grill or the Old Agness Store

**Quality (out of 5):** 3.5

**Raft Recommendations:** Yes, all types

Mule Creek Canyon (Mile 21, counting from Grave Creek), the most stunning single section on the run, marks the beginning of the next substantial section of whitewater. Here the river funnels down into a narrow gorge characterized by continuous, confused and powerful hydraulics. At flows between 1,000-5,000 cfs, the gorge is essentially a series of back-to-back Class III rapids. Between 6,000-15,000, it is continuous with more powerful hydraulics, but otherwise no more or less difficult. At flows above 25,000, the gorge itself is covered and the hydraulics in the canyon can become very powerful, unpredictable and spontaneous.

*Continued on page 360*

9

Keel Brightman
Some of Oregon's finest camping

359

# THE ROGUE RIVER

Soon after passing through the Coffee Pot (the final bowl of confused hydraulics in Mule Creek Canyon), the inner gorge walls begin to recede back out into the broader canyon and Stair Creek Falls comes into view on river-left. (The falls have been run during high-water events, and the ambitious, exploratory paddler might well find a gem of a steep creek in its upper reaches.)

For the next 1.5 miles, the canyon begins to widen before depositing paddlers at the Rogue's steepest and most notorious rapid, Blossom Bar. Locals describe Blossom Bar as a Class II move with Class V consequences, especially in a raft. Many competent oarsman have ended up with their rafts stuck on the group of rocks called the Picket Fence. Scout from above on the right and the line is reasonably obvious. Left to middle at the top then pick your way. At flows over 6,000 cfs, some prefer to run the right the entire way. At flows over 20,000 cfs, Blossom Bar becomes a big-water wave train (with deceptively powerful compression waves).

Immediately below Blossom Bar is Devil's Staircase (Class III), after which the river mellows out considerably offering only one more Class III rapid before the takeout, Clay Hill. The section between Blossom Bar and Foster Bar houses many of the rivers premier campsites.

—*Aaron Lieberman and Erik Weiseth*

## SHUTTLE DIRECTIONS

For the Grave Creek launch, exit I-5 at Exit 61. Head west for 19 miles until crossing the river the second time. Grave Creek launch is on your immediate left after the second river crossing **(42.650428, -123.585819)**. Groups looking for a few miles of Class II warmup will launch at Almeda four miles upriver. Almeda also has a nice campground for groups coming in the night before. To get to the Foster Bar takeout in summer: Drive back toward the interstate and immediately after the small town of Galice, take the right on Bear Camp Road and follow signs to Agness. This 37-mile road is 95 percent paved but is steep, windy, and one lane. When at the end of Bear Camp Road, take a right turn on South Bank River Road. After about 2 miles cross the river and take the first right. Follow this well-paved road for 4 miles before turning into Foster Bar at the bottom of hill **(42.632453, -124.049333)**. In the winter, when snow blocks the high-elevation Bear Camp Road, a longer shuttle must be taken. Expect this lower-elevation route to take a few hours and bring a map. From the Graves Creek put-in, take Galice Rd. south into Merlin for a right turn onto Robertson Bridge Rd. Where this road Ts at state Hwy. 260, turn left (south). Proceed to the Redwood Highway (U.S. 199) and turn right (southwest) which you follow for over an hour to U.S. Hwy 101. At this point head north on U.S. 101 to Gold Beach. Just before crossing over the Rogue River turn right onto 595, staying on the river-left bank as the road changes to NF 33, which you follow through Agness to Foster Bar. USING A SHUTTLE SERVICE IS HIGHLY RECOMMENDED.

Keet Brightman
Floating through the canyon walls of the mighty Rogue River

# NATURAL BRIDGE

## OF THE NORTH FORK ROGUE

Natural Bridge is a great section to take intermediate boaters looking to expand within and outside Class III. The rapids are still fun enough to entertain paddlers of any skill level and the scenic beauty is hard to beat. Natural Bridge starts with a bang: The first rapid below the put-in is a longer Class III, scoutable from a walking bridge spanning the NF Rogue. Expert paddlers can also tackle the Class V rapid visible upstream of this bridge. A winter 2015 high-water event created a new logjam on the left side of the rapid. It's easy to avoid on the right and lines you up for a fun boof before moving back to the center. Below here, more shallow ledges await. It's best to pick the line with the most water.

For about a half-mile, the run continues through some flatwater and small pool-drop Class IIs. This is one of the best times to soak in the scenery the NF has to offer. Soon the river will make a big bend to the left, signaling the nearness of Karma, a good Class III+ or IV- (depending on the line and flow). Scout on the left side. Both middle and left are open and tons of fun. Directly below is another fun Class III that lands in a pool.

After another half-mile of "scenic" water comes the biggest hazard of the run. The river takes a hard right and starts to pick up speed. Eddy out on the left before the river turns back to the left to portage Knob Falls. This 20-foot falls has been run many times in the past, but the high consequences of a missed line usually send boaters walking up the hill on the left. Carry to the end of the pool then slide in off the rocks; below starts the read-and-run section of the NF, with plenty of Class II and some tricky Class III drops sure to keep paddlers entertained.

Once Woodruff Bridge is in sight, continue down on the right side, running though a tight mossy channel. From the pool there, you get a final 5-footer to end this section.  The left side of this final bedrock formation is hazardous. Take out on river-left.

—*Hunter Connolly*

### SHUTTLE DIRECTIONS

Take state Hwy. 62 east from Medford. Stay on 62 the whole time. You will pass over Lost Creek Lake, marking about 20 miles out. Once past Prospect, turn left at the sign for Woodruff Bridge. Continue down the dirt road until you hit the bridge, which is the takeout (**42.862540, -122.505106**). To Natural Bridge, head back to OR 62 and head east once more. Turn left at the sign for Natural Bridge and continue down to a large parking area, which is the put-in (**42.888516, -122.466351**).

### THE RUNDOWN

The river follows the path of lava flows from the eruption of Mount Mazama—apparent once you arrive at the put-in, where the entire river is channeled through a lava tube just upriver!

**Difficulty:** Class III-IV (V)

**Gauge:** USGS #14328000— Rogue River above Prospect

**Flow Min-max:** 300-1,500 cfs

**Gradient:** 42 fpm

**Takeout:** Woodruff Bridge

**Put-in:** Natural Bridge viewpoint (be sure to put in below the natural bridge itself). During the winter months (November to April) the Forest Service closes the gate leading from the highway to the main parking lot, requiring a short walk in on the access road.

**Length:** 3 miles

**Hitchability:** Hitching a ride from put-in to takeout might pose some difficulty due to being back off the main highway. Bike shuttle is a much better option.

**Season:** Year-round

**Camping:** Optional. There is great access to camps on river-right by Woodruff Bridge. It makes for a great weekend getaway spot.

**4WD Needed?** No

**Best Close Food/Beers:** Prospect Pizza. Located off Mill Creek Drive in the town of Prospect.

**Quality (out of 5):** 3+ (great year-round fun)

**Raft Recommendations:** Rafts are not recommended as the tight streambed may prove difficult. If you are an ambitious rafter interested in this section anyway, shoot for higher flows in early spring. The portage around Knob Falls is a bear.

9

Nate Pfeifer
Roman Androsov enjoying the whitewater
on the Natural Bridge run

# TAKELMA GORGE

## OF THE NORTH FORK ROGUE

Takelma Gorge is a full step up from Natural Bridge. Many, including the author, like to run NB as a warmup for Takelma Gorge. You should not enter this stretch without experience in Class IV and V whitewater. It's best to go with someone who knows the run and can lead and/or provide beta. Once you are in the gorge there is no way out. Even though the gorge is short, vertical walls lock in all the drops.

Starting from Woodruff Bridge, the river evinces a similar character to the Natural Bridge run, with similarly stunning views. Once the water starts to pick up and the river banks begin to rise into walls, take it slow. Soon comes the rapid that marks the entrance to the gorge. The entire gorge can be scouted on river-left via a trail, though this trail cannot be accessed once the gorge has been entered. The entrance is a long Class III run down the middle; eddy out at the bottom and take a peek at the next drop.

Here starts Takelma Gorge, and the first Class IV: Number 1. Starting on the right side, this drop calls for good speed, driving left. Make sure to take a big stroke at the bottom as a strong hole is waiting. Use caution on this next part, for this is no pool and a large sieve sits in the middle of the river. Go far left or far right of the sieve. Once below there is a slow-moving recovery pool.

Next is Number 2. This rapid sits below the outflow from the first pool. Move down the center and take some solid strokes to gain speed. As the lip of the next drop becomes apparent, line up to the center-right, and take a good boof stroke. In most cases this creates so much speed you just blow through the bottom, avoiding a strong eddy that pushes into the wall on the right. There is no undercut or cave, just an easy paddle-out if you get stuck.

Next up is a portage. Eddy out on the right when the old-growth log across the river comes into view. There is a tailor-made place to get out right above the logjam. Just take it slow. There is an easy walk along the river-right side. From here, scout the whole next rapid, plus there are a variety of places to re-enter the water. Pick the spot you like best and go for it! It's all good below the portage.

Above the next drop, Number 4, there is a place to scout on the left. Number 4 is a must run. Move down the right; first up is a 8-ish-foot boof on the far right of the river. Take a big right stroke to keep off the wall. Once landed, move to the left. Watch out for the hole in the middle. At higher flows, the river tries to push you to the right. Boof the bottom ledge on the left. Another pool awaits directly below.

## THE RUNDOWN

If you are looking for more action and commitment from the Natural Bridge Section, this run delivers!

**Difficulty:** Class IV+ (V)

**Gauge:** USGS #14328000—Rogue River above Prospect, OR

**Flow Min-max:** 300-1,500 cfs

**Gradient:** 38 fpm. Put-in elevation: 2,480 feet.

**Takeout:** River Bridge

**Put-in:** Woodruff Bridge

**Length:** 3 miles

**Hitchability:** Not recommended. Limited road access makes it difficult. Bike shuttle is a better option. If running Natural Bridge and Takelma together, it is about 45 minutes on a bike.

**Season:** Year-round

**Camping:** Optional. More great places to camp on a dirt road that parallels the river on river-right.

**4WD Needed?** No

**Best Close Food/Beers:** Prospect Pizza, located in the town of Prospect. Or Becky's, with the best pie in Oregon.

**Quality (out of 5):** 4

**Raft Recommendations:** Rafting is not recommended, but can be done by Class V rafters (R-2 preferred). There have been multiple incidents in Takelma Gorge involving inexperienced rafters, some ending in tragedy. Kayaks are the way to go.

Up next is the fifth and final rapid of the gorge. There is a big pyramid rock in the middle of the river with water moving around both sides. Both sides go, but the right is narrower and has a mixed history of lodged wood. It's better going down the left side, riding the flow off of the rock. At higher flows, ride higher on the rock for a tricky but fun boof off the left side.

Once through, turn back and enjoy the magic of such a rad place. Another mile of beautiful scenery and flatwater with sporadic, read-and-run Class IIs finish out the run to the takeout at River Bridge. This run is rightly considered a gem among Southern Oregon paddlers.

—*Hunter Connolly (additions from Aaron Lieberman)*

9

Nate Pfeifer 📷

Jim Reed navigating the gorge on the Takelma run 👁

## SHUTTLE DIRECTIONS

Use the previous same directions to Woodruff Bridge, the Takelma put-in **(42.862650, -122.505167)**. The turn to the River Bridge takeout is located 5 miles before Woodruff Bridge on state Hwy. 62 **(42.821135, -122.494273)**. Both these locations are clearly marked by road signs that give you plenty of notice.

9

9

365

# NORTH FORK OF THE UMPQUA RIVER

This run is only 30 minutes off of I-5 near Roseburg and runs year-round. Considered too dangerous by the novices who seek out the splashy and scenic upper reaches, the Narrows offer expert boaters a nice, quick run in the area.

Put in at one of the roadside pull-outs about a half-mile above Deadline Falls. Eddy out below the first Class III rapid to scout Deadline Falls. Deadline has a major hole in the middle that most choose to avoid. The main line is off a nice flake center-left, with a sneak route far right. Very low flows open lines closer to the center. Between here and the Narrows proper are a few Class II-III rapids and a small wave or two to keep paddlers entertained. At the Narrows, the river pinches down into a turbulent chute on the left. At normal flows, scouting is available on either side. Around the corner is one more ledge into a hydraulic before the river flattens, broken up by Class II down to Glide with a number of roadside takeouts available.

If you want more whitewater, add Rock Creek at the end of the day if levels are over 1,500 cfs. Access this Class IV-V run via Rock Creek Road, starting near Anabel Road to cut off the upper flat stretches.

—*Jacob Cruser*

## THE RUNDOWN

The 30 miles upstream of this section house quality intermediate roadside whitewater. Put-ins and takeouts abound.

**Difficulty:** Class IV-V

**Gauge:** USGS #14318500—North Umpqua at Glide

**Flow Min-max:** 400-5,000 cfs

**Gradient:** 30 fpm. Put-in elevation: 800 feet

**Takeout:** Near Idleyld Park or roadside pull-outs

**Put-in:** Half-mile above Deadline Falls

**Length:** 2+ miles

**Hitchability:** A reasonable option

**Season:** Year-round

**Camping:** Plenty of options around

**4WD Needed?** No

**Best Close Food/Beers:** Roseburg

**Quality (out of 5):** 3

**Raft Recommendations:** You bet, the sections upstream are more family friendly though

## SHUTTLE DIRECTIONS

From I-5 turn east onto the N. Umpqua Highway (OR 138) and follow to the town of Glide. There is a takeout here at Colliding Rivers Park, or, to skip some of the flatwater, continue upstream from the bridge over the Little River. Between 2.8 and 5 miles, are a few roadside pull-outs that can be used for takeouts throughout this section of road **(43.322587, -123.056922)**. From the takeout, head east on the N. Umpqua Hwy. to the bridge over Rock Creek and continue upriver another 0.7 miles to the put-in at a small parking area off the highway **(43.320142, -122.984895)**.

Ben Sigler
Deadline Falls on the NF Umpqua

# TOKETEE FALLS

Toketee Falls sits in the upper reaches of the North Umpqua River drainage, in the heart of the Umpqua National Forest. Long considered and visited by Southern Oregon paddlers but little known outside the area, it was finally run in April 2012. The falls is a series of intimidating ledges formed by broken and spectacular columnar basalt. The main falls consists of roughly 6-, 20-, and 60-foot drops. Shifting wood is always a concern and the cave at the base of the falls is a hazard that requires great contemplation and safety set. The cave is on the left, behind the falls and becomes more consequential with more water. Scout all the moves in sequence from river-right. Bring a rope and walk carefully as the ground is unstable and every step is exposed to the vertical canyon.

Access is easy, but consequences could be great. The falls should absolutely be considered by waterfall experts only.

*—Chris Korbulic*

## SHUTTLE DIRECTIONS

Head east out of Glide on state Hwy. 138 for about 45 minutes and follow the signs. Put-in and takeout: **43.264040, -122.427423**

## THE RUNDOWN

3.5 miles of fun Class II-IV+ water exists between Toketee Falls and a bridge near Slide Creek.

**Difficulty:** Class V+

**Gauge:** USGS #14315500—North Umpqua at Toketee

**Flow Min-max:** minimum-max: 250-500 cfs

**Gradient:** 120 feet in less than a quarter-mile

**Takeout:** Pool below Toketee Falls or Slide Creek

**Put-in:** Toketee Falls Trailhead, or just above the falls.

**Length:** 0.75 mile or less depending on launch point

**Hitchability:** N/A

**Season:** Spring, release dependent

**Camping:** Toketee Campground (Umpqua Hot Springs nearby)

**4WD Needed?** No

**Best Close Food/Beers:** Narrows Tavern near Glide, OR

**Quality (out of 5):** 5+ (for the falls, not the bar)

**Raft Recommendations:** An attempt would likely result in injury or worse

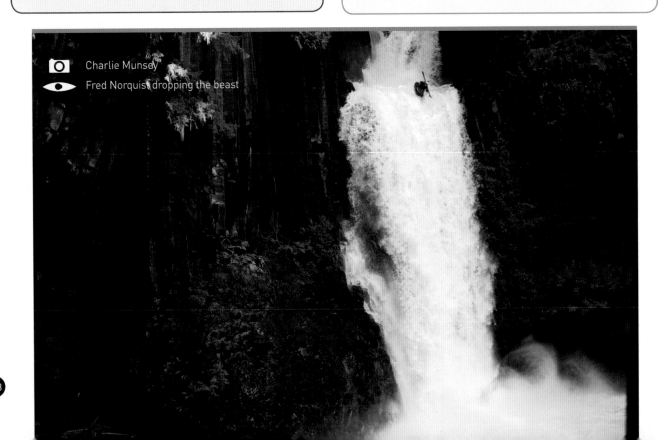

Charlie Munsey

Fred Norquist dropping the beast

Charlie Munsey

Katrina Van Wijk on Toketee

# BLACK ROCK FORK

## OF THE SOUTH UMPQUA

In 2007, Jason Rackley received word from Chad Bevill that this Creek might be worth the drive south into the headwaters of the South Fork of the Umpqua River. We took a chance on the Black Rock Fork and got lucky. We found classic pool-drop-style rapids with manageable gradient in a beautiful, remote location. With the predictable flow window we had a trip worth going back for! The Black Rock Fork merges with the Castle Rock Fork just downstream of the takeout to form the South Fork of the Umpqua River.

The takeout is just off the side of the road, upstream of the confluence, downstream from a 6-foot ledge drop. This is a good place to gauge the flow for the run as well. If the flow coming off this ledge looks manageable to you, then you will enjoy the run. We had enough water going off this ledge to barely touch any rock going off of it in the center.

Now for the fun. Just downstream of the put-in creek, after some small, fast and creeky rapids, the canyon walls appear for Entry Falls. On our trip, a large piece of old-growth blocked Entry—without it, this would be a great set of runnable ledges dropping around 20 feet over three drops. After a portage on the right are a few sliding ledges that lead down to what the locals call Deer Lick Falls (which you can see from the road on your way to the put-in). I mentioned it looked like a Box of Rock from the road on our trip and that seemed to stick. Box of Rocks starts with a small ledge pouring into a swirly boxed-out pool that pushes chaotically toward a 10-foot-wide exit and over the exit ledge/spout that spits you out like a watermelon seed.

Downstream is a very large logjam that was easy to portage up and over. The next mini-gorge, Zodiac Gorge, was beautiful, but closed out at the very bottom into a mess of boulders and wood. There is an easy portage on the left. Below are several fun read-and-run rapids with various character from boulder gardens to clean, sloping ledges. The next large horizon line drops into another mini-gorge called Comfort Zone. Comfort drops about 25 feet in the first drop into a bad-looking hole as the walls constrict at the bottom. There is one eddy on the left before the gorge pinches down again and drops another 8 feet into an angled wall on the left. You need to be far right on this ledge to avoid contact and make it through.

Not far downstream comes It's on like Donkey Kong. Imagine paddling hard, taking your last powerful paddle stroke, planting it perfectly and crushing your boof. You will still probably get slammed on this drop. At the lip of the 6-foot constricted ledge

## THE RUNDOWN

You can spend a weekend in the area and paddle the three falls section of the South Umpqua or any of the numerous tributaries as well.

**Difficulty:** Class IV-V (suggested portages—Entry Falls, the Filter, and Comfort Zone, which may become un-runnable at high flows)

**Gauge:** USGS #14308000—South Umpqua at Tiller

**Flow Min-max:** 1,000-3,000 cfs (best at 1,500-2,000 cfs and dropping)

**Gradient:** Manageable pool-drop

**Takeout:** NF-28 near the takeout ledge

**Put-in:** NF-28 bridge over the Black Rock Fork

**Length:** 2 miles

**Hitchability:** Not Recommended

**Season:** Spring, fall

**Camping:** Quality camping all around (great campsite at the put-in)

**4WD Needed?** No

**Best Close Food/Beers:** Your best options will be in Canyonville near I-5. There is a convenience store in Tiller.

**Quality (out of 5):** 4

**Raft Recommendations:** Not recommended

the water violently folds to the right and into the narrow landing against the right wall. James Bagley Jr., ran this drop on our trip, took the hit and turned out fine (in other words, it looks terrible, but it goes). Just downstream is the Filter, which looks more like a cool piece of geology by the large rock slabs that filter the river into three extremely tight channels, than any kind of runnable whitewater. The takeout ledge quickly appears downstream and the run comes to an end.

Note: There is also talk of a tough, but runnable 15-foot drop a half-mile above the normal put-in and just below the Prong Creek confluence.

—Ryan Scott

SHUTTLE DIRECTIONS

To reach the takeout, from Interstate 5 south of Roseburg, take Exit 98 toward Canyonville/Days Creek. Turn left onto 1st St., then right on SE Main St., proceed two blocks and then take a left onto SE 3rd St. This will turn into Douglas Co. Hwy. Continue about 23 miles to the town of Tiller. Take a left on South Umpqua Rd. before crossing the river. Stay on this road, it will eventually turn into NF-28/S. Umpqua Rd. About 26 miles from Tiller, the Castle Rock Fork pours in on the opposite side of the river. Just upstream, look for the pull-out and the takeout ledge **(43.088934, -122.624968)**. There is also a bridge a mile downstream of here, but there might be a portage or two as well. For the put-in, continue 2.2 miles up NF-28 to the bridge that crosses the Black Rock Fork **(43.132750, -122.579539)**.

Jason Rackley
E. J. Etherington charging through Box of Rocks

# THE KLAMATH RIVER

The Upper Klamath is one of the best summer whitewater trips in Oregon. Due to releases from John C. Boyle, the river flows nearly every day of the year. In the late summer months, when other rivers in the area are experiencing lower flows, the Upper Klamath has plenty of water and the same great whitewater that keeps boaters coming back for more.

The first 5.5 miles from Spring Island to Frain Ranch feature beautiful scenery, wildlife sighting opportunities, and mainly Class II rapids with the occasional Class III (Osprey). From Caldera to Stateline Falls (5.5 miles), the river steepens to 80 feet per mile and offers continuous Class III and IV with two Class IV+ rapids (Caldera and Hell's Corner). Stateline Falls to Access 1 (the top of Copco Lake) is 6 miles of nothing more than Class II along grazing land.

The bulk of the whitewater and all the significant rapids occur between Frain Ranch and Stateline Falls. Caldera (IV+) kicks things off and is a long rapid worth scouting from river-left or -right. After Caldera, the whitewater is continuous Class III+ like Branding Iron (the "branding iron" is the large wave at the bottom of this rapid), punctuated by a couple notable Class IV rapids, Gunslinger and Satan's Gate.

Satan's Gate marks the entrance to Hell's Corner, which is often thought of as the crux of the Upper Klamath canyon. Hell's Corner is the longest rapid of the trip and is difficult to scout, though the entrance can be scouted from river-left immediately below Satan's Gate. After Hell's Corner, the whitewater continues with rapids like Fluffy Bunny, Horseshoe, Ambush, and Ol' Bushwhacker.

Below Ol' Bushwhacker, the pace slows briefly as you pass the Salt Caves (river-left), which are a sacred Native American site prohibiting you from stopping on river-left for about half a mile. It is also the site of a dam that would have been built had the river not been designated Wild and Scenic.

At this point, all the Class IV rapids are over, however, there is still a handful of good Class III. Captain Jack, Snag Island, Wells Fargo, Razor Rock (aka Don't Kill The Piano Player) and Stateline Falls finish the run in California. If you are continuing to Copco Lake (Access 1), there six remaining miles of Class II. All takeouts are on river-left.

—Will Volpert

## THE RUNDOWN

The Upper Klamath cuts through the Cascade Mountain Range. This section of river was slated to be dammed before it was designated Wild and Scenic.

**Difficulty:** Class IV (IV+)

**Gauge:** USGS #11510700—Klamath below John C. Boyle Power Plant

**Flow Min-max:** 800-4,000 cfs

**Gradient:** 40 fpm

**Takeout:** Varies (popular is Stateline and Access 1 "Copco")

**Put-in:** Spring Island or Frain Ranch

**Length:** 17 miles, Spring Island to Copco; 11 miles, Spring Island to Stateline; 5.5 miles, Frain Ranch to Stateline; 11.5 miles, Frain Ranch to Copco.

**Hitchability:** Not going to happen

**Season:** Flows year-round

**Camping:** Yes

**4WD Needed?** If putting in at Frain Ranch, absolutely. If putting in at Spring Island, no

**Best Close Food/Beers:** Put-in—Klamath Falls, OR; takeout—Hornbrook, CA

**Quality (out of 5):** 4

**Raft Recommendations:** This is a good run for rafting

## SHUTTLE DIRECTIONS

The shuttle is awful with a one-way drive time of 2.5 to 3 hours. If you don't have a shuttle driver, you will probably want to put in at Frain Ranch (42.023710, -122.105332), although this requires a four-wheel-drive vehicle. Otherwise, from Spring Island (42.089389, -122.072206), drive to Ashland, Ore., taking state Hwy 66. In Ashland, take Interstate 5 south to Hornbrook, Calif. (second Hornbrook exit, #789). Turn left onto Copco Rd., and turn right on Ager Rd. (bridge over the Klamath). Turn left onto Ager-Beswick, which eventually takes you to Copco Lake, Access 1 (41.965405, -122.253600), and Stateline (42.006111, -122.189848).

9

# JENNY CREEK

Below the put-in, Jenny meanders down through a couple of miles of relatively easy Class III-IV rapids in an open, basalt-lined gorge. Soon the creek turns left and splits around an island, signaling Entrance Drop, a steep boulder garden that has been run down the right channel, but should be scouted for wood before committing.

Immediately below Entrance Drop, the creek enters an impressive vertical-walled gorge and drops out of sight with an huge roar, signaling Upper Jenny Creek Falls. This waterfall is marginally runnable, cascading about 40 feet over jagged rocks; portage on the right. Immediately below is Lower Jenny Creek Falls, a relatively benign 15-foot broken ledge-falls that has been run middle-left.

Downstream of the lower falls, the creek rolls through a long series of Class IV-IV+ boulder gardens in a very narrow streambed with tiny eddies. At high water it would be difficult to stop, so bear that in mind before you put on.

*—Jason Rackley*

## THE RUNDOWN

Jenny Creek is a small, remote, high-desert stream that starts in Oregon and ends in California. Any run down Jenny is an adventure because the shuttle is very long and there is a time-consuming portage around a huge, marginally runnable waterfall. Get an early start!

**Difficulty:** IV(P) to V+, depending on flows and number of portages

**Gauge:** N/A

**Flow Min-max:** There is no gauge. Estimate flow by monitoring the inflow into Iron Gate Reservoir. Has been run with an estimated 200 cfs at the put-in.

**Gradient:** 215 fpm

**Takeout:** North side of Iron Gate Reservoir, Copco Road

**Put-in:** Hwy 66 outside of Ashland

**Length:** 4.3 miles

**Hitchability:** No

**Season:** April and May on normal snow years

**Camping:** Mallard Cove

**4WD Needed?** No

**Best Close Food/Beers:** Allstar Liquor Express, Ashland or Yreka

**Quality (out of 5):** 3+

**Raft Recommendations:** NO, there is some barbed wire in the creek in places, leftovers of old fences across the creek

## SHUTTLE DIRECTIONS

Copco road is the most direct route, but has a gate that forces a very long shuttle around 90 minutes one way. To get to the put-in from Ashland, take state Hwy. 66 east 19 miles to the bridge over Jenny Creek—impossible to miss as the Pinehurst Inn is right next to the bridge. Cross Jenny Creek and continue uphill about a quarter-mile until you come to Copco Road on the right. Turn here and drive about eight miles to the gate across the road. Veer right and continue on the main road until you see the power lines. Reaching the power lines, follow them down a secondary road to the top of Jenny Creek Gorge. From here it is a technical hike (requiring boat lowering in spots) to the creek **(42.018619, -122.362395)**. To get to the takeout, drive OR 66 back to south Ashland, head south on I-5 20 miles until you get to the Hornbrook exit. Head east on Hornbrook-Ager Rd. for 15 miles (Hornbrook-Ager becomes Copco Road), staying on the north side of Iron Gate Reservoir until the road crosses the reservoir. Jenny Creek comes in here, leave your car near the bridge **(41.976289, -122.400113)**.

Jason Rackley 📷
Jesse Coombs running Lower Falls 👁

9

375

# HONORABLE MENTIONS

## O F   S O U T H W E S T   O R E G O N

**The Three Falls Run** on the South Fork Umpqua is a 6.7-mile, Class-IV section highlighted by South Umpqua and Campbell falls, with a couple other fun drops thrown in the mix. Look for 1,000-3,000 cfs on the SF Umpqua gauge at Tiller (USGS #14308000) for this run with easy access and quality whitewater. Takeout: 43.044053, -122.786766. Put-in: 43.054869, -122.686660

**Grave Creek** is a bouldery run near Grants Pass split in two by I-5. The steep upper stretch ends near Placer and is Class IV-V (takeout: 42.633301, -123.298435; put-in: 42.647397, -123.250624). There is also a 6-mile Class III stretch ending at the Rogue confluence (takeout: 42.650361, -123.585839; put-in: 42.651270, -123.511112). There is a gauge on the most downstream, river-right pylon of the I-5 south bridge (42.636000, -123.385339), visible from Frontage Road. Ask locals about flow correlations, but a ballpark for the upper is when the USGS 14309500 WEST FORK COW CREEK NEAR GLENDALE, OR is reading between 1,000-2,000 cfs.  The lower section can be run a little lower or higher.

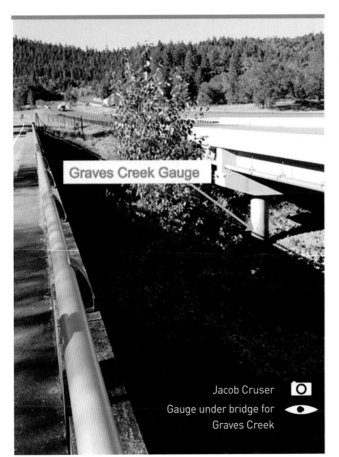

Graves Creek Gauge

Jacob Cruser

Gauge under bridge for Graves Creek

**The Smith River** drainage (near Gasquet, Calif.) becomes a go-to destination when the state of Oregon begins to dry up. The middle and south forks both have powerful, Class IV-iV+ gorges just above where they merge, as well as longer beginner through expert runs available upstream. The north fork is a world class scenic intermediate run with classic whitewater that is often done by rafters as well as kayakers. For flow information and shuttling, call Bearfoot Brad at (707)457-3365 or visit americanwhitewater.org. Brad posts the flow information on dreamflows.com each morning. The two most common sections are the middle and south fork gorges (Oregon Hole takeout: 41.801560, -124.053533) (SF Gorge takeout: 41.797072, -124.054353).

**Copeland Creek** was once considered a classic, though this Class IV stream doesn't see much attention after rumors spread of cluttered wood. The stream has since cleaned up and provides a good trip when USGS 14316495 BOULDER CREEK NEAR TOKETEE FALLS, OR is between 3.7 and 5.0 feet. Look out for the three standout rapids: Paul Bunyan Falls, Sneaky Snake, and Fountain of Youth. Putting in at the first bridge over Copeland Creek (43.236413, -122.526708) upstream of the N. Umpqua Hwy. takeout bridge (43.291706, -122.545341) will avoid Paul Bunyan Falls (a likely portage).

**Calapooya Creek** is a neat intermediate run a half-hour east of I-5 near Sutherlin. Putting in at Nonpareil Rd. (43.408742, -123.164885), the stream incises through cow pastures into a scenic gorge with Class III-IV whitewater. Take out in Fair Oaks (43.414833, -123.214383). The Elk Creek gauge near Drain (USGS #14322000) needs to read at least 2.5 feet (5 feet is not too high).

**The South Fork Chetco River** requires some map work before an attempt at this Class IV-V run. The Chetco needs at least 3,000 cfs for this run to thrive, though it would not be surprising if it could be done lower. Reports are that this 7 mile run is worth doing, boasting a handful of fun rapids as it flows through a classic Kalmiopsis gorge (cobalt blue water and rugged terrain) 6,000 CFS was a medium flow USGS 14400000 Chetco River Near Brookings, OR Takeout: 42.186571, -124.134924. Put-in: 42.169603, -124.057466

**Jackson Creek** is a classic Class IV stream in the South Umpqua drainage. It boasts nearly 20 miles of runnable whitewater.  High up near Falcon Creek the stream has some IV+ action.  As Jackson Creek gets closer to the South Umpqua, the stream eases to II-III with the occasional IV.  The South Umpqua needs at least 1,500 cfs at the Tiller gauge (USGS # 14308000). Lowest takeout: 42.965754, -122.887325. Uppermost put-in: 42.997444, -122.577759.

**Steamboat Creek** is a nice run in the Umpqua drainage with two small, but tricky waterfalls. Most of the creek is Class II-III with a couple of challenging IVs. (Flows: 800 cfs or higher on USGS #14316700). Lowest takeout: 43.345325, -122.736211. Uppermost put-in: 43.498071, -122.599703.

**Canton Creek** is a tributary of Steamboat with a number of ledges and a portage. The Steamboat Creek gauge (USGS #14316700) needs to read at least 1,000 cfs. Takeout: 43.349849, -122.729626. Put-in: 43.455707, -122.763600.

**The Rogue River Powerhouse Run** is only a couple minutes off I-5 near Gold Hill, where a short section of the Rogue serves as a local training ground. The main event is the final rapid named Powerhouse (access: 42.445337, -123.044097), which has three channels each with its own flavor. Paddlers can spend an afternoon running laps on each. There is also a short Class II-III stretch starting a few miles upstream where the Gold Ray Dam used to be. And there is still always enough water to paddle this stretch of whitewater. Takeout: 42.430606, -123.044280. Put-in: 42.436787, -122.983558.

**Lower Rogue River Tributaries:** When the Rogue hits 10,000 cfs in Grants Pass (USGS #14361500), many of its tributaries become runnable. A trip down the Wild and Scenic section allows paddlers to hike up some of these tributaries for bonus whitewater. Mule Creek comes in just above Marial Lodge and has nice intermediate whitewater in a tight gorge. Stair Creek has a double-drop coming in from the left: The bottom one is shallow but the top is good to go! There may be a run accessible from logging roads as well. Taylor Creek and Galice Creek have road access for day-trips, while many other tributaries await exploration. Take your pick of adventure.

**The Illinois River Tributaries** are similar to the Rogue's, but a half-Class harder both to run and access. Check out the following creeks to get started, then find your own to explore: Briggs, Josephine, Rough and Ready, Indigo, EF Illinois, Collier and Lawson. 5K cfs in the Illinois is a good level for exploring the tributaries. Check nwrafting.com/trip-reports and sundancekayak.com/tag/exploratory for more info.

Priscilla Macy
A tributary to the Wild and Scenic section of the Rogue River

Jacon Cruser

Emile Elliott kicks off the North Fork of Silver Creek

Jacon Cruser
Entrance to the gorge on Calapooya Creek

# CENTRAL OREGON

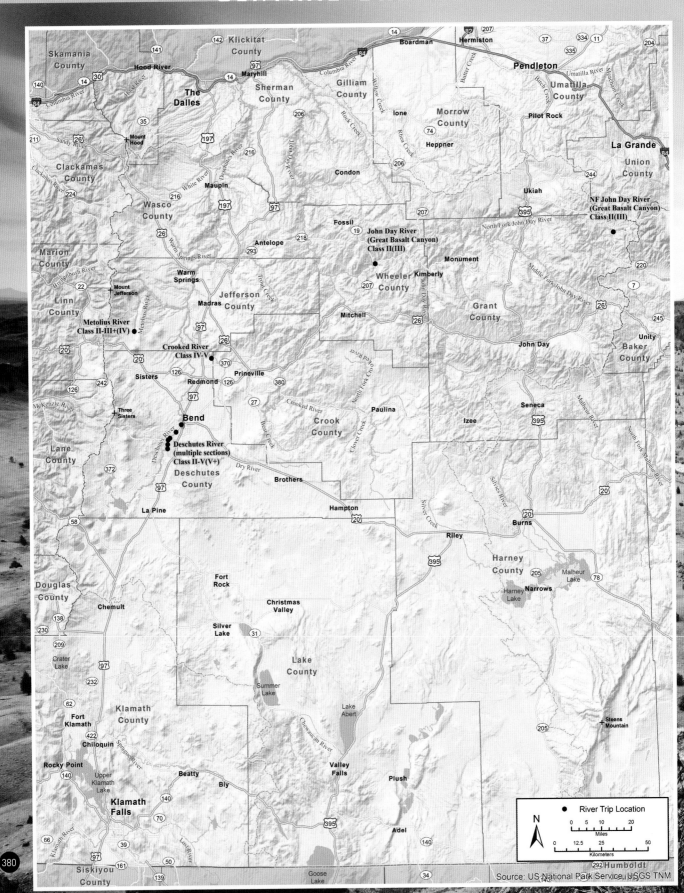

Skamania County
Klickitat County
142
141
Hood River
30
14
Maryhill
97
Columbia River
Boardman
14
84
Hermiston
82
207
37
334
11
204
335
Pendleton
Umatilla River
Umatilla County
La Grande
84
Union County
244
220
7
245

Mount Hood
35
The Dalles
197
216
Deschutes River
White River
Sherman County
206
Gilliam County
Ione
Rock Creek
Rhea Creek
Morrow County
74
Heppner
206
Condon
Pilot Rock
Ukiah
395
North Fork John Day River
NF John Day River (Great Basalt Canyon) Class II(III)

Clackamas County
224
Wasco County
Maupin
197
97
216
26
Warm Springs River
Antelope
293
218
Fossil
19
John Day River (Great Basalt Canyon) Class II(III)
Monument
Middle Fork John Day River
26

Marion County
22
Mount Jefferson
Breitenbush River
Warm Springs
Metolius River Class II-III+(IV)
Metolius River
Jefferson County
Madras
97
26
Trout Creek
Wheeler County
207
Kimberly
Grant County
John Day River
Mitchell
26
John Day
Unity
Baker County

Linn County
Crooked River Class IV-V
20
370
126
Prineville
380
Crooked River
North Fork Crooked River
Paulina
Seneca
395
Izee
Malheur River
North Fork Malheur River

Sisters
126
242
Three Sisters
Redmond
27
Crook County
Clover Creek
20

McKenzie River
Bend
Deschutes River (multiple sections) Class II-V(V+)
372
Deschutes County
97
La Pine
Bear Creek
Dry River
Brothers
Hampton
20
Silver Creek
Silvies River
Burns
20

58
Douglas County
136
230
209
Crater Lake
97
Chemult
Fort Rock
Christmas Valley
Riley
395
Harney County
205
Malheur Lake
78
Harney Lake
Narrows

232
62
Fort Klamath
Klamath County
422
Chiloquin
Silver Lake
31
Summer Lake
Lake County
Chewaucan River
Lake Abert
205
Steens Mountain

Rocky Point
Upper Klamath Lake
140
Beatty
Bly
Valley Falls
Plush

Klamath Falls
70
140
395
Adel
140

66
39
50
Klamath River
Sprague River
Lost River
161
139
Siskiyou County
Goose Lake
34
292 Humboldt

Sandy River
211
140
14
Columbia River
84
26

Source: US National Park Service, USGS TNM

River Trip Location

N

0  5  10       20
Miles

0   12.5    25        50
Kilometers

10

Keel Brightman

# BENHAM FALLS

## OF THE DESCHUTES RIVER

Benham Falls is only a half-mile long, but it packs a heavy punch. Scouting is possible via the river trail on left. Scout from the rocks up high, and also from river level to get true feel of the power—it is bigger and plusher than it appears. At the bottom of falls there is old-growth log that extends into the river, ideal for setting good safety. Depending on the flow, Benham can be run center moving left or right.

Not really much of a warmup, so come ready to fight. The top half has four ledge-holes getting stickier as you move downriver. During winter flows, you can eddy out above the canyon on the left to scout lower Benham. During summer flows you are committed to kayak through lower Benham for a minimum of three seconds more. (Lower Benham has four ledges with no pools in between.) During the summer, tourists from Sunriver cheer you on from the lookout. Below Benham, be on your toes because there is fun mile of Class III with wood-choked side-channels to the takeout.

Completing the 'Triple Crown of central Oregon' (Benham, Dillon and Lava) is a must for any Class V paddler visiting the area with a full day to paddle.

*—Scott Baker*

## THE RUNDOWN

Kayaking in front of a live audience.

**Difficulty:** Class V+

**Gauge:** USGS #14064500— Deschutes at Benham

**Flow Min-max:** 400-2,300 cfs

**Gradient:** 62 fpm (153 fpm in Benham Falls)

**Takeout:** Slough Camp

**Put-in:** Benham Falls

**Length:** 1.8 miles

**Hitchability:** Hard, but an easy hike back to the car

**Season:** During the winter, access to the put-in and takeout may be blocked by snow. Fall and spring offer lower water for a safer descent down the falls. Summer offers high water and a very powerful V+ rapid.

**Camping:** No

**4WD Needed?** No

**Best Close Food/Beers:** Bend— Parrilla Grill (fish burrito), Cascade West Grub and Alehouse

**Quality (out of 5):** 5

**Raft Recommendations:** above 1,400 cfs

## SHUTTLE DIRECTIONS

From Bend, drive southwest on Century Drive toward Mount Bachelor. Turn left on FS Road 41 and follow to a left at Benham Falls **(43.930468, -121.411761)**. The takeout is about 1.2 miles before Benham Falls at the Slough Day Use Area **(43.945250, -121.430472)**.

Katey Kelley

Scott Baker and Matt King R-2 through the chaos of Benham Falls

# DILLON FALLS

## OF THE DESCHUTES RIVER

The excitement starts with a bang! Dillon Falls is a classic pool-drop rapid. Put on at the boat ramp, enjoy the scenery and admire the flatwater boaters warning you of the hazard downstream. If you didn't scout prior, paddle 100 yards downriver and scout on left along the river trail. Dillon Falls is a horseshoe-shaped 8- to 12-foot waterfall that leads into a quarter-mile-long canyon. It is runnable year-round, though be aware that the lines and character change with flows.

At summer flows (1,650 cfs and up), the line is on the left using one of three flakes to boof. At winter flows (500-1,200 cfs), the normal route is down right off the ledge. Many kayakers fall off the ledge to the left into the horseshoe and are OK.

The river-wide Dill Hole lurks right below the falls. It's hungry if you are off-line, otherwise, the seam will let you though. The canyon continues for a quarter-mile and is read-and-run Class IV. Paddle to Bend, downriver to the Lava Island (43.986992, -121.398946) or Meadowcamp sections, or, right before the flatwater, look for the trail on river-left to hike back for another lap.

*—Scott Baker*

### SHUTTLE DIRECTIONS

From Bend, head southwest on Century Drive toward Mount Bachelor, turning left on FS Road 41/Conklin Rd., just past Seventh Mountain Resort. Take the second left toward the Big Eddy Trailhead/Aspen Day Use Area takeout **(43.9729881 -121.4099418)**, or continue to the next left for Dillon Falls. Put in on the boat ramp **(43.957194, -121.416616)**.

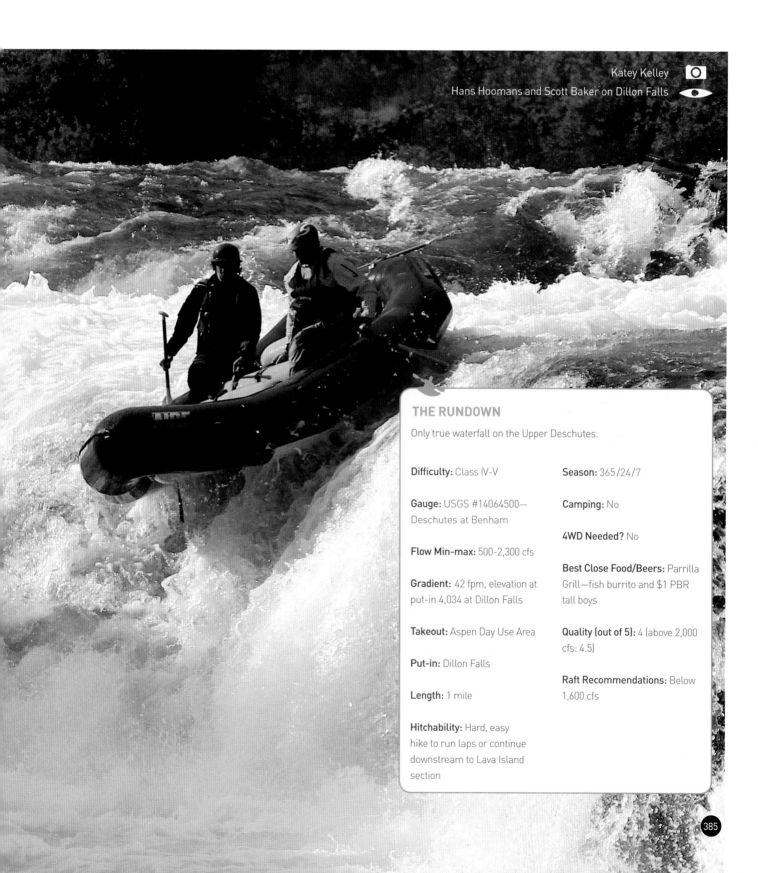

Katey Kelley

Hans Hoomans and Scott Baker on Dillon Falls

## THE RUNDOWN

Only true waterfall on the Upper Deschutes.

**Difficulty:** Class IV-V

**Gauge:** USGS #14064500—
Deschutes at Benham

**Flow Min-max:** 500-2,300 cfs

**Gradient:** 42 fpm, elevation at
put-in 4,034 at Dillon Falls

**Takeout:** Aspen Day Use Area

**Put-in:** Dillon Falls

**Length:** 1 mile

**Hitchability:** Hard, easy
hike to run laps or continue
downstream to Lava Island
section

**Season:** 365/24/7

**Camping:** No

**4WD Needed?** No

**Best Close Food/Beers:** Parrilla
Grill—fish burrito and $1 PBR
tall boys

**Quality (out of 5):** 4 (above 2,000
cfs: 4.5)

**Raft Recommendations:** Below
1,600 cfs

# THE CROOKED RIVER

This is one of the most scenic and best Class IV runs in Oregon. The run starts off slow with a scenic 2.5-mile warmup until the first rapids. Look for the aqueduct (large tube) to warn you of the first rapids, which consist of 1.5 miles of fun Class III-IV read-and-run right down the middle. After this warmup, the Crooked goes flat and does a loop through Smith Rock. Here you will encounter rock climbers and hikers. Enjoy the float and look for the Monkey Face. Past Smith Rock is your first real rapid, Number 1—look for the horizon line of mist and scout on the right. Most run it down the right, but there is a line down the middle next to some holes. You can self-rescue before the next rapid, where there is also a great beach on river-left. Next up is Number 2 after a sharp left turn where the river divides in two channels; scout on the right. Both channels are runnable and both get sticky with higher flows. At Mile 10.5 is Wap-Te-Doodle, the best rapid and one big splashy ride; scout left or run right down the middle. At 2,300 cfs or higher, there is a fun boof over a monster wave in the middle. After Wap-Te-Doodle is fun Class III and IV rapids in the most remote part of canyon. The last rapid is the most feared: No Name. Scout or portage down the trail on river-right. The hole at the bottom is sticky; run left or right of it and avoid any swims as there are no pools. Below No Name, the Crooked has a few more Class II and IIIs. The last rapid is China Dam; scout either left or right. Most run China Dam on the right. There is a hole in middle but you can punch it right though. The takeout is on the left, either before China Dam or below it. Look for the trail and get ready for 1.5-mile climb/slog to Hollywood Road. Don't forget beers at takeout.

—*Scott Baker*

## SHUTTLE DIRECTIONS

From U.S. Hwy. 97 in Terrebonne, follow signs north to Crooked River Ranch. When you reach CCR, turn right, drive past the clubhouse and park in a gravel pull-out. Do not block the green gate **(44.424269, -121.235637)**. To get to the put-in, from U.S. 97 in Terrebonne, drive east toward Smith Rock State Park. Continue past Smith Rock for 3 miles until you reach Lone Pine Bridge. Park on the right. To shorten the run, put in 1 mile east of Smith Rock at the aqueduct **(44.349234, -121.082694)**.

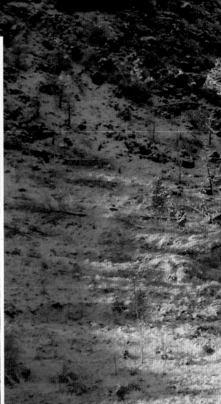

David Chatham

Priscilla Macy 📷
The Crooked River flowing by
Smith Rock in the winter

## THE RUNDOWN

Best Class IV in Oregon.

**Difficulty:** Class IV-IV+

**Gauge:** Crooked River at Smith Rock

**Flow Min-max:** 1,200-4,500 cfs

**Gradient:** 36 fpm

**Takeout:** Hollywood Road/ Crooked River Ranch (don't park in front of the gate)

**Put-in:** Lone Pine Bridge

**Length:** 18 miles

**Hitchability:** Tough (but when it's running, other boaters are around)

**Season:** March-April usually, but only during very wet years

**Camping:** at Smith Rock

**4WD Needed?** No

**Best Close Food/Beers:** Pump House Bar & Grill in Terrebonne

**Quality (out of 5):** 4 (above 1,800 cfs: 5)

**Raft Recommendations:** 1,800 cfs

# MEADOWCAMP

### OF THE DESCHUTES RIVER

Meadowcamp is an awesome run for solid Class IV paddlers. It is within the Bend city limits and runs reliably all summer long. Best first-time level is 1,700-1,900 cfs. Above 2,000 cfs, Meadowcamp gets quite pushy and continuous, with more of a big-water feel than most runs in the region. Unless you are a Class V boater, it is a good idea to have a guide for your first run. There are no shortage of locals willing to show you down. The Bend Whitewater Facebook group is a great way to find paddling partners.

From the put-in at River Rim Park, the first rapid starts about 200 yards downstream. If you want a bit more of a warmup, put in at the Meadow Picnic Area off of Century Drive to add 2 miles of Class I-II. Playtime (Class IV) consists of three distinct drops, with the first being the biggest. Run down the right, or go for the S-turn move on the left. There are two consecutive holes to avoid in the middle. The second drop can be run pretty much anywhere. The final drop is a river-wide wave/hole. Stay right to avoid the hole, or boof far left into the eddy. About 50 yards below this ledge, a canal intake on river-right removes a large portion of the river's flow. The intake is a significant hazard and has caused some scary situations in the past.

The intake also marks the largest rapid on this section, Dammit (IV+), which can be scouted on the left or portaged on the right. Boof the 4-foot entrance ledge on either side of the middle chute and stay center-right down the steep tongue that follows. If possible, catch the eddy on the left to set up for the next move. Here, a pipe shoots water back into the river at head height on river-right, which creates a very strong push into a catcher's mitt on river-left. Drive hard to the right across the diagonal formed by the pipe, or catch the eddy on the left (directly across from the pipe) and make an intimidating but easy ferry out. After a half-mile of read-and-run Class III, the river turns dramatically to the right, signaling the top of the next rapid.

Amazing (IV) is pretty straightforward, but can be intimidating the first time down. Run the lead-in to the right of a small island, then run the rapid down the middle, moving to the right as the river turns the corner. Just be sure to avoid the far left, as there is pin potential. After a couple mellow Class II ledges, you arrive at the next rapid, Marioland (III+), which is a maze of boulders and logs. Enter in the middle, then immediately move to the right for the easiest line. This rapid is very manky at low water, and gets significantly easier as flows rise. It offers some great eddy hopping and a couple of good boofs toward the bottom. Roughly a half-mile of flatwater brings you to an obvious horizon line, marking the final rapid of the run.

## THE RUNDOWN

Urban kayaking.

**Difficulty:** Class IV+

**Gauge:** USGS #14064500—Deschutes at Benham

**Flow Min-max:** 1,600-2,300 cfs

**Gradient:** 70 fpm

**Takeout:** Intersection of Ashwood Dr. and Cedarwood Rd.

**Put-in:** River Rim Park

**Length:** 3 miles

**Hitchability:** Difficult, but it is easy to find people to paddle

with during the summer. It is also possible to bike or run the shuttle.

**Season:** Late April to mid-September

**Camping:** No

**4WD Needed?** No

**Best Close Food/Beers:** Bend—Brother John's, the Lot

**Quality (out of 5):** 3.5 (4 above 2,000 cfs)

**Raft Recommendations:** Above 1,800 cfs

## SHUTTLE DIRECTIONS

From the takeout parking lot (corner of Cedarwood Rd. and Ashwood Dr., **44.037366, -121.327719**), go back out to Reed Market Rd. and head east, up the hill. At the first roundabout, take a right onto Brookswood Blvd., follow it until you pass an elementary school on the left, and then take a right onto River Rim Dr. Follow River Rim until it dead ends at the park. Park on the right and walk down the path to put in (**44.014912, -121.355928**).

One Hundred Percent (IV) can be scouted from the paths on either side of the river. If you decide to scout, make sure to give yourself enough room to make the ferry, as the run in is quite shallow. Drive slightly left to right across a large diagonal at the entry, and make sure to stay upright as you careen down between large boulders and through a few crashing waves. Move left to avoid a large hole, or boof the rooster tail on the far right. At high flows, this hole has served up some beatdowns. A shallow Class II-III runout continues around the corner, making swims very unpleasant. Another half-mile of flatwater separates you from the takeout on river-right. If you are looking for more excitement, put in at Lava Island Falls (V) and run all the way down to the Meadowcamp takeout. This run, referred to locally as Lavacamp, is about 6 miles.

—*Matt Deacon*

Scott Baker

Kyle _____ in Pipe Move

# THE DESCHUTES WHITEWATER PARK

There are three channels and river-left is the safe passage allowing floaters to continue to Drake Park. River-right is the fish passage. The middle is the whitewater park. There are four play-features. The top wave is called Eddie's Miller Wave, designed for board surfing and kayaking. The second feature is another great surf wave. The third feature is named after the late Kricket Serota and is kayak rodeo hole. The fourth and final feature is the Jason Mitchell wave/hole. Big thanks and shoutout to Bend Paddle Trail Alliance for making this a reality.

—Scott Baker

## THE RUNDOWN

Urban kayaking and surfing.

**Difficulty:** Park and play

**Gauge:** USGS #14064500—Deschutes at Benham

**Flow Min-max:** 400-2,300 cfs

**Gradient:** Total drop about 10 feet.

**Takeout:** McKay Park

**Put-in:** McKay Park

**Length:** 0.25 mile

**Hitchability:** Park and play

**Season:** Year-round

**Camping:** No

**4WD Needed?** No

**Best Close Food/Beers:** Longboard Louie's Westside

**Quality (out of 5):** Something for everyone

**Raft Recommendations:** See safe passage channel

## SHUTTLE DIRECTIONS

Park at McKay Park **(44.050062, -121.320756)**. Another option is parking at Tumalo Creek Canoe and Kayak and hiking back to your car on the river-right trail.

Jesse Polay

# LOWER DESCHUTES RIVER

Keel Brightman

The final section of the Deschutes runs from Sherar's Falls to the Columbia. This is a handy run given its proximity to population centers and reliable flows. With 44 miles of Class II cruising and a handful of Class III rapids, it is a wonderful family float trip, and often less busy than the Whitehorse section. The basalt canyon presents a lovely series of walls to enjoy, and the brisk current makes miles roll by easily. A long weekend is a nice pace, and longer trips are possible.

The run's whitewater is well-spaced. Wreck, III+, at river Mile 39 is the first significant rapid; run center or far right. The river continues with Class I and II water with lovely walls and grassy hillsides, with occasional camps. Six miles above the mouth, Class III Gordon appears. Here the river drops abruptly and busy water continues for some distance.

Colorado, Class III, comes 2 miles below Gordon and has perhaps the biggest waves on this float. In another mile, Class III Green Narrows offers many route choices amongst grass-covered midstream rocks. If Hobbits ran whitewater through the Shire, this is what it would look like.

The Green Narrows leads directly into Class III Rattlesnake, the biggest drop on the Lower Deschutes. A steep entry leads to a powerful hole that can be safely passed on the left. Scouting is possible from either bank. The final Class III, Moody, lies within sight of the takeout, I-84, and the Columbia.

—*Brian Vogt*

## SHUTTLE DIRECTIONS

To get to the put-in, take state Hwy. 216 to Shearer's Falls and a launch at the bridge **(45.263980, -121.023048)**, or drive down river-right to a number of roadside put-ins. To reach the takeout, follow OR 216 to either U.S. Hwy. 97 or U.S. 197 and head north to I-84. Follow I-84 to Exit 97 and the takeout park **(45.633027, -120.914846)**.

## THE RUNDOWN

World-class fishing.

**Difficulty:** Class II-III+

**Gauge:** USGS #14103000—Deschutes at Moddy, near Biggs

**Flow Min-max:** 3,000-10,000 cfs

**Gradient:** 8 fpm

**Takeout:** Heritage Landing Park

**Put-in:** Below Sherar's Falls

**Length:** 44 miles

**Hitchability:** Maybe, rural highways.

**Season:** Year-round dam release

**Camping:** Open desert benches, some light shade. Trains.

**4WD Needed?** No

**Best Close Food/Beers:** Hood River

**Quality (out of 5):** 3.5, you can be back in town in an hour. Try that from Otter Bar.

**Raft Recommendations:** Great training run

# THE METOLIUS RIVER

The Metolius is a beautiful spring-fed river that provides intermediate boaters with ample year-round flows and some exciting whitewater. From the put-in just upstream of Gorge Campground, the river is shallow with gentle gradient until entering a small gorge punctuated by a couple of straightforward Class II-II+ drops that ends in a large open meadow with great views of Mount Jefferson. Two low bridges in this section will require most rafts to portage. After about 1.5 miles, a large spring enters on river-right indicating Class III Ledge Drop. Boaters can run to the right or left of the center ledge-hole or punch through the middle with some speed. A series of Class II rapids follow for a half-mile leading into Class III Plop Plop with many routes for boaters to take.

Bedrock ledges begin to emerge in the riverbed leading up to Class II-III Horseshoe in the river-left channel, with a sneak to the right. Class II+ Wizard Falls comes soon after. Though not a true falls, this rapid does provide a narrow turbulent channel to navigate with a low bridge at the bottom. Rafts may need to portage. Bridge 99 (Lower Bridge), 2.5 miles downstream of Wizard Falls, marks the beginning of the lower canyon and the last access point until the takeout near Lake Billy Chinook about 14 miles downstream. Class III+ Candle Creek Rapid comes soon after Bridge 99 with continuous Class II-III for miles below. About 9 miles after Candle Creek is the most difficult stretch of the run, a long Class III-IV rapid. A few more miles of Class II leads to the takeout on river-right. Wood is always a hazard on this run so be sure to scout accordingly.

—*Lucas Rietmann*

## THE RUNDOWN

A few miles above the put-in, the Metolius emerges from Black Butte. The landscape goes from dry ground to a river with over 1,000 cfs in a single stride, making it one of the largest spring-fed rivers in the U.S.

**Difficulty:** Class II-III+ (IV)

**Gauge:** USGS #14091500—METOLIUS RIVER NEAR GRANDVIEW, OR

**Flow Min-max:** The Metolius is nearly always between 1,000-2,000 cfs, which happens to be the optimal flow range

**Gradient:** 50 fpm. Put-in elevation: 3,000 feet

**Takeout:** Drift Campground

**Put-in:** Boater access just upstream of Gorge Campground

**Length:** 21 miles

**Hitchability:** Not a good option.

**Season:** Year-round, cold in the winter.

**Camping:** At the takeout or near the put-in at Gorge, Pine Rest, Smiling River, or Camp Sherman campgrounds. Along the river at Lower Bridge Campground, then anywhere you can pull over with space below that on river-right.

**4WD Needed?** No, lots of gravel roads though

**Best Close Food/Beers:** Camp Sherman in Sisters

**Quality (out of 5):** 3

**Raft Recommendations:** This run is raftable, wood can be an issue

## SHUTTLE DIRECTIONS

A good map of the area is recommended to navigate the shuttle route, which typically takes 1.5-2 hours one way. The put-in is located 2 miles north (downstream) of the small town of Camp Sherman, just upstream of Gorge Campground on Metolius River Rd. **(44.4839, -121.6382)**. To reach the takeout from Gorge Campground, continue north on Metolius River Rd. for 0.5 miles and merge onto NF-14 and continue north for 4.3 miles. Turn right onto NF-1490 (gravel) which will switchback up Green Ridge proper for 6 miles. Keep left onto NF-1140 (Green Ridge Rd.) for 0.4 miles and turn right onto SW Prairie Farm Rd. for 1.7 miles. Take a slight right onto SW Alder Springs Rd. and continue for 3 miles. At a major four-way intersection, keep straight on NF-1170 for 0.7 miles and then merge right onto SW Prairie Farm Rd for 4.2 miles until the intersection with Montgomery Rd. (64 Rd.). Turn left and travel northeast on Montgumery Rd. for 7.6 miles until reaching Drift Campground on the right, about a mile up from the slackwater of Lake Billy Chinook **(44.6291, -121.4876)**.

Nick Hinds
Alyson Hinds

# THE JOHN DAY RIVER

The longest undammed river in Oregon offers a mix of ranch lands, remote canyons, and mellow whitewater. Major access points are at Service Creek, Twickenham, Clarno, and Cottonwood. This river is predominately Class I and II, with Clarno Rapids offering a Class III punch, especially at high water.

But the excellent feature of this river tour is the geology laid bare by the canyon. The Wild and Scenic canyon offers glimpses of the painted hills seen in splendor at nearby John Day Fossil Beds National Monument. You'll also see some spectacular basalt formations. Some are orderly and tall, marching in file across the cliff. Others are a frozen moment of chaotic currents exposed in solid rock. The canyon is often austere, then sublime, in turns.

The whitewater, however, is gentle. Most of the river follows Class I meanders. The afternoon upstream winds or cold spring squalls pose more danger than the rapids. There are many nice camps, but holiday weekends tend to be quite crowded. The run has a new and evolving BLM permit process, so check to see if permits are still unlimited in advance of your planned trip.

The river offers three Class II rapids above Clarno. The first is Russo Rapids, 6 miles in, where rocks present obstacles down the left. Stay right and avoid the headwall at the bottom. Good waves form at some flows, and this rapid can be scouted. The second rapid, Fossil, comes 18 miles below Service Creek. It is a shorter and steeper drop than Russo. Avoid the cliff on the right at the bottom. In 4 miles,

## SHUTTLE DIRECTIONS

Service Creek is located at the junction of state highways 19 and 207, some 26 miles north of U.S. Highway 26 **(44.796023, -120.002958)**. To reach Clarno, drive northwest on OR 19 from Service Creek, then west on OR 218 to the bridge and hamlet of Clarno. To reach the Cottonwood access, drive OR 218 from Clarno east to Fossil, then take OR 19 north to Condon. Take OR 206 northwest to Cottonwood Bridge **(45.477015, -120.470018)**. Beware Tumwater Falls below the takeout.

Joe Vogt

Classic raft touring through the Great Basalt Canyon

Burnt Ranch Rapids occurs where the river bends left. Scout from the left and look for a rock near midstream at the top.

Below Burnt Ranch the river enters a lovely remote gorge, the scenic heart of the upper run. Many great camps and side hikes dot this stretch. The takeout at Clarno Bridge is on the right and can be muddy, and crowded.

Below Clarno Bridge, the river floats through an open ranching valley for 2.5 miles before Clarno Rapids, the only Class III water on the river. Clarno is a long section and has some Class II entry water. The main drop can be scouted from the left and can feature powerful waves, particularly at high water when it may reach IV-.

There are numerous Class I riffles along the trip. Class II rapids occur occasionally. Basalt Rapids is a named Class II where large basalt boulders obstruct the channel, and comes 15 miles below Clarno Bridge.

There are many scenic delights, sublime camps, and tantalizing hikes tucked throughout this lower canyon, sometimes called the Great Basalt Gorge. A lovely narrows occurs at Basalt Rapids. It's worth several trips to explore and find your favorite spots. For any trip, be sure to plan adequate river time, as low gradient and strong winds can make progress slow. River time just seems slower on the John Day than anywhere else. Savor it!

—*Brian Vogt*

## THE RUNDOWN

A 147-mile-long Wild and Scenic River.

**Difficulty:** Class II (III)

**Gauge:** USGS #14046500—John Day at Service Creek

**Flow Min-max:** 1,200 -10,000 cfs

**Gradient:** 8 fpm (upper), 11 fpm (lower)

**Takeout:** Cottonwood Bridge

**Put-in:** Service Creek

**Length:** 147 miles

**Hitchability:** Nope

**Season:** Snowmelt. Usually becomes low in June.

**Camping:** Arid canyon benches

**4WD Needed?** No

**Best Close Food/Beers:** The Dalles

**Quality (out of 5):** 4

**Raft Recommendations:** All craft recommended.

Joe Vogt

The open varied terrain of the John Day canyon

# HONORABLE MENTIONS

## OF CENTRAL OREGON

**The Deschutes' Riverhouse** section is an in-town, intermediate run that flows when the diversion canals are shut off in the winter. There are a number of intermediate rapids. The highlight is the 20-foot runnable dam at the put-in (portage if the flows cause the hydraulic at the base to be retentive), located at Riverview Park in Bend. Take out where O.B. Riley Rd. crosses the Deschutes. (Flows: 500-1,500 cfs in the Deschutes below Bend.) Takeout: 44.129460, -121.331480. Put-in: 44.075432, -121.306986

**The Middle Deschutes**, from Steelhead Falls to Lake Billy Chinook, is a great stretch beginning with 20-foot Steelhead Falls and continuing 8 miles through quality read-and-run Class III-IV+ rapids and stunning canyon walls to the slack water of Lake Billy Chinook. There is a lot of overgrowth on the banks in this section making scouting tough, but many of the rapids are easy to read and run. One section of note is at the Squaw Creek confluence where a Class IV+ rapid may require careful scouting. You will need to paddle another 2 miles of flatwater to the take out on the lake or call for a pickup at the Deschutes arm bridge. Takeout: 44.547566, -121.279210. Put-in: 44.411110, -121.293110.

**The Deschutes' play-spot** Deschutes Playspot is 3 miles up from its confluence with the Columbia River in Colorado Rapid. At lower summer flows, the C Wave stands up and creates a dynamic, action-packed surf wave for paddlers willing to put in the work to get there. Park at the Deschutes River State Park Recreation Area and hike or bike up the trail. A few miles in, when the trail splits, stay low and continue up until you can ferry across to access the wave from river-left. Parking: 45.629344, -120.907975. Wave: 45.587653, -120.895718

**The North Fork Crooked** features a couple of waterfalls and also a lot of flatwater. This remote run through the heart of Oregon provides more aesthetics than action, but where there is whitewater, it is challenging. Takeout: 44.116775, -120.245950. Put-in: 44.326318, -120.047969.

**Fall Creek** offers a stream full of wood and waterfalls flowing off South Sister that runs from snowmelt. The highest put-in is at Green Lakes and it is probably worth a hike without your boat first to scout the sections of interest—it is rare to run the first mile below the lake. Takeout: 44.031467, -121.736127. Put-in: 44.081924, -121.734879.

David Spiegel

Will Stauffer-Norris on Steelhead Falls, Deschutes River

# HONORABLE MENTIONS

## OF CENTRAL OREGON

Priscilla Macy

**The Upper North Fork John Day** is a rugged multi-day trip, with just over 40 river miles to negotiate. The river is mostly Class II-III+ with many continuous sections. There are also some Class IV rapids and one rapid that rates a V at some flows at the confluence with Granite Creek. Be ready to make your own decisions and probably a portage or two whether it be for wood or whitewater. Put in where FS Road 52 crosses the NF John Day (44.912909, -118.400293) and take out in the town of Dale (44.999180, -118.948088).

**Granite Creek** into the North Fork of the John Day River is rarely run, but features remote Class III-IV continuous boulder gardens in a deep Blue Mountain canyon that leads about 4 miles into the NF John Day. A single Class V (IV at low flows) sits at the confluence, easily portaged on the right via the river trail. The fun Class II-III continues 26 miles down to Dale, with great camping throughout. Run when the NF John Day is 1,000 cfs and above. Takeout: 44.9991111, -118.9480000. Put-in: 44.841210, -118.487781

**Whychus/Squaw Creek** has an oddly long season for such a small stream, funneling the snow of South Sister into its canyon for a Class IV-V upper run, a Class IV lower stretch, and then a Class IV canyon just above the confluence with the Deschutes that runs at high water. There are many stretches to choose from; seek local beta. Lowest Takeout: 44.525293, -121.299131. Uppermost put-in: 44.165722, -121.674020.

**The White River** is a fast-paced Class III+ river flowing off the south side of Mount Hood (1,000 cfs is a good flow). Be cautious of wood and bring a sturdy vehicle. There is good whitewater from Barlow Crossing (45.185530, -121.586113) down to Tygh Valley, but the best stretch is from Keeps Mills (45.154707, -121.520678) to White River Crossing (45.159591, -121.312516). If Scenery is the ticket for the day, the canyon between White River Crossing and Tygh Valley (45.234876, -121.160841)houses less rapids, but provides better views and wildlife opportunities. Downstream from Tygh Valley is

Celestial Falls, an ultra-clean 50-foot waterfall sandwiched between a nasty 90-foot drop and a runnable but consequential 20-footer a couple hundred yards downstream (45.242563, -121.096470). It is illegal to run this drop anymore, and there is a guard there in the summer. This drop is typically run between 200-700 cfs. Below the White River Waterfalls two miles of intermediate whitewater continues down to the confluence with the Deschutes: 45.233255, -121.067189

**Tumalo Creek**, above Tumalo Falls – Main Stem V-V+: This would be a classic without wood. There are a lot of waterfalls on Tumalo Creek culminating at 90+ foot Tumalo Falls, just upstream of the parking area. A maintained trail leads upstream revealing more and more waterfalls the further you go. Some of the larger falls are on the main branch of the Tumalo, each with their own character. If you want to try a different access to other falls further up the North Fork and Middle Fork you can access the North Fork via a short trail here, 44.053509, -121.614967. A small group who put on the NF in 2006 (44.053509, -121.614967) and paddled down to Tumalo Falls reported the first big waterfall runnable, with a big portage over

to the WF where you can pick and choose to paddle what you like. Alternately you can portage and paddle your way down the north fork to the confluence with the middle fork, then hike up as far as you wish to pick off rapids on the middle fork. It is usually runnable at the peak of snowmelt. Parking area at Tumalo Falls: 44.031953, -121.566438.

**Shitike Creek** has a steep half-mile Class V section a short way upstream of Warm Springs. It can be run lower, but ideally look for 400+ cfs on the Shitike gauge (USGS #14093000). Access is via Wolford Canyon/Shitike Creek Rd. Takeout: 44.772273, -121.305868. Put-in: 44.786619, -121.345272. There is some hiking involved with this route.

**The Lower John Day** is mostly flatwater, but the Class V Tumwater Gorge waits 9.5 miles upstream of the Columbia. Tumwater Gorge. Not to be confused with Tumwater Canyon of the Wenatchee or the Stehekin, the Tumwater Canyon of the John Day is short, but packs a punch with class V Tumwater falls and the ledges in the Narrows: 45.657765, -120.502044

Ryan Scott
Justin Wiley playing around at the C Wave at prime flows

# EASTERN OREGON

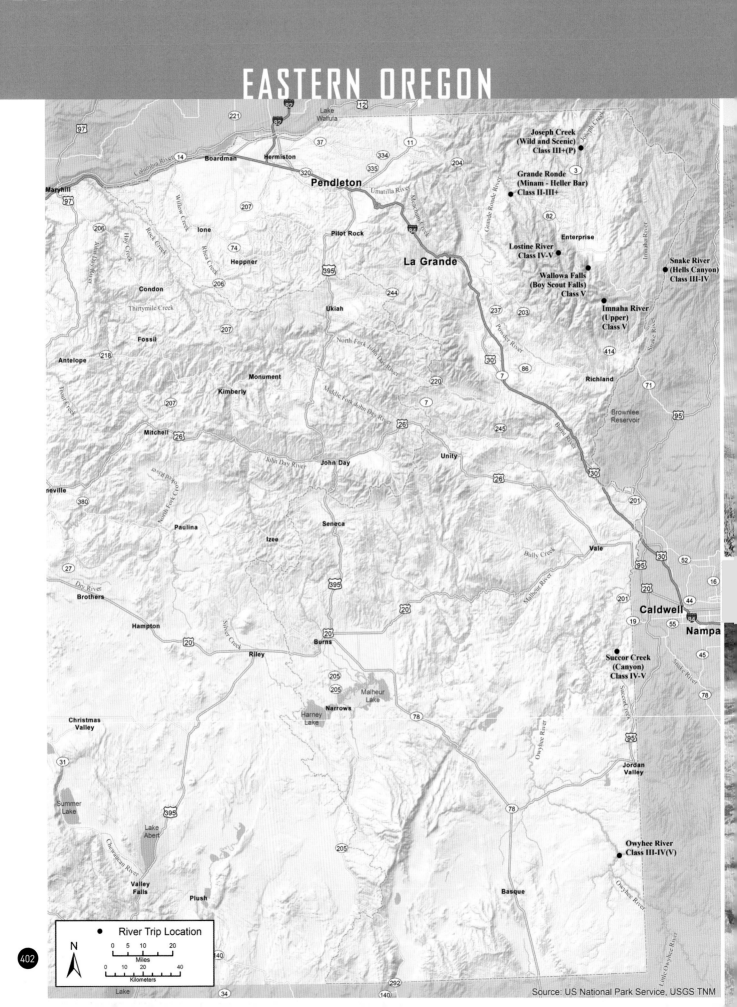

Joseph Creek
(Wild and Scenic)
Class III+(P) ●

Grande Ronde
(Minam - Heller Bar)
Class II-III+ ●

Lostine River
Class IV-V ●

Wallowa Falls
(Boy Scout Falls)
Class V

Snake River
(Hells Canyon)
Class III-IV ●

Imnaha River
(Upper)
Class V ●

Succor Creek
(Canyon)
Class IV-V ●

Owyhee River
Class III-IV(V) ●

● River Trip Location

N

0   5   10        20
Miles
0   10   20        40
Kilometers

402

Source: US National Park Service, USGS TNM

Priscilla Macy

Jeff Moag

Nick Hinds drops into the
widow maker

# THE LOSTINE RIVER

The Lostine really stands out in the Eagle Cap Wilderness. It's a deep granite canyon with lots of steep sections and a road that more or less follows the creek way up into the mountains. The easy access, great camping, and quality of the run make it the favorite local river when spring snowmelt brings the flows up. The Lostine is continuous, steep, and constantly changing, with endless boulder gardens that morph into eddy-less wave trains at high water. This is definitely a run where some local knowledge helps, with rocks and wood moving around each spring.

Williamson Campground serves as the perfect put-in: an idyllic riverside campground with mountain views and a placid pool. There's even a staircase down to the river (if the bottom stair is in the water, put your game face on!). About a mile of warmup water and a log portage lead you into a blind right turn with a visible landslide coming off the river-right slope, with a short scout available on the right. Tailspin then drops like a rock around the corner, with a stout lead-in to miles of continuous water.

After countless boofs, lots of wave-holes and a quick log portage, a trailer-sized boulder in the middle of the river marks the most rarely run drop on the river, Condemnation Corner. A huge log used to block almost the entire river, and we've had some sketchy moments, including a swim and some lost gear on our exploratory descent years ago. Some good Samaritans cut the log out a few years back, only to reveal a really retentive ledge with a ping-pong lead-in. Condemnation can be scouted and portaged on the left through a boulder field.

More fun read-and-run boofs and waves lead you into the final gorge, Last Delight. The gorge is the icing on the cake and can be scouted/portaged in part on river-left. A series of irregular ledges from 2-4 feet tall lead into the only truly vertical feature on the river, an 8-foot ledge that is typically run off a flake on the left, though the middle line temps paddlers who want to go big. After the ledge is the marque move for the whole stretch: a speeding logjam duck that careens into a boulder-pile zigzag marking the exit to the gorge and spitting paddlers out underneath Pole Bridge, the takeout. The exit to Last Delight is not portageable without some serious rock climbing, so if it doesn't look good, go back upstream and cross to river-right to hike up to the road. At the time of press, the river had only one mandatory log portage in the upper sections.

## THE RUNDOWN

A kayak guardian angel down the road likes to provide motorcycle shuttles and party favors free of charge. If some rando turns up with a dirtbike and some Keystones, just strap on your helmet and hop on back!

**Difficulty:** Class IV-IV+ (V) from 350-600 CFS, Class V above 600

**Gauge:** NOAA -LOSTINE RIVER ABOVE LOSTINE

**Flow Min-max:** 450-600 cfs is optimal first-time flow. The high end is limited by a logjam that blocks the exit to the final gorge at flows above 900 cfs.

**Gradient:** 250 fpm

**Takeout:** Pole Bridge Picnic Area

**Put-in:** Williamson Campground

**Length:** 4 miles

**Hitchability:** Never had to wait more than 15 minutes

**Season:** Late spring-early summer, sometimes rain on snow can bring it in during fall

**Camping:** The river corridor is full of fantastic campspots, both developed and undeveloped.

**4WD Needed?** No

**Best Close Food/Beers:** The Lostine Tavern or the quintessential Wallowa County eatery, Terminal Gravity Brewing

**Quality (out of 5):** 4

**Raft Recommendations:** Hasn't been done yet, final logjam would be tough to duck

There are a few drops worth running upstream of this section, though the farther upriver you go, the more wood you find. Another section below Pole Bridge can be fun for boaters not looking for a Class V experience, and for those who want to take out at the Lostine Tavern for a beer.

—*Matt King*

Matt King

Ty Overeem below the 8-foot vertical ledge in Last Delight Gorge

Matt King

Ryan Scott and Jacob Cruser in Last Delight Gorge

# BOYSCOUT FALLS

## OF THE WEST FORK WALLOWA

Many people have seen the grandeur of Wallowa Lake, its proud moraines and towering peaks. People come from all over to swim in the clear alpine waters coming out of the heart of the Wallowa Mountains, to take the tram up to Anaroid Peak and peer across Hells Canyon into the vast Idaho wilderness, and to enjoy the bucolic countryside of Wallowa County.

That stuff is cool and all, but it ain't the main event. There lies a hidden gem at the head of the lake that has been overlooked by tourists and locals alike. The West Fork of the Wallowa has a trail that begins along a boxed-in granite gorge that you can't avoid if you're on the trail. As it nears the lake, it takes a turn to the west and drops over a hidden waterfall, with no good viewpoints unless you're standing right over it. The vast majority of folks who have been up the trail (at least the ones I've talked to) have no idea there is a 40-foot series of drops right before the creek flattens out and hits the lake.

What you find is a beautiful piece of whitewater, technical, big, and consequential. The drop consists of a 5-foot ledge into an 8-foot ledge, similar to Double Drop on the Truss, but smoother and smaller. The second drop slams into a giant boil, turns 70 degrees to the left, splits into two flows, then careens off a 25-footer, sloping on the left with a reconnect and spouting on the right out of a bathtub-sized slot. Add a deep cave on the left and a nasty pocket on the right and you've got yourself a nice little stout, one we lovingly call Boy Scout Falls for the Boy Scout camp just downstream.

I have stood above the falls and stared into the canyon dozens of times, at all manner of flows, and only a few times have I decided to go back to the car, gear up and go for it. When it's too high, the boil off the wall consumes the whole flow and the pocket and cave combo at the bottom looks marginally survivable at best. When it's too low, the top ledges get chunky, the reconnect looks painful on the left, and the bathtub line would do an awful number on your elbows and/or face. That leaves a limited flow window that's fortunately pretty reliable before and after Lostine season, so we always get the chance to run it in early spring and mid-summer.

—Matt King

## THE RUNDOWN

The falls actually had another tier of about 12 feet following the final plunge that was filled in with gravel and sediment following a mudslide in 2002. The same mudslide destroyed much of the Boy Scout camp and marooned a home when it changed the course of the river.

**Difficulty:** Class V

**Gauge:** Visual

**Flow Min-max:** Personal choice

**Gradient:** Park and huck

**Takeout:** Wallowa Falls Campground (same spot as put-in)

**Put-in:** West Fork Wallowa Trailhead

**Length:** Park and huck

**Hitchability:** N/A

**Season:** Early spring and/or late summer, sometimes rain on snow can bring it in during fall

**Camping:** There are some campgrounds at the lake, and innumerable campsites in the Wallowa National Forest.

**4WD Needed?** No

**Best Close Food/Beers:** Terminal Gravity Brewing in Enterprise

**Quality (out of 5):** 4

**Raft Recommendations:** No, it hasn't been done yet

## SHUTTLE DIRECTIONS

From the Wallowa Trailhead, hike up about 5 minutes on the West Fork Trail and take a peek into the gorge. Turn right (downstream) to find the hidden falls, and give it a close look. If you choose to run it, you can boat down to the campground after (45.267040, -117.212931).

11

Scott Baker
Jacob Cruser on Boy Scout Falls

# SUCCOR CREEK

The Succor Creek whitewater run is in eastern Oregon, right on the border with Idaho. This run has become a favorite among Boise paddlers for very good reason. This tiny creek is steep and tight and depends almost entirely on a rain on snow event or a very good snowpack for optimal flows. It consists of a dozen or more Class IV and V drops, some extremely tight, and is only navigable via whitewater kayak. It's set in a stunning and secluded desert canyon. Among this region's abundant kayaking opportunities, Succor Creek is very unique and possibly the best creeking near Boise.

The whitewater starts off about a quarter-mile below the put-in with Rattlesnake. If this rapid is outside your comfort zone it probably best to hike your boat out because things only get more challenging downstream with rapids named Swisher Sweets, the Italian Pinch, Vietnam, Scary Falls, Lost and Found, D-bag, Skate Park, Bar-fight, and many others. The most dramatic series of rapids is in Scary Canyon where 5 or 6 very unique drops culminate in the tallest single ledge known as Scary Falls. This canyon can all be scouted/portaged easily on the left from a cow path. About a quarter-mile below Scary Falls is one sieve-filled rapid that has yet to be run; portage/scout on the left. You are about halfway done with the run at this point. Lots of rapids remain as well as a very spectacular final canyon.

Succor Creek has been run as low as 60 cfs with a number of portages, but the minimum recommended flow is 140 cfs, and it's best between 180 and 260 cfs. As the creek approaches 300 cfs and beyond, things start to get rowdy but super-fun if you are familiar with the run. With such a small window for optimal flows, figuring out when to go is one of the biggest challenges. There's a gauge in Homedale below the run, but it runs about 12 hours behind what's

## THE RUNDOWN

The scenery is phenomenal with multi-colored cliffs, spires, and arches.

**Difficulty:** Class IV-V

**Gauge:** National Weather Service: Succor Creek near Homedale

**Flow Min-max:** 140-300 cfs

**Gradient:** medium/steep

**Takeout:** Succor Creek State Recreation Area

**Put-in:** 7 miles up from the takeout (42.193175, -111.778349)

**Length:** 7 miles

**Hitchability:** Limited traffic on gravel road, so don't count on it. Not a bad bike shuttle.

**Season:** February, March, April, May (dependent on snowpack and winter rain events)

**Camping:** Free camping at takeout. Outhouses and fire rings, no water.

**4WD Needed?** No

**Best Close Food/Beers:** Nearest town is Homedale

**Quality (out of 5):** 4

**Raft Recommendations:** Not recommended

happening on the whitewater run upstream. There's also a gauge at Jordan Valley above the run, but it only represents a portion of what's going on in the canyon downstream and is only a good gauge when the water is coming from snowmelt later in the season. On low-water years this creek may run for only a day or two. Or not at all. However, on really good water years, paddlers have enjoyed this run from early February through mid-June.

The rapids in Succor Creek are created by large, round polished rhyolite boulders and ledges, which aren't as sticky as the basalt features you find on other runs in southwest Idaho and southeast Oregon. All of the rapids are easily scouted and portaged. Wood is typically not an issue with this run being in the desert, but watch out for barbwire fences, which seem to change from year to year. Unlike most paddling in this area, the gravel road is generally in good shape, even during rain events.

*—Mike Copeland*

## SHUTTLE DIRECTIONS

To reach the takeout from Oregon, take I-84 east to Exit 374. Turn right onto OR 201 S/U.S. 30. Drive 11.3 miles and turn right onto Columbia Ave. In 1 mile, turn left onto Clark Blvd., and in 2.6 miles, stay right following OR 201/Succor Creek Hwy. In 17.4 miles, turn right onto Succor Creek Rd., and approximately 15.5 miles later, the Succor Creek State National Area takeout is on the left, (42.193183, -111.778518). To reach the put-in, continue up 7 miles above the canyon to where the road nears the creek, and a short hike over to the water (42.263876, -111.752478).

# HELLS CANYON

## OF THE SNAKE RIVER

Tamed by the Snake River dams, most of the whitewater in Hells Canyon lies buried beneath the reservoir upstream. Yet this Wild and Scenic river offers some of the biggest big water in the Northwest. Popular with whitewater boaters, jet boaters, hunters, fishermen, and even hikers, the Snake is a river of many uses. It is also part of the Four Rivers Lottery system, so plan early in the year or look for cancellation permits. Good river maps are available from a variety of sources and most detail the various camps.

This float trip begins at Hells Canyon Dam. The dramatic setting is picturesque if bittersweet. Though rarely visible from the depths of the canyon, nearby peaks may be between 5,500 and 9,000 feet above the river. The big-water nature of the run matches this scale. Immediately below the dam, where Hells Canyon Creek enters, Class II whitewater awaits. Stay off the walls and watch out for turbulent eddylines.

A few camps are available before Mile 5.8, where Wild Sheep, Class IV, offers a couple of route choices before the wide entrance constricts into a powerful exit. Watch out for the big hole top-center at high water; scout left.

A few more camps are dispersed amongst the rocks until Granite Creek enters at Mile 7.3. Less than a half-mile below lies Granite Creek Rapid, Class IV. A gargantuan boulder midstream forms a menacing hole top-center. At high flows, a green breaking wave forms. Run either side, with left being favored. Granite can be scouted either side. This rapid may push Class V at flows over 50,000 cfs.

At Mile 11, Saddle Creek enters from the left. Class II+ Bernard Creek Rapid follows, then Lower Bernard, Class III, in quick succession. After 2.5 miles, Class III Waterspout can be tricky at low flows.

Brian Vogt

Johnson Bar

At Mile 15.5 is Rush Creek Rapid, a significant Class III which gets worse at higher flow. Watch for the big hole top-center. Class II water follows.

Kirkwood Historic Ranch at Mile 26 is a worthwhile stop. There is a museum and drinking water. Pittsburg Landing at Mile 32 offers an early exit for a short trip. Water below here is Class I and II and the canyon opens up through Pleasant Valley. An historic sign at Mile 50.5 marks where the Nez Perce crossed the Snake in their effort to reach Canada.

The Imnaha River enters from the left at Mile 55 and Imnaha Rapid, Class III, follows the confluence. A farther 3.5 miles on, the Snake meets the Salmon at a massive confluence of huge canyons, truly one of the special places in the West.

Below this confluence, the river enters Snake Lake, a slow Class I section of moving pools. Boaters who follow the currents will be rewarded, especially when fighting the afternoon upstream winds

Weather seems to be the biggest variable in a Hells Canyon trip, followed by water level. High summer can be punishing with little escape from the heat. Yet the canyon offers extended shoulder seasons which might be a bit cold but promise a less busy river corridor. The wise trip leader will pace the flatwater miles carefully, and make the most of the scenic splendor of the canyon. Hikes, pictographs, and wildlife are plentiful.

—*Brian Vogt*

# HELLS CANYON

## OF THE SNAKE RIVER

Brian Vogt

Hells Canyon Wild Seep

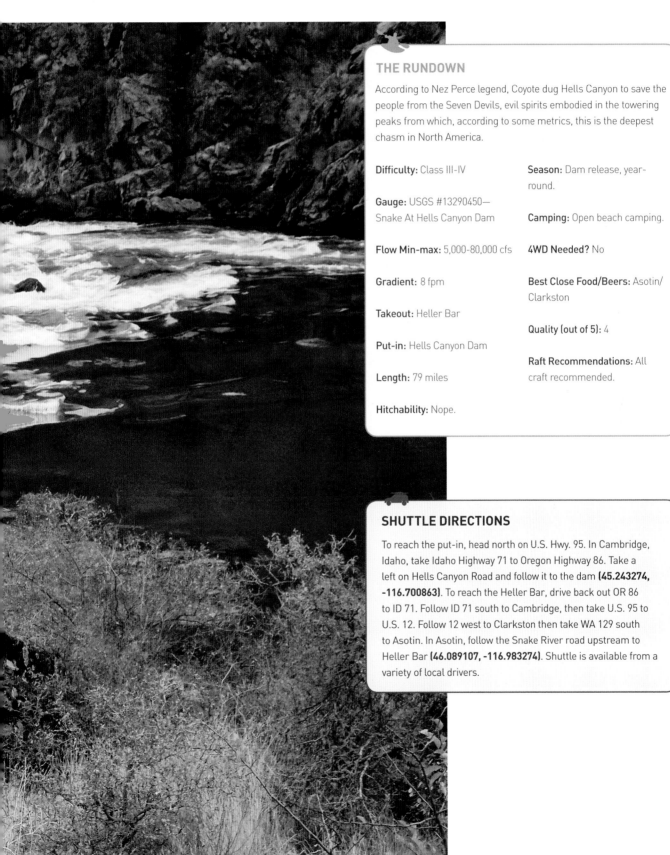

## THE RUNDOWN

According to Nez Perce legend, Coyote dug Hells Canyon to save the people from the Seven Devils, evil spirits embodied in the towering peaks from which, according to some metrics, this is the deepest chasm in North America.

**Difficulty:** Class III-IV

**Gauge:** USGS #13290450—Snake At Hells Canyon Dam

**Flow Min-max:** 5,000-80,000 cfs

**Gradient:** 8 fpm

**Takeout:** Heller Bar

**Put-in:** Hells Canyon Dam

**Length:** 79 miles

**Hitchability:** Nope.

**Season:** Dam release, year-round.

**Camping:** Open beach camping.

**4WD Needed?** No

**Best Close Food/Beers:** Asotin/Clarkston

**Quality (out of 5):** 4

**Raft Recommendations:** All craft recommended.

## SHUTTLE DIRECTIONS

To reach the put-in, head north on U.S. Hwy. 95. In Cambridge, Idaho, take Idaho Highway 71 to Oregon Highway 86. Take a left on Hells Canyon Road and follow it to the dam **(45.243274, -116.700863)**. To reach the Heller Bar, drive back out OR 86 to ID 71. Follow ID 71 south to Cambridge, then take U.S. 95 to U.S. 12. Follow 12 west to Clarkston then take WA 129 south to Asotin. In Asotin, follow the Snake River road upstream to Heller Bar **(46.089107, -116.983274)**. Shuttle is available from a variety of local drivers.

# JOSEPH CREEK

Joseph Creek is a unique mini-expedition trip for seasoned wilderness paddlers. It has no gauge, a short snowmelt season, tricky access, and continuous intermediate whitewater darting through blind wood-infested channels. This
is not a boat-scout float trip, but it is an isolated Wild and Scenic canyon full of surprises. You should have solid Class IV boat handling, rescue, and wilderness skills to attempt this run.

The top is boney and narrow until Swamp Creek enters. The gradient is gentle in the upper sections and the water is very shallow. Be careful of logs and of blind corners, and be prepared to portage. Most spots can be scouted or portaged, but eddies can be tight and crowded by trees. The canyon is only just poking its bones out of the hills, and bedrock begins to appear.

As the canyon deepens and widens the rapids also solidify. Continuous II builds to continuous III, with brushy banks. Swamp, Rush, Peavine and Tamarack creeks all add significant flow, and after each, the whitewater intensifies. There is one standout IV-drop, and some nice headwall drops deep in the gorge. No one rapid is difficult, but swimmers would be at the mercy of midstream trees and hard-pressed to get out of the river safely. The moves and consequences stack up, magnified by high water. I've had trips with no portages, and trips with 6 wood portages. Always expect wood.

In the lower canyon, it is not only driftwood that is in play. The trees overgrow the riverbed enough to dictate your paddle placement. In some ways, Joseph Creek is as much about wood as water. It's hard to describe how uniquely fun this gauntlet of moves becomes, and it makes for thrilling paddling. "You'll be coughed out of the canyon in a whitewater fit" is an apt description, and indeed the rapids crescendo into a continuous blur of waves and channels. The decisions come fast and furious and eddies are scarce indeed.

Eventually you'll see the walls open up, where a bridge crosses and a ranch adorns the verdant lower valley of Joseph Creek. Take out at the second bridge, or continue onto the Grande Ronde, or on even farther to the Snake at Heller Bar.

Camping is plentiful on the many benches, but of dubious legality. It is best to use a GPS and a good map to ensure your spot is on public land. There are many public parcels, old homesteads, and private holdings scattered throughout the canyon.

But if the trees are leafing out, your downstream visibility will be impaired, so go early!

## THE RUNDOWN

Asking permission beats the hike from the rim.

**Difficulty:** III+(P)

**Gauge:** Historical WA Dept of Ecology

**Flow Min-max:** 300-1,000 cfs (visual)

**Gradient:** 50 fpm

**Takeout:** Chief Joseph Wildlife Refuge

**Put-in:** Near Crow Creek

**Length:** 48 miles

**Hitchability:** No

**Season:** Early snowmelt

**Camping:** On public parcels

**4WD Needed?** No

**Best Close Food/Beers:** Asotin/Clarkston

**Quality (out of 5):** 4

**Raft Recommendations:** Only with machetes

You may takeout at Heller Bar, along the Grande Ronde, or along Joseph Creek Road. The put-in is more difficult as up top, land on both sides of the river and road is private. There is a small public parcel extending to the river 1.25 miles upstream from the final, locked road gate.

Nine Bark Outfitters operates the property behind the locked gate and boaters must obtain permission before floating through. Nine Bark operates out of Joseph, not at the ranch behind the locked gate. Contact them in advance of your trip (ninebarkoutfittersatgmail.com or 541-426-4855). They may also run shuttles or allow access to the end of the road.

Joseph Creek's status as a navigable river is questionable, so it is not clear the public enjoys the right to boat through private land to access public land. Please be respectful of private property so that others can enjoy this special place.

—Brian Vogt

Brian Vogt

1000 cfs makes for scenic bank-full fun
on Joseph Creek

## SHUTTLE DIRECTIONS

To reach the put-in, head north on state Hwy. 3 out of
Enterprise. Take a right on Starvation Rd. or FR-46. Stay on 46
heading downstream. Road 46 will become 4600. Take a left on
Crow Creek Rd., then left again on Joseph Creek Rd. Choose
your own put-in below here **(45.714103, -117.154066)**. To
reach the takeout, follow OR 3 north into Washington, where it
becomes WA 129. South of Anatone, turn right on Montgomery
Ridge Rd. Go straight onto Appleford Rd., then right on Edeburn
Gulch Rd. Next, take a left onto Couse Creek Rd.., and after a
right onto Snake River Rd, you'll drive to Heller Bar. You can
follow Snake River Rd up the Grande Ronde to a takeout, or
continue upriver and take a left on Joseph Creek Rd. There
is public parking (Discover Pass required) at the first bridge
across Joseph Creek **(46.031143, -117.016153)**.

Brian Vogt

Joseph Creek flows through a Classic
ponderosa-lined basalt canyon, often
with overgrowing trees

# THE GRANDE RONDE RIVER

Brian Vogt

The Grande Ronde Wild and Scenic River is a choice overnight trip with excellent canyon scenery, wildlife, abundant camping, and a long season. This means on holiday weekends the river will be packed with boaters. Try to offset your trip a day or two so as not to be in competition at peak times for camps. Memorial Day weekend is especially crowded. Trips of 1 night or 7 are possible.

The Grande Ronde has three sections: A 39-mile stretch from Minam to Powwatka, a 26-mile run from Powwatka to Boggan's Oasis, and a 26-mile run from Boggan's Oasis to Heller Bar. The runs may be linked together for one of Oregon's longest trips.

The upper run begins in Minam, at the Minam-Wallowa confluence. The river here is fast and continuous Class II. Two miles below Minam a large breaking wave-hole on the outside of a right bend may catch boaters by surprise. This is the Class II+ Minam Roller and a good playspot. The character of the canyon is steep basalt cliff bands, grassy hillsides, and ponderosa benches with comfortable camps.

Shortly below the Minam Roller and some small camps, you'll run House Rock Rapid, Class II. Here, a large rock splits the river. Either channel is usually runnable, but left is larger and easier to see.

Shortly below House Rock, power lines cross the river, indicating the approach of Blind Falls, Class II+. This is the longest and steepest drop on the upper run. The rapid can be run center through a nice wave, but be careful not to get too far right, where the blind ledge lurks with exposed rocks at low flow, and a powerful hydraulic at higher flows.

At Mile 10, the Grande Ronde enters from the left at Rondowa. Though the Wallowa carries more water, the longer Grande Ronde keeps its name. Here, the train tracks on river-right cross the river and leave the canyon. A roadless Wild and Scenic river corridor awaits. Camps of spacious and elegant appointment dot the canyon.

Sheep Creek rapids, Class II, awaits below the confluence. The final named rapid on the upper run comes at Martin's Misery, a splashy left bend best run left. It comes about 10 miles below Sheep Creek. The final 15 miles to Powwatka Bridge are straightforward water with occasional riffles. There is a campsite void the last few miles above the bridge. Takeout at Powwatka on the right below the bridge, or float down into Troy.

*Continued on page 418*

## THE RUNDOWN

The best non-permitted raft camping trip in Oregon!

**Difficulty:** Class II-III+

**Gauge:** USGS #13333000—Grande Ronde at Troy

**Flow Min-max:** 1,000-15,000 cfs

**Gradient:** 20 fpm to Troy, 17 fpm below. Put-in elevation: Minam 1,720 feet

**Takeout:** Troy, Boggan's Oasis, Heller Bar

**Put-in:** Minam

**Length:** 91 miles

**Hitchability:** Not recommended. Shuttle services exist.

**Season:** Snowmelt, but runnable flows nearly year-round. A great winter trip.

**Camping:** Excellent established camps

**4WD Needed?** No

**Best Close Food/Beers:** Boggan's Oasis

**Quality (out of 5):** 4

**Raft Recommendations:** Flows below 1,000 cfs will be technical and bony

## SHUTTLE DIRECTIONS

Minam is located on state Hwy. 82, 34 miles northeast of La Grande where state Hwy. 82 crosses the Wallowa. There is access at the Minam Hotel on the right and at the public launch on the left downstream of the bridge **(45.621835, -117.721462)**. There is also the state park 2 miles downstream with camping and possible access. To reach Powwatka, drive east on OR 82, then take OR 3 north near Enterprise. Drive roughly 34 miles then turn west 3 miles to Flora. Follow the signs to Troy and drive upriver 7 miles to the bridge at Powwatka. To reach Boggan's Oasis, drive the dirt road downstream from Troy. Heller Bar, just below the mouth of the Grande Ronde, can be reached by driving WA 129 north from Boggan's Oasis. Follow 129 to 1.5 miles south of Anatone and go right on Montgomery Ridge Road. Drive some 15 miles then head upriver along the Snake to Heller Bar **(46.079970, -116.979059)**.

# THE GRANDE RONDE RIVER

The lower Grande Ronde is a mostly arid, open canyon with Class I and II water. Double Eddy, 5.5 miles below Powwatka can be turbulent at high water. Seven miles below Powwatka is river access at Troy, and the Wenaha enters on the left, a wilderness hike-in run in its own right.

Boggan's Oasis: 19.5 miles below Troy is another access spot. Stop above the bridge on the right. Below Boggan's Oasis, the canyon becomes more remote. Lazy meanders amongst islands offers mostly Class I and II water.

There is one standout rapid, the Narrows, above the Joseph Creek confluence. This is a Class III+ rapid and is steep and constrained by bedrock. It is easily scouted on the left and the line is straightforward. At low flows this channel can be only 10 feet wide.

At high flows the whole river is busy Class II, with a bit of push and few eddies, and water can be cold. The Minam to Powwatka section can be done in a day at high flows. Lower flows make for calm, slow pools alternating with shallows which add more drift time. On busy weekends, the lower may offer more solitude. Weather may be inclement and snow is possible into May. Be prepared for remote wilderness river conditions and cold water.

—Brian Vogt

Jason Shappart

Blind Falls at low water

The vast sprawling sage canyonlands of southeast Oregon are home to one of the finest multi-day river trips in the West. The Lower Owyhee is a classic float trip through open desert country featuring spectacular canyons and plentiful side hiking.

The run begins at the hamlet of Rome along state Hwy. 95. The river here is open and rangeland dominates the first five miles or so before you enter Sweetwater Canyon with its series of Class II and III rapids. The standouts are Upset and Bull's Eye. Lines may become technical at lower flows, but moderate flows bring fun rolling wave trains.

*Continued on page 387*

## SHUTTLE DIRECTIONS

The put-in is located where state Hwy. 95 crosses the Owyhee **(42.839910, -117.621319)**. To reach the takeout at Leslie Gulch, head east on OR 95 into Idaho and take a left onto McBride Creek Rd. Take a right onto Succor Creek Road, then another right to stay on Succor Creek Rd., then left onto Leslie Gulch Road **(43.322730, -117.323651)**.

Matt Vogt 📷

Niki Vogt in Iron Point Canyon, Lower Owyhee 👁

# LOWER OWYHEE RIVER

Around Mile 20 the whitewater picks up again. First Read-it-and-Weep, then Artillery offers some excitement. A worthwhile side-hike to the Rustler's Cabin on the right offers geologic and historical interest, as well as a hot spring.

This open section of canyon offers many great camps and loads of hiking. The Lambert Rocks, near Mile 28 and Dog Leg rapid, are of particular interest and are worth a day's exploration from all angles. Erosion has laid bare many treasures, many best seen up close. Near Mile 30 look for Potter's Cave, another side-hike of note.

Next comes Iron Point Canyon, a steep-walled inner gorge of hard rhyolite. You will drift between sheer walls of towering hoodoos, amphitheaters, and caves in a place so inhospitable, only the most frugal or acrobatic life seem to find a home. This section is reminiscent of its sister drainage, the Jarbidge-Bruneau to the east in Idaho.

Iron Point canyon isn't all scenery though. Watch for Whistling Bird, III+, on a sweeping left bend where a large slab has fallen into the water from river right. The line is straightforward but the hazard created by the sieve behind the slab is significant. Scout or line left. More heavy water follows near Mile 32 beginning with Rock Trap. Next up is Squeeze. Both are straightforward IIIs. Montgomery, III+, finishes the set of heavy water. This long drop runs along a big wall on the left and has some obstacles at the bottom. Pull right or find a clean chute.

Whitewater continues intermittently as the canyon opens up. Morcum Dam can be an obstacle at low flows. The hot springs at Mile 44 are a favorite stop on cold spring trips when freezing temps are possible. Please run the rapid and land below to hike back up to the springs to protect sensitive riparian habitat.

Boaters can take out at Birch Creek, where the improved road can still pose a challenge for long trailers and two-wheel-drive vehicles, or at Leslie Gulch, following a 10-mile reservoir row. Boat tows are available and the lower sections are lovely in their own right.

—*Brian Vogt*

## THE RUNDOWN

Hot springs, geology, homesteading history, and petroglyphs with a bit of whitewater sprinkled in.

**Difficulty:** Class II-III+

**Gauge:** USGS #13181000—Owyhee near Rome

**Flow Min-max:** 600-10,000 cfs

**Gradient:** 13 fpm

**Takeout:** Leslie Gulch

**Put-in:** Rome

**Length:** 65 miles

**Hitchability:** Could take days

**Season:** Spring rains and early runoff, best March to June

**Camping:** Premier wilderness multi-day

**4WD Needed?** Required for any dirt road in Owyhee country unless bone dry.

**Best Close Food/Beers:** This is a joke, right?

**Quality (out of 5):** 5, about as deep as wilderness gets in the Lower 48

**Raft Recommendations:** A quintessential raft run

Matt Vogt

# UPPER & MIDDLE OWYHEE

## OF THE OWYHEE RIVER

The vast sprawling sage canyonlands of southeast Oregon are home to a stash of the finest multi-day river trips in the West. The Upper Owyhee's intricate network of canyons offers endless combinations for adventure. Run 40 miles on Deep Creek for its willow-lined, narrow intimacy. Or enjoy 55 miles on the South Fork, taking out above the confluence and the Upper Owyhee for a Class III trip. Want more challenge? Put on the East Fork and deal with all the problems: around Owyhee Falls only to Thread the Needle past the South Fork, then down the Upper Owyhee through twisting Cabin, and the ledges of Cable. If the 86 miles down the East Fork to Three Forks aren't enough, the 37-mile Middle Owyhee and Widowmaker's Class V water (or walk) await.

I see I've failed to mention the point: These amazing gorges. Ancient rhyolite floes, solidified and eroded, roll by in varied hue and form. This a true wilderness expedition that blends tricky logistics, fickle flows, and deeply wild canyon country traveled easily only by boat.

*Continued on page 424*

### THE RUNDOWN

You can boat more contiguous free-flowing miles on the Owyhee than a Grand Canyon trip!

**Difficulty:** Class III-IV (V)

**Gauge:** USGS #13181000— Owyhee near Rome

**Flow Min-max:** 1,000-5,000 cfs

**Gradient:** 15 fpm

**Takeout:** Rome

**Put-in:** Various

**Length:** 35-140 miles

**Hitchability:** Could take days

**Season:** Spring rains and early runoff, best March - June

**Camping:** Premier wilderness multi-day

**4WD Needed?** Oh yeah. How many spares ya got?

**Best Close Food/Beers:** This is a joke, right?

**Quality (out of 5):** 5, about as deep as wilderness gets in the Lower 48

**Raft Recommendations:** Pack to portage

Bill Cavali

Deep Creek bedrock

Bill Tuthill 📷
Owyhee Falls from above 👁

# WIDOWMAKER SECTION

## OF THE OWYHEE RIVER

The first challenge is deciding where to launch. Most popular is Three Forks, offering a 37-mile run down the Middle Owyhee to Rome. The Upper Owyhee, with Class IV+ Cabin and Class V Cable, runs the 36 miles from the East and South Fork confluence to Three Forks, with a launch at Crutcher Crossing. Above the Upper Owyhee there is the Class III South Fork, and the varied runs of the East Fork and Deep Creek, both quite placid save for cataclysm of Owyhee Falls.

The South Fork is best for rafts because there are no portages. You can launch at YP Ranch (41.8046540, -116.473918), 90 miles above Three Forks, or the Pipeline Road (41.9479048, -116.672755), or the 45 Ranch (42.1725959, -116.873320). Arrange permission to access ranch land in advance. But that's just the South Fork.

The East Fork is best in small light craft because of portages. Launch 65 miles above Three Forks at Garat Crossing (42.169439, -116.501968), or add the IV-V Garat Gorge by launching upstream from Duck Valley. Or choose to run 40 miles on Deep Creek (42.5808625, -116.675813) from Brace Crossing into the East Fork, entering 10 miles above the confluence with the South Fork for 86 miles of wild canyon adventure. Crutcher Crossing, just above the South Fork confluence and 37 miles above Three Forks is the last access on the East Fork, and the most direct launch for the Upper.

**SHUTTLE DIRECTIONS**

The takeout is located where OR 95 crosses the Owyhee in Rome **(42.839879, -117.621448)**. Your put-in logistics are best vetted with a local shuttle driver, a good weather report, and a good map.

If boating from the East Fork side, enjoy the many mellow miles of scenic Class II canyon. The action picks up in the last 10 miles above the confluence when Class III Rockfall rapid marks the entrance to Lambert Gorge, a deep defile host to Owyhee Falls, a Class VI rapid with an arduous mandatory portage along a high trail for 100 yards. Two miles below is Thread the Needle, a portage for all but the smallest boats even at high flows. The East Fork is a trip unto itself, and it is possible to takeout at Crutcher Crossing (42.260271, -116.869371) or via a hike-out option at Rickert Crossing.

If coming down the South Fork side, you'll have less portaging and more Class II and III runnable water. The canyon is equally as stunning, if less obstructed. The BLM guide has good maps on all of these canyons, helpful as well as all of their access roads present challenges.

Jason Shappart

Scouting Cable Rapid

Beginning below Crutcher's Crossing and the EF/SF confluence, the Upper Owyhee flows some 36 miles to Three Forks. The two biggest obstacles in this stretch are a pair of big rapids. First is Cabin, a series of bends studded with huge boulders rated IV+ that can be run after a careful scout. A mile below, the shorter Class V Cable is often portaged or lined along the right. At low flows rock sieves present hazards, and at high flows, river-wide hydraulics develop. The deep rhyolite gorge continues throughout this stretch, and a spectacular wilderness hot spring awaits just above Three Forks.

From Three Forks, another access point (42.546271, -117.168942), the Owyhee enters the Middle Owyhee Canyon, the most consolidated whitewater stretch on the river. The action picks up in 1.5 miles with the Ledge, a long steep Class IV boulder garden.

After another seven miles, a long IV called Half Mile is best scouted right. This long S-bend has two sections but runs together into one rapid at higher flows, and is followed closely by Class III Raft Flip. Subtle Hole and Bombshelter Drop, Class III and III+, come a few miles farther on.

Class V Widowmaker, 15 miles above Rome, is the crux of the Middle Owyhee canyon. This drop has many hazards, and is best scouted from the right. Stop above the III lead-in, and expect the portage to be a herculean task amongst car-size boulders. The discerning boatman will line gear boats with a good plan and crew. Below Widowmaker the canyon quickly opens up into Jordan Valley and the flatwater float to Rome.

—*Brian Vogt*

Mike Quigley

Upper Owyhee canyon scenery.

# HONORABLE MENTIONS

## OF EASTERN OREGON

**Upper Imnaha**: Hike in to Deadman's Crossing. The Class IV-V run down to Indian Crossing weaves in and out of gorges with fantastic whitewater. Scout often. (Flows: 500-2,000 cfs). Takeout: 45.111515, -117.014986. Put-in: 45.111641, -117.120601.

**Donner and Blitzen** is a Class III overnight (or long day) trip at the foot of the Steens Mountains. The gauge should read over 300 cfs to justify the drive. Takeout: 42.805500, -118.867916. Put-in: 42.638562, -118.764317.

**Eagle Creek** helps capture water flowing south from the Eagle Cap Wilderness. There is good Class III-IV(V) whitewater between Paddy Creek and Skull Creek. There are a number of takeouts to choose from. The forks of Eagle Creek also have some serious whitewater on them. This drainage usually has water when the Lostine and Imnaha are running, and it also handles high water well. There is a good campsite (44.890611, -117.262316) at the confluence with Little Eagle Creek. Takeout: 44.874856, -117.245433. Put-in: 44.951535, -117.337524

**The Lower Imnaha** has many miles of easy to intermediate floating from Indian Crossing down to the Snake. The last 4 miles are the best part of this section. Hike back out to Cow Creek or continue to Heller Bar. The river can be run with as little as 700 cfs in the Imnaha gauge from snowmelt, and has been run at over 3,000 cfs— when the river is big-water fun! Takeout: long shuttle, 46.088992, -116.983020; must hike out, 45.816937, -116.764786. Upper put-in: 45.559384, -116.834115; lower put-in: 45.763235, -116.748276.

**The Minam River's Wild and Scenic section** requires either flying into Minam Lodge or hiking in 7 miles from Moss Creek Trailhead. In 2014 the flight was $200 via Spence Air Service, and certainly part of the trip's intrigue. The stretch of river from Minam lodge is 22 miles and mostly continuous Class II. The range of flows is 800-3,000 cfs; watch out for blind corners with potential wood hazards at the higher end of the range. There is one Class III rapid that tapers to significant Class II for about 5 miles. Most people will do this as an overnight (a great campsite exists on river-right near Trout Creek). Farther upstream paddlers will find more difficult whitewater (III-IV+) as well as more difficult logistical challenges. The entire river has world-class fishing at lower levels. The surf wave at Minam State Park near the takeout is the best play around above 3,000 cfs in the Grande Ronde. Takeout: 45.621626, -117.721587. Put-in: 45.353980, -117.631780.

**Hurricane Creek** is a hike-in run with a next-level gorge and some manky floating. There is a short Class IV stretch accessible by road that runs when the Lostine is at a low, but runnable level. Takeout: 45.348992, -117.269537. Trailhead: 45.311373, -117.307247. Put-in: 45.265056, -117.316151.

Matt King

Earning strokes in the Wallowa's

**The Powder River** is a scenic run with abundant wildlife and an officially designated Wild and Scenic section. The put-in is a short hike down from the Thief Valley Reservoir boat launch down to the dam. A fence lurks right below the dam, so keep a look out. About a mile in, the remoteness of the canyon becomes clear, with little evidence of human impacts and wonderful scenery. One Class III punctuates an otherwise Class II river. Great fishing. Portage the small diversion dam once you exit the canyon about a mile before the takeout at the Medical Springs Hwy. Some boaters may be interested in tackling the Hole in the Wall Landslide rapid about 25 miles downstream (44.806565, -117.313775). Takeout: 44.913974, -117.671878. Put-in: 45.012579, -117.781061.

Matt King
The Imnaha River a couple miles above Indian Crossing

Dave (demshitz) Fusilli